Perspectives on Social Power

ALDINE TREATISES

IN SOCIAL PSYCHOLOGY

edited by M. Brewster Smith

Perspectives
on Social Power

edited by
James T. Tedeschi
SUNY Albany

ALDINE PUBLISHING COMPANY chicago

ABOUT THE EDITOR

James T. Tedeschi is Professor and Director of the
Social Psychology Program, State University of New
York at Albany, and is the author of numerous theoretical and research papers on the topics of power
and influence. He received his Ph.D. in psychology
from the University of Michigan in 1960 and is a
fellow of the American Psychological Association.

First published 1974 by
Aldine Publishing Company
529 South Wabash Avenue
Chicago, Illinois 60605

ISBN 0-202-25117-9 clothbound edition
Library of Congress Catalog Number 73-89516

Printed in the United States of America

In Memory of Bertrand Russell

Contents

Contributors

David A. Baldwin, Government Department, Dartmouth
College, Hanover, New Hampshire

Martha R. Burt, Sociology Department, University of
Minnesota, Minneapolis, Minnesota

Robert M. Carmack, Anthropology Department, State University of New York, Albany, New York

Daniel Durckman, Research Program in Child Development,
Institute for Juvenile Research, Chicago, Illinois

James P. Gahagan, Psychology Department, Antioch
College, Yellow Springs, Ohio

William A. Gamson, Sociology Department, The University
of Michigan, Ann Arbor, Michigan

Herbert C. Kelman, Department of Ethics and Social Relations, Harvard University, Cambridge, Massachusetts

David Kipnis, Psychology Department, Temple University,
Philadelphia, Pennsylvania

Bruce D. Layton, Psychology Department, State University
of New York, Albany, New York

H. Andrew Michener, Sociology Department, University of
Wisconsin, Madison, Wisconsin

Dean G. Pruitt, Psychology Department, State University
of New York at Buffalo, Buffalo, New York

Bertram H. Raven, Psychology Department, University of
California at Los Angeles, Los Angeles, California

William H. Riker, Political Science Department, University of Rochester, Rochester, New York

Richard Rozelle, Psychology Department, University of

Houston, Houston, Texas

John Schopler, Psychology Department, University of North Carolina, Chapel Hill, North Carolina

James T. Tedeschi, Psychology Department, State University of New York at Albany, Albany, New York

Preface

The first two annual Albany Symposia on Power and Influence were supported by funds provided by the Institutional Grants Committee of the State University
of New York at Albany. Each of the meetings was held
over a three-day period: October 11-13, 1971, and
October 9-11, 1972. During the symposia each participant read all or part of his prepared paper and the
other participants engaged in open discussion of the
paper. The formal symposium consumed six hours of
each day, but the participants continued their discussions informally throughout the three-day period.
At times the differences between participants grew
heated. These exchanges were important to the final
papers. Almost all of the contributors revised their
papers in some respect as a result of the interchanges.
The cold glare of print does not completely capture
the spirit of the meetings, but the papers do provide
the reader with the interesting and important ideas of
the contributors.

The editor would like to thank the following peo-
ple for performing the many chores that enabled the
symposia to function as smoothly as they did: Thomas
Bonoma, Robert C. Brown, Vincent Franconere, Bob Helm,
Joanne Joseph, Thomas Kane, Frank Monteverde, Pete
Nacci, Barry Nelson, Barry Schlenker, R. Bob Smith,
Terry Stapleton, Richard Stapleton, Peg Tedeschi, and
Richard Teevan.

Perspectives
on Social Power

Introduction and Overview

James T. Tedeschi

The first book explicitly devoted to reporting empirical work on the topic of social power was published in 1959. Dorwin Cartwright, the editor and a major contributor to this important book, rued the fact that so little *scientific* work had been done on so obviously important a phenomenon. A few years later Kenneth Clark (1965), another prestigious psychologist, lamented the apparent lack of commitment by the scientific community to the development of an understanding of social and political power and urged social psychologists to focus more of their research time and skills on the problem. Simultaneously (during the 1960s), shouts of black power, student protests, and antiwar demonstrations reverberated through the legitimate institutions of the United States, and presidential commissions investigated violence and disorder. Unfortunately, social scientists possessed little accumulated knowledge that could be applied to help solve the social problems of the day.

THE CONCEPT OF POWER

Whether or not one agrees that little effort has been invested in the scientific study of power depends upon what one means by the concept. Controversy among social scientists of all disciplines about a "correct" definition has been quite intense over the last two

1

decades. Each definition that is proffered turns out
upon examination to serve as a nominalistic device
either for identifying a set of phenomena or for making a distinction between types of phenomena that the
theoretician considers to be quite important. Naming
events or discriminating among them may be important
as a first step to theory building, but it should be
clear that such rough, intuitive typologies are not
sophisticated scientific theories. Two theorists may
classify events differently but agree on the basic
laws regulating the referent events. Thus, although
one theorist may prefer to restrict the referent class
of events subsumed under the label of power to the
successful exercise of threats in gaining compliance
(Bachrach and Baratz 1963), and a second theorist may
define power as coextensive with all interpersonal
causation (Morgenthau 1960), the two may actually agree
on the conditions that lead to the successful use of
threats.

George Kennan once remarked that American foreign
policy and public opinion might well be more clear-
eyed and realistic if the word communism were purged
from the vocabulary. The label carries such negative
connotations and obscures so many possible discrimi-
nations--say, between the communisms of China, Cuba,
Yugoslavia, and the Soviet Union--that decisions are
made on the basis of myths and abstractions rather
than realities. Riker (1964) has made the same argument with respect to the use of the concept of power
by social scientists. Seldom, if ever, does the use
of the concept of power by an author do more than
serve as a convenient way to refer to a set of complex phenomena. There is nothing wrong with trying
to find simple ways to communicate with one another
so long as the simple linguistic device is not decoded
to mean more than it does. The "noise" that occurs
between communicators results from the fact that each
is using the concept of power to refer to a different
set of phenomena. There is much less disagreement and
misunderstanding when the referent phenomena are directly discussed.

The papers in this book reveal that little consensus exists about the referent phenomena to be identified by the concept of power. Schopler and Layton

and Pruitt and Gahagan define power as an indication
of change in another person, where change may be identified in many ways--attitudinal, behavioral, intentional, motivational, or directional. Both Kelman and
Raven identify as social influence actual change in a
person's cognitions, attitudes, or behaviors that has
its origins in another person or group and reserve the
concept of power to refer to potential influence that
an agent can exert on another person. Gamson suggests
that the concept of power be restricted only to control over behavior and that changes in internal states
of the target individual be left for other subfields
of social psychology to explain. Druckman and Rozelle
define power as control over resources that may be
used to gain influence over the decisions of others.
Carmack uses the concept of power to refer to interpersonal or intergroup influence directed toward
change and involving manipulatory and contested modes
of influence. Carmack's purpose in defining power in
this way is to make a clear discrimination between
power and authority. Authority refers to delegated
influence in a hierarchy where compliance is obliga-
tory and the purpose of influence is to maintain the
status quo. Thus, power is used to influence public
decisions, while authority is used to execute politically determined decisions.

FACILITATING THEORY DEVELOPMENT

It is important to recognize that this diversity in
defining the concept of power does not signify that
the theorists disagree about fundamental processes or
functions. On the other hand, the definition given
does often indicate the distinctions, emphases, weight-
ings of variables, and focus of interest of the theorist. The differences in definition are therefore not
trivial in understanding the thrust of the theorist's
thesis.

The processes and relationships referred to by the
above definitions of power are the bases of much social psychological research. Why then are appeals
made to social psychologists to give more attention to
the study of power? It is the editor's view that the
state of dissatisfaction is traceable to the inade-

quacies of all the available theoretical formulations
of the social influence processes. Without a sophisticated scientific theory, action-oriented social scientists find themselves in the position of being
sought after by political decision-makers (just as
would be desired, presumably) but finding that there
is little besides intuitions and values as a foundation
for offering policy advice. Whenever a particular behavioral scientist believes he can give sophisticated
rationales for his advice, he discovers that others
are offering conflicting counsel. The policy-maker is
left confused and frustrated by conflicting advice and
has only his own part experience, intuition, and values
as guidelines for devising policy. The source of frustration among social psychologists about the state of
knowledge about power, therefore, lies in the absence
of sophisticated and well-accepted theories of the
social influence processes.

The Albany Symposia on Power and Influence are an
attempt to facilitate the development of theories of
power and influence. Of all the social scientists,
social psychologists are probably most prone to frac-
tionate their interests into small subareas of research and to develop miniature theories to handle the
data in their domains of research. When viewed from
the perspective of social power, these subareas may be
organized on the basis of broad principles. A yearly
symposium devoted to fostering theoretical discussion
among sociologists, anthropologists, political scientists, and social psychologists may act as a catalyst
for theoretical growth.

ATTRIBUTIONS OF POWER

The order of presentation of the papers in this volume
is intended to maximize comparisons among them. Part
I is devoted to two papers concerning the perception
of power by human observers of events. William Gamson,
whose paper was probably the most controversial and
provocative of those presented at the meetings, asked
the very basic question, How do we know that power has
been exerted? This is an operational question posed
in the context of a definition of power as a change in
the probability that a target person will choose an al-

ternative preferred by an influencer. Gamson proposed
that a panel of informed judges be used to gain a true
subjective probability that the event will occur and
then, soon after an intervening influence attempt has
been made by significant others, that a second true
subjective probability estimation be obtained from the
same knowledgeable judges. A difference between the
first and second estimations would identify that power has occurred. Gamson does not treat the problem of
identifying the causes of change in this paper, but he
assumes that the reader is aware that he has proposed
such a theory in his book *Power and Discontent*.

Schopler and Layton were also interested in the
identification of effective power in social relationships. But their focus was not so much on whether
power is *really* exerted as on the conditions that will
lead persons to *attribute* power to others. Schopler
and Layton, like Gamson, also drew from Dahl's formulation of power as a change in probabilities from time
1 to time 2. In general, a source will be perceived
as having power over a target when the target's behavior at time 2 was not expected from what was known
about him at time 1 but was expected from knowledge of
the source's intervention. Attributions of power depend upon the context of interaction, the outcomes for
the parties involved, and the perspective of the observer (source, target, neutral third party). Schopler
and Layton's theory is rich with implications for research.

THE SOURCE OF POWER AND INFLUENCE

The social influence process minimally involves a
source, a message or influence mode, and a target.
There has been an almost exclusive focus in social
psychology upon the target of influence. Research
topics and miniature theories center upon such matters
as attitude change, conformity to group pressures, behavioral compliance to various forms of influence, and
imitation or modeling. But one must sift and strain
through the social psychological literature to find
scientific work directed toward an understanding of
the factors that contribute to the source's use of power and influence. Even the study of leadership tends

to center upon the degree to which the leader is responsive to his followers, rather than upon how the
leader exercises influence over them. In their contributions, both William Riker and David Kipnis have
given their full attention to the source of influence.

The ubiquitous problem faced by a source is how to
maneuver the target into making the response desired
by the source. Presumably, the source tries to exercise influence because he cannot gain reinforcements
by his own responses. A self-reliant individual need
not be concerned with influence because his rewards
and/or punishments are not interdependent with the reinforcements of other people. It is usually assumed
that once the source decides that he wants something
that he cannot attain by his own behaviors, he must
choose to influence someone else to mediate the com-
modity or sentiment desired. William Riker's analysis suggests that trust may be an alternative to influence.

Trust is behavior based on a decision to be dependent on other people in risky situations. Whether a
source should trust others or, instead, influence them
to gain his objectives requires that he analyze the
situation, ascertain what the interests of the relevant others are, and predict what others will do. When
the interests of relevant others coincide with the interests of the source, the source can act in concor-
dance with those others and both will presumably gain
their objectives. However, when there is conflict between the interests of interdependent parties, trust
becomes irrelevant and the parties will attempt to influence one another. In order to determine whether he
can rely upon the interests of others to bring about
the desired states of affairs or whether it will be
necessary to bring influence to bear, the source must
learn to distinguish situations in which trust is and
is not appropriate. Riker suggests some "rules of
thumb" that have been developed to answer the question,
Is he trustworthy?

David Kipnis views the source of influence within
the context of institutions. Asymmetrical superordi-
nate-subordinate relationships are typical of many interactions in institutions. Often the motive for exercising power is provided by an institution, as are

the resources and the means that can be used to gain
compliance. Access to institutional resources ele-
vates the source's self-esteem and encourages him to
perceive himself as a locus of control. After factor-
ing out the important features of an influence relationship, Kipnis carefully examines the evidence concerning a source's use of promises and rewards, persuasion, or threats and punishments as power tactics.
Rewards are provided as workers merit them, but are
also given to those who ingratiate themselves with the
supervisors. Persuasion is most likely to be directed
to subordinates who display positive attitudes but who
reveal their ineptness in the execution of institutional
tasks. Coercion is used against subordinates who show
poor attitudes and deny the legitimacy of the superordinate and the goals of the organization. The use of
punishments is also associated with sources who lack
self-confidence, are oppressed by feelings of powerlessness, or have so many subordinates that they cannot devote much personal attention to them. Coercion
also appears to be the means of last resort after other modes of influence have failed to gain compliance
from the target. These and many other principles are
derived from the literature on the uses of institutional power.

THE TARGET OF INFLUENCE

Herbert Kelman has the longest history of contribution
to the study of power and influence among the contributors to this volume. His paper is the fullest statement of his theoretical posture to date. The three influence processes of compliance, identification, and
internalization are linked to both antecedent and consequent factors. Furthermore, Kelman links these psychological processes to social system processes.
Viewed from the perspective of the individual, the responses of the target are conceptualized as social influence, but from the perspective of the system the
same patterns of interaction of source and target may
be conceived as problems of social control. Kelman
limits his presentation to positive modes of influence.
   The individual faces inconsistency dilemmas stemming from concern for standards of individual propriety

(i.e., individual perspective) and standards of responsibility and morality (i.e., social perspective).
The former involve a specific influence agent and direct material rewards and punishments for the target
person, while the latter involve standards in the form
of rules, norms, role expectations, and values, and
imply social rewards and punishments for the target.
Resolution strategies used by individuals to solve inconsistency dilemmas and the role these strategies
play in legitimizing the system complete this powerful
theoretical statement.

Bertram Raven was one of the contributors to Cartwright's pathbreaking book on social power. In their
original theory, French and Raven proposed that compliance by a target would be significantly affected by
the bases of power controlled by the source. These
bases included the source's coercive and reward power
and his attractiveness, expertise, and legitimacy. In
his contribution, Raven has carefully articulated some
distinctions that are often overlooked in the original
formulations of the theory. In particular, the distinction between informational influence and the other
bases of social power is emphasized. Raven reported
several studies on the perception of power and the preferred modes of power used in conjugal and teacher-
student relationships. The comparisons he made between his theory and Kelman's are enlightening since
they help both to sharpen concepts and functions and to
correct hasty judgments of similarity between concepts
that have a different meaning for the two theorists.
Finally, Raven relates his theory of power to the incident at My Lai in South Vietnam and to Frantz Fanon's
view that violence may be necessary for the development of self-respect among the oppressed peoples of the
world.

FORMAL ANALYSIS OF
INDIVIDUAL-SYSTEM RELATIONSHIPS

Druckman and Rozelle take an empirical approach to
model construction. They are concerned with building
structural and contemporaneous situational variables
into simulation experiments so that the interaction of
both system and social psychological factors can be
methodically explored. Their task is to create labo-

ratory situations of increasing complexity in the context of which persons form facilitating or blocking
coalitions with respect to particular group goals. A
potential set of ecumenical coalitions are provided to
groups of subjects with different ideological and mate-
rialistic goals. Within each group, the distribution
of control over the resources necessary for the success of a coalition is varied. Multiple regression
analyses reveal the relative contributions of ideology,
materialism, and initial funding potential (i.e., power) as sources of variance in predicting both facilitating and blocking coalitions. The resulting model
is bound to generate future experimentation on interparty decision-making in the context of institutions
that require a balancing of material utilities and
ideologies.

POLITICAL POWER

[When a particular individual, group, or institution
has widespread influence over others, we may speak of
political power. The possessors of political power
may be generally accepted by a constituency and in
fact be in control of relevant offices, resources, and
decision-making apparatus. Or, a political group may
represent a minority or even a revolutionary group
which is not widely accepted in the society and which
does not possess desired control over important institutions.] Questions important to social psychologists that arise in the study of political power include the sources of institutional authority, the basis
of legitimacy of those who hold office in the political
system, and the processes which tend to undermine authority and to produce revolution or insurrection. Despite the fact that Michener and Burt, Carmack, and
Pruitt and Gahagan view such problems from the very
different perspectives of sociology, social psychology,
and anthropology, the language of their theories does
not disguise some basic agreements among them.

 Robert Carmack has searched through the anthropological literature on tribal societies in order to discover what is truly basic in human institutions. In
the absence of laboratory or field experiments, research involving natural observations is the basic
method employed in comparing simple tribal societies

with modern social systems. Carmack finds that both
power and authority are involved in all social relationships. Power refers to the capacities of persons
and groups to affect competitive decision-making,
while authority refers to administrative offices created to execute politically determined decisions.
Mystical symbols legitimate and dramatize society's
ownership of administrative offices and limit the extent of the officeholder's authority. Vestigial law
is found in all tribal societies, if law is defined
as rules mutually recognized by tribal members and
backed up by authority. Even kinship lineages and rituals and wife exchanges are clearly manipulated for
purposes of political advantage. Carmack's stress on
the ubiquitous influence of the group on the beliefs,
decisions, and behaviors of individuals might well
have been expected from a political anthropologist,
but his view is strikingly similar to Kelman's position that the individual is faced with inconsistency
dilemmas between what he wants and what the system requires or approves. Carmack also apparently believes
that the individual can become the willing captive of
his cultural milieu and that to be powerful means to
be free from dominating cultural forces and at the
same time able to satisfy individual (alienated) desires.

Most of the papers in these proceedings devote some
space to the problem of legitimate power. Legitimate
power refers to the target person's belief that a
source of influence has the right by virtue of his role
position to expect deference from the target. The role
position vests authority in a person, and the exercise
of the prerogatives of an office depends largely upon
a constituency's perception of the officeholder's legitimacy. Kelman suggests that legitimacy is based on
three factors: *(a)* ideological integration of the individual into a system of shared symbols; *(b)* role-
participant integration, in which the individual derives rewards and self-identification through engaging
in roles within the system; and *(c)* normative integration, in which acceptance of authority is based on
commitment to the state as a sacred object or on commitment to the legal system as a guarantor of equitable
procedures. Except for minor language differences,

Carmack's position appears to be quite similar to Kelman's.

The problem of authority or legitimate power is implicit in Kipnis's discussion of the institutional powerholder and is briefly discussed by Raven. Michener and Burt concentrate their attention on the problem of legitimacy. They find that legitimacy is based on several processes that have different antecedents and consequences and that may vary independently of one another. An officeholder or leader may receive the endorsement of his group. Endorsement is a measure of the degree of support that a group gives a leader, presumably based on how satisfied the group is with the way the role position has been exercised. Election or removal from office are two means of showing endorsement or a lack thereof. Endorsement, then, refers to collective attitudes regarding the officeholder. Normativity refers to the collective sentiment that creates and supports the office or role position apart from whoever fills the position. [Social groups are careful to establish rules to regulate the functions of an office, including procedures for making decisions, solving problems, and settling disputes.\

Michener and Burt proceed to specify the antecedents of endorsement, which include the success or failure, competence or incompetence, fairness, and selfishness or altruism of the officeholder and the degree of support he is perceived to have from other group members. Strong endorsement by the group apparently makes the leader resistant to influence from his followers and encourages him to use noncoercive modes of influence. However, at the moment the evidence shows that strong endorsement does not gain the leader more compliance from his followers.

Normativity is described in terms of the approval or disapproval of various behaviors by a group's members, the intensity of the norms, the positive and negative sanctions associated with them, the degree of consensus in the group about the norms, and the existence of an implicit coalition in the group which is ready to impose sanctions for deviant behavior. Each of these elements of normativity is related to the behavior of group members towards the leader. For example, lack of consensus about norms lowers the probabil-

ity that the leader will gain compliance to his requests or commands and increases the probability of
insurgent behavior against him. The virtue of the entire analysis of legitimacy provided by Michener and
Burt is the care with which functional relationships
are specified and the obvious concern for empirically
testable hypotheses. The experimental development of
revolutionary coalitions under specifiable conditions
is an exciting example of this approach to the study
of legitimacy.

Dean Pruitt and James Gahagan examined legitimacy
and revolutionary behavior in a more realistic and direct fashion. They report a case study of a violent
campus confrontation between students and the "Establishment" at the State University of New York at Buffalo. Throughout the conflict the two authors participated in the events they report, but their perspectives were quite different. They participated on different sides during the conflict. Pruitt was involved
in the Administration's efforts to find a resolution
to the conflict, and Gahagan was involved in the leadership of the student revolutionary group. Pruitt and
Gahagan kept diaries and engaged in dialectic with
each other over the rather long period of the conflict.

Three different models are used to examine the details of the conflict: the aggressor-defender, conflict spiral, and structural change models. The authors argue that the last model is the most comprehensive and is capable of incorporating the other two
models. Central to the conflict escalation at SUNY-
Buffalo were attributions of blame and the erosion of
legitimacy. Each side in the dispute viewed the other's actions as aggressive, while perceiving its own
actions as defensive and morally correct. Each action
was followed by a reaction: hence a conflict spiral
clearly occurred. During the conflict spiral, changes
took place in the motives, attitudes, images, or com-
mitments of one or both of the contending parties.
Thus, the character and intensity of a conflict may
change over time as a function of structural changes
taking place in the participants. In the Buffalo instance, a struggle organization emerged, and a polarization took place within the university community between members and supporters of the Strike Committee

and of the Administration.

   Pruitt and Gahagan draw some clear lessons from the Buffalo conflict. They propose strategies that would have helped either side to resolve the conflict in a manner to its own liking. On the one hand, strategies which could be used by an administration to blunt the thrust of campus revolutions are advanced. Alternatively, strategies that could be used to further polarize issues and bring about bargaining advantages for the revolutionaries are also considered. Thus, the different perspectives of the two authors provide a heuristic basis for theory development and for showing how the same theory can be used for opposite social or political purposes.

THE MEANS OF INFLUENCE

Both individuals and nations can choose between a rather large array of means (or tactics) to achieve influence. Threats, promises, punishments, rewards, persuasion, third-party interventions, and nonverbal or tacit communications may all be employed in order to gain compliance from a target. The effectiveness of a particular means depends upon the situation, the history of interactions, the goals of the source, and the characteristics, costs, and gains to the target. For example, if two parties are involved in an intense conflict, where significant interests of both parties are at stake and neither party trusts the other, it is unlikely that persuasion or promises will contribute to conflict resolution. Under such conditions, each party is more likely to seek third-party intervention or to resort to coercive influence means, depending upon the perceived probability that such tactics would be successful in achieving its minimum goals.

   David Baldwin draws upon economics and small group research to develop a set of hypotheses regarding the use of economic means of influence in international relations. These tentative formulations are developed by comparing economic with military influence techniques. The failure by decision-makers to carefully consider positive and negative economic sanctions often creates a distinct preference for using military power. Since it is important to find alternatives to military sanc-

tions if world peace is to be achieved, Balwin's paper
serves the function of focusing scholarly attention on
a little-discussed topic. Although the unit of analysis is the national decision-maker in the context of
the international system, interesting implications for
interpersonal behaviors can easily be drawn from the
hypotheses offered.

PERSPECTIVES ON POWER

The Albany Symposia were described to the participants
as an interdisciplinary attempt to organize, develop,
evaluate, and interpret *scientific* theories of social,
political, and economic power. The papers show a clear
shift from the typical focus on the passive target of
influence, who, at least in laboratory situations, is
the recipient of threats, promises, or persuasive communications and who then must react in a binary choice
situation (i.e., comply or not comply, change or not
change his attitudes, etc.). New hypotheses have been
proffered about the perception of the origins of behaviors in influence situations, the source's choice of
targets and means, the linkages of the individual to
the social system, and legitimacy and authority. If
these theoretical innovations and changes of focus generate new directions for research, the purpose of the
symposia will have been achieved.

The papers in this collection show a rather disdain-
ful view of the so-called levels of analysis problem.
The very existence of power is a matter of individual
or collective perceptions, according to Gamson and
Schopler and Layton. For Gamson, the nature of the
event, individual or collective, is not as relevant as
the procedure for determining whether power has occurred. The method is the same, presumably, whether
the events at issue are considered psychological, economic, sociological, political, or international in
character. Kelman, Michener and Burt, Carmack, Druckman and Rozelle, and Pruitt and Gahagan deal explicitly
with the articulation between system characteristics
and individual decision-making.

Traditionally, sociological theory has been concerned with finding and specifying linkages between the
individual and the system. Grand theories in the man-

ner of Talcott Parsons (1967) have been quite heuristic, but, unfortunately, they appear to be immune to
empirical tests. The failure to develop an empirically
accessible theory linking the individual with the system has meant that research has often ignored cultural
and societal factors in explaining human behavior. The
result has been that the many generalizations of social
psychology often seem to imply that individuals are
rootless and normless. If one can judge from the papers contributed over the two years of these symposia,
there is a concerted effort underway to carefully specify individual-system linkages so that proposed hypotheses can be experimentally tested.

I

ATTRIBUTIONS
OF POWER

Power and Probability *1*

William A. Gamson

The area of interpersonal power is beset by a handicap
that analysts of community, national, and international
power have been able to avoid. The handicap is the apparently innocent assumption that interpersonal power
should be thought of as the power that one individual
has over another. Even when it is recognized, as it
frequently is, that such power relations may be a two-
way street, the assumption remains a straitjacket.

The problem with thinking of power as a relationship
between people is that it deprives the discourse of an
intellectual apparatus that has proved very useful in
talking about power relations in larger units. Only
the slightest change is necessary to make this apparatus available. First, let's speak of power over behavior rather than power over a person. This means that
we relinquish our claim to be dealing with changes in
attitudes, values, learning, and other internal states
except insofar as we must invoke such concepts to explain the mechanisms by which power operates on behavior. We leave the domain of explaining changes in internal states to other subfields of social psychology
--moral and cognitive development, value and attitude
change, and the like.

Second, let's think about the behavior being explained in a specific way--as the decisions or the
choice among alternatives that an individual makes.
This is hardly any limit at all because it is a sim-

19

ple matter to cast most behavior in these terms. Virtually any action may be viewed as an implicit choice
among possible alternatives even if the other members
of the decision set were never consciously considered.
Many choices will be trivial ones of little interest
or concern, so we must specify the domain that is important to us--the choice of a political candidate to
vote for, the decision to take a job or buy a product,
the choice of a policy to advocate and support, and so
forth.

What I am proposing is that we redefine the task of
an interpersonal power analysis. Instead of attempting to make statements about how much or what kind of
power A has over B, we should speak instead of how much
and what kind of power A has over a specified domain of
B's decisions. The dividend we receive for this change
is the employment of the highly useful conceptualization of power as a change in probability.

THE PROBABILITY CONCEPTION OF POWER

The explicandum for interpersonal power analysis is the
set of decisions that an individual makes. But only
part of the explanation lies within the realm of power.
Many effects on a person's decisions may have nothing
to do with the behavior of other actors but may reflect
his internal states, natural events, the physical environment, and so forth. Clearly, a power explanation
has certain more specific characteristics.

For an intuitive feeling of where the explanation
lies, I like the story about the man who enthusiasti-
cally and repeatedly threw bits of newspaper in the
street. One morning, a woman who had watched this performance for several months approached him and asked
him what he was doing. "I'm throwing this paper down
to keep the elephants out of the streets," he told her.
"But there are no elephants in the streets," she re-
proached him. "That's right," he said triumphantly,
"Effective, isn't it?"

Clearly, the exercise of power must imply some
change over the kind of decision that an individual
would make in the absence of its exercise. But what
of a situation in which I would probably have voted
for Candidate X anyway but became more certain of the

decision as a result of a conversation with a respected friend? Surely there is some kind of influence or power being exercised here, but can one say
that my decision was altered if I probably would have
voted the same way anyhow?

We can say this quite easily if we conceive of the
exercise of power as an act which increases the probability that I will choose a preferred alternative of
the influencer. To conceive of influence as a shift
of probability is one of Robert Dahl's (1957) several
magnificent and seminal contributions to the area of
power analysis.[1] In the example above, my probability
of voting for Candidate X was, let us say, .7 before
talking to my respected friend and .9 after the conversation. The shift from .7 to .9 in the probability of
my choice represents the exercise of power or influence.

It will be useful to have some specific terms to refer to these probabilities in a more general way. First,
we need to refer to the probability that a person will
choose a given alternative before the alleged exercise
of power has occurred. Let's call this the *before* probability or P_b. Second, we need to refer to the probability that a person will choose a given alternative
after the alleged exercise of power has occurred. Let's
call this the *after* probability or P_a. Power has been
successfully exercised if and only if there is a difference between P_a and P_b.

The simplicity of this definition is deceptive.
There are an array of both conceptual and operational
problems. The conceptual issues include such nettles
as anticipated reactions, the stimulation of counter-
activity by one's actions, and negative power. I have
had my say on these matters elsewhere (Gamson 1968,
pp. 68-91) and have nothing to add here. The operational difficulties are formidable enough and will occupy the balance of this essay.

OPERATIONALIZING POWER:
OBJECTIVE PROBABILITY

One may wonder when confronting the problems of operationalizing the probability conception of power, whether the dividend I have offered with such glowing pro-

mises is any blessing at all. If it brings some conceptual clarity, perhaps this is offset by the difficulties of putting it into practical use in research.
Perhaps the touted dividend will turn out to be a
white elephant which has somehow gotten into the
streets after all.

Here's the problem. Imagine that we want to know
whether Mr. A exercises influence over the voting decisions of Senator X and, if so, to what degree. Our
initial approach to this question might consist of the
following easily made observations. We observe the
total set of Senator X's voting decisions. We note
those occasions on which Mr. A has attempted to influence the outcome of Senator X's vote. We can then calculate two conditional probabilities:

(1) The probability that Senator X will vote for
Mr. A's preferences when Mr. A does not attempt influence;

(2) The probability that Senator X will vote for
Mr. A's preferences when Mr. A actively tries to get
Senator X to do so.

If we have a substantial number of cases in each
class, we can compare these conditional probabilities
and we should be able to make meaningful statements
about the power Mr. A has exercised. More specifically, if the probability of Mr. A's getting favorable
votes is higher when he attempts influence than when
he doesn't, we have apparent evidence that he has exercised power over Senator X's decisions. Furthermore, the degree of difference between these two probabilities gives us an apparently precise measure of
the exact amount of power that Mr. A was able to exercise.

I use the word apparently because this procedure
is, in fact, fraught with difficulties. First, there
is the problem of the equivalence of decisions. It is
simply not true for most purposes that a vote is a
vote is a vote. Any comparison of probabilities must
assume that there are certain equivalences in the
classes of votes being compared. But imagine a situation in which Mr. A is active only on pork-barrel issues while he does not attempt influence on such major
policy questions as inflation and unemployment. We
must also assume that he expresses his personal pre-

ferences to an investigator on the issues on which he
is inactive--only thus can we calculate the probability of his getting what he desires in the absence of
influence attempts.

How meaningful can it be to compare Mr. A's probability of getting his preferred alternative in these
two situations--one in which he attempts influence and
one in which he does not? We might easily exaggerate
his power by the following reasoning: Senator X is
personally indifferent and especially open to influence on most pork-barrel issues, but on major policy
questions he is constrained by his own opinions and
those of his vocal constituents. Since Mr. A is only
active on issues that are easy to influence and never
tries the hard ones, he may look very powerful indeed.
On the other hand, we may just as easily *underestimate*
Mr. A's influence. Perhaps he already agrees with
Senator X on most major policy issues and thus has no
incentive or need to exercise influence on such questions. On pork-barrel issues, however, he must go all-
out, since Senator X is generally resistant to special
interest legislation. The result in this case will be
to reveal Mr. A as having a net minus power score. When
he is inactive he almost always gets his preferred alternative, but when he is active and tries hard, his
percentage of success is much lower.

This example does not seem too farfetched, and yet
it leaves our comparisons of probabilities a meaning-
less shambles. Nor is the problem solved by drawing
narrower content categories of decision--for example,
tax votes or foreign policy votes. The assumption of
equivalency within such categories remains and is just
as difficult to meet. Specifically, there must be
equivalency with respect to two things for the probability comparisons to be meaningful:

(1) The average before probability (P_b) must be the
same for the two classes of decisions--those in which
Mr. A attempts influence and those in which he doesn't.

(2) The average degree of competitiveness and attempted influence from others must be the same for the
two classes of decisions.

These are extremely formidable equivalency require-
ments--formidable enough to render the above operation
of questionable usefulness in practice.

As serious as this problem is, there is another
that is perhaps even more so. The probability definition of power seems to lead us off in a direction that
is not really where we want to go. To switch meta-
phors, it is the wrong tool for the job. What we want
is an apparatus that will allow us, among other things,
to make power statements about unique, nonrecurring
situations. We are led instead to compare classes of
decisions so that we can examine the relative frequency of preferred alternatives in the presence or absence of alleged influence.

What does this conception allow us to say about
whether Robert F. Kennedy's sympathy call to Mrs. Martin Luther King influenced the outcome of the 1968
election or whether Dwight D. Eisenhower's pledge to
go to Korea influenced the outcome of the 1952 election? Or, at an interpersonal level, can it tell us
whether Smith's passionate plea swayed the Board of
Trustees from its apparent earlier inclination to cut
the funds for the new building? Our conception of
power ought to allow us to make statements about
classes of events that have only one member--the one
we're really interested in talking about.

OPERATIONALIZING POWER:
SUBJECTIVE PROBABILITY

To talk about power over a single decision, we must
necessarily abandon the notion of objective probability. Objective probability is inseparable from the
idea of the relative frequency of a given outcome, and
there is no meaningful way of talking about the relative frequency of an outcome on a unique occasion--
the outcome either occurs or it doesn't.

Subjective probability is a different matter, and I
offer it as our salvation. The fact is that we talk
all the time about the probability of single events,
and we act on these subjective probabilities. A whole
industry is built very successfully around such probabilities, and its members would have been happy to
quote you precise odds on a wide variety of unique
events--the probability that Baltimore would win the
world series, the probability that the Detroit Lions
would win the Super Bowl, or, lest anyone think I am

being frivolous, the probability that Richard Nixon
would be reelected.

The first thing we must struggle against is the notion that because a judgment is subjective it is unreliable, unstable, idiosyncratic, or unmeasurable. Subjective probabilities are stable, reliable, and measurable. As a collective phenomenon, they are an objective part of the social world, independent of our
whims and wishes.

To make this clearer, let me introduce a new con-
cept--that of the "true" subjective probability of a
given event. The true subjective probability is the
mean probability of a distribution of subjective probability judgments by informed observers. By an informed observer, I mean one who possesses all the information that is available for forming a judgment. Because there are many factors, the judgments of informed observers will have some variance, but there is
reason to expect these judgments to be normally distributed except when the event in question has an extremely high or low subjective probability of occurrence.

It is, of course, not easy to know what this true
subjective probability is. Even if we are ourselves
informed observers, we may be deviant or idiosyncratic
in our judgment. A sample of one to represent the mean
of a distribution is inadequate no matter how percep-
tive the one may be. In short, one's own estimate of
the probability should not be used as a measure of the
true subjective probability.

Gamblers have an excellent device for estimating the
true subjective probability of a given population. They
offer odds and adjust them to the way in which the population places its bets. Let us say that they placed
the odds at 2-1 against Muskie's gaining the Democratic
presidential nomination. If they found that many were
willing to bet on Muskie at these odds and few were
willing to bet against him, they would lower the odds--
perhaps to 3-2. On the other hand, perhaps many might
have been willing to bet against Muskie at the original
odds and few would take a chance in his favor--then
gamblers would have raised the odds, perhaps to 3-1.
The shifts in odds were a search for the true subjective probability, and they would stabilize when they

reach the mean--about as many people would bet for
Muskie as against him. The variance around this mean,
of course, is what makes horse races and election bets.

Once the idea of a true subjective probability has
been accepted, we can--with some additional specifica-
tions--use it in measurement of the exercise of power.
First, if we are interested in power, we must limit our
attention to those events which are under the control
of targets of potential influence. In other words, the
events must be the decisions of men. In studying social power, we are not interested in the subjective
probability of whether it will rain tomorrow; we are
interested in the probability that the state legislature will pass a proposed no-fault insurance bill, that
voters will pass a proposed school bond issue, or that
the president will withdraw troops from Europe. To be
related to a measure of power, the subjective probability in question must refer to the probability that a
particular alternative will be chosen by an actual or
potential *target of influence*.

The most meaningful subjective probabilities are
those held by such targets of influence. Even if the
target is a single individual, the idea of subjective
probability remains valid. To illustrate this, assume
that the decision of concern is whether Professor Jones
will accept an attractive offer from another university.
He has promised to give an answer in thirty days, but
he is able to tell us that he "probably" will accept
the offer. When pressed to be specific, he tells us
that there are two chances in three that he will accept.
Subsequently, his wife is offered an attractive position at his present university and a new interview reveals a change in his subjective probability. He now
suggests that he is quite likely to remain at his present job, rating the chances of accepting the competitive offer at only one in five. Here we have a situation in which the target's subjective probability has
changed significantly, and we can infer influence even
though the actual decision has still not actually been
made.

The measurement process is similar when the decision
is a collective one. Members of the group are asked
to estimate the probability that the decision-making
body of which they are a member will act in a particu-

lar fashion. Thus, they are asked to report partly on
their own actions and partly on their anticipation of
the actions of others. They are, in effect, serving
as particularly well-informed observers who have two
advantages over other observers. First, they have special and unparalleled access to their own reactions,
and second, they have a high probability of exposure
to the thinking and feelings of other members of the
decision-making body.

These advantages distinguish them from other observers only in making them better informed. Empirically, this presumption may turn out to be false in
some cases. Some set of observers, by their more systematic efforts and attention, may be better informed
than members of the target group on the likely actions
of that body. A journalist who regularly covers Congress may be in a better position to know how congress-
men are leaning on an upcoming vote than are many members who are junketing, repairing fences in their home
district, or otherwise preoccupied. Similarly, the
president's analyst may be a better judge than the
president himself of his likely decision on a matter
in which unconscious impulses are heavily involved.

The point of these examples is to underline the fact
that the essential prerequisite for judging subjective
probability is being an informed observer of the body
making the decision. The focus on the judgments of the
decision-making group itself rests on a presumption
that may well be discarded in given cases--that a group
is likely to be especially well-informed on its own
likelihood of taking particular actions.

One final element is necessary to use subjective
probability as a measure of how much influence has occurred. So far, we have suggested that we ask a group
of decision-makers or other informed observers to estimate the probability at time 1 that the group will
make a particular decision. We then repeat this same
question to the group at some subsequent time. If we
find a difference in the two subjective probability
estimates (beyond any fluctuations that could be attributed to measurement error), we have merely established an effect. Something has influenced our decision-makers, but we cannot yet say that an act of social influence has done so. It may have been some fac-

tor beyond the conscious control of men or some unintended by-product of unrelated decisions. Our difference between P_b and P_a establishes a *necessary* but not
a sufficient condition for inferring that social influence has occurred. If there is no difference, we
can dismiss any claims about the success of influence
attempts; if there is a difference, we are still left
with the problem of identifying social influence as
the cause.

Only those effects on subjective probabilities which
can be attributed to the acts of men aimed at altering
the outcome of a decision should qualify as social influence. Unintended acts of men can have important effects on decisions, but it merely contributes conceptual confusion to include these as acts of influence.
Social influence is clearest when a single act of intended influence has occurred between the measurement
of P_b and P_a, a situation which is most likely to occur when we take frequent readings of subjective probability. If we then find a difference between the
before and after probabilities in the intended direction, we can say that social influence has occurred,
and the difference in size tells us how much. Thus we
have a neat way of using the probability concept of
power to allow us to make precise, measurable statements about the exercise of power in the case of single, nonrecurring events.

I'm sure I will have to defend this idea, so let me
deal with several possible objections. What I am arguing is sometimes misunderstood in the following way.
"You are dealing with reputation for influence," I am
told, "rather than actual influence. Maybe the reputation is deserved in some cases, but these informant
judgments about influence are notoriously unreliable.
There is no guarantee that someone has really exercised
power just because a lot of people happen to think this
--they may be subject to similar perceptual distortions.
You can fool all of the people some of the time."

Now I completely agree with the above argument, but
it happens to be quite irrelevant to my suggestion a-
bout measuring the exercise of power. The argument assumes that people are being asked to make judgments a-
bout whether an act has been influential or not, but I
am not suggesting anything of the sort. The only judg-

ment the informed observers are asked to make concerns
the probability of the outcome of a given event at different points in time. The best technique for discovering their subjective probability is to offer them
bets on the outcome at various odds, asking them to
choose which side they would bet on. Their indifference point--the point at which they can't decide which
way they would bet--establishes their individual subjective probability about the outcome. Nowhere are
they asked to make any judgment about *why* they may
have changed an estimate; nowhere are they asked to
speculate on whether any given act led them to change.
They are simply being used to establish the existence
and degree of a shift in the probability of an outcome
--not the causes of the shift.

One might argue that their attributions of causality are inevitably affecting their judgment. Perhaps
Congress has been considering a bill which has only
lukewarm administration support. The president then
goes on national television and strongly endorses the
bill, implying a willingness to put further efforts behind it. Isn't a congressman who raises his estimate
before and after the speech relying on his (perhaps
faulty) attribution of the president's influence on
Congress?

There is no doubt that the attributions which observers make are affecting their subjective probabilities. Still, there is a difference in estimating the
probability of an outcome and in estimating what *caused*
an increase or decrease in probability. Perhaps in
many cases these judgments will be perfectly correlated
-- the more influence one thinks that the president has
over Congress, the greater will be the rise in subjective probability that Congress will pass the bill after
the president supports it.

However, there is an important, systematic bias in
certain attribution judgments that is attenuated or absent when one is merely judging the likelihood of outcomes. The bias stems from the general unwillingness
of targets of influence to attribute influence to
agents whose tactics they dislike. Pressure may work,
but it is a rare politician indeed who admits he acted
because of it. Thus, there is some reason to expect
systematic denial of certain kinds of attributions, but

there is little or no reason for distortion if one is
merely asked to state the present probability of an
outcome without regard to the tactics that may have influenced it. Of course, if the informant is aware of
the nature of the inferences being made from his probability estimates, he may be tempted to distort his reports to affect the inferences. But the separation of
the attribution task from the estimate of probable outcome promises to reduce, if not to fully eliminate this
tendency.

Even if we accept the fact that the observers are
providing us with honest judgments, perhaps they are
ignorant and incompetent. If one uses unreliable informants, here as in any other study the resulting
measures will be correspondingly less reliable. Those
who know little and are bad judges have difficulty making judgments and will produce a high variance in any
test-retest reliability check. But surely one is not
helpless here. I have suggested picking the decision-
makers themselves as particularly well-informed observers. If many of them are ill-qualified to judge the
probable outcome, one is free to establish stricter
qualifications. Clearly, any investigator using this
technique will face the challenge of showing that his
informants were in a position to make intelligent judgments about how the decision-making body would act--
that they had the information, access, and interest to
make their collective judgment an informed one.

Suppose one's observers are well-informed but biased.
There is some reason to suspect that subjective probability judgments are not independent of one's feelings
about the desirability of an outcome. Wishful thinking may be affecting the judgment of many observers,
perhaps quite unconsciously. Thus, they may exaggerate
the likelihood of getting a desired outcome and bias
the measure.

This argument may hold for individual judgments, but
its implications are much less clear for the collective
measure. To the extent that there is a division among
the raters on the outcome desired, they will shift
their estimates in opposite directions. This will have
the effect of increasing the variance of the subjective
probability estimate. But even if there is bias here,
it appears to be a constant bias as likely to be pres-

ent at both time 1 and time 2. If there is a change
between these two periods, it is hard to see how one's
feelings about the outcome could produce the shift.

Another problem centers upon disentangling any single influence attempt from a whole variety of events
and actions that may have occurred in the interval between time 1 and time 2. This problem must also be
viewed in a more general context. Measuring the effect
of an attempted act of influence is a special case of
causal analysis. The problem we face is no different
from the general one of asserting that variable X has
affected variable Y. It is always possible that our
statement is false because of spurious effects--that
both variables were being independently affected by
variable Z, for example.

The approach to this problem is essentially the same
with regard to the measurement of power as it is more
generally. We try as much as possible to isolate the
effect of the act of interest from other possible
causes. One may do this by using small time intervals
--that is, by measuring the true subjective probability
as soon as possible after any act of interest or any
contaminating event has occurred. Let us say, for example, that we are interested in whether the endorsement of Candidate X by Senator Y has improved the candidate's chances of election. It also happens that
Candidate X fathered an illegitimate child in his youth
and that this fact has been brought to light a few days
before the endorsement. If we have a panel of informed
observers, we measure the true subjective probability
before either the endorsement or the revelation; we re-
measure it after the revelation of youthful indiscre-
tion but before the endorsement; and we measure it
again after the endorsement.

Clearly, this will not work if acts and events occur
simultaneously. We will have only net effects here,
and we must rely on whatever outside evidence and argu-
mentation we can muster to disentangle the elements in
the net. There might be some limited value in obtaining hypothetical subjective probability judgments. For
example, what odds would you have accepted on Senator
Edward M. Kennedy's being nominated for president if
Chappaquiddick had not occurred? Such judgments should
be taken with a heavy grain of salt since changing one

important element forces us to make a host of assumptions about secondary effects on other elements. Since these assumptions are likely to be highly variable and implicit, the reliability of the attendant judgment is dubious. Nonetheless, viewed as an attempt to decompose and assess simultaneous events or acts, they may give a few useful clues on relative weights.

SUMMARY

I am arguing for a rather simple and straightforward way of measuring the exercise of power over specific decisions of interest. First, one creates a panel of informed observers. These panel members are assumed to have or are given a common set of relevant information and are asked to fill out a short questionnaire which measures whether they are sufficiently knowledgeable about the situation being studied. Those who fail to meet some threshold of knowledge are eliminated.

The panel members are then given a certain amount of money—real or hypothetical—and asked to consider whether they would bet this money for or against a given outcome at various odds. For any given set of odds, one will then have a percentage of bets for or against the alternative. The entire distribution of odds will enable one to establish the point at which exactly half the informed observers bet each way. One can also gain a measure of confidence by allowing people to reduce the amount they would bet as they approach their subjective indifference point. This also opens the possibility of using a weighted mean of subjective probability judgments—weighted by the degree of confidence that each individual places in his judgment. This procedure is then repeated at regular intervals during a period in which attempts to influence the outcome are occurring and as soon as possible after any influence attempt of special interest.

Does one need a large panel? This depends on the variance of the subjective probability judgments. My hunch—and it is only a hunch—is that the variance is surprisingly low and that a very small panel would do the job. I have found, for example, that I can rather accurately predict the odds that will be available on major sports events with a panel of as few as five or six people. The more important the event and, hence, the more attentive the observers, the lower the variance and the smaller the panel needed to accurately estimate the true subjective probability. If one is talking, for example, about the outcome of a presidential election, I would guess that a panel of thousands would offer little improvement over a panel of only twenty or thirty close election watchers. However, if the decision of interest is obscure, one would expect the variance of subjective probability judgments to rise considerably, and a somewhat larger panel would be necessary to measure the true subjective probability within a given range of error.

So, the promised dividend is, I claim, of considerable value after all. The probability conception of power is not only measurable but, if one relies on subjective probability, may be a first-class bargain. I offer the probability conception to students of interpersonal power as a Best Buy.

NOTE

1. Some people incorrectly credit Weber with this idea because he spoke of power as "the probability that one actor within a social relationship will be in a position to carry out his will despite resistance." (1947, p. 152). One shouldn't be tricked here by the common appearance of the word *probability*, since Weber's definition is not at all the same as the idea of power as a *change* in probability contingent on the actions of the influencer.

REFERENCES

Dahl, R. A. 1957. The concept of power. *Behavioral Science* 2: 201-18.
Gamson, W. A. 1968. *Power and discontent*. Homewood, Ill.: Dorsey Press.
Weber, M. 1947. *The theory of social and economic organization*. New York: Oxford University Press.

Attributions 2
of Interpersonal Power
John Schopler and Bruce D. Layton

Man is distinct from other animals not only because he
makes promises, but also because he needs to identify
the causes of perceived effects. A myriad of events
in our daily lives, ranging from a presumed slight by
a friend to an unexpected job promotion, impel us to
seek explanations. Despite the epistemological dilemmas contained in the logic of specifying causes (e.g.,
Russell 1929), the human mind does not rest easy until
effects are attributed to causes.

The present paper will focus upon those social situations in which individuals may reasonably be considered as potential causal agents. We will attempt to
specify a simple framework consisting of two major components and a set of situational considerations for
predicting the amount of power attributed to an actor,
or to the self, from a knowledge of the course of a
particular interaction. Attributions of power made by
the self, by the person being influenced, and by an
outside observer will be examined in the context of
this framework.

DETERMINANTS OF ATTRIBUTIONS OF POWER

Interpersonal power, as Schopler (1965) has noted, is
typically defined as the induction of change in another person. The attribution of interpersonal power--

The preparation of this paper was facilitated by NSF Grant
GS-2563, to the first author.

perceiving that person A has caused a change in person B--involves a judgment about how much of the change observed in B was caused by A. The perception of interpersonal power is thus an instance of the general attributional problem of specifying how a perceiver allocates the origins, or causes, of a particular effect or effects (Heider 1944, 1958; Kelley 1967). Because the manifestation of power is assumed to be in the induction of influence, attributed power and influence are equivalent. Certain formulations of power, particularly the analysis suggested by March (1957) and extended by Dahl (1957), are explicitly grounded in an equivalence between power and influence. Dahl has identified two components which are basic determinants of an individual's amount of power. We will discuss our modification of these components first, before turning to a discussion of situational factors.

The two components determining power can best be described by reference to the simplest imaginable interaction in a dyad. Let us assume we are watching the mythical person A who is interacting with the hypothetical person B. For example, imagine that A is a mother who enters the family room while her daughter, B, is watching television. The mother says, "It is time to practice the piano," and the daughter turns off the television set and begins to play the piano. As observers of this poignant drama, we would correctly conclude that A has influenced B. The ingredients required for such an attribution are a knowledge of B's state at time 1 (watching television), of A's behavior toward B or merely of A's intervention ("It is time to practice the piano"), and of B's state at time 2 (playing the piano).

In general terms, the sequence of events defining interpersonal power is roughly as follows: given B's state at time 1, person A is seen to have influence over person B if A directs a behavior to B who subsequently does something at time 2 which does not follow from his state at time 1, but which does follow from A's behavior. Considered by itself, B's state at time 1 generates expectations about the next behaviors B will enact. Component 1 is defined in terms of the single subjective probability value linking B at time 1 with B at time 2. The lower this probability, that is, the less likely that B's time 2 state has followed

from her time 1 state, the more potential for attributing power to A. Component 2 is also defined in terms
of a single subjective probability value. It encom-
passes the expectations generated by A's behavior with
respect to B's time 2 state. Given B at time 1, what
is the likelihood that A's intervention will produce B
at time 2? The higher this probability value, the more
potential for attributing power to A. In general, then,
person A will be seen as having maximum power over person B if B's behavior at time 2 was not expected from
what was known about her at time 1, but was expected
from knowledge of A's intervention. The basic elements
in being a powerful witch doctor or teacher require demonstrating that the patient's, or student's, improvement at time 2 would not have been expected from what
was known about him at time 1, but was perfectly predictable from knowledge of the interventions.

The ease or clarity of making power attributions
will vary depending upon circumstances and the type of
relationship linking A with B. The clearest circumstance, for example, is when A and B are in a "closed"
system, that is, a system in which no outside events
can intervene between time 1 and time 2. In closed
systems, the causes for B's behavior must be allocated
between A and B. (Though in some situations "luck" may
also be viewed as a cause.) In an "open" system the
occurrence of outside events require additional judgments about their causal connection with B's state at
time 2. Thus, power attributions about A may be more
ambiguous in open than in closed systems. Power attributions will also be affected by the extent of cooperation or competition existing in the relationship between A and B. Because both components contain estimates of B's state at time 2, attributions of power will
occur most readily when A and B are in a competitive
relationship, or, in the terms of Thibaut and Kelley
(1959), a relationship characterized by noncorrespond-
ence of outcomes. In such relationships, B's state at
time 1 reflects preferences or wishes which are opposed to those of A. The resolution of such a conflict, reflected in B's state at time 2, provides a
clear basis for attributing power. The power attributed to A will be high if the resolution is in keeping with his wishes and will be low if it is not. Rela-

tionships which are not purely competitive, however,
also provide a basis for attributing power. In circumstances of pure cooperation, when A's and B's outcomes are in perfect correspondence, actual power considerations are irrelevant, but attrbutions of power
may still occur.

Finally, it should be noted that it is not essential
for A to represent a single individual. In a recent
New Yorker article, Harris (1971), writing about the
influence of campaign contributions on politicians,
noted that during his senatorial campaign James L.
Buckley "clearly indicated" that if elected he would
oppose the SST program. Harris also wrote that the
Republican party, which was committed to the SST, fun-
neled sizable contributions to Buckley's campaign and
that "the first important vote he cast when he reached
the Senate was in favor of the SST" (p. 57). Given
this set of information, the reader was bound to attribute power to the Republican party.

Component 1: The Subjective Probability of B
at Time 2 from B at Time 1

The first component determining the attribution of power is based on the probability generated by B's state
at time 1 with respect to his state at time 2. There
are several features of this component which require
elaboration. In order for this component to have any
research use, it must be possible to define B's state
at time 1. Despite the arbitrariness of any definition of time 1, observations must begin at some point
in time. Time 1 refers either to the starting point
or to the state immediately preceding the intervention.
In many research settings, defining time 1 will probably prove to be a minor problem and could be operationalized as a subject's state at the beginning of the
experiment or, similarly, a student's performance at
the start of school. Defining time 1 in ongoing interactions, however, presents greater problems. One
possibility is to define it as the state of B which is
closest to A's intervention. Any subsequent state of
B could then serve as the time 2 state. The length of
time spanning time 1 and time 2 is probably an important determinant of power attributions. In general, it

seems likely that the events most proximal to the time
2 state are the most compelling candidates as causes.
If A can obtain B's immediate compliance to a request,
he will probably be seen as more powerful than if B's
compliance is delayed.

Finally, it should be noted that measurement of the
probability value required by component 1 can be accomplished either before B's state at time 2 is known
or after it is known. Observers in the real world typically make the calculations specified by this component after the state at time 2 is known, and this is
the perspective of the present analysis. An investigator, however, could obtain probability estimates of
various potential time 2 states before it is known
which one has actually occurred. The use of this method is likely to produce lower probability values because an event which might occur may not be seen to be
as probable as events which have occurred.

When component 1 is defined in terms of expectations,
two different sequences are treated as identical. Person B's state at time 2 can be unexpected either because B enacts an unexpected response or because B does
not enact an expected response. The former sequence,
ending with B's unexpected response, is probably more
typically associated with power than the latter sequence. The blocking or prevention of an expected response, however, should have comparable importance for
attributing power. It is reminiscent of the power one
would have attributed to Winston Churchill if one knew
the results of his command to an erratic colleague,
"Don't just do something; stand there!"

*Component 2: The Subjective Probability of B
at Time 2 from A's Intervention*

The second component determining the perception of power is based on the probabilities generated by A's intervention with respect to B's state at time 2. The
higher these probabilities, of course, the higher will
be A's attributed power. The meaning of A's intervention is intended to be a broad category, inclusive not
only of verbal responses, but also of the mere presence
of A and whatever relevant attribute he possesses. Certainly, the class of verbal responses which are intend-

ed to influence B, such as commands or requests, are
the clearest examples of interventions which generate
probabilities with respect to B's compliance at time
2, because they specify the direction of change desired
by A. The analysis, however, need not be restricted
only to these responses. Any attribute of person A
which is likely to raise the probability that his intervention will result in B's state at time 2 should increase A's attributed power regardless of the knowledge of B's state at time 1. Person A's high status
or expertness, for example, can be seen as attributes
which increase this probability. In addition, the differences between a demand, a request, and a hint can be
seen in terms of the decreasing probabilities they generate for compliance. It is thus understandable why
people who wish to be seen as having power are fond of
making demands and why people who do not wish to be
seen as having been influenced are reluctant to comply
with demands.

Combining Components to Predict Attributed Power

The relative magnitudes of the probabilities associated
with component 1 and component 2 predict attributed
power. Each of the probabilities represents a separate index of attributed power. The relationship between each index and attributed power can best be established empirically. In the absence of any data on
which to base rules for combining the two indices, we
have made the guess that simple subtraction will be an
adequate starting point. The attributed power of A,
therefore, can be written as:

$$\text{Attributed power of } \overset{\bullet}{A} = v_2 - v_1,$$

where v_2 is the value of the conditional probability of
B's state at time 2, given A's intervention, and v_1 is
the value of the conditional probability of B's state
at time 2, given B's state at time 1. The formula is
similar to the one suggested by Dahl for determining
actual power.[1] It makes two very strong assumptions.
In the first place, it assumes that the values of both
components are equally weighted. Second, it assumes
equal interval scaling for the probability values as-

sessing each component.

The formula gives an aura of precision which is admittedly unwarranted, but it is presented as a convenient way to illustrate our general intentions in deriving attributed power. The lower the probabilities associated with component 1 and the higher the probabilities associated with component 2, the greater will be A's attributed power. Maximum attributed power exists when B does something unpredictable which is perfectly predictable from A's intervention. The value of attributed power would then be equal to +1. Minimum attributed power is defined by a -1. It exists when B does domething predictable which is not predictable from A's intervention. The positive and negative values of attributed power are probably not symmetrical. It seems intuitively correct to assume that attributed power will already be low whenever the indices equal zero. Whenever what B has done at time 2 is as likely to follow from his state at time 1 as from A's intervention, attributions of power will be ambiguous and are likely to be low. Increasing negative values, then, will not reflect a continuous loss of attributed power. They may, however, be useful in distinguishing among variations in B's amount of control over his own outcomes. As the values become more negative, B has greater control over his own outcomes and hence more responsibility for those outcomes.

Self-Relevance

The two components discussed so far could be used to determine actual amounts of power, as well as the amount of power attributed to A by a disinterested observer. If, however, the course of an interaction has relevance for the person making power attributions, such relevance will affect his attributions. For example, the participants in the interaction are likely to see their own actions in the most favorable light possible. Balance principles suggest that a person will be more likely to take credit for causing a benefit to another or to himself than to take the blame for causing negative outcomes. Whenever B's state at time 2 is evaluatively positive or negative, in the phenomenology of the participants, their power attributions will be directed toward maintaining self-esteem. Furthermore, even if the outcomes at time 2 are neither positive nor negative, B will generally be more resistant to attributing a change in his own behavior to A than would A or an outside observer. The consequences of self-enhancement tendencies are assumed to be manifested by their impact on the probability judgments defined by the first two components. They imply the necessity of taking into account whether B's outcomes are good or poor and the role of the person whose judgments of attributed power are being investigated.

APPLICATIONS OF THE FRAMEWORK TO PREVIOUS RESEARCH

Attributions of power are determined by the two components contained in any interaction sequence and by the self-enhancing tendencies of the individual making the attributions. The consequences of self-enhancing tendencies differ, depending upon whether power attributions are made by an outside observer, the person who makes the influence attempts, or the target of influence. Research from each of these perspectives will be reviewed and reinterpreted in terms of our framework. Because none of these studies have used the probability values specified by the framework, the research cannot be a test of the framework, but is merely illustrative of its applicability.

Attributing Own Influence

According to the proposed framework, person A will attribute power to himself if his interactions with B lead to a change in B which was not predictable from B's initial state but was predictable from A's interventions. The consequences of A's interventions depend not only upon the characteristics of his responses --their strength and direction--but also upon B's characteristics. Commands or requests directed toward high-status persons are likely to be seen as less predictive of conformity than those directed toward low-status persons. This was the basic assumption in the well-known Thibaut and Riecken (1955) experiment.

Each of Thibaut and Riecken's subjects was required

to make identical requests of two persons, one of whom
was of high social status, the other of low social status.   In one study, for example, the subject had to de-
vise a persuasive appeal to induce the two persons to
donate to a Red Cross blood campaign.   After several
influence attempts, both the high- and low-status persons, who were actually confederates, always complied
by indicating that they were persuaded by the subject.
Thibaut and Riecken predicted that subjects would view
the high-status person's conformity as being internally
caused because a high-status person had sufficient power to resist a request.   They also predicted that compliance by the low-status person would be viewed as externally caused by the force of the power relationship.
The predictions were confirmed.

In terms of the present framework, the Thibaut and
Riecken results can be understood as a manipulation of
the values of component 2.   The power to resist, which
was presumed to be associated with status, can be
viewed as meaning that the probability of a request's
producing conformity is lower when directed toward a
high-status person than toward a low-status person. Actual compliance by both persons then leads to attributing less power over the high-status person than over
the low-status person, and, respectively, attributing
an internal and an external locus of causality.   The
contribution made by component 1 (the probability of
someone's being willing to donate blood) to the results
seems negligible.   If high-status persons are seen as
more likely to donate blood than low-status persons,
however, the power attributed over the high-status person would be correspondingly smaller.   Finally, it
should be noted that in this experiment identical
amounts of change occurred in both the high- and the
low-status person.   The amount of power the subject attributed to himself presumably differed because of the
difference in status of the persons upon whom influence
attempts were made, suggesting that amount of change
alone is not a sensitive index of attributed power.

By extending Thibaut and Riecken's reasoning, Strickland (1958) predicted that trust for another would be
enhanced if his compliance were obtained freely (internally) rather than by an enforced power relationship
(externally).   The experimental setting required sub-

jects to act as supervisors who differentially monitored two fictitious workers on ten trials. At the
end of the ten trials, the subjects learned that both
workers had met a high production standard and had
equal work outputs. On each of the trials in a second
set, the supervisor was free to monitor the worker of
his choice. Strickland found that in the second set
of trials supervisors were more likely to monitor the
worker who had been heavily monitored in the first set
and to trust him less than the infrequently monitored
worker. These results have been recently replicated
by Kruglanski (1970).

It is probably evident by now how the Strickland experiment relates to our two components. Given the iden-
tically good work records, the supervisor's (A) self-
attribution of power over the heavily monitored worker
(B) must have been higher than his self-attribution of
power over the infrequently monitored worker (C). Trust,
obtaining conformity without the exercise of power, was
therefore greater for worker C than for worker B. Consider the information available to the subjects about
worker C. His high productivity would not appear to
have been caused by the subject's minimal intervention.
It would be more likely to be seen as predictable from
his state at time 1. Because the subject's intervention accompanied the productivity of B, B's productivity is likely to be seen as having depended more upon
A's intervention than upon B's initiative. That is,
with respect to B the probability value of component 2
was higher than the value of component 1.

The two experiments cited above are limited to situations in which A obtains uniformly positive outcomes,
that is, in which the target persons either comply with
a request or achieve high productivity. The first two
components of our framework, however, predict that any
change in B's behavior following A's intervention will
be attributed to A's power. This generalization is
qualified by the factor of self-relevance, which suggests that a person will be more likely to take credit
for causing a positive outcome than to take blame for
causing a negative outcome.

An experiment reported by Johnson, Feigenbaum, and
Weiby (1964) is another illustration of the framework
within which positive and negative outcomes have been

used. In a simulated teaching situation, student-
teachers were to instruct fictitious target persons
on arithmetic multiplication tasks. The experiment
was divided into two parts. Each teacher was faced
with two "students." One of these students performed
consistently well. The experimental manipulation consisted of varying the performance of the second "student." He performed poorly on the first part and either remained incompetent or improved on the second
part. Perceived influence was felt over the student
who improved, but not over the student who remained incompetent. (No ratings of perceived influence over the
consistently good student were obtained.) A uniformly
poor performance was attributed to qualities inherent
in the student. On the surface, these results fit our
framework. Consider the poor performer who improves.
His state at time 2 is both evaluatively positive and
not predictable from his state at time 1. The positive
end state at time 2 is likely, however, to have been
produced by the teacher's intervention. Consequently,
there is a self-attribution of power by the teacher. A
different set of circumstances holds for the student
whose performance was consistently poor. His state at
time 2 is characterized as being predictable from his
state at time 1, not expected from the teacher's intervention, and evaluatively negative. It is not surprising, then, that the teacher feels little influence over
his student's performance.

Because of certain limitations in the experimental
design, the results of Johnson, Feigenbaum and Weiby
must be interpreted with a degree of caution. For example, the subjects were actual student-teachers who
believed that they were to be evaluated on the basis of
the performance of their "students." This feature
would tend to enhance the self-relevance of attributions and could account for the results. What may be
more to the point, however, is that perceived influence
was confounded with performance. It is impossible to
determine from this design whether teachers believed
they had influence only when their students changed or
only when they performed well. There is no indication
of whether deteriorating performance would result in
self-attributions of power.

Further research in this area has been recently recently reported by Beckman (1970). Beckman's subjects taught two fictitious students at the same time. One of these students performed consistently well throughout a series of four trials. The experimental manipulation was induced by varying the performance of the second student, which was programmed from one of three patterns. These patterns were: *(a)* low initial and low final performance, *(b)* low initial and high final performance, and *(c)* high initial and low final performance. Data were also collected from observer-subjects, who merely read a stylized transcript from one of the three experimental conditions.

For the present our concern will be limited to the active participants. Coding of a set of open-ended measures concerning the perception of causality for the student's performance revealed that teachers attributed causality for a student's performance to themselves only when their students improved. In contrast, when the student performed poorly, responsibility was attributed to various causes external to the teacher, such as the child's motivation or situational factors. This was true regardless of whether the pattern for failure was low-low or high-low. The affective significance of failure, then, eliminated self-attributions of influence.

Our framework, however, would have predicted that affective significance would reduce, but not eliminate, attributions of influence in a change situation leading to failure. As Beckman has noted, it is possible that the subjects, who were actual student-teacher volunteers, were responding to the starkness of the teaching situation in disclaiming responsibility for failure. In addition, it must be remembered that each subject simultaneously "taught" a student who performed in a consistently successful fashion. Comparisons between the performance of the two students would certainly be inevitable, and would probably foster ego-saving mechanisms. The teacher at least knows that her interventions are not invariably accompanied by low performance.

One of the problems in the studies of Johnson et al. and Beckman is the experimenter's lack of control over the nature of the influence attempt. In both experiments the teacher-subjects were free to do and say almost whatever they wished. In addition, there was a

clear emphasis on the superior-subordinate relationship between teacher and student. These factors also
add to the likelihood of perceiving improvement as influence and failure as situationally determined.

In a recent investigation stemming directly from our
framework (Schopler and Layton 1972), we attempted to
control these variables. Each subject (A) was paired
with one partner (B) who had previously performed well
or poorly on a social judgment task. There were no social status differences between partners. The partner's previous level of performance was used to manipulate the subject's expectations about performance on
the next set of trials. During the next set of trials
the subjects were asked to take an advisory role with
respect to their partners. The strength of the subject's intervention was held constant by limiting his
communication to the sending of answers which B was
free to accept or reject. After completion of the second set of trials the subject learned how well his
partner had done. The partner's performance was presented as having remained the same (low-low or high-
high) or as having changed (low-high or high-low). The
major dependent variable was attributed influence over
the partner.

The presumed value of component 1 was manipulated by
making the partner's performance at time 2 expected or
unexpected from his previous performance. Self-relevance was also manipulated by having the partner's second performance represent success or failure. The value of component 2 was not directly manipulated. It
was predicted that more influence would be attributed
to a partner whose performance changed than to a partner whose performance remained the same. This prediction was confirmed. Attributed influence was greater
when B performed at time 2 in a manner that was unexpected from his performance at time 1 (low ability B,
success; high ability B, failure) than when his performance was expected (low ability B, failure; high ability B, success). The effects of self-relevance were
also evident. Subjects believed themselves to be more
influential when B succeeded than when B failed. Furthermore, the results showed the basic difference between the consequences of expecting a good or a poor
performance. As was noted earlier with respect to the

Johnson et al. experiment, a student who performs poorly at first should provide the clearest evidence for
attributing influence. His success is unexpected.
Therefore, the implications of both the value of component 1 and the factor of self-relevance are in the
direction of inducing a self-attribution of influence.
If he fails, his failure is expected. The implications
of neither the value of component 1 nor self-relevance
are in the direction of self-attribution of influence.
The consequences are different for a subject whose
partner's initial performance was good. Both the partner's unexpected failure and his expected success pit
the implications of component 1 and self-relevance
against each other. The occurrence of a change is accompanied by negatively valued outcomes. Expected performance is accompanied by positively valued outcomes.
The pattern of means corroborates this analysis. The
most influence was attributed to the partner whose initial performance was poor and who subsequently succeeded. The least influence was attributed to the
partner whose performance was poor initially and remained poor.

Component 2, the probability of the intervention's
producing B's state at time 2, was not manipulated in
our experiment. The fact that individuals attribute
more influence to themselves for a partner's success
than for his failure may be partly a function of the
value of component 2. From A's point of view his own
interventions may simply appear to be more predictive
of success than failure. Indeed, except for relationships in which A and B are competing, A's interventions
are typically intended to produce success and may actually be more predictive of success than failure. Phy-
sicians, parents, teachers, or psychotherapists undoubtedly believe that their interventions will produce
good outcomes for their respective Bs. If it were demonstrated that success, compared to failure, generated
higher probability values for component 2, it would not
be clear whether such asymmetry was in the service of
self-enhancement or of a realistic assessment of the
base-rate consequences of the particular intervention.

The conditions specified by the present framework
are sometimes contained in research not explicitly investigating power. Although a number of experiments

might be cited, it will be sufficient to illustrate
this point by discussing one such study. Aronson and
Linder (1965) tested the effects of differing sequences
of personal evaluation upon interpersonal attraction.
It was their idea that a gain, or a loss, in self-esteem would be a more important determinant of attraction than would uniform evaluations. Female subjects
interacted with another subject (who was actually a
confederate) over a series of seven meetings. Following each meeting, the subject "overheard" an interview
between the experimenter and the confederate in which
the confederate made evaluative remarks about the subject. The sequence of evaluations over the interviews
constituted the major manipulation. Four sequences
were used. One group heard uniformly positive evaluations about themselves, while a second group heard uniformly negative evaluations. A third group heard negative evaluations first, followed by positive evaluations, while a fourth group heard positive evaluations
first, followed by negative evaluations. As predicted,
the negative-positive sequence resulted in significantly higher liking than the positive-positive sequence.
The positive-negative sequence resulted in more liking
than the negative-negative sequence, although the difference was not significant. These results were for a
single item measuring liking. On trait ratings, however, the significant effect was absent, and for three
of the fourteen traits used a significant reversal was
found. Compared to the negative-positive confederate,
the positive-positive confederate was rated as nicer,
warmer, and more friendly.

The present framework suggests that Aronson and
Linder created differences in the subjects' attribution
of power to themselves. Consider the differences between the negative-positive and the positive-positive
condition. In the former the confederate changed to an
end state which was favorable toward the subject. This
would represent the conditions for inducing maximum
power. The accomplice's end state is not expected from
the state at the start and is evaluatively positive.
Furthermore, it is expected from the subject's own interventions. The uniformly positive other, however, is
more predictable from time 1 to time 2. It must further be assumed that individuals who feel they have in-

fluenced another to like them will reciprocate greater liking than those who have not had such influence.

The reversals found for the trait ratings are also interpretable by our framework. If the confederate's change from negative to positive evaluations was attributed to influence, the occurrence of positive evaluations does not provide stable indices of enduring, positive traits. The uniformly positive confederate, whose end state is predictable from time 1, is more likely to be seen as possessing such traits as friendliness and warmth.

The research discussed in this section on self-attributions of influence supports the framework originally presented. This research, however, has been limited essentially to closed systems. There is very little chance in these experiments for the subjects to attribute influence for B's state at time 2 to any factor other than themselves or B. In these closed systems the behavior change from time 1 to time 2 may be so overwhelming as to lessen the likelihood of a subject's searching for causal factors other than his own intervention. For example, in our experiment we had expected that subjects might attribute their partners' unexpected failure to a reduction in the partners' effort or motivation rather than to their own intervention. There was, however, no evidence to support this interpretation. The perceived effort of B was constant regardless of B's success or failure. If, in other situations, several possible causal sources were present, we could expect that individuals would be more likely to attribute negative outcomes to these sources and positive outcomes to themselves.

B's Attribution of Influence to A

There is surprisingly little research devoted to understanding how the target of influence preceives the causes of any change which has been induced in him. Although countless studies have investigated various variables which produce change in subjects, to our knowledge no subjects have ever been asked to identify the causes of their own change. Such disproportionate experimental emphasis may be unwitting testimony to the fact that people feel reluctant to admit to others that

they have been influenced. Experimenters may not have
asked such questions because subjects would not have
answered them. Certainly, a number of writers have
stressed the psychological importance of feeling free
from influence. This is the theme contained in concepts of self-consistency (cf. Brown's [1965] interpretation of dissonance effects), of being the origin of
one's acts (de Charms 1968), or of avoiding constraints
on one's behavioral freedom (Brehm 1966).

In keeping with the factor of self-relevance, a person's reluctance to proclaim that he has been influenced is probably mitigated by whether he views his
state at time 2 as being positive or negative. If B
has obtained good outcomes he is likely to discount A's
power. If B has obtained poor outcomes he is likely to
elevate A's power. It serves self-interest to attribute superior performance, correct decisions, and positive interpersonal experiences to oneself, while attributing poor performance, decisions, and interpersonal
experiences to another.

The implications of this reasoning suggest several
basic differences between A's and B's attributions of
power. These differences will be the focus of the remainder of this section.

If self-relevance is an important consideration, it
will affect B's attributions in an opposite way to A's
attributions when the time 2 state has similar evaluative meaning for both of them. Both A and B will have
a tendency to ascribe the credit for good outcomes to
themselves, but to blame the other for poor outcomes.
Under such circumstances A's and B's attributions will
be discrepant. When B's state at time 2 has opposite
evaluative meaning for A and B, the force of self-relevance will be in the same direction for both participants. For example, if B dislikes doing the things required by A, but A likes them, they will both wish to
attribute B's conformity to A's power.

Another implication of the self-enhancement assumption is that the optimal conditions for exercising power are those in which B's desired behaviors are obtained in a context which is sufficiently ambiguous to
permit B to discount the role of A's power and to enhance the perception of his own control. Such conditions are met, for example, when A links the behavior

he desires to accepted norms (Thibaut and Kelley 1959),
or when his intervention provides valid information
about environmental entities (Kelley and Thibaut 1969).

According to Thibaut and Kelley, by linking a desired behavior to an accepted norm, A can avoid the use
of personal power to obtain conformity. The use of a
normative referent presumably makes obtaining conformity more likely. It may also create ambiguity for B
with respect to assessing the causes of his conformity.
In B's eyes, the norm rather than A's intervention may
be seen as the major determinant of his change. The
value of component 2 would thus be lowered. Furthermore, any behavior which is consistent with a norm represents a class of behaviors that other people would
also enact. A conforming B may believe that it was
very likely that he would have performed the behavior
without A's intervention. That is, he has some reasons
to raise the value of component 1. Either of these
consequences would serve to lower B's attribution of
A's power.

In a similar way, when A's intervention provides B
with information about particular behavioral entities,
some ambiguity is created about the cause of B's change.
Raven and Kruglanski (1970) have noted that even though
A is the purveyor of B's new knowledge, the information
provided may rapidly become independent of A. For example, when a teacher instructs her pupils on the rule
for multiplying a number by 10 in a specific arithmetic
problem, the students will probably attribute their
changed behavior at time 2 to the teacher's instruction. But since the students have now been given a
general rule to follow for other problems, they will
probably attribute the cause for their behavior in
these later situations to their own knowledge of the
multiplicative rule rather than to the teacher. Thus,
once B has acquired and mastered the new information,
he is likely to feel free of A's power and to use his
own initiative in situations which follow time 2. Although A may be prone to continually recall B as he was
at time 1 and to see evidence of his own power in B's
use of the information, B is likely to have a shorter
memory span. Parents and teachers tend to persist in
the annoying habit of remembering previous states that
their children or students consider to be irrelevant

history. It is an intriguing, albeit unresolved, problem to specify what processes determine the point at
which any B considers new information as belonging to
himself.

This problem could be examined by an extension of
the experimental format used by both Beckman (1970) and
Schopler and Layton (1972). In keeping with the latter paradigm, a subject (A) might be asked to give what
he considers as the correct answer to another subject
(B) over a long series of trials. Changes in A's perception of his influence could be assessed over time.
Similarly, by placing the subject in the role of B,
B's attribution of influence by A could also be examined over time.

As a final point, it might also be noted that B's
attributions of power may be affected by whether his
behavior at time 2 necessitates a further response from
A. It is likely that the power attributed to A will be
less if he must make a response contingent upon B's behavior at time 2. Various authors have suggested that
A's use of reward or punishment has different consequences for his relationship with B (cf French and
Raven 1959; Collins and Raven 1969; Raven and Kruglanski 1970); in addition, there may also be differences
in attributions of power. If A is using rewards to obtain conformity, he must make another response when B
conforms, that is, A must reward B. It may be that
from B's point of view conformity exerts some control
over A and lessens A's attributed power. In the extreme case in which conformity is always followed by a
reward, B can easily invert the power relationship. It
is like the situation depicted in a well-known cartoon
a number of years ago. A rat in his home cage is saying to his cagemate, "I've really got this psychologist
conditioned; every time I press the bar, he gives me a
pellet of food." The use of punishment, in contrast,
requires A to do nothing if B has complied. In this
situation, B can only exert control if he does not conform and thus requires A to make a response. B can
only increase his sense of control, and lower A's attributed power, by conforming to rewards and not conforming to punishment.

Observer's Attribution of Influence

The framework should remain a valid predictor of attributed influence when an observer views the situation
facing A and B. As in self-attributions of influence,
when B's state at time 2 is predictable from his state
at time 1, an observer would probably attribute B's
second performance to characteristics within B. When
B's state at time 2, on the other hand, follows from
A's intervention but is not predictable from B's state
at time 1, the observer will attribute influence to A.
Although the basic components of the framework predict
attributed influence for observers and participants,
the self-relevancy considerations which qualified the
attributions made by the participants will not be important for the observers. We would not expect an uninvolved observer to be influenced by the valence of
the outcomes for B at time 2. His perceptions of causality for the change in B's performance would not be
biased by the same defensive self-attributions that
are present when A perceives himself as the cause of
B's failure. For observers, thus, we would not expect
any differential estimates of A's influence to result
from B's success or failure.

This is also the approach taken by Beckman (1970) in
her investigation of attributional differences between
participants and observers. She hypothesized that observers would not be affected by the "ego relevancies"
of the experimental situation. Observers read a story
which was a partial replica of the situation actually
faced by the teacher-participants. Only in what Beckman called the "ego enhancing" condition, where the
student performed poorly at first and then improved
over time, did observers differ from participants in
the open-ended attributions of causality. In this condition participants were more likely to take credit for
the improvement than observers were willing to grant
them. Observers and participants, however, did not
differ in their causal attributions in the "ego protec-
tive" conditions, where the student failed. Unfortunately, participant-observer differences may have been

obscured both by the incomplete transcript presented to
the observers and by the general drawbacks of the design, which were discussed earlier. Despite the problems with this study, to the best of our knowledge it
is the only experimental attempt aimed at investigating differences between participants and observers with
respect to causal attributions of influence. It remains important because of the basic questions it
raises.

Other experiments have collected data which are relevant to the observer-participant distinction. For
example, in a series of investigations Alex Bavelas and
his associates (Bavelas, Hastorf, Gross, and Kite 1965;
Hastorf, Kite, Gross, and Wolfe 1965) have demonstrated
the basic similarity of observer and participant attributions of influence. In the initial experiment Bavelas et al. examined sociometric ratings and verbal output from the four members of a discussion group. After
determining a base rate of verbal output for each member in the first discussion period, Bavelas et al. selected one of the quieter members of the group as the
target person whose behavior they were primarily interested in changing. Through a system of red and
green lights used in the second discussion period, the
target person was rewarded for participating and punished for remaining silent. At the same time, the other group members received an opposite reinforcement
schedule: they obtained rewards for remaining silent
and punishments for talking. It was found that the
participation of the target person increased significantly during the second discussion period compared to
the first discussion period. In addition, the target
person was rated by the other group members as being
more effective in guiding the discussion and in general leadership ability than he had been in the first
discussion period. All the participants, however, were
unaware of the precise contingencies used by the experimenters in their assignment of rewards and punishments.

In a similar experiment, Hastorf et al. reasoned
that the extent of an observer's knowledge of the reinforcing contingencies producing the behavioral change
might differentially affect the ratings of the target
person. Hastorf et al had observer-subjects listen to
two taped discussions of a three-man group. In the

second discussion one of the group's participants increased his verbal output; another decreased his verbal
output; and the verbal output of the third participant
remained the same. When the two group members who
changed were rated by observer-subjects who were ignorant of the contingencies, the results essentially replicated those of Bavelas et al. The change in participation from time 1 to time 2 was seen both as internally controlled and as varying in quality directly
with the quantity of participation. When the group
members were evaluated by observer-subjects who were
informed of the experimental reinforcement contingencies, however, the two group members who changed were
seen as externally controlled. Awareness of the reinforcement contingencies used by the experimenter evi-
dently made the group members' change appear to be
caused by the experimenter's power. When observers
were faced with essentially the same situation as participants, attributions of causality for a participant's changed behavior and perceptions of effectiveness and leadership were identical for observers and
participants. If the observers were aware of the experimenter's intervention, however, the changed participation was attributed to external factors, that is,
to the experimenter's power.

The discussion thus far on participant-observer differences has suggested that participants' attributions
of power are influenced by some affective considerations which are rather unimportant for the observers'
assignments of responsibility. There are certain affective considerations, however, which may be more important to the observer than to the participant. These
considerations involve the observer's evaluation of
both A and B independently of, and in relation to, the
outcome at time 2. For example, the attributed influence of a dissertation chairman in the production of a
brilliant dissertation is likely to be enhanced by the
observer who likes the chairman and dislikes the student. Conversely, if the dissertation is a catastrophe,
the liked professor's attributed influence will probably drop. The consequences of these affective considerations are thought to be manifested by their impact
on the probability values defined by the two components
of our framework.

OVERVIEW

The present framework attempts to predict the amount of
power attributed to person A in a particular relationship. The predictions require obtaining the probability values of two components. These components can be
seen as instances of a naive version of J. S. Mills'
method of differences. Kelley's (1967) analysis of
attributional processes defines this method as the
"basic analytical tool" determining attributions. He
has summarized it as follows, "The effect is attributed to that condition which is present when the effect is present and which is absent when the effect is
absent" (p. 194). Application of the method of differences implies the necessity for having, at a minimum, two occasions for making observations. Causal
attributions and, specifically, attributions of influence can be made from a single observation if prior expectations exist about the relationship between a condition and an effect. The attributions specified in
the present framework are determined by the match between what is expected and what is observed.

Although no direct empirical tests of the framework
exist, its applicability to previous research seems to
warrant some guarded optimism about its research utility. Furthermore, the measurements specified by the
two components should be relatively easy to obtain and
could be applied in a variety of settings. It is also
recognized that the framework, as presently constituted,
has definite limitations. Chief among these is its restriction to predicting attributed power for a particular dyadic relationship. Comparisons of attributed
power among different relationships could be made by
taking into account additional variables. For example,
such comparisons could include measurements of the importance to B of the behavior being changed, as well as
of the number of Bs over which a given A can exercise
power.

We should note an apparent paradox with respect to
power research. Despite the obvious importance and
relevance of power formulations, the amount of research
they have generated is dismayingly small. While the
general themes of influence and induction of change are

dominant themes in social psychology, formulations of
interpersonal power seem to have had little impact on
research. We would attribute the existence of this
paradox to at least two causes. In the first place,
when interpersonal power is defined in terms of amount
of influence, there is no way to generate meaningful
hypotheses relating power to influence. Amount of power and amount of influence must covary by definition.
An experiment which manipulated A's power in order to
assess his influence over B would merely be providing
evidence about the validity of the operations used to
define power. This is not the case if amount of power
is related to a dependent variable other than influence, such as the permanence of change or the attractiveness of A. It is not surprising that the more interesting power hypotheses usually involve dependent
variables other than amount of influence or change. The
second cause, as has been noted in previous reviews
(Schopler 1965), involves the difficulty of meeting the
measurement specifications required by various power
formulations. The procedures required to obtain the
requisite data have either been unspecified or have
been quite difficult to manage. Although any analysis
of power, including our framework, is vulnerable to
these problems, a focus on the attribution of power reduces their impact. As has been noted above, the measurement problems are not formidable. In addition, because the components in our framework define states not
uniquely related to power, predictions of their relationship to influence have general relevance. Amount
of influence, therefore, remains an important dependent
variable.

In summary, we have proposed a framework for predicting attributions of interpersonal power based upon
two subjective probability estimates. Given an influencing agent (A) and a target of influence (B), predictions of attributed power depend upon the likelihood
of the occurrence of B's behavior at time 2 given his
behavior at time 1 and upon the probability of B's behavior at time 2 given that A has intervened between
time 1 and time 2. Attributed power is defined as the
difference between these two probability estimates. The
probability estimates can be affected both by objective
properties of the situation, such as A's acknowledged

expertness, and by relatively subjective factors, such as self-enhancement tendencies. These latter factors of self-relevance determine the differing attributions of power that are made by the person who makes the influence attempt, the target of influence, and an outside observer. The framework specifies that person A will attribute power to himself when B's behavior at time 2 is not predictable from B's initial state but is predictable from A's intervention. Furthermore, when B's state at time 2 is evaluatively positive, the likelihood of A's attributing power to himself should be markedly greater. Self-enhancement effects assume even greater importance when B is attributing power to A. For example, when B has obtained good outcomes, he is likely to discount A's power, but when poor outcomes have been obtained, he is likely to elevate A's power. Finally, the basic components of the framework predict that power attributed by an outside observer will be the same as that attributed by a participant if self-relevancy considerations for the observer and the participant are the same.

NOTE

1. Dahl defines power as the probability of B's enacting a response in A's presence minus the probability of B's enacting that response in A's absence. In circumstances where A's intervention results in B's not enacting a response he would otherwise always make, the power index has a negative value and Dahl speaks of negative power. Because our framework utilizes expectations rather than overt acts, amount of power is equal where B's response at time 2 represents the blocking of a usual response or the induction of an unusual response. Negative values in the present framework are therefore not the same as in Dahl's formulation.

REFERENCES

Aronson, E., and Linder, D. 1965. Gain and loss of esteem as determinants of interpersonal attractiveness. *Journal of Experimental Social Psychology* 1: 156-71.

Bavelas, A., Hastorf, A. H., Gross, A. E., and Kite, W. R. 1965. Experiments on the alteration of group structure. *Journal of Experimental Social Psychology* 1: 55-70.

Beckman, L. 1970. Effects of students' performance on teachers' and observers' attributions of causality. *Journal of Educational Psychology* 61: 76-82.

Brehm, J. W. 1966. *A theory of psychological reactance*. New York: Academic Press.

Brown, R. 1965. *Social psychology*. New York: Free Press.

Collins, B. E., and Raven, B. H. 1969. Group structure: attraction, coalitions, communication, and power. In G. Lindzey and E. Aronson (Eds.), *The handbook of social psychology*. 2d ed. Vol. 4. Reading Mass.: Addison-Wesley, pp. 102-204.

Dahl, R. A. 1957. The concept of power. *Behavioral Science* 2: 201-18.

de Charms, R. 1968. *Personal causation*. New York: Academic Press.

French, J. R. P., Jr., and Raven, B. 1959. The bases of social power. In D. Cartwright (Ed.), *Studies in social power*. Ann Arbor, Mich.: Institute for Social Research, pp. 150-67.

Harris, R. 1971. Annals of politics: a fundamental hoax. *New Yorker* August 7: 37-64.

Hastorf, A. H., Kite, W. R., Gross, A. E., and Wolfe, L. J. 1965. The perception and evaluation of behavior change. *Sociometry* 28: 400-410.

Heider, F. 1944. Social perception and phenomenal causality. *Psychological Review* 51: 358-74.

------. 1958. *The psychology of interpersonal relations*. New York: Wiley.

Johnson, T. H., Feigenbaum, R., and Weiby, M. 1964. Some determinants and consequences of the teacher's perception of causation. *Journal of Educational Psychology* 55: 237-46.

Kelley, H. H. 1967. Attribution theory in social psychology. In D. Levine (Ed.), *Nebraska symposium on motivation, 1967*. Lincoln: University of Nebraska Press, pp. 192-238.

Kelley, H. H., and Thibaut, J. W. 1969. Group problem solving. In G. Lindzey and E. Aronson (Eds.), *The handbook of social psychology*. 2d ed. Vol. 4. Reading, Mass.: Addison-Wesley, pp. 1-101.

Kruglanski, A. W.   1970.   Attributing trustworthiness in supervisor-worker relations. *Journal of Experimental Social Psychology* 6:   214-32.

March, J. G.   1957.   Measurement concepts in the theory of influence. *Journal of Politics* 19:   202-26.

Raven, B. H., and Kruglanski, A. W.   1970.   Conflict and power. In P. Swingle (Ed.), *The structure of conflict*. New York: Academic Press, pp. 69-109.

Russell, B.   1929.   *Our knowledge of the external world*. New York: Norton. Reprinted as: On the notion of cause, with applications to the free-will problem. In H. Feigl and M. Brodbeck (Eds.), *Readings in the philosophy of science*. New York: Appleton-Century-Crofts, 1953, pp. 387-407.

Schopler, J.   1965.   Social power. In L. Berkowitz (Ed.), *Advances in experimental social psychology*. Vol. 2. New York: Academic Press, pp. 177-218.

Schopler, J., and Layton, B.   1972.   Determinants of the self-attribution of having influenced another person. *Journal of Personality and Social Psychology* 22: 326-32.

Strickland, L. H.   1958.   Surveillance and trust. *Journal of Personality* 26:   200-215.

Thibaut, J. W., and Kelley, H. H.   1959. *The social psychology of groups*. New York: Wiley.

Thibaut, J. W., and Riecken, H. W.   1955.   Some determinants and consequences of the perception of social causality. *Journal of Personality* 24:   113-33.

II

THE SOURCE
OF POWER
AND INFLUENCE

The Nature of Trust 3

William H. Riker

Trust is, in some sense, an alternative to power. One can coerce other people to bring about a result one desires or one can trust them to bring about a desired result without coercion. The distinction is not quite this neat, however, for it is rare that force and trust are in fact directly substitutable devices. Rather, in some situations force is the only or the most realistic method; in other situations trust is; and in still other (possibly quite a few) situations the methods are interchangeable. To instance one extreme, one's opponent cannot reasonably be trusted to contribute to one's success in a battle or chess game. In general, whenever the situation is zero-sum, so that the winner gains exactly what the loser loses, two opponents have no motive to help each other. Hence each must rely on his own resources. This means each must try to win by coercion, that is, either by the use of physical force or by the selection of a superior strategy to outwit the opponent. At the other extreme, when a situation is wholly cooperative so that each participant gains only if he helps the other participant or participants to gain, force is superfluous. If, for example, several participants are trying to find each other in the absence of perfect instructions for doing so (which is Schelling's example of what he calls games of coordination), one must rely wholly on the good sense and goodwill of the others. In this kind of situation, trust

63

is a sufficient (and indeed the only) device to produce gains for everybody. In between these extreme examples are many kinds of situations in which either
trust or force might work or in which both may be present in varying amounts. Consider businessmen who make
bargains in a market. If the market is international,
so that buyer and seller are under different jurisdic-
tions, the main device to induce them to carry out the
terms of a bargain is their trust in each other, trust
based on their experience of previous trades and on
their expectation of future trades. But standing behind the trust may be power, the threat that if the
buyer, say, reneges, the seller's government may coerce
the buyer's government, which in turn will coerce the
buyer. If, however, the market is local, an organized
exchange under one government, then the sanctions of
the exchange and the government are ever-present
threats guaranteeing fulfillment. Still, if one had
to resort to sheriffs to enforce every contract, not
much business would get done. Even where there is government and hence power, much of the cement of negotiations is trust. I reiterate, then, that power and
trust are alternatives but not exclusive alternatives.
It seems appropriate, therefore, that any systematic
examination of power and force and coercion ought also
to include an investigation of trust and agreement and
mutual aid. Such an investigation is the purpose of
this paper. In particular, I shall define the notion
of trust as precisely as possible and explain in considerable detail when trust is an appropriate device
to bring about a desired result and when it is not.

1

Consider the sentence, "After I vote for your bill, I
trust you to vote for my bill." Assume that it is ut-
tered in a legislature where the members are roughly
equal, and assume also that the body itself is an independent branch of government. Then there is no recognized authority to enforce the vote trade. It is
conceivable that the speaker may have some unmentioned
threat over the auditor, but typically "I trust you"
implies that the speaker has no threat. Indeed, he appears to be placing his fate and his hope in the hands
of the auditor.

So it is, generally, with the common sense of trust. One trusts in God, which is to say that one relies on God to bring about a state of nature that satisfies the trustor, a state of nature, furthermore, that the trustor cannot bring about himself. And God, of course, may or may not turn out to be reliable. In law the trustor who for some reason (such as death or incapacity) cannot act for himself counts on the trustee to carry out his (the trustor's) wishes with respect to some beneficiary. Being human, the fiduciary may betray his trust. The lender trusts the borrower, which means that the lender expects the borrower to repay the loan, though of course it may happen that the borrower goes bankrupt or absconds. In all these cases the trusting person places some portion of his fate in the hands of the person trusted, and this trustee may either justify or betray the trust.

In the notion of trust expressed in these usages there seem to be at least three features worthy of comment:

(1) Trust is an action, a piece of behavior, something somebody does. It is, of course, an internal event like choosing, judging, preferring, etc. and cannot, therefore, be directly observed. But internal events result in physical actions (e.g., speech and movement), and from these one infers the internal behavior.

(2) Trust is a decision to be dependent on other people. It can be contrasted, therefore, with various kinds of self-reliance.

(3) Furthermore, trust involves risk, since the other people on whom one has decided to depend may or may not prove worthy. These last two features are what make the act of trusting such a complicated event, meriting on this account detailed examination.

2

To say that trust is a decision to be dependent on another person (or persons) is to say that it is a decision not to be self-reliant. We can use this distinction between trust and self-reliance to analyze trust negatively, to specify what it is not. This procedure is useful because it helps to reveal the nature of a trusting dependence on others.

   Self-reliance, interpreted most crudely and obviously, is a function of power. If one has power over other people, or simply power over outcomes, then one can
by definition control events, bringing them to a desired conclusion. In this sense the man of power need
not trust others to do what he wants because he can coerce them instead.

   But it is possible to be self-reliant without being
able to control people or outcomes. Even the powerless
man can adjust his expectations to the conditions of
the world, choosing as a goal only what he can guarantee for himself by himself. When he achieves this minimally satisfactory outcome, he is fully self-reliant,
as much so as a man of power. In this way the man of
modest (or realistic!) expectations also has no need to
trust anyone because he is able to get what he wants
all by himself.

   These several kinds of self-reliance can be described with vocabulary from the theory of games. In a
game with two players, 1 and 2, let each one have a
set, A and B, respectively, of possible alternative actions. For 1, $A = (\alpha_1, \alpha_2, \ldots, \alpha_n)$, and for 2, $B =
(\beta_1, \beta_2, \ldots, \beta_m)$. The choice of alternatives by the
players determines outcomes, O_{ij}, $i = 1, 2, \ldots, n$, and
$j = 1, 2, \ldots, m$. The outcomes are payoffs to each
player, a_{ij} for 1 and b_{ij} for 2. A game may be depicted with a matrix in which 1's alternatives form
the rows and 2's alternatives the columns and in which
each cell of the matrix contains, first, 1's payoff,
and second, 2's payoff:

$$
\begin{array}{cccccc}
 & & 2 & & & \\
 & \beta_1 & \beta_2 & \cdot\ \cdot\ \cdot & \\
\alpha_1 & (a_{11}, b_{11}) & (a_{12}, b_{12}) & \cdot\ \cdot\ \cdot & (a_{1m}, b_{1m}) \\
\alpha_2 & (a_{21}, b_{21}) & (b_{22}, b_{22}) & \cdot\ \cdot\ \cdot & (a_{2m}, b_{2m}) \\
 & \cdot & \cdot & \cdot & \cdot \\
1 \quad \cdot & \cdot & \cdot & \cdot\ \cdot\ \cdot & \\
 & \cdot & \cdot & \cdot & \cdot \\
\alpha_n & (a_{n1}, b_{n1}) & (a_{n2}, b_{n2}) & \cdot\ \cdot\ \cdot & (a_{nm}, b_{nm})
\end{array}
$$

FIGURE 3.1   A Two-Person Game

The first kind of self-reliance (involving power over people) can be illustrated by a two-person game with outcomes such that $p > q$ for both players:

$$2$$

	β_1	β_2
α_1	p, q	q, p
α_2	p, q	q, p

1

FIGURE 3.2.   A Two-Person Game Where $p > q > 0$

If 1 has power over 2, he can coerce 2 into the choice of β_1, which is highly advantageous to 1--because then 1 is sure to get his best payoff--and highly disadvantageous to 2--because then 2 is sure to get his worst payoff.   Typically, 1 coerces 2 by reformulating the payoffs to 2 with sanctions so that $p - k > q$, and the matrix is rewritten:

$$2$$

	β_1	β_2
α_1	p, q	$q, p-k$
α_2	p, q	$q, p-k$

1

FIGURE 3.3.   1 Has Power over 2

Thus revised, the objective situation requires that 2 change his behavior.   If he preferred β_2 in figure 3.2, now in figure 3.3 he surely prefers β_1 because it is more profitable for him as well as for 1.   In practice, 1's power over 2 is 1's ability to subtract the sanction k from some of 2's payoffs.   And 1's self-reliance consists of his use of his power to impose this sanction.

Power over outcomes, on the other hand, involves less manipulation of the opponent's motivation than does power over people.   Nevertheless, it is self-reliance by means of power.   Consider the game:

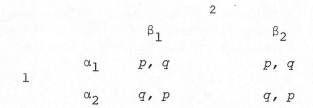

FIGURE 3.4. 1 Has Power over His Outcome

Here, as before, $p > q$ for both players. In this situation, 1 can by his choice of α_1 guarantee his preferred outcome regardless of what 2 does. Indeed,
there is really nothing for 2 to do. Clearly, 1 needs
to rely only on himself.

The world is not always so kind or so cruel. Often
neither player has sanctions over the other, or an alternative that leads inevitably to his preferred outcome. Instead, what each player gets may be quite dependent on what the other player does. Nevertheless,
despite this dependence, each player may be entirely
self-reliant. This situation is best illustrated, I
think, by zero-sum games in which the payoffs to the
two players sum to zero, i.e., for O_{ij}, $a_{ij} = b_{ij}$ so
that $a_{ij} + b_{ij} = 0$. Conventionally, in zero-sum two-
person games one writes only the payoff to the row
player inasmuch as we know that the payoff in any particular cell to the column player is always the negative of the row player's payoff in that cell.

In figure 3.5, there is a clear kind of self-reliance even though neither player can impose a sanction
on the other and even though neither can individually
obtain his most preferred outcome. Player 1 might
achieve as much as p if 2 helped him to do so by choosing β_1 or β_2. But since 1's gain is 2's loss, 2 has
no apparent motive to help 1 by choosing actions that
lead to 2's worst outcomes, $- p$ and $- q$. Therefore, 1
is constrained to seek only that maximum which he alone
can guarantee himself. To discover that maximum, consider the worst that can happen to 1 if he chooses α_1.
This worst is that 2 choose β_3 so that 1 gets his
minimum, s, of that row. In a final column to the
right of the matrix is recorded the worst that can happen to player 1 for each choice of an alternative α_i.

The best of those worst payoffs is identified as the maximum of the row minima, the so-called maximin. This is what 1 can certainly guarantee himself by himself. In figure 3.5, by choosing α_2 he can guarantee himself at least r. And if 1 insists on no more than r, then he can be wholly self-reliant.

2

	β_1	β_2	β_3	row minima
α_1	r	q	s	s
α_2	q	q	r	r ←maximum of row
α_3	p	p	s	s minima

1

column maxima p p r

$\Big($minimum of column maxima

FIGURE 3.5.   A Zero-Sum Game (Where $p > q > r > s > 0$)

Furthermore, r is as much as 1 can reasonably think he is likely to get. If player 2 makes a similar analysis to determine what he can guarantee himself, the worst that can happen to him for each choice of β_j is set forth in a row beneath the matrix. Since 2 receives the negative of 1, p is 2's worst, q his next to worst, ..., and s is 2's best. Thus the worst for 2 is the maximum of each column and the best of the worst is the minimum of the column maxima, the minimax, which here is r. Hence 2 can be wholly self-reliant if he expects as much and no more than $-r$.

The outcome which each can achieve by himself, in this case r and $-r$, is called the *security level*. When, as here, the security levels for each player are the negative of each other and in the same cell, then neither player can expect the other to be generous, for to be generous means to give the other fellow more than his security level by taking for oneself less than one's own security level. Consequently, in this zero-sum situation each player is in effect forced to be self-reliant. While this is a different kind of self-reliance from those of figure 3.3 (power over persons) and figure 3.4 (power over outcomes), it shares with them the feature that trusting behavior is inappropriate. In figures 3.3 and 3.4, player 1 can achieve all that he might want without needing to trust player 2. In the zero-sum situation, without additional detail about the other player's motives, intelligence, etc., there is no reason to expect him to be generous and hence no reason to trust him. By default, the players must be self-reliant.

3

Contrasting with the situations in which trust is neither necessary nor advantageous are those in which it makes sense to depend on others. In such situations there is always some chance of getting more than one's security level by trusting the other person or persons, although of course one often runs some risk as well.

In two-person, non-zero-sum games it is sometimes advantageous for both players to agree to help each other. Furthermore, it is often also advantageous to keep the bargain. One well-known example of such gains from trade is the so-called Battle of the Sexes:

		2	
		β_1	β_2
1	α_1	p, q	$-q,-q$
	α_2	$-q,-q$	q, p

FIGURE 3.6. The Battle of the Sexes
(Where $p > q > 0$)

Here 1 most prefers (α_1, β_1) and secondarily (α_2, β_2), and 2 reverses this order. Both agree that (α_2, β_1) and (α_1, β_2), each of which gives each player the security level of $-q$, are undesirable. If each insists on his or her own first choice and refuses to trust the

other in a bargain, then they are likely to end up at
the undesirable outcome (α_1, β_2). But if they agree on
either (α_1, β_1) or (α_2, β_2) or some combination like
"a one-half chance of (α_1, β_1) and a one-half chance of
(α_2, β_2)," then each can surpass his or her security
level. Hence, it makes sense to trust each other, not
only because each can make more by trusting than by not
trusting, but also because each can easily see that the
other has some motive to be trustworthy.

In zero-sum games, the security level, or what the
player can guarantee for himself, is often higher than
the worst that can happen to a player, as is readily
seen in figure 3.5. On the other hand, in cooperative
games, such as Battle of the Sexes, it is often the
case that the security level is also the worst that one
can do. Hence, there is an evident motivation for the
players to bargain, to agree, and to trust each other.
If they do not they are likely to bring about the worst
possible result. So, if they play at all, it makes
sense to trust each other for, with trust, something
approaching the best possible result is obtained.

This is particularly evident in games with three or
more players. If it is possible for players to cooperate at all, then the main feature of such games is
making coalitions of a set of players who, together,
can determine the outcome. Even if the game is zero-
sum, coalition formation is the essential activity. And
trust is, of course, the cement that holds a coalition
together.

One can describe games of three or more players with
a statement of the minimum amounts that each possible
coalition can win. This is the so-called characteristic function. In a situation in which the main activity is forming coalitions, the worst that can happen to
a player is to be left all alone. If an attempt is
made to force a player to do worse in a coalition of
two or more people than he can do all alone, then that
threatened player has, wholly within his own resources,
a perfect defense, viz., to resign from the oppressive
coalition and to play all alone. The amount that a
person receives in a "coalition" of himself alone may
be thought of as the security level in a game played by
three or more persons, because that is what he can
guarantee for himself. It is symbolized as "$v(\{i\})$"--

meaning the value, v, of the coalition, $\{i\}$, of just
one person, i--and may be normalized to zero: $v(\{i\}) =$
0. The members of any larger coalition must then be
able to guarantee that they, taken together, receive
at least as much as, and in some cases more than, zero.
If they cannot so guarantee, there is no point to forming the coalition. So, in general, for any coalitions
S and T, it must be true that

$$v(SUT) \geq v(S) + v(T)$$

which is to say that there is some advantage in forming a larger coalition (SUT) out of smaller ones, (S)
and (T).

Consider, then, the game of Couples, a three-person
game in which the only action is that each player
chooses another. If two players choose each other,
they are a coalition and receive a payoff of one unit.
Otherwise, no payments are made. The characteristic
function, where the players are labeled 1, 2, and 3, is:

$v(\phi) = 0$, where ϕ is the empty coalition
$v(1) = v(2) = v(3) = 0$
$v(1,2) = v(1,3) = v(2,3) = 1$
$v(1,2,3) = 0$

By definition, the players in this game cannot coerce
one another. Suppose 1 were stronger than 2 and 3 together and could thus coerce one of them to join him.
the situation would then be described by: $v(1,2) =$
$v(1,3) = 1$, $v(2,3) = 0$. So, to say that the value of
all two-person coalitions is the same is to say that
initially no player is stronger than either of the others. If, instead, the players are unequal in strength,
then the two strongest bid for the weakest, and thereby the weakest has the best position--so the last is
indeed first. But where the players are roughly equal
in strength, the only thing to do is to find someone to
trust.

It is, of course, true that this game could be
played without trust. Suppose each of the players behaved self-reliantly and chose another randomly, without investigating the possibilities of bargains, alli-

ances, or trust. Then each player could expect to be in a winning coalition with a probability of one-half, thus:

Case 1: 1 chooses 2, 2 chooses 1, 3 chooses 1,
  so (1,2) and (3) form.
Case 2: 1 chooses 2, 2 chooses 1, 3 chooses 2,
  so (1,2) and (3) form.
Case 3: 1 chooses 2, 2 chooses 3, 3 chooses 1,
  so (1), (2), (3) form.
Case 4: 1 chooses 2, 2 chooses 3, 3 chooses 2,
  so (2,3) and (1) form.
Case 5: 1 chooses 3, 2 chooses 1, 3 chooses 1,
  so (1,3) and (2) form.
Case 6: 1 chooses 3, 2 chooses 1, 3 chooses 2,
  so (1), (2), (3) form.
Case 7: 1 chooses 3, 2 chooses 3, 3 chooses 1,
  so (1,3) and (2) form.
Case 8: 1 chooses 2, 2 chooses 3, 3 chooses 2,
  so (2,3) and (1) form.

If we assume that members of two-person coalitions divide the payoff equally, then, in this circumstance of self-reliant random choice, the expected value for player i, $E(v_i)$, is:

$$E(v_i) = .25,$$

because half the time player i has a chance to be in a two-person coalition from which he will receive one half unit. Of course, however, if two players trust each other so that some coalition (i,j) is certain to form, then, for each of these players, the expected value doubles:

$$E(v_i) = E(v_j) = .50,$$

because (i,j) is sure to form and each member gets one-half the payoff. For the third player, untrusted or untrusting, $E(v_k) = 0$.

There is thus a strong incentive in this game for people to trust each other. If the trust is warranted, players double their expected values; and even if it is

unwarranted, they at least do no worse than obtain
their security levels. In this version of Couples,
which some scholars regard as the essential model of
political life, not only does it make sense to depend
on others, it is, moreover, the only sensible thing to
do.

   When we turn to the form of Couples that some scholars regard as the essential model of economic life (or
at least of the free market economy), the incentive to
coalesce, to trust, is even greater. The characteristic function of this (economic) form of Couples is:

$$v(\phi) = v(1) = v(2) = v(3) = 0$$
$$v(1,2) = v(1,3) = v(2,3) = 1$$
$$v(1,2,3) = 2$$

Here it makes sense to form a coalition of everybody
because in such a coalition *every* smaller coalition can
obtain at least its security level and perhaps more.
(Games with this property are, in technical language,
said to have a core.) It is hard to imagine a player
in this game refusing to trust others. Without trust,
he is consigned to his security level. With trust, he
is *certain* to do better. And at no risk. Only the
pathologically suspicious would refuse to behave trust-
ingly in this circumstance.

   In all the games so far considered in which trust is
advantageous, it is unambiguously so. That is, there
is no danger in trusting others. So one might as well
trust. But there are games in which, while one can
gain by trusting, one runs the risk, when one trusts,
of receiving less than one's security level. An example is the well-known game of Prisoners' Dilemma, in
which there is a motive for trust but also a motive for
betrayal, as can easily be seen in figure 3.7.

		2	
		β_1	β_2
1	α_1	b, b	d, a
	α_2	a, d	c, c

FIGURE 3.7. Prisoners' Dilemma
(Where $a > b > c > d > 0$)

Since each player can guarantee himself at least c by choosing his second alternative, c is the security level, which is exactly what both will get if each acts independently and self-reliantly. Furthermore, since the payoffs from the second alternative are better, regardless of what one's opponent does, than the payoffs from the first alternative, i.e., $a > b$ and $c > d$, each player has a strong motive to act in a self-reliant way. So the players end up at (α_2, β_2), where each receives his security level payoff. By trusting each other, however, it is possible, if neither betrays the trust, to end up at (α_1, β_1), where each gets more than his security level. Thus there is a real motive in this game for trust. But there is also a motive for betrayal of trust: if one player is convinced that the other is trustworthy (i.e., will choose the first alternative), then the player so convinced can choose his second alternative and the result is either (α_2, β_1) or (α_1, β_2), where the untrustworthy player makes the best possible return. Then the reward for the trusting innocent is his worst possible outcome, worse indeed than his security level. The Prisoners' Dilemma is thus a classic example of the benefits and perils of trust. Self-reliant players are likely to do no better than their security levels, but trusting players may do both better and worse.

4

In the last two sections I have described situations in which there is, first, an advantage in self-reliance and, second, an advantage in trusting other people. The fact that one can distinguish situations in which trust is and is not appropriate indicates that trust is a matter of choice and hence a kind of behavior rather than a state of mind. It is true that we often speak of trust as if it were a characteristic of personality --we say, for example, "he has a trusting nature." Still, it is clear from the situations just described that when we trust we do something such as choose alternative α_1 over alternative α_2 or choose as partner player 2 rather than player 3. In that sense, trust is a piece of behavior, not a trait or predisposition.

The essential ingredient in this act of trusting is a decision on the nature of the risk, an estimate of

the gamble. When we decide to depend on others for the
sake of gain, we do so because we anticipate that some
gain will be forthcoming. Prior to the decision, we
have necessarily, therefore, assessed the risk of
trusting and have decided that the risk is worth taking. The decision to trust thus involves initially an
evaluation of evidence. In order to understand the behavior of trust, then, it is necessary to analyze the
way in which risks are evaluated; and this section is
devoted to some comments on that task.

The risk that potential trustors evaluate is, of
course, a risk about what someone else, a potential
trustee, will do. The problem of evaluating risk is,
therefore, the problem of predicting the behavior of
another person: What will the other guy do?

Preliminarily, it should be noted that this question
is probably not universal but exists only in specific
historical contexts. It arises with special force in
modern complex civilized society. In the primitive
world of face-to-face contact among a few people who
live entirely dependently on each other, trust is so
fundamental and self-reliance so rare that most people
probably live completely trusting lives without ever
consciously assessing the risk of trust. When to trust
and whom to trust are, in such societies, so thoroughly
regulated by habit and custom that the act of assessment is seldom necessary. It is only with the introduction of civilization, which replaces the invariant
loyalty of blood, tribe, and cult with the conditional
loyalties of bureaucratic states, market economies, and
competing sects, that the assessment of risk becomes a
matter of daily routine. In the Indian tribe, chief
and brave need not rationalize trust because most of
the time their interests are identical, but this is
rarely true of presidents and citizens. In the markets
of peasant and mostly subsistence agriculture, trading
is merely barter and requires little trust; but in the
modern market trust is necessary not only for credit
but for the very use of money. In the primitive world
there is nothing akin to that bureaucratic organization
of the state and the economy which characterizes civilization, and bureaucracies depend entirely on the trust
that all members have in the viability of the system.
Even such routine daily activities as motoring depend

on an immense amount of trust that other (unidentified) drivers will follow the rules of the road. Indeed, civilization may be described as that state of society in which trust is elevated from an unconscious to a conscious activity. This is why the question "What will the other guy do?" is a peculiarly modern question.

The usual way that contemporary humans respond to general questions of this sort is to seek a scientific answer. In the study of human motives, however, a scientific answer does not exist. We have, of course, many theories about the "other guy" that purport to describe what, in general, the class of "other guys" will do. Unfortunately, these theories are not very useful, either as practical guidance for persons who actually have to trust or as theoretical guidance for the social scientist who is trying to interpret trust. Consider psychoanalysis, a typical example of such theory, which fails for a variety of reasons. For one thing, it is vastly too expensive for ordinary use. Imagine a bank officer seeking psychoanalytic advice to determine whether or not a borrower is trustworthy. However, most bank officers probably would not do this even if they could, simply because it does not appear likely that they would be any better off if they did. As a metatheory, as a method, that is, of constructing a particular theory about a particular personality, psychoanalysis fails to pass the usual test for the adequacy of a metatheory, which is whether or not the particular theories generated from it are correct. I have no intention of elaborating the debate on this subject because the mere existence of the debate is enough to decide its outcome. If insiders cannot agree that particular theories allow accurate predictions (and hence cures) with more than chance frequency, then the outsider can only conclude that the metatheory is in practice inadequate. Furthermore, if this metatheory is not useful in practice where users are willing to expend great energy and much money to make it work, then it cannot be of much value as a theoretical explanation of behavior.

As with psychoanalysis, so in general with psychological theories of personality and behavior. So also with sociological theories of interaction. None of these are of much significance for the ordinary trust-

or, called upon to assess the risk of what the other
guy will do. Were such theories adequate, in the sense
that by using them one could predict behavior with more
than chance accuracy, one could be sure they would be
used. And in the absence of use, one can be fairly
sure that they are not in general useful as descriptions of behavior.

Faced with the question of what the other guy will
do and unable to answer it in a scientific way, people
evaluate risk by the use of a lot of rules of thumb.
Each rule is, indeed, a kind of theory for its users,
though inadequately formulated and seldom rigorously
tested.

Such ad hoc theories vary in quality, of course.
Some are based on an interpretation of wholly superficial cues, such as dress, manner, appearance, sex, age,
and other characteristics unlikely to be closely related to how a trusted person will behave. Typically,
there is some articulable basis for such superficial
rules, but only rarely do they effectively discriminate between the trustworthy and the untrustworthy.
Even so, such rules are sometimes better than nothing.
It is probably more likely that the child who follows
the advice never to trust a stranger will survive to
adulthood unmolested than one who does not, if only because the advice narrows the circle of potential mo-
lesters to friends and relatives. Since most child mo-
lesters *are* friends and relatives, the rule probably
doesn't increase the chance of survival very much, but
it can be argued that any increase, however small, is
worthwhile. On the other hand, these superficial rules
of thumb might be counterproductive. A youth who re-
solutely followed the advice not to trust anyone over
thirty would find himself exposed to intense competitors of his own age and denied access to help from
quasi-parental figures. The justification of the rule
--offered, of course, by those very competitors under
thirty--is that, however good the intention, quasi-
parental aid is smothering and corrupting. Possibly
so; but it is aid, and the aid is sacrificed if the
rule is followed.

Most sensible people are not satisfied, therefore,
with untested, and indeed untestable, rules of thumb
based on superficial cues. Such rules have about the

same intellectual status as weather wisdom, which, typically, operates with no more than chance success. But it is not easy to develop better rules of thumb simply because it is not easy to find more significant attributes as cues. For example one commonsensical, but probably useless, rule for selecting an investment adviser, a rule that appears to be, but probably is not, based on a significant cue, is to choose an adviser who has previously succeeded more often than not in predicting fluctuations of security prices. Assuming, however, that such prices reveal a random walk, previous success is probably no better a cue than sex or hair color or personality features.

Since untested rules of thumb, even when based on apparently significant cues, are not very useful, some risk takers find it worthwhile to subject rules of thumb to systematic tests. This development has been carried to greatest lengths in the insurance business, where the actuary with his statistical methods of hypothesis testing now dominates all decisions about whom to trust and whom not to trust. There is no question that tested rules of thumb are a great improvement over untested ones. In the absence of good actuarial work, some insurers would charge too little and go bankrupt while others would charge too much and lose sales. Furthermore, it often does not make much difference for the health of the insurance enterprise whether or not the rules of thumb embody dubious theory. For example, one popular rule specifies higher premiums for young male drivers, which apparently reflects a theory that they are more careless than old male drivers. It may well be a better theory that inexperienced male drivers, old or young, are more careless than experienced male drivers. For the most part, however, inexperienced male drivers are young, so that statistical tests of the two theories raise problems of multicollinearity. In this circumstance, it does not make much difference to the actuary whether the underlying theory is true or false. If the overlap of classes is nearly complete, the rule of thumb operates about as well as can be expected, whichever theory is offered to explain the regularity.

This is the power and attraction of the statistical method of assessing risk, but it is also the Achil-

les' heel. If the multicollinearity is not complete,
the firm whose actuary has the better theory will tri-
umph in the market simply because it can assess risks
better. Consequently, even more important, in the long
run, than testing hypotheses is the task of determining
which hypotheses are worthwhile. For this one needs a
meta-rule of thumb, a rule of thumb by which to assess
particular rules of thumb.

One such meta-rule is that the trustee is more
trustworthy when an action in the trustor's interest
is also in the trustee's interest than when an action
in the trustor's interest is not in the trustee's interest. It seems reasonable that I am more likely to
be better off if the trustee in whose hands I have
placed my fate finds it personally advantageous to make
things turn out nicely for me. This meta-rule is based
on the assumption that everybody, including trustees,
is interested in making things turn out nicely for himself. It may be that there exist in this world some
true altruists, that is, people who get their satisfactions from helping others. If so, one would be wise to
place one's fate in their hands. But true altruists
seem to be quite rare outside of the love relationships
in the family. So for ordinary trusting it seems wise
to find a trustee who is himself better off because he
has helped the trustor.

Given the fact that the modern world is peculiarly
dependent on conscious trust, it is not surprising that
this meta-rule has in the last few centuries been developed into a philosophical doctrine, namely, utilitarianism. The contemporary form of this doctrine is
the notion of expected utility, which is the assertion
that each person chooses that action (out of the actions available) which maximizes his expected utility.
Since utility is defined as a measure of the intensity
of one's preferences among outcomes, to maximize one's
expected utility is to choose what one wants most, not
what someone else (such as a trustee) wants or what
someone else says should be wanted.

It is probably the case that very few trustors consciously judge their rules of thumb by the utilitarian
standard. Yet almost all contemporary social scientific descriptions of behavior are utilitarian in their
interpretation of what people do. This is particularly

true for economics and politics, but it is also true
even in social psychology, which, despite its tradition
of concern for specific motives like love and hate,
envy and pride, etc., makes use of essentially utilitarian notions in learning theory. Since the contemporary philosophical interpretation of behavior is over-
whelmingly utilitarian, it seems likely that more and
more rules of thumb will come to be judged by the utilitarian meta-rule.

It also seems likely that successful trustors are
those who use the utilitarian meta-rule, selecting as
trustees those who have a coincidence of goals with
the trustor. If utilitarianism reflects a real feature of the problem of trust in the modern world, then
the utilitarian trustor should in fact be more successful than those who use rules based on superficial cues
or ad hoc hypotheses. At any rate, this is a matter
that can be empirically investigated, and indeed such
investigation seems to be just about the most significant thing that social scientists could do now to improve our understanding of the behavior of trust. How,
in fact, do people go about assessing the risks of
trust? Are those who use utilitarian rules more successful in assessing risks than those who do not?

Most of the scientific investigations of trust that
have hertofore been undertaken have been concerned
mainly with finding out whether or not trusting behavior occurs and with identifying personality attributes
of trustors. If the understanding of trust set forth
here is reasonable, however, the interesting questions
concern not the occurrence of trust, but the way trusting is done. The need is not to find out what kind of
people push the trusting button in Prisoners' Dilemma
experiments but rather to find out how people generally
assess the risk of pushing one button instead of the
other.

The Powerholder 4

David Kipnis

The newspaper columnist James Kilpatrick recently began an article by saying: "The name of the game is power. Nothing else. Who has power. How he gets it. How power is delegated. How power is restrained. How power is exercised. These are the questions that absorb us." And these are the questions that have also absorbed many psychologists who have become involved in the dynamics of the social issues of contemporary Western society.

Unfortunately, there has been little in the way of psychological theory to guide our understanding of the forces shaping the actions of those in positions of authority when they are deciding whom to influence, the kinds of demands to make, and what resources to invoke in order to bolster their demands. Shall one focus on the process of interaction between the powerholder and his target of influence (Thibaut and Kelley 1959)? On the powerholder's personality (Rogow and Lasswell 1963)? On the kinds of resources he has available to influence others (Cartwright 1965)? On the social context in which power is exercised (Deutsch 1969)? On the resources and needs of the target (French and Raven 1959)? The reason for this current dilemma in psych-

The author wishes to express his appreciation to Jeffrey Goldstein, Barry Goodstadt, Ury Gluskinos, Louise Kidder, and Ralph Rosnow for their helpful comments while he was preparing this paper.

ology is that the mainstream of social psychological
thought and research has been concerned with how individuals and groups respond to social forces designed
to change beliefs, cognitions, and behaviors. With but
few exceptions, social psychologists have tended to ignore the person trying to change those beliefs, cognitions, and behaviors.

This paper is concerned with the individual doing
the influencing. Given that he has access to resources
that are needed or valued by others, we are concerned
with the circumstances that influence his use of such
resources and how this use feeds back on his self-perceptions and his perceptions of others. The paper will
focus mainly on the individual who has access to institutional resources, such as money, law, and military
force. Access to these institutional resources may be
a result of the person's role in an institution, his
wealth, or special friendships that give him "behind
the scenes" influence. Less attention will be paid to
individuals whose resources are based upon personal
qualities, such as beauty, strength, or intelligence.
This is because access to institutional resources allows even the most ordinary of persons to extend their
influence over others to a far greater degree than is
true for the same persons acting alone. Politicians
control patronage; bankers, money; military officers,
weapons; college professors, the baccalaureate degree.
In all instances, access to these institutional resources increases the individual's potential for controlling the behavior of others and for shaping society.

The paper will first present a descriptive model of
the power act from the point of view of the powerholder.
This model is basically an attempt to describe the
chain of events that culminates in the decision of the
powerholder to invoke his resources as a means of influencing others. The next section summarizes the results of a series of field and laboratory studies carried out by the author and his colleagues in order to
identify the circumstances that affect the powerholder's choice of means of influencing others. The final
section examines how access to institutional forms of
resources--or the "pooled energy of many," to use
Mott's (1970) definition of power--may influence the
powerholder's views of himself and of the less powerful.

DESCRIPTION OF THE POWER ACT

The use of resources to influence another's behavior
has been examined from a bewildering array of views.
Cartwright (1965) has provided what may be the most
useful classification of these many perspectives in a
recent review article. Figure 4.1, a partial adaptation of Cartwright's classification system, with addi-
tions by the present author, presents the power act
from the perspective of the powerholder.

Step 1. Power Motivation

Our starting point is the initial motivation of the
powerholder to influence others. We begin by asking
why power is exercised. That is, why does a powerholder want to make a target do something he ordinarily would not do? The answer originates of course in
man's dependency on others to mediate important outcomes for himself. When this dependency on others is
combined with the belief that others are unwilling to
provide the powerholder with what he wants, then the
powerholder experiences an inclination to influence
others, and so gain satisfaction. We designate these
inclinations to influence others as power motivations.
*Power motivations arise when an individual experiences
an aroused need state that can only be satisfied by inducing appropriate behaviors in others.* Power motivations are reduced when the target performs the desired
behavior.
    Most conventional wants of modern man can be viewed
as instances which involve the arousal of power motivations. The individual's need for affection and material goods are all instances which arouse these motivations as is the need of a supervisor to increase the
effort of his workers. *These conventional wants can
only be satisfied by inducing appropriate behaviors in
others.*
    Let us briefly examine some of the more important
reasons why power motivations may be aroused. By so doing, we can distinguish between different conceptions
of power motivation as these are currently emphasized
in the literature.

Power Motivation as Irrational Impulse. Power motivation is frequently defined in psychology as gaining
satisfaction from manipulating and influencing others.
When defined in this way, the act of manipulation is
seen as both the means and the end in itself. In essence, the powerholder derives satisfaction from perceiving that he has shaped outcomes for others, either
because he derives enjoyment from such activities
(Christie and Geis 1970; McClelland 1969) or because
such activities allow him to avoid feelings of weakness and a loss of control (Veroff and Veroff 1972).
Dynamically oriented psychologists have variously
ascribed the origins of the need to influence others
either to the developing individual's way of responding
to an absence of love (Horney 1950), or to his feelings
of inferiority (Adler 1964), or to continual anxiety
(Fromm 1959). It should come as no surprise, therefore, that when we talk of power motivations in terms
of gaining satisfactions from influencing others, most
persons see the power need as representing the irrational, neurotic, and perverted aspects of man's nature.

Power Motivation as Role Behavior. Deriving satisfactions from manipulating others describes only one,
possibly minor, source of power motivations. A more
pervasive reason why people attempt to influence the
behavior of others derives from involvement in institutional roles. Here, the needs to be satisfied originate in the individual's desire to do his work well.
When the powerholder perceives that other persons in
his "role set" (Kahn, Wolfe, Quinn, Snoek, and Rosenthal 1964) are behaving in ways that interfere with
the goals of his organization, feelings of distress are
aroused within the powerholder which subsequently lead
him to attempt to correct this deviant behavior. It is
important to note that under these circumstances the
powerholder may not experience any personal satisfaction from influencing others, and indeed may find the
act of influencing distasteful (Milgram 1963). In a
sense the individual is trapped by his own loyalties to
a legitimate authority, so that he discovers that it is
almost impossible to ignore the authority's demands.
Adolph A. Berle (1967), in speaking of the demands
placed upon individuals given access to institutional
powers, has put the surrender of voluntary actions in

this way:

> One of the first impacts [upon assuming office] is
> the realization that the obligations of power take
> precedent over other obligations formerly held near-
> est and dearest. A man in power can have no friends,
> in the sense that he must refuse to the friends con-
> siderations that, power aside, he would have ac-
> corded. (p. 58)

When power motivations arise as a result of institutional involvement, the individual frequently finds
himself forced to deliver noxious stimuli to a target
in order to influence his behavior. On the surface
the individual should experience shame and guilt over
his own actions, and over time he should refuse to continue this kind of influence. Yet this rarely happens.
  What mechanisms allow individuals in their institutional roles to carry out behaviors that they would
condemn if these occurred outside the institution? The
answer appears to be that the individual believes that
the institution has granted him absolution for his
acts. Since the individual perceives that he has no
choice but to obey, he also sees himself as not being
responsible for the suffering he causes. He views himself as a "pawn" rather than as an "origin of behavior,"
to borrow de Charms' (1968) phraseology. Blame, if
placed, is directed toward the institution, the ration-
alization being, "If I don't do it, someone else will."
Thus, the banker who forecloses, the instructor who
flunks a student, the supervisor who makes a worker
redo a job, the mother who spanks, may all believe
themselves absolved from blame because they are "doing
their duty."
  Power Motivation as a Universal Drive. A third and
equally important reason why people are motivated to
use power arises from the fact that the induction of
behaviors in others can be instrumental in obtaining
rewards for oneself. This source of power needs is
frequently associated with the view that power motivation is a universal attribute of man (e.g., Hobbes and,
more recently, Mulder 1963). When power motivation is
viewed as a universal drive, the emphasis is on the
pursuit of resources which, in turn, enhance man's

ability to influence others and to enjoy the "good
life." In contrast, there is a de-emphasis on the enjoyment of seeing others "dance to your tune." Cartwright (1965) describes this general version of power
motivation as follows: "All men seek to influence
others and to strive for positions of influence, because they seek certain objectives whose attainments
require the exercise of influence" (p. 7). Both the
criminal's need for money and the lonely man's need
for affection can only be satisfied by convincing someone else to take appropriate actions, i.e., to part
with money in the first instance and to return affection in the second.

In summary, power motivations arise when people have
needs that can only be satisfied by inducing appropriate behavior in others. Three reasons why these motivations arise have been described. It is proper to assume that the three reasons mentioned here can overlap.
In addition to his need for money, the criminal may
come to enjoy frightening his victims and seeing them
grovel. The police officer may use the authority of
his office to "finagle" a bribe from a motorist. There
are obviously many other reasons for power motivations
to arise. Frequently the mere possession of institutional resources can instigate new needs, setting up an
endless procession of reasons for influencing others.
We stress, however, that what is common to all these
reasons is the fact that they can only be satisfied by
inducing appropriate behaviors in others.

Step 2. Request for Compliance.

resistance from target

Given an aroused need, the next step, as shown in figure 4.1, is for the individual to induce appropriate
behavior in a target that will satisfy this need. In
theory, this induction begins with a simple request;
for example: "I love you. Will you marry me?" Frequently, of course, this step is omitted since the individual anticipates refusal. The consumer knows that
without money his request for a new car from the auto-
mobile dealer will be refused, and the criminal knows
that a polite request for money from passersby will often be ignored. Let us assume that the target has re-

fused to comply. It is suggested that at this point
the individual is tempted to invoke whatever resources
are available to him in order to obtain the compliance
of the target.

Step 3. Resources

Figure 4.1 lists some of the common resources available
to individuals in our society. We have found it useful to distinguish between resources that reside within the individual (personal resources) and resources
available to the individual by reason of his institutional role.
    Personal resources are fashioned out of each indi-
vidual's unique endowments and include such things as
superior intelligence that can be used to persuade the
target to comply, superior physical strength to inti-
midate the target, personal beauty to seduce the target, and the ability to grant or withhold affection and
services. The reader may think of many other personal
resources that can be used as a base of influence.
    The second grouping of resources available to the
individual is derived from his participation in institutional life. Access to these resources will vary according to the individual's institutional position. Individuals with high status and great offices may have
unlimited access to resources, while those with less
status, such as supervisors or teachers, will have limited access. Among the resources referred to in figure 4.1 are control over money, the law, military
forces, and so on. Frequently, it is more economical
to classify institutional resources in terms of a particular institution than to develop general classification schemes. Dahl (1957), for instance, lists the
resources available to politicians as including access
to money, credit, and wealth, control over jobs and information, and esteem, or social standing, as well as
the legitimacy of the political role, which, if accepted, allows the individual to influence others.
    Several points need to be made in connection with
the control of resources. It was mentioned that if the
individual's request for compliance has been refused,
the next step in the power act is to invoke resources
as a means of inducing compliance. If the individual

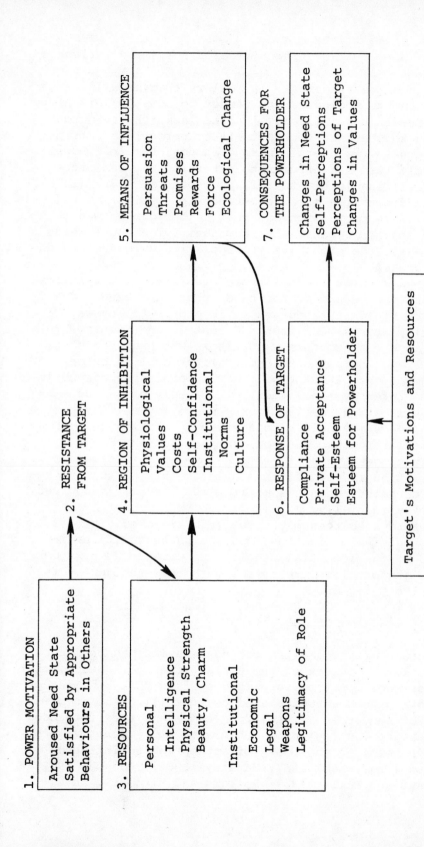

FIGURE 4.1. A Descriptive Model of the Power Act

from the perspective of the power wielder

1. POWER MOTIVATION

Aroused Need State
Satisfied by Appropriate
Behaviours in Others

2. RESISTANCE
FROM TARGET

3. RESOURCES

Personal
Intelligence
Physical Strength
Beauty, Charm

Institutional
Economic
Legal
Weapons
Legitimacy of Role

4. REGION OF INHIBITION

Physiological
Values
Costs
Self-Confidence
Institutional
Norms
Culture

5. MEANS OF INFLUENCE

Persuasion
Threats
Promises
Rewards
Force
Ecological Change

6. RESPONSE OF TARGET

Compliance
Private Acceptance
Self-Esteem
Esteem for Powerholder

7. CONSEQUENCES FOR
THE POWERHOLDER

Changes in Need State
Self-Perceptions
Perceptions of Target
Changes in Values

Target's Motivations and Resources

has few or no resources, it follows that he will cease
his attempts to induce the target to comply. His needs
must remain unfulfilled, since he lacks the resources
needed to convince others to take appropriate actions.
Of course, if a need is strong enough, the individual
may well turn his efforts to obtaining the resources
that will enable him to influence others. Gurr (1970),
in his discussion of circumstances precipitating political violence, points out that as the gap between
needs and the capabilities for satisfying those needs
increases, the probability of political violence tends
to increase.

Another point is that there are functional relations
between the nature of the needs that have been aroused
and the kinds of resources it is proper to invoke. For
example, it has been found (Goodstadt and Kipnis 1970)
that in a work context supervisors who had choice between invoking personal and institutional resources to
influence the behavior of their subordinates overwhelm-
ingly preferred the latter. The theory of resource exchange (Foa and Foa 1971) presents evidence that particular needs may only be satisfied by a reliance upon
particular resources. For example, Foa and Foa's
theory suggests that to obtain love and affection from
a target an individual should invoke his persuasive resources rather than his military or economic resources,
at least initially.

Before resources may actually be invoked, there is a
region of inhibition that must be successfully navi-
gated by the potential user of resources. We next consider the problems presented to the powerholder by this
inhibitory region.

Step 4. Region of Inhibition

The study of factors inhibiting behavior has been a
traditional concern of the social sciences. Hence, the
reader should not be surprised to find that a number of
factors have been postulated as inhibiting the invocation of resources to satisfy needs. Some theorists conceptualize the region of inhibition at a cognitive level in terms of the costs of attempting to influence
others (e.g., Dahl 1957; Harsanyi 1962; Tedeschi 1972;
Thibaut and Kelley 1959; Pollard and Mitchell, in

press). As Cartwright (1965) points out, "When an
agent is deciding whether to exercise influence, it
must be assumed that he calculates in some sense the
net advantage to him of making an influence attempt"
(p. 8). If the results of his calculations indicate
that he will lose more than he will gain, presumably
the individual does not attempt to influence others.
Thus, what inhibits the invoking of resources at this
level of abstraction is a hedonic calculus that yields
negative results.

Others view the problem of inhibition in terms of
subjective values and attitudes (Berkowitz and Daniels
1963; Leventhal and Lane 1970; Pepitone 1971; Staub
1971; Walster, Berscheid, and Walster 1970). Despite
the fact that the individual may gain substantial advantages by invoking his resources, it frequently happens that he inhibits the invoking of resources because he questions the propriety of the act. Hence,
the need to act in an egalitarian manner overrides the
temptation to maximize gains.

We note that impulses toward equality appear to be
most likely to occur when power differentials are at a
minimum or when the interaction is between peers. There
is reasonably strong evidence to support the generalization that as an individual's resources increase in
comparison to those of others, the person controlling
greater resources is tempted to allocate more of the
available rewards for himself and, accordingly, to provide the less powerful with a smaller share (Tedeschi,
Lindskold, Horai, and Gahagan 1969; Shure, Meeker, and
Hansford 1965). Such temptations to act in an objec-
tively inequitable manner apparently occur because the
powerholder convinces himself that his inputs into any
situation, as represented by his resources, are greater
than those of the less powerful and that, accordingly,
he deserves a larger share of the outcomes. Limitations to departures from equality occur mainly when the
less powerful succeed in making these departures too
costly for the powerholder (Gruder 1970; Thibaut and
Faucheux 1965).

Many studies suggest that inhibitions against invoking resources can be related to stable individual differences in personality and values (Christie and Geis
1970; Kohlberg 1964; Loevinger 1966; Megargee 1971).

For example, in several studies that have directly investigated individual differences in relation to the
choice of resources (Kipnis and Lane 1962; Goodstadt
and Kipnis 1970; Goodstadt and Hjelle, in press), it
has been found that appointed leaders who either lacked
self-confidence or perceived themselves as externally
controlled were reluctant to invoke personal resources
as a means of inducing behaviors in others. Rather
than trying to persuade others to comply, less confident or externally controlled individuals either did
nothing or else relied exclusively on institutional resources.

Finally, still other investigators discuss factors
inhibiting the invoking of resources in terms of re-
straints that originate in the norms of groups, institutions, and societies (Berle 1967; Kaufman 1970). Powerful guidance in the use of resources is given by
laws, traditions, and values. While not absolute,
these written and unwritten norms tend to form a moral
climate which serves to restrain the use of resources,
even though their use might be considered completely
appropriate in a different moral climate. Today, managers of modern corporations are restrained by law from
using their vast economic resources to openly intimi-
date potential business competitors, although in the
late nineteenth century the use of economic resources
for this purpose was not uncommon (cf. Tarbell 1904).
The decision of President Truman to use the atomic bomb
at Hiroshima could only have been made against the
background of continuous killing and destruction of the
Second World War. Proposals to use far less destructive forms of thermonuclear weapons in Vietnam and
Korea were continually restrained, and I believe that
this restraint was in part due to the overwhelming rejection of these means by most Americans.

From these remarks it can be seen that inhibition
against invoking resources may act in one of two ways.
First, it may diminish the individual's power motivations. Thus the taking of the "power pill," to para-
phrase Clark (1971), may eliminate the ruler's desire
to dominate and manipulate others. Second, the individual may have to use different resources than those
initially preferred in order to satisfy his needs, as
may be true in the case of thermonuclear weapons. In

this second instance, the need remains, but the individual must shift to a reliance upon different resources
to induce behavior in the target.

Step 5. *Means of Influence*

If the individual is not restrained by the various
sources of inhibition mentioned above, the next step
in the power act, as shown in figure 4.1, is to invoke
his resources in order to induce compliance from the
target. At this step the question is, How shall the
resources be presented to the target--as a promise or
as a threat? Both Dahl (1957) and Cartwright (1965)
have discussed in detail the various ways in which resources may be used. Cartwright suggests that the powerholder may exploit a base of power by (*a*) exercising
physical control over the target or the target's environment, (*b*) exercising control over the gains and
costs that the target will actually experience, (*c*)
exercising control over the information available to
the target, or (*d*) making use of the target's attitudes
about being influenced.

Here again--though not shown in figure 4.1--re-
straints exist which shape the particular means of influence chosen by a powerholder. For instance, discipline in the armed forces can no longer be maintained
by arbitrary threats of loss of leave and furlough, although this means of influence was acceptable prior to
revisions in the Uniform Code of Military Justice. Or
again, union contracts markedly limit the range of influence supervisors may use with their workers.

As might be expected from an examination of figure
4.1, there is also a relation between the resources invoked and the means of influence that are attempted.
Some resources, such as guns and knives, are particularly suitable for threatening and intimidating targets. Others, such as the possession of superior knowledge, mainly favor the use of persuasion. Money provides the powerholder with a broad spectrum of influence means, particularly rewards and punishments.

The relations between resources and means of influence have far-reaching consequences for the kinds of
social relations that evolve between powerholders and
targets. Etzioni's (1968) classification of institu-

tions in terms of the means of influence available indicates that institutions whose representatives can only rely on coercion produce hostile and destructive forms of interpersonal relations. A study of this issue by Berger (1972) found that managers in a simulated organization who were delegated only coercive means to influence their workers (i.e., deduct pay) generally believed that their workers disliked them, whether or not the managers invoked coercion. Further, Berger found that the managers who possessed only coercive means directed most of their attention toward marginal workers as the most suitable potential targets of this means of influence. Satisfactory workers were ignored. These results seem consistent with Etzioni's assumption that the kinds of means available structure both the sorts or relations powerholders may enter into with others as well as the powerholders' feelings about those others.

Step 6. The Target's Response to the Influence Attempt

Consider now the target's response to the powerholder. Does he comply with the request? If so, is his compliance willing or is it given grudgingly? Does the target ignore or actively resist the powerholder's influence? And assuming that the target resists, what happens next? In figure 4.1 it is suggested, though not shown, that the powerholder must recycle through earlier stages. Depending upon the strength of the original power needs, the resources available, and the strength of the restraining forces, the powerholder may decide either to modify his original needs, to abandon his influence attempt, or to persist in it by invoking different means of influence. If he persists, the question of tactics becomes important. What new means of influence are likely to convince the target? While in many instances these new means of influence will take harsher forms, as will be discussed subsequently, this is not always the case. Rather, the new means of influence will be selected to increase pressure for change on the target. They may include not only threats, but also promises of additional rewards, or greater reliance on informational modes of influence.

⟨Basically, the choice of means depends upon the powerholder's ability to diagnose the causes of the target's
resistance. A wrong diagnosis may increase rather than
decrease resistance.⟩ This cycling through various
means of influence in order to induce compliance is
well illustrated in the government's attempts to
achieve racial balances in public schools. At various
times, threats of economic sanctions, new information
on integration, the use of court orders, and even military force have been invoked.

Step 7. Consequences for the Powerholder

The act of influence has consequences not only for the
target but for the powerholder as well. If his influence attempt is successful and his needs are reduced,
the powerholder should experience satisfaction. By
contrast, if his influence attempt is resisted and his
needs remain unfulfilled, the powerholder should experience frustration and self-doubt. Hence, the last
step in the descriptive model is concerned with the
reactions of the powerholder to his own use of power.
I call these reactions the metamorphic effects of
power.

In addition to effecting the immediate consequences
associated with the satisfaction of needs, the use of
resources to influence others--as has been suggested by
many writers in political science and sociology (e.g.,
Sampson 1965; Sorokin and Linden 1959)--may change the
powerholder's views of his own worth, his values and
standards, and his views of the worth of the less powerful. Since these changes influence the powerholder's
subsequent use of power, it is appropriate to speculate
on why they occur.

One plausible reason for shifts in self-regard is
that the powerholder receives false feedback concerning his own worth. Because of the resources he controls, the powerholder may find that his ideas and
opinions are readily agreed with. This public compliance may lead the powerholder to believe falsely that
his ideas and views are superior to those held by other persons, when in fact compliance is based not on the
superiority of his ideas, but on the superiority of his
power. In addition, the powerholder's views of himself

may be further distorted by the flattery and well-
wishes he receives from the less powerful who are anx-
ious to keep in his good graces. If it is not recognized as such, this flattery may also contribute to
the powerholder's idea that he is something special.

Changes in values and normative beliefs may also
occur because of the powerholder's attempts to preserve and extend his influence. Machiavelli argued
that if a prince is to retain power he must learn how
not to be good. A study of present-day business executives (cited in Sorokin and Lunden 1959) found that
they led a double life with respect to values, having
one set for the office and another for the home. Apparently, the control of resources demands that the
individual adopt values consistent with the kinds of
resources he controls and the kinds of influence he
exerts. For instance, Galbraith (1967) has said that
managers in large corporations are practically forced
to make decisions that minimize risks to corporate investments, despite the fact that these decisions violate laws and the general welfare of the public. Thus,
in this instance, the standards and values that develop serve to justify managers' attempts to protect and
extend corporate power and resources.

Finally, changes in the powerholder's views of the
worth of the less powerful can also be traced to the
control and use of resources. Devaluation of the less
powerful may occur because the powerholder believes
that the behavior of the less powerful is not completely autonomous, but is in part caused by the powerholder's orders and suggestions. As a result, the less
powerful person is not given full credit for his own
performance, and the locus of control is seen to reside in the powerholder, who believes that he has
shaped the behavior of the target. In addition to de-
valuing such targets, powerholders frequently express
preferences for maintaining social distance from them.
One explanation, offered by Fiedler (1967), is that is
is easier to influence others if psychological distance is maintained and emotional involvement is kept
to a minimum. This is especially true if the powerholder thinks it likely that he will order the less
powerful to carry out distasteful behaviors. Insofar
as the powerholder feels sympathy for the position of

the less powerful, he may be reluctant to issue such
orders.

Summary

From the point of view of the powerholder, the power
act is like a game. Each step flows from the previous
one, and penalties blocking progress continually arise.
The contingencies are such that without a need, influence is unlikely to be attempted. Without resources,
influence is unlikely to be attempted. In the presence
of strong inhibitions, influence is unlikely to be attempted. Without the proper means of influence, influence is unlikely to be attempted.

The initial sequences of the power act can be described in terms of an instrumentality view of motivation. The perception that others mediate desirable
outcomes for the powerholder provides the incentive to
take action. The expectancy of successful influence,
the second major variable in instrumentality theories,
is provided by the kind and amount of resources available. The more resources available, the higher the expectations of successful influence. As the individual
proceeds from step to step in the power sequence, the
expectancies of success and the incentives for influencing the target take on new values. Further, the
region of inhibition adds negative values to the instrumentality model. Several other investigators
(Pollard and Mitchell, in press; Tedeschi, Schlenker
and Lindskold 1972) have also noted the usefulness of
some form of instrumentality theory for explaining the
power act. An added value of the present analysis is
that it considers how the availability of resources
can shape the initial expectations of the powerholder.

FACTORS AFFECTING THE MEANS OF INFLUENCE

In hierarchically organized work settings, appointed
leaders are delegated a range of means for influencing
their subordinates' behavior. These means of influence
extend the supervisor's potential for influencing others and allows him a central role in mediating outcomes
for his workers. Pelz (1951) and Godfrey, Fiedler, and
Hall (1959) have found that when appointed leaders were

deprived of such institutionally based means of influence, they were less able to influence their subordinates' behavior. Clearly, in institutional settings
personal charm and charisma may have only limited value
for inducing behaviors when they are unaccompanied by
institutional means of influence.

   Given the array of means of influence available to
appointed leaders, a question of some interest is why
a particular means is used in one situation but not in
another. Why does a supervisor in one instance spend
long hours training an incompetent worker to reach acceptable levels of performance, but in another instance
fire an equally incompetent worker?

   Raven and Kruglanski (1970) have suggested that the
powerholder anticipates the possible effectiveness of
each of his bases of power and avoids using those he
believes will be ineffective. In essence, the powerholder must first diagnose the reasons for the target's
resistance and then select the means of influence most
likely to overcome this resistance. To use the medical
term, there is a "treatment of choice" associated with
each diagnosed kind of resistance. Limitations upon
this search pattern are imposed upon the powerholder by
(*a*) the institution, which may not allow him to use the
proper means of influence, as, for example, when a supervisor is not given the authority to promise pay
raises; (*b*) the supervisor, whose inexperience may
cause him to misdiagnose the causes of his subordinate's resistance and hence apply the wrong means of
influence.

   We now turn to field and laboratory research done by
my colleagues and myself that has been concerned with
the particular means of influence that supervisors select when attempting to correct substandard behavior.
It can be shown that the choice of means is, as Raven
and Kruglanski have suggested, guided by the powerholder's expectations of successful influence. It can also
be shown that expectations are influenced not only by
the behavior of the target but also by the situation in
which the influence is attempted and by certain personal characteristics of the powerholder.

   In the field studies supervisors were asked to describe a recent incident in which they corrected the
behavior of a subordinate. They were asked to describe

what the problem was and what they or someone else did
about it. A content analysis of this latter information provided data on the kinds of influence means
available to supervisors for the intended purpose and
the relative frequency with which such means were invoked. Supervisors were also asked to provide background information surrounding the incident, such as,
for example, the number of workers they had been super-
vising at the time.

We have classified supervisors' influence attempts
as follows: (a) coercive power, in which the subordinate is threatened with demotion or actually demoted,
assigned to less pleasant or less remunerative work, is
given reduced responsibilities, receives official letters of warning, or is suspended or fired; (b) ecological control (to use Cartwright's 1965 term), in which
the subordinate is shifted to a new job, work shift, or
job location; (c) expert power, in which new information or new skills are imparted to the worker; (d) legitimate power, which is expressed in terms of direct
requests or orders for change.

In addition to these institutional means of influence, supervisors also relied upon their personal powers of persuasion to convince subordinates to change by
praising the subordinate, reprimanding the subordinate,
and encouraging the subordinate to expend additional
effort.

One of the clearest findings that has emerged from
these studies is that there is a "treatment of choice"
associated with the selection of means of influence
(Kipnis and Cosentino 1969). That is, the kind of influence invoked by the supervisors was found to vary
systemically with the nature of the problem presented
by the subordiante. As the supervisor's diagnosis of
what was causing the poor performance changed, so too
did his means of influence. For instance, when the
supervisor attributed the subordinate's unsatisfactory
performance to a lack of motivation, persuasive power
was a frequently evoked means. The supervisor's concern was to find out the causes of the subordinate's
poor attitudes and, if possible, to persuade him to
change. If, however, the supervisor attributed the
subordinate's poor performance to ineptness, persuasive means of influence were rarely attempted. Rather,

the supervisor invoked his expert powers and devoted
time to training his subordinate.

If the problem manifested by subordinate was complex, with elements of both ineptness and poor attitudes, then the supervisor increased the number of
means of influence directed toward the subordinate. For
instance, 76 percent of a sample of Navy supervisors
invoked two or more means of influence (e.g., increased
training and change of job) when subordinates' problems
were complex. When the subordinates evidenced a simple problem, however, only 41 percent of the Navy supervisors invoked two or more means of influence. Also,
when subordinates manifested complex problems, a significantly preferred means of influence was for the supervisors to exercise power by ecological control. That
is, a subordinate might be transferred to a new job, or
a new shift--the reasoning of the supervisor apparently
being, "If he's causing so much fuss on this job, let's
try him somewhere else."

Rewards

Because our field studies focused on attempts to elevate subordinates' performance to an acceptable level,
the studies provided no insight into what caused appointed leaders to use their powers to reward in order
to obtain compliance. No mention was made of rewards
in this context. Apparently, organizations do not encourage the use of rewards as a means of changing the
performance of noncompliant workers. Such use of power
might be viewed as a "bribe" and, hence, illicit. Pay
raises, promotions, favorable performance reviews, and
the like are used either to *maintain a target at some
acceptable level of performance* or to *encourage a target to exceed this level*.

Information on factors influencing the use of rewards is available however, from several experimental
simulations of organizations carried out by Goodstadt
and Kipnis (1970) and Kipnis and Vanderveer (1971).
These simulations will be described in more detail
later. Briefly, subjects were appointed as managers of
a business and required to direct the performance of
varying numbers of workers, who ranged from poor to
above average in performance. Among the means of in-

fluence provided the managers was the authority to
award pay increases.

In these studies, the following circumstances were
found to be associated with the decision to use rewarding power:

(1) The most rewards were given to superior workers, the next most to average workers, and the fewest
to inferior workers. This finding is hardly surprising
and merely confirms the commonplace observation that
good work is usually better rewarded than bad work.

(2) The presence of noncompliant workers, who deliberately refused to obey the manager's directions,
increased the number of rewards given to compliant
workers. Fewer rewards were given to compliant workers
when all workers were compliant (Goodstadt and Kipnis
1970). While several plausible explanations of this
finding are available, an experimental follow-up
(Kipnis and Vanderveer 1971) suggested that the presence of noncompliant workers provided the manager with
new standards for judging the worth of compliant workers. By analogy, if a father has only dutiful and compliant sons, his evaluation of their worth might tend
to be less favorable than if one of his sons has proven
to be a continued disgrace. Under the latter circumstances, he would appreciate his remaining sons far
more intensely. Or, to give another example, in the
late 1960s, when political dissent was at it height,
the silent majority was most highly praised by President Nixon.

(3) Fewer rewards were given for superior performance when managers were directing a large number of
subordinates rather than a small number. Apparently,
overburdened managers are just too busy to notice or
reward superior performance.

(4) It has long been recognized that "buttering up
the boss" is the royal road to organizational advancement and success. Support for this belief was provided
by the finding that managers gave more rewards to an
ingratiating worker than to an equally competent nonin-
gratiating worker. At times, the ingratiator received
as many rewards as the best worker in the organization.
It is unclear from our data whether the added rewards
were given the ingratiator because his flattery had
convinced the manager that the ingratiator's perfor-

mance was superior or because the manager wished to
continue to receive compliments and was willing to pay
for them. Perhaps both explanations are correct.

In any case, the findings on the use of rewards are
consistent with Raven and Kruglanski's suggestion that
the powerholder uses those means of influence most
likely to overcome the target's resistance. By extension, when the target is carrying out behaviors that do
satisfy the powerholder's needs, rewards will be invoked to maintain and reinforce this state of affairs.

Coercion

Goodstadt and Hjelle (in press) have been specifically
concerned with circumstances that cause an appointed
leader to invoke coercive means. These authors proposed that expectations of successful influence mediate
the use of coercion. That is, as the powerholder's expectations are lowered, he is increasingly tempted to
increase the amount of pressure placed upon the target
by invoking coercive means. Milder forms of influence
are reserved for instances in which the powerholder believes that the target is not completely resistant to
change. When are targets seen as most resistant to influence? Goodstadt and Hjelle suggest that expectancies of successful influence are lowest when the target
is seen as deliberately and willfully defying the powerholder's influence. That is, when the target's resistance is attributed to motivational causes ("I refuse") rather than to a lack of ability (I don't know
how"), expectations of successful influence are lowest.

Several studies have tested the implications of this
expectancy view of when coercion will be invoked. In a
field study among first-line supervisors, Kipnis and
Cosentino (1969) found that 63 percent of those supervisors who attributed the cause of their workers' dis-
satisfactory performance to a lack of motivation, invoked coercive means in attempts to alter this behavior. Among supervisors who attributed the dissatis-
factory behavior to ineptness, only 26 percent invoked
coercion. We have generally found that more workers
are fired for poor attitudes and lack of discipline
than for lack of ability.

Similar results were found in an experimental simulation of an organizational setting (Goodstadt and Kipnis 1970). In this simulation, subjects were appointed
as managers of a manufacturing organization and requested to direct the performance of a group of workers. The managers were provided with a range of institutional means of influence (power to reward, to
train, to punish, etc.). It was left to them to decide
which, if any, of these means would be used. The experimental manipulation involved programming one of the
workers to work at a substandard level. In one condition, the reason for this poor performance was ascribed
to the ineptness of the worker. In a second condition,
the same poor performance was ascribed to a lack of motivation. As was true in the field studies, it was
found that significantly more managers threatened to
deduct pay, actually deducted pay, and fired the worker
when his poor work was due to a lack of motivation than
when the poor work was due to ineptness. Similar findings have been reported in experimental simulation
studies by Goodstadt and Hjelle (in press) and Rothbart
(1968).

Other evidence that targets who willfully resist a
powerholder's influence invite punishment can be summarized as follows:

(1) In a questionnaire study among middle-level
executives employed by a major oil corporation (Kipnis
1972b), direct support was found for the assumption
that expectations of successful influence mediated the
use of coercion. These executives read eight case histories about employees who were performing at below
average levels. In four of the case histories, the
poor performance was attributed to a lack of motivation.
In the four remaining case histories, the poor performance was attributed to a lack of ability. After reading each case, the managers stated their expectancies
of being able to improve the employee's performance. In
addition, the managers rated the appropriateness of using coercive means to correct the employee's performance. It was found that the managers had far lower
expectations of improving the performance of employees
who lacked motivation. The managers were also significantly more willing to recommend the use of coercive

means among such employees. Finally, of particular interest in the present context is the finding that, regardless of the reason for the employee's poor performance, if managers rated themselves as having low expectations of influencing that performance, they endorsed the use of coercion. The correlation between
expectations of improving the employee's performance
and endorsement of the use of coercion was -.41 (*p* <
.05). The lower the expectations, the more frequently
coercion was recommended.

(2) A final illustration of the way in which motivational forms of resistance are associated with the
use of coercive means is found in a study of factors
causing police to arrest a male offender for disorderly
conduct (Kipnis and Misner 1972). This is a violation
that allows police officers enormous latitude in deciding how to respond. Aside from ignoring the situation,
the police officer may attempt to persuade the offender,
make his presence known, use physical force, or actually make an arrest. To examine what guided the decision
to make an arrest, thirty police officers were asked to
describe the most recent incident in which they had arrested a male offender for disorderly conduct. Another
thirty police officers described a similar incident in
which *no* arrest was made. Content analysis of the incidents found that neither the kind of incident (domestic fight, traffic violation, street corner disturbance, etc.) nor the presence of initial violence differentiated when an arrest would be made. What clearly
determined when an arrest would be made was whether the
offender continued to resist the police officer's orders. As resistance and the concurrent threat of violence grew, the probabilities of an arrest increased
sharply. If the offender quieted down and complied in
some form with the police officer's request, then the
incident terminated without arrest.

Taken together, then, the findings from these various studies are consistent with the belief that underlying an appointed leader's choice of coercive means of
influence is the perception that the target's resistance is willful and voluntary. In turn, this perception generates the conviction that less harsh means of
influence are inadequate to obtain compliance.

Situational Influences on Expectancies

Many will argue that there is nothing surprising in the
finding that powerholders use coercion when they believe that strong and deliberate resistance has been
encountered. What is of interest, however, is that the
powerholder's expectancies can also be shaped by a wide
variety of social influences that have nothing to do
with the target's behavior. Under stress, for example,
the powerholder may miscalculate the amount of resistance that will be shown by a target. An overworked executive may take a worker's misunderstanding of a poorly communicated order as evidence of calculated inso-
lence. A teacher who is told that a new student is
hostile is far more likely to perceive deliberate resistance in any mistakes made by the student. In
short, the target's behavior is only one of the factors
that may affect the powerholder's expectations of successful influence. Our research has found that more
coercive means were invoked by supervisors in the following situations: (a) when the supervisors were directing large numbers of workers; (b) when the supervisors were directing union workers; (c) when white
supervisors were directing black workers (Kipnis and
Cosentino 1969; Kipnis, Silverman, and Copeland, in
press).

What all these situations may have in common is that
they serve to reduce supervisors' expectations of being
able to influence subordinates successfully. A large
span of control reduces the amount of time that supervisors can spend with any subordinate, in turn reducing
their confidence that even simple suggestions will be
carried out without surveillance. The presence of
unions creates a situation approaching bilateral power
in which, with the support of the union, subordinates
can actively resist the demands of their supervisors.
In this climate, the supervisor may again come to doubt
that even simple suggestions will be carried out. Finally, while it may be argued that the greater reliance
on coercion by white supervisors among black workers is
due to blatant prejudice rather than lowered expectations of successful influence, our follow-up interviews

with supervisors suggested that such an explanation is
only partially correct.

That is, when supervisors were informed of the results, they denied any malicious intent. Rather, they
stressed the lower ability and dependability of black
workers as a justification for the use of coercion.
Since our analysis found that the problems attributed
to black subordinates were not different in kind or
severity from those attributed to white subordinates,
it seems probable that prejudice acted in this instance
by affecting the supervisors' expectancies of successful influence. The same problem was perceived as more
difficult to correct when manifested by a black subordinate than when manifested by a white subordinate.

Individual Differences in Expectancies

Individual differences in beliefs about one's own effectiveness may also help shape expectancies of successful influence. A person who doubts his own competence
as a source of influence may be more likely to see others as resisting that influence, when in fact such resistance may not exist at all.

There is good evidence that in situations in which
it is possible to influence others only by relying on
personal powers of persuasion, persons low in self-esteem and self-confidence do not attempt influence
(French and Snyder 1959; Hochbaum 1954). What happens,
however, when these same individuals are given access
to a range of institutional means of influence? Are
they still passive? We have not found this to be the
case (Kipnis and Lane 1962; Goodstadt and Kipnis 1970).
While still not relying on persuasive means, less confident supervisors remain active by relying extensively
on their institutional means of influence. Moreover,
less confident officeholders tend to be attracted
toward harsher means of influence, involving administra-
trative punishments. In one study (Kipnis and Lane
1962), for instance, it was found that Navy noncommissioned officers who stated that they had little confidence in their leadership abilities recommended placing
troublesome subordinates on official report more often
than did confident Navy noncommissioned officers. Placing a subordinate on report is a first step leading to
court-martial.

Similar findings have been obtained by Goodstadt and Hjelle (in press) in a laboratory study in which persons who perceived themselves to be either powerless or powerful (using Rotter's Locus of Control measure) were given access to a range of means for influencing a target. Persons who perceived themselves to be powerless chose to invoke coercive means of influence far more frequently than persons who perceived themselves to be powerful. The latter attempted to produce change in the target through persuasion.

Apparently, having lower expectancies of being able to influence others, less confident leaders avoid gentle means of influence, such as persuasion, since they believe that "no one will listen to them anyhow." Accordingly, they are attracted to those means that will be obeyed. These findings remind one of Fanon's (1963) view that persons who feel ineffective and powerless are drawn to the use of coercion when attempting to influence others. While Fanon was concerned with the exploited and downtrodden, his views have implications for understanding the use of power in institutional settings. That is, it appears that those who are most passive and timid in noninstitutional settings tend to be transformed into the most severe of taskmasters when given access to institutional means of influence. Interestingly enough, Raser (1966) reached somewhat similar conclusions in a biographical analysis of the personalities of totalitarian and democratic political leaders. Totalitarian leaders were more insecure in private life and lower in self-esteem. Force, then, as Fanon has suggested, seems the main means for satisfying the power needs of those who, by nature or circumstance, are passive.

Sequential Use of Coercion

It is important to note that anger and hostility are not the main instigators of the use of coercion in the instances discussed above. Rather, instigation to use coercion arises from cognitions concerning the best means of inducing compliance. The distinction here has to do with the timing of the delivery of coercive stimuli to a target. When angry and seeking revenge, the powerholder may immediately seek to invoke whatever personal or institutional means are available. The

sequence described by Berkowitz (1969) of arousal, disinhibition, and the immediate evoking of coercive means
applies here. Despite the fine old Elizabethan observation that "revenge is a dish that is best eaten cold,"
most angered persons prefer immediate retaliation. In
contrast, most officeholders, whose power needs originate from their institutional roles, prefer to use coercion as a last, rather than a first, resort.[1] Exceptions to this generalization exist, of course, such
as the previously mentioned less confident officeholders, who are drawn rather rapidly to harsher means.

   Some evidence that invoking harsher means of influence is deferred until gentler means have been ex-
hausted is available from the previously cited experimental study of Goodstadt and Kipnis (1970). This
study had six work periods during which data on the
output of the workers were brought to the managers.
Thus, it was possible to examine the means of influence invoked by managers during the earlier and later
work periods.

   During the first half of the experiment, the preferred means used to influence the performance of the
below average worker were ecological control (i.e., assigning the worker to a new job), persuasion (i.e.,
pleading with the worker to improve), expert powers,
and threatening to deduct pay from the worker's salary.
During the last half of the experiment, deducting pay
from the worker's salary, threatening to fire the worker, and actually firing the worker were the preferred
means of influence. This trend toward reliance on
harsher means was less advanced for the worker who was
inept than for the worker whose resistance was based
upon poor attitudes. However, since both workers' outputs had been programmed to stay below average, an increasing reliance upon coercion was apparent for both
workers.

   Thus, given the availability of a range of means of
influence, it appears that there will be a progressive
scaling of means from less harsh to most severe. University instructors will first discuss with and give
extra instruction to a failing student before recom-
mending dismissal, and diplomats prefer to "jaw, jaw,
jaw," to quote Winston Churchill, before proceeding to
"war, war, war."

THE METAMORPHIC EFFECTS OF POWER

Our interest in the power act also includes examining
how the control of resources may influence the powerholder's self-regard and his regard for the less powerful. In this final section, I would like to summarize
some ideas about how self-evaluations and evaluations
of others are formed in institutional settings in which
power is only minimally resisted. At the outset I will
label these ideas as speculative, since psychologists
have written very little about the metamorphic effects
of power. On the basis of the literature reviewed in
the first section of this paper, however, and of some
data to be presented in the following pages, I would
suggest that access to institutional resources triggers
the following chain of events:

(1) *Access to institutional resources increases the*
    probability that powerholders will attempt to
    influence others.
As suggested previously, needs are more likely to be
satisfied when the individual has the necessary means
of reinforcing his orders. In this regard, Cartwright
(1959) has suggested that when a powerholder has
"strong acts" in his repertoire he is more likely to
attempt to influence others. Of course, the relation
between the possession of resources and their use to
satisfy a power need is not inevitable. Studies of
community power, for example, have reported instances
in which the power elite refrained from influencing
community issues, despite their personal interest in
the outcome (Hawley and Wirt 1968). However, there
does appear to be at least a moderate relation between
the possession of resources and their use, if for no
other reason than that those without resources are not
likely to attempt to influence others (Deutsch and
Krauss 1960; Lippitt, Polansky, Redl, and Rosen 1952;
Zander, Cohen, and Stotland 1959).
More recently, the relation between influence attempts and access to institutional resources was reported by Kipnis (1972a). In this study, subjects were
appointed as managers of a simulated business, and in
one condition--the power condition--they were given a

broad range of institutional powers to influence their
subordinates' behavior (i.e., power to give pay raises,
to deduct pay, to fire, to train, to transfer). In a
second condition--the no-power condition--managers were
given no means of influence beyond being informed that
they were the managers. As a result, in this latter
condition, managers could rely on only two bases of
power when attempting to influence their workers--their
legitimate powers as managers and their personal powers
of persuasion. It was found that managers in the power
condition made more than twice as many attempts to influence their workers as did managers in the no-power
condition. Since, in this study, all workers were performing at satisfactory levels, the reticence of those
without institutional resources cannot be attributed to
their not having appropriate means of influence. Personal persuasion and encouragement would have been completely appropriate. Nevertheless, those with institutional means of influence were far more active in their
attempts to influence.

> (2) *The more a powerholder attempts to influence*
>   *others, the more likely he is to believe that*
>   *their behavior is not self-controlled, but is*
>   *caused by the powerholder. This belief be-*
>   *comes stronger when the means of influence are*
>   *based on institutional rather than personal*
>   *resources.*

We have stated previously that the availability of
resources increases the probability that the powerholder will attempt to influence others. Here we are
concerned with the next step in this sequence: how the
act of influencing shapes the powerholder's views of
the target. It is suggested that when the powerholder
brings "strong means" of influence to bear on the target, i.e., institutional means, he is more likely to
believe that he has "caused" the target's behavior. In
this regard, Raven and Kruglanski (1970) have pointed
out that a powerholder's reliance on persuasion alone
allows the target a good deal of latitude in deciding
whether or not to obey. As a result of the target's
freedom to choose, the powerholder cannot be certain
that his orders were the cause of the target's behavior. Restricting the target's freedom of choice, however, by promising, for example, to increase his pay

in exchange for compliance, is more likely to convince
the powerholder that any subsequent compliance was due
to his influence. This is not to say that strong means
of influence cannot be fashioned out of personal resources. The local bully may be firmly convinced--and
correctly so--that his threats of a physical beating
have caused others to accept his influence. Our point
is that means of influence fashioned out of institutional resources contain more "muscle," over a broader
range of influence modes, than means of influence fashioned from personal resources.

Evidence to support this view is found in the previously cited industrial simulation study of Kipnis
(in press), in which the amount of power available to
managers was varied. In the condition in which managers were delegated a broad range of institutional powers, there was a correlation of .65 between the frequency of use of these institutional powers and the
managers' endorsement of the statment, "My orders and
influence were the main reason for the amount of work
done by the workers." The more managers invoked institutional means for influencing their workers, the
more they believed that they "caused" their workers'
behavior. In the second condition, in which managers
could rely only on their persuasive powers to influence
their workers, the correlation between frequency of the
use of persuasion and endorsement of the above statement was .39, much lower. It should be noted that
since the workers' performance in this study was pre-
programmed, the managers had no actual influence on
their behavior. Thus, any attribution of causality was
made strictly on the basis of the managers' evaluations
of their own actions rather than on the basis of actual
changes in their workers' performance.

Similar findings have been reported by Berger (1972),
who also used the same industrial simulation design. In
Berger's study, influence attempts by the manager were
coded into those in which managers made explicit reference to institutional means of influence (e.g., If you
increase production by ten units, I'll give you a pay
raise") and those that relied on persuasion (e.g., "Try
harder next time--we need more production"). The correlation between frequency of use of formal institutional means and the manager's belief that he had

"caused" the worker's behavior was .40 (*p* < .01). When persuasion was used as the means of influence, the correlation was .23, again lower.

In short, these findings are consistent with the generalization that the more powerholders attempt to influence others, the more likely they are to believe that they have caused the targets' behavior. This belief becomes stronger when the means of influence that are used are based on institutional rather than personal resources.

(3) *To the extent that the powerholder believes he*
       has caused the target's behavior, there is a
       devaluation of the target's behavior.

If you believe that you have caused someone else to do something, it is likely that you will minimize the other's contributions. For example, I have frequently heard fellow instructors "put down" the talents of a student by implying that all the student had done was carry out the detailed instructions of the instructor. It is important to distinguish, in this regard, between devaluation of a target which is attributable to the belief that one has "caused" the target's behavior and devaluation of a target which originates in attempts to justify exploitative behavior (Walster, Berscheid, and Walster 1973). In the first instance, the powerholder makes the inference that the target's performance is simply an extension of the powerholder's ideas and orders. Hence, full credit is not given the target for any outcomes he may achieve. In the second instance, more dynamic processes are at work, designed to justify some decision or action of the powerholder which has caused others to experience pain and suffering. Here, derogation of the target (e.g., "The poor are shiftless and deserve no better") serves to protect the powerholder from feeling guilty over his actions. Further, as Walster et al. suggest, derogation allows the powerholder to avoid compensating the target by shifting the blame for exploitative behavior from himself to the target.

Some experimental evidence concerning the relation between the belief that one has "caused" a target's behavior and derogation of the target is found in the previously cited industrial simulation study by the present writer. In this study it was found that mana-

gers who controlled a wide range of institutional powers evaluated the performance of their workers significantly less favorably than managers without institutional powers. Managers without institutional means of
influence were far *more* appreciative of the quality and
quantity of their workers' performance. Apparently,
since managers with institutional power believed that
they caused their workers' performance, they discounted
the worth of their workers' contributions. Similar
findings were obtained by Berger (1972), who reported a
negative correlation of -.31 (*p* < .01) between managers'
evaluations of their workers' performance and managers'
attributions of causality for their workers' performance. Lower evaluations were given when the managers
believed that they had caused the workers' performance.

   We may now ask an external validity question regarding the range of situations to which these particular
findings can be generalized. For instance, we may ask
whether directive psychotherapists think less of their
clients than nondirective psychotherapists. Again, do
"hard sell" salesmen rate their customers' judgment
lower than "soft sell" salesmen? Or, do husbands who
make most of the decisions have a lower opinion of
their wives' ability than that held by husbands whose
wives share decisions (Sampson 1965)? In short, is the
act of influencing by the use of strong means invariably associated with a downgrading of the worth of the
target? For the time being, this question can only be
raised. Unfortunately, there is no research available
to provide the answers.

   (4) With increased access to, and use of, institu-
        tional means of influence, forces are generated
        within the more powerful which increase their
        psychological distance from the less powerful.

   This generalization is intended to reflect the widespread observation (e.g., Jackson 1964; Sorokin and
Lunden 1959; Zander, Cohen, and Stotland 1959) that
those in positions of power "move away" from social
contacts with the less powerful. That is, there is a
preference among powerholders for social exchanges with
those of equal or higher status, and a tendency to a
avoid social "chitchat" with those of lesser rank. Mulder (1963) has argued that this behavior reflects "power
gradient" motivations in which individuals are contin-

ually attracted to regions containing greater resources than they own and away from regions containing
fewer resources than they own. Distrust of the motives
of the less powerful has also been suggested as a partial explanation of this "movement away" from the less
powerful. Sampson (1965) has observed that some persons in positions of power are repelled by the obse-
quiousness of the less powerful, their lack of candor,
and their penchant for flattery. There is a suspicion
that whatever is said by the less powerful is designed
to obtain favors. These suspicions contribute to a
preference for social distance. A final possible explanation is suggested by B. F. Skinner, who points out
that Western man balks at information which sets limits
on his conception of himself as an agent possessing
free will. By extension, we may also desire to avoid
those persons who appear not to be in control of their
own behavior but to be controlled by us. Fundamentally,
then, it may be the target's lack of freedom of choice
that provokes this "movement away" from his company.

   *(5) Access to and use of institutional powers
          elevates self-esteem.*

The control of resources is considered by many to
be a basic prerequisite for psychosocial development.
At the individual level, as students of Rotter (1966)
have found, those who control few resources of a material, social, or intellective kind have been found to
act passively and to believe that luck or chance controls their fate.

Resources enhance feelings of well-being in several
ways. Most obviously, they allow the individual to
live a more comfortable life. In addition, as we indicated in the first section of this paper, those who
have access to valued resources are more likely to receive flattering feedback from the less powerful. Even
the most foolish of suggestions may be carried out by
a target who wants to keep in the good graces of a powerholder. The potential mental health benefits accru-
ing to those with access to institutional resources was
suggested in a review by Porter and Lawlor (1965) of
factors influencing the morale and satisfactions of
business executives. It was found that the higher the
status level of the executive, the more likely were his
important need systems to be satisfied. Top executives

were far more fulfilled than executives of lower rank
in terms of needs for esteem, autonomy, and self-ac-
tualization. Of course, these kinds of findings are
open to many other explanations aside from the belief
that the executives' positive mental health was due to
their access to resources. For example executives who
rose to the top may have been more satisfied and men-
tally healthy to begin with.

I am not aware of any controlled studies, aside from
those to be discussed below, that have examined the relation between access to and/or use of power and
changes in self-esteem. The previously cited studies
by the present writer (Kipnis 1972 and Berger 1972) did
examine, with mixed results, how self-esteem was influenced by the use of power. In my study no relation was
found between managers' evaluations of the quality of
their performance and access to institutional power.
Managers with a wide range of institutional powers did
not perceive themselves as having done a better job
than did managers without those powers. Further, there
was no relation between the frequency of use of institutional powers and gains in ratings of one's own performance.

In Berger's study, however, which varied the means
of influence available to managers (rewards plus coercion, rewards only, coercion only), there was evidence
that the use of institutional means elevated self-esteem. These findings were restricted to managers with
access to the broadest range of institutional means of
influence. At the end of Berger's study, managers
evaluated themselves in their roles as managers on
three semantic differential scales that measured potency, activity, and evaluation. The scales were
adopted from Helm, Bonoma, and Tedeschi (1971). It was
found that frequency of use of institutional means was
positively related to managers' self-evaluations for
potency ($r = .35$, $p < .01$), activity ($r = .40$, $p < .01$),
and for evaluation ($r = .41$, $p < .01$) in the reward
plus coercion condition. The more managers in this
condition invoked institutional means to influence
their workers, the more they described themselves in
favorable terms, i.e., powerful, active, and worthy.
No relation was found between self-evaluations and the
frequency with which managers used persuasion. Further-

more, in conditions in which managers had access to a restricted range of means of influence, these findings did not obtain. Thus, in addition to supporting the idea that influencing others may raise self-evaluations, Berger's findings suggest added complexities. That is, the use of institutional powers may enhance self-evaluation only if subjects have access to a broad range of means of influence.

CONCLUDING REMARKS

Adolph A. Berle (1967) has wisely argued that the use of power is inevitable, since it is only through the transformation of resources that men and societies survive. It follows that attempts to condemn or forbid or somehow eliminate the use of power are shallow and irrelevant. While the tenor of my remarks may give the impression that the possession and use of power is necessarily a bad thing, this has not been my intent. Rather, I have sought to outline how the unchallenged use of resources may alter the kinds of relations that are possible between the more powerful and the less powerful. The real problem for psychologists, as most recently stated by Kenneth B. Clark (1971), is to understand and control the tendencies of those having access to vast resources to submerge their "uniquely human, moral, and ethical characteristics of love, kindness, and empathy, in favor of the primitive propensities of man" (p. 1055). The process by which this estrangement may occur has been suggested in the last section of this paper. An interesting question for future research is to more intensively investigate how this cycle of institutionally based influence attempts and subsequent estrangement can be disrupted without destructive conflict.

NOTE

1. In a recent article analyzing the use of sanctions in international relations, Baldwin (1971) has proposed that the use of threats and punishments increases rather than decreases as expectations of successful influence increase.

REFERENCES

Adler, A. 1964. *Superiority and social interest.*
H. L. Ansbacher and R. R. Ansbacher (Eds.). Evanston, Ill.: Northwestern University Press.

Baldwin, D. A. 1971. Inter-nation influence revisited.
Journal of Conflict Resolution 15: 471-86.

Berger, L. S. 1972. Use of power, Machiavellianism,
and involvement in a simulated industrial setting.
Unpublished doctoral dissertation, Temple University.

Berle, A. A. 1967. *Power.* New York: Harcourt, Brace
& World.

Berkowitz, L. 1969. The frustration-aggression hypothesis revisited. In L. Berkowitz (Ed.), *Roots of
aggression.* New York: Atherton Press.

Berkowitz, L., and Daniels, L. R. Responsibility and
dependency. *Journal of Abnormal and Social Psychology* 66: 429-36.

Cartwright, D. 1959. *Studies in social power.* Ann
Arbor, Mich.: Institute for Social Research.

------. 1965. Influence, leadership, and control. In
J. G. March (Ed.), *Handbook of organizations.*
Chicago: Rand McNally, pp. 1-47.

Christie, R., and Geis, F. 1970. *Studies in Machiavellianism.* New York: Academic Press.

Clark, K. B. 1971. The pathos of power. *American
Psychologist* 26: 1047-57.

Dahl, R. A. 1957. The concept of power. *Behavioral
Science* 2: 201-15.

de Charms, R. 1968. *Personal causation.* New York:
Academic Press.

Deutsch, M. 1969. Conflicts: productive and destructive. *Journal of Social Issues* 25: 7-41.

Deutsch, M., and Krauss, R. M. 1960. The effect of
threat upon interpersonal bargaining. *Journal of
Abnormal and Social Psychology* 61: 181-89.

Etzioni, A. 1968. Organizational dimensions and their
interrelationships. In B. P. Indik and F. K.
Berrien (Eds.), *People, groups, and organizations.*
New York: Teachers College Press.

Fanon, F. 1963. *The wretched of the earth.* New York:
Grove Press.

Fiedler, F. E. 1967. *A theory of leadership effectiveness.* New York: McGraw-Hill.

Foa, U. G., and Foa, E. B. 1971. Resource exchange: toward a structural theory of interpersonal communication. In A. W. Siegman and B. Pope (Eds.), *Studies in dyadic communication*. New York: Pergamon Press.

French, J. R. P., Jr., and Raven, N. B. 1959. The bases of social power. In D. Cartwright (Ed.), *Studies in social power*. Ann Arbor, Mich: Institute for Survey Research, pp. 150-67.

French, J. R. P., Jr., and Snyder, R. 1959. Leadership and interpersonal power. In D. Cartwright (Ed.), *Studies in social power*. Ann Arbor, Mich.: Research Center for Group Dynamics.

Fromm, E. 1959. Individual and social origins of neurosis. In C. Kluckhohn and H. A. Murray (Eds.) *Personality in nature, society, and culture*. New York: Knopf.

Galbraith, J. K. 1967. *The new industrial state*. Boston: Houghton Mifflin.

Gamson, W. A. 1961. An experimental test of coalition formation. *American Sociological Review* 26: 565-73.

Godfrey, E. P., Fiedler, F. E., and Hall, D. M. 1959. *Boards, managers, and company success*. Dansville, Ill.: Interstate Press.

Goodstadt, B., and Hjelle, L. A. In press. Power to the powerless: locus of control and the use of power. *Journal of Personality and Social Psychology*.

Goodstadt, B., and Kipnis, D. 1970. Situational influences on the use of power. *Journal of Applied Psychology* 54: 201-7.

Gruder, C. L. 1970. Social power in interpersonal negotiation. In P. Swingle (Ed.), *The structure of conflict*. New York: Academic Press.

Gurr, T. R. 1970. *Why men rebel.* Princeton, N. J.: Princeton University Press.

Harsanyi, J. C. 1962. Measurement of social power, opportunity costs, and the theory of two-person bargaining games. *Behavioral Science* 7: 67-79.

Hawley, W. D., and Wirt, F. M. 1968. *The search for community power*. Englewood Cliffs, N. J.: Prentice-Hall.

Heider, F. 1967. *The psychology of interpersonal relations*. 2d ed. New York: Wiley.

Helm, B., Bonoma, T. V., and Tedeschi, J. T. 1971. Counteraggression as a function of physical aggression. Paper presented at the meeting of the American Psychological Association, Washington, D. C.

Hobbes, T. 1968. *Leviathan*. Middlesex, England: Penguin Books.

Hochbaum, G. 1954. The relation between group members' self-confidence and their reactions to group pressure to uniformity. *American Sociological Review* 19: 678-87.

Horney, K. 1950. *Neurosis and human growth*. New York: Norton.

Jackson, J. M. 1964. The organization and its communication problems. In H. J. Leavitt and L. R. Pondy (Eds.), *Readings in managerial psychology*. Chicago: University of Chicago Press.

Kahn, R. L., Wolfe, D. M., Quinn, R. O., and Snoek, J. D. 1964. *Organizational stress*. New York: Wiley.

Kaufman, H. 1970. *Aggression and altruism*. New York: Holt, Rinehart & Winston.

Kipnis, D. 1972a. Does power corrupt? *Journal of Personality and Social Psychology* 24: 33-41.

------. 1972b. Expectations of successful influence and the use of coercive means of influence. Manuscript in preparation, Temple University.

Kipnis, D., and Cosentino, J. 1969. Use of leadership powers in industry. *Journal of Applied Psychology* 53: 460-66.

Kipnis, D., and Lane, W. P. 1962. Self-confidence and leadership. *Journal of Applied Psychology* 46: 291-95.

Kipnis D., and Misner, P. R. 1972. Police actions and disorderly conduct. Mimeographed manuscript, Temple University.

Kipnis, D., Silverman, A., and Copeland, C. In press. The effect of emotional arousal upon the use of coercion among Negro and union employees. *Journal of Applied Psychology*.

Kipnis, D. and Vanderveer, R. 1971. Ingratiation and the use of power. *Journal of Personality and Social Psychology* 17: 280-86.

Kohlberg, L. 1964. Development of moral character and

moral ideology. In M. L. Hoffman and I. W. Hoffman
(Ed.s), *Review of child development research*. Vol. 1.
New York: Russell Sage Foundation.

Leventhal, G. S., and Lane, D. W. 1970. Sex, age, and
equity behavior. *Journal of Personality and Social
Psychology* 15: 312-16.

Lippitt, R., Polansky, N., Redl, F., and Rosen, S. 1952.
The dynamics of power. *Human Relations* 5: 37-64.

Loevinger, J. 1966. The meaning and measurement of
ego development. *American Psychologist* 21: 195-206.

McClelland, D. C. 1969. The two faces of power. *Journal of Interpersonal Affairs* 24: 141-54.

Megargee, E. L. 1971. The role of inhibition in the
assessment and understanding of violence. In J. L.
Singer (Ed.), *The control of aggression and violence*.
New York: Academic Press.

Milgram, S. 1963. Behavioral studies in obedience.
Journal of Abnormal and Social Psychology 67: 371-78.

Minton, H. L. 1972. Power and personality. In J. T.
Tedeschi (Ed.), *The social influence processes*.
Chicago: Aldine-Atherton, pp. 100-149.

Mott, P. E. 1970. Power, authority, and influence.
In M. Aiken and P. E. Mott (Eds.), *The structure
of community power*. New York: Random House.

Mulder, M. 1963. *Group structure, motivation, and
group performance*. The Hague: Mouton.

Pelz, D. C. 1951. Leadership within hierarchical organizations. *Journal of Social Issues* 7: 49-55.

Pepitone, A. 1971. The role of justice in independent
decision-making. *Journal of Experimental Social
Psychology* 7: 144-56.

Pollard, W. E., and Mitchell, T. R. In press. A decision theory analysis of social power. *Psychological
Bulletin*.

Porter, L., and Lawlor, E. 1965. Properties of organization structure in relation to job attitude
and job behavior. *Psychological Bulletin* 64: 23-51.

Raser, J. R. 1966. Personal characteristics of political decision makers. *Peace Research and Society
(International) Papers* 5: 161-81.

Raven, B. H., and Kruglanski, A. W. 1970. Conflict
and power. In P. Swingle (Ed.), *The structure of
conflict*. New York: Academic Press.

Rogow, A. A., and Lasswell, H. D.   1963. *Power, cor-
    ruption, and rectitude*. Englewood Cliffs, N. J.:
    Prentice-Hall.
Rothbart, M.   1968.   Effects of motivation, equity,
    and compliance on the use of rewards and punish-
    ments. *Journal of Personality and Social Psycho-
    logy* 9: 353-62.
Rotter, J. B. 1966.   Generalized expectancies for in-
    ternal versus external control of reinforcement.
    Psychological Monographs 80, No. 1 (Whole No. 609).
Sampson, R. V., 1965. *Equality and power*. London:
    Heinemann.
Shure, G. H., Meeker, R. J., and Hansford, E. A.   1965.
    The effectiveness of pacifist strategies in bargain-
    ing games. *Journal of Conflict Resolution* 9: 106-17.
Sorokin, P. A., and Lunden, W. A. 1959. *Power and
    morality: who shall guard the guardians?* Boston:
    Sargent.
Staub, E. 1971. The learning and unlearning of ag-
    gression: the role of anxiety, empathy, efficacy,
    and prosocial values. In J. L. Singer (Ed.), *The
    control of aggression and violence*. New York:
    Academic Press.
Tarbell, I. M. 1904. *The history of the Standard Oil
    Company*. New York: Macmillan.
Tedeschi, J. T., Lindskold, S., Horai, J., and Gahagan,
    J. P. 1969. Social power and the credibility of
    promises. *Journal of Personality and Social Psycho-
    logy* 13: 253-61.
Tedeschi, J. T., Schlenker, B. R., and Lindskold, S.
    1972. The exercise of power and influence: the
    source of influence. In J. T. Tedeschi (Ed.), *The
    social influence processes*. Chicago: Aldine-
    Atherton, pp. 287-345.
Thibaut, J. W., and Faucheux, C. 1965. The develop-
    ment of contractual norms in a bargaining situation
    under two types of stress. *Journal of Experimental
    Social Psychology* 1: 89-102.
Thibaut, J. W., and Kelley, H. H. 1959. *The social
    psychology of groups*. New York: Wiley.
Veroff, J., and Veroff, J. 1972. Reconsideration of
    a measure of power motivation. *Psychological Bulle-
    tin* 78: 279-91.

Walster, E., Berscheid, E., and Walster, G. W. 1970.
    Reactions of an exploiter to the exploited: com-
    pensation, justification, or self-punishment? In
    J. R. Macaulay and L. Berkowitz (Eds.), *Altruism
    and helping behavior*. New York: Academic Press.
------. 1973. New directions in equity research.
    Journal of Personality and Social Psychology 25:
    151-76.
Zander, A., Cohen, A. R., and Stotland, E. 1959. Power
    and the relations among the professions. In D.
    Cartwright (Ed.), *Studies in social power*. Ann Ar-
    bor, Mich.: Research Center for Group Dynamics.

III

THE TARGET
OF INFLUENCE

Further Thoughts on the 5
Processes of Compliance,
Identification, and Internalization

Herbert C. Kelman

INTRODUCTION

In the early 1950s I developed a theoretical framework
for the analysis of social influence, based on a qualitative distinction between three processes of influence: compliance, identification, and internalization.
For each of these, a distinct set of antecedents and
consequents is postulated. The model is particularly
concerned with specifying the conditions under which
changes induced by social influence attempts are temporary and superficial and, by contrast, those under
which such changes are lasting and integrated into the
person's belief and value systems. A summary of the
model and of the research based on it was published
over ten years ago (Kelman 1961). Several experimental tests of the model have been reported (Kelman
1958; Kelman 1960; Kelman and Cohler 1965; Kelman and
Eagly 1965). Furthermore, the model has been extended
to the study of attitude-discrepant behavior (Kelman
1962; Kelman, Baron, Sheposh, and Lubalin, forthcoming)
and applied to the analysis of influence processes in
psychotherapy (Kelman 1963), in international educational exchange (Bailyn and Kelman 1962), and in the
integration of individuals into the national system

This paper is a product of a research program on social influence
and commitment to social systems, supported by Grant MH-17669-04 from
NIMH, United States Public Health Service. 125

(Kelman 1969). A full presentation of the theoretical
framework and of the experimental work based on it,
however, has not yet appeared in print. Although I had
completed a monograph many years ago (Kelman 1956) and
even signed a contract to publish it, I was reluctant
to let it go to press without making some further revisions and collecting some more data. As a result of
this youthful discretion, the monograph remains unpublished to this day.

In the intervening years, I have continued to work
on and with the three-process model. I remain committed to its basic outlines (since I obviously cannot af-
ford to change my views too drastically until the book
is completed!), but my thinking has developed in a number of directions. In particular, as I shall try to
point out in the present paper, I have come to see the
three processes of influence as representing different
types of linkages between the individual and the social
system. When my book finally appears, it will reflect
these revisions and extensions of my own thinking--as
well as the enormous growth of the literature on social
influence and attitude change that has taken place within social psychology. In the meantime, I have taken
advantage of the opportunity offered me by the Albany
Symposium to present a partial status report on my
thinking about the three processes of influence, dwell-
ing especially on some features of the model that have
not so far appeared in published form.

To provide a context for my work on social influence,
let me note that it began within the experimental tradition of the Yale attitude change program under the direction of Carl Hovland (see, for example, Hovland,
Janis, and Kelley 1953). From the very beginning, my
own work within the Yale program focused on differences
in the nature of changes produced by persuasive communications along a "depth" dimension. Thus, my early experiments were concerned with determinants of public
versus private changes (Kelman 1953) and of immediate
versus delayed changes (Kelman and Hovland 1953). My
concern with the depth of change was reinforced by my
interest in developing a model of social influence that
would encompass not only the effects of persuasive communications, but also the effects of more powerful influence attempts, such as psychotherapy, brainwashing,

and conversion to social movements. These are the
kinds of interests that eventually led me to the distinction between the three processes of influence (having started with a simpler public-private dichotomy),
and to the hypotheses specifying their distinct antecedent and consequent conditions.

My approach to social influence is closely linked to
two other traditions within social psychology: Lewinian
field theory and functional theories of attitudes (Katz
1960; Smith, Bruner, and White 1956). The starting
point of my model is an analysis of the influence situation from the point of view of the person being influenced, with special reference to the social norms and
the power relationships that characterize that situation for him. This type of analysis has many points of
contact with the Lewinian formulations of induced behavior, and especially with the distinction between different bases of power developed by French and Raven (1959).
In distinguishing different types of change produced by
social influence, the model focuses on the nature of
the person's concerns activated in the influence situa-
tion--the kinds of motives that are aroused and the specific meaning the situation has for him in view of his
efforts at coping with the environment and achieving
his goals. Its orientation is, thus, very similar to
that of functional theories, such as those of Katz and
Smith, which postulate different conditions for attitude change depending on the motivational basis of the
attitude to which the influence attempt is directed.
However, though my approach is clearly functional and
fully compatible with those of Katz and Smith, it draws
a different set of qualitative distinctions. Their
schemes distinguish the different meanings that atti-
tudes--and hence influence attempts designed to change
those attitudes--may have in terms of the different coping processes in which the person may be engaged. My
scheme, as I have increasingly come to view it, distinguishes the different meanings that an influence
situation may have in terms of the different types of
social integration to which the person may be oriented.
In other words, the three-process model is very much in
the functionalist tradition, in that it focuses on the
person's concerns and coping efforts within the influence situation; unlike the other schemes, however, it

is a classification of different types of linkages between individual and social system, rather than of different types of personality functions.

In the present paper I shall attempt to relate the
three processes of influence to both a situational and
a functional analysis. More specifically, I shall
trace the distinction between the three processes to an
analysis of the structure of the social influence situation in general. I shall then proceed to illustrate
some of the implications of the distinction for the
ways in which individuals relate themselves to their
various social systems. Before turning to these issues,
however, I need to say something about the definition
and the scope of social influence, as I use the term.

DEFINITION AND SCOPE OF SOCIAL INFLUENCE

The term social influence is used here to refer to socially induced behavior change. Thus, social influence
can be said to have occurred whenever a person (P)
changes his behavior as a result of *induction* by another person or group (the influencing agent, or O). The
terms induction and change, as used in this definition,
require some further elaboration.

I will speak of induction whenever O offers or makes
available to P some kind of behavior and communicates
something about the probable effects of adopting that
behavior. In other words, O points a way for P--he provides a direction in terms of which P can then select
his own responses. The new behavior made available by
O is not necessarily a specific response; it may be a
new pattern of behavior which challenges P's existing
beliefs and opinions.

Induction may be deliberate and intentional, as in
those cases in which O tries to persuade, order, threat-
en, express expectations to, or provide guidelines to P.
On the other hand, induction may also be unintentional
to varying degrees, as in the case where O sets an example or serves as a model for P. In the limiting case
of unintentional induction, O may serve as a model for
P without even knowing of P's existence. Often, induction represents a mixture of intentional and unintentional elements; this would be true, for example, when
O is unaware of the extent to which he is directing P's

behavior by subtly communicating his own expectations and preferences.

Induction may take place through direct or symbolic contact with the influencing agent. That is, O may induce behavior in P in the course of face-to-face interaction. Alternatively, induction may occur in the course of P's exposure to mass communications or to various institutional symbols (e.g., a flag, a uniform, an official setting) representing an influencing agent.

We would speak of change as a result of induction to the extent that P's behavior following induction is different from what it would have been in the absence of such induction. Thus, the definition of social influence implies at least some degree of resistance to change that has to be overcome. The degrees of resistance, of course, may vary widely. Phenomenologically, there may be influence situations in which the person experiences no resistance at all; he may, in fact, be eagerly seeking guidance and direction. Even in such cases, however, change implies that O's induction has diverted P's behavior into new directions. Theoretically, therefore, I would conceptualize P's original behavioral tendencies as sources of resistance, even though their competitive strength might be negligible.

Changes resulting from induction may be overt or covert. That is, they may take the form of concrete actions or of new attitudes and beliefs, with the possibility of various combinations of changes at these two levels. Furthermore, changes may be positive or negative. We would speak of positive influence if the individual adopts the induced behavior. Thus, positive influence is the equivalent of conforming behavior, if we use that term in a strictly descriptive sense. Negative influence refers to a change in a direction opposite to that induced by the influencing agent. Negative influence is clearly different from resistance to change, in that P's behavior is very definitely affected by O's induction. In Willis's (1965) terms, negative influence constitutes anticonformity rather than independence. There is also the possibility of changes that are directly stimulated by the induction, but that cannot be characterized as either positive or negative. The induction may lead P to engage in a process of reconsidering his behavior, but the changes re-

sulting from that process may not be clearly related to
the direction induced by the influencing agent. Perhaps such changes can be reanalyzed as representing
some combination of positive and negative elements,
along with elements of independent movement.

Though my definition of social influence is rather
broad, it is not intended to cover all changes resulting from social interaction. Thus, for example, I
would not consider the acquisition of skills in a particular social learning environment to be an instance
of social influence, although attitude changes accompanying this process would clearly fall within my definition. Similarly, I would not view the moment-to-moment adjustments in behavior that people make in the
course of any social interaction--in the interest of
both effective communication and impression management
--as instances of social influence. Many of the changes
that I would exclude from my definition could probably
be analyzed in social influence terms, but a social influence model would not be particularly useful for these
purposes. Other models--such as a social learning model for analyzing the acquisition of skills or Goffman's (1959) dramaturgical model for analyzing self-
presentation in social interaction--would probably be
more parsimonious. A social influence model of the
type that I am proposing is likely to be useful only if
the following conditions are met:

(1) There is some meaningful connection--recognized
in the wider society--between the induced behavior and
the influencing agent. The agent is not just trans-
mitting stimuli or reinforcers but is inducing behavior
that is in some way linked to him--that represents him,
or is tied to his values, or reflects his expectations.
Social influence therefore represents an aspect of the
relationship between P and O within a social system in
which both occupy specified positions. The nature of
O's role and of P's role relationship to him have a
direct bearing on the meaning of the induced behavior.
In this sense, the transmission of information and
skills would not represent an instance of social influence, but the transmission of an attitude about such information and skills would.

(2) There is a clear induction. O is not merely
providing the stimulus for some new behavior by P but

is actually making such behavior available to P--he is
pointing a direction for him. Take, for example, an
interaction situation in which P has said or done something inappropriate and O has somehow communicated to
him what behavior is expected in this situation. P may
respond immediately by engaging in various maneuvers
designed to save face, to reduce embarrassment, and to
ingratiate himself. He may also develop a new view of
the norms governing the situation and change his behavior accordingly. The latter response would clearly
meet my conditions for a social influence analysis,
while the former would not.

(3) The behavior change resulting from the interaction is relatively gross. It represents a learning
that the person carries away with him from the interaction situation rather than a moment-to-moment adjust-
ment within that situation. This does not necessarily
mean that the change is highly durable or generalized;
it may vary considerably along these dimensions. It
simply means that the focus of the analysis is on ex-
portable products of the interaction, in the form of
norms, expectations, attitudes, opinions, or action
preferences.

THE STRUCTURE OF A SOCIAL INFLUENCE SITUATION

In keeping with the definition of social influence that
I have just presented, we can describe an influence
situation--in its most general form--as one in which an
influencing agent offers some new behavior to a person
and communicates to him, in some fashion, that adoption
of this behavior will have certain implications for the
achievement of his goals. Presumably, P will be positively influenced if he anticipates that adoption of
the induced behavior is likely to facilitate goal
achievement. He will be negatively influenced if he
anticipates that a behavior contrary to that induced is
likely to facilitate goal achievement. What can we say
about the characteristics of an influence situation
that is conducive to such outcomes?

My answer to this question is diagramed in figure
5.1, which represents the structure of a social influence situation as seen from P's point of view. The
situation depicted in the diagram is one that culmi-

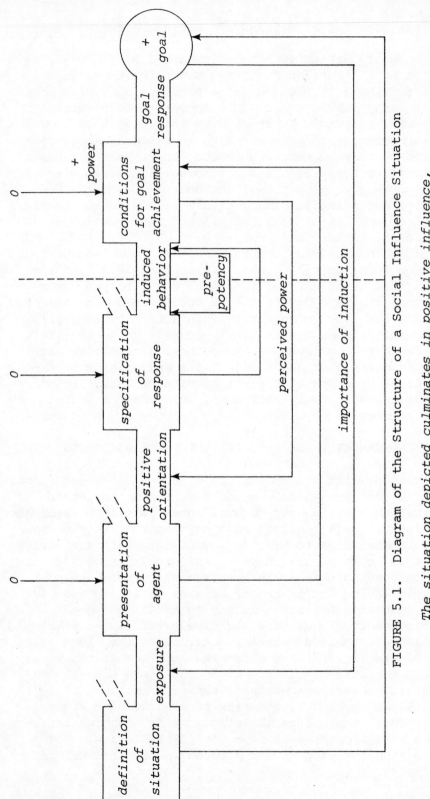

FIGURE 5.1. Diagram of the Structure of a Social Influence Situation

The situation depicted culminates in positive influence,
i.e., acceptance of induced behavior.

nates in positive influence. A comparable diagram
could be constructed for the case of negative influence. However, since my work so far has largely focused on positive influence, most of my discussion will
deal with that case. The diagram applies to unintentional as well as intentional induction, although--for
the sake of convenience--I shall sometimes refer to
what an influencing agent would have to do if he wanted
to facilitate positive influence.

The diagram is based on the assumption that three
things must happen in an influence situation if positive influence is to take place: (1) A goal important
to P must be activated, so that he will be responsive
to the induction and expose himself to it. (2) P must
perceive O as having some relevance to the achievement
of the goal that has been activated, so that he will be
positively oriented to an induction coming from O.
(3) The specific behavior induced has to constitute
a sufficiently "distinguished path," so that P will
select it in preference to other response alternatives
available to him. All three of these conditions are
necessary for the occurrence of positive influence. If
no important goal is activated, P lacks the motivation
to search for new behavior and is unlikely, therefore,
to expose himself to the induction. If an important
goal is activated, but P perceives O as irrelevant to
the achievement of that goal, he lacks the motivation
to accept O's induction and is likely to turn elsewhere in his search for new behavior. If both the
first and the second conditions are met, then there is
sufficient motivation to accept the induced behavior.
This motivation is not likely to be translated into
specific action, however, unless the third condition is
met as well--i.e., the induced behavior stands out relative to the other behavioral options.

Let us examine figure 5.1 in more detail. The left-
hand side of the diagram (i.e., the portion to the left
of the vertical broken line) sketches out what actually
happens in the influence situation from P's point of
view. The boxes represent the different kinds of information with which the situation provides P; roughly
speaking, they can be characterized as stimulus elements. The channels represent P's responses to the information. The diagram specifies three kinds of informational input:

(1) *Definition of the situation.* Through deliberate efforts by the influencing agent and/or through other features of the influence situation, P is informed about the nature of the situation in which he finds himself and, more particularly, about what is at stake for him in this situation. Typically, in a deliberate influence attempt, the influencing agent tries to present an effective challenge to P's existing beliefs, attitudes, or actions--to show that these are not maximally conducive to the achievement of P's goals. More often than not, such a challenge takes the form of bringing some discrepancy to P's awareness--a discrepancy between P's beliefs or attitudes and the evidence of reality, or between P's own attitudes and the attitudes of important others, or between P's attitudes and his own actions. If the challenge is successful, then P will be motivated to reconsider his current behavior. In the search for alternative approaches, he will be ready to expose himself to the induction as a possible source of new directions. If the challenge is unsuccessful--if P remains unconvinced that important goals are at stake in the situation--then he will be inclined to leave the field. The broken-lined channel leading out of the first box in the diagram represents the latter case. That is, the influence situation fails to culminate in positive influence because P has not been motivated to expose himself to the induction; in other words, he has been "lost" to the influence attempt at this initial point.

(2) *Presentation of the agent.* The influence situation conveys to P--deliberately or otherwise--information about the characteristics of the influencing agent. This information may refer to O's status, prestige, special knowledge or expertise, group membership, representativeness of certain points of view, control of certain resources, ability to apply sanctions, or the like. In a deliberate influence attempt, this information is designed to demonstrate, in a way maximally persuasive to P, that what O says or does may have considerable relevance to P's goal achievement. If this communication is successful, then P will be inclined to give serious consideration to behavioral possibilities that O makes available to him--in other words, he will be positively oriented to O's induction. If the communication is un-

successful--if P remains unconvinced that O is relevant
to the achievement of his (P's) goals--then he will
turn elsewhere for direction and remain uninfluenced by
O's induction. If P is convinced that O is detrimental
to the achievement of his goals (e.g., because O represents a negative reference group or a hated ideology,
or because he is publicly identified with illegal or
socially disapproved activities), then he may actually
be influenced in a negative direction. The broken-
lined channel leading out of the second box in the diagram represents failures in positive influence arising
from the fact that P has not been persuaded to orient
himself positively to the influencing agent. This is
the second point, then, at which P may be lost to the
influence attempt.

(3) *Specification of the response.* The influence
situation conveys to P the precise nature of the response that is being induced and facilitates the performance of that response. In other words, the induced
behavior is made readily available to P, both perceptu-
ally and behaviorally. In a deliberate influence attempt, the influencing agent would try to demonstrate
the unique relevance of that response (in contrast to
various other possible alternatives) to P's goal
achievement. He would try to reduce whatever ambiguities might arise about the form and content of that response, to overcome P's resistances to performing the
response, and to find ways of easing P into performance
of the response (e.g., through social facilitation,
step-by-step involvement, or limited commitment). If
these efforts are successful, then P will be both willing and able to adopt the induced behavior. If the efforts are unsuccessful--if the form and content of the
behavior remain ambiguous or resistances to its performance have not been overcome--then P is likely to opt
for one of the alternative courses of action available
to him. The broken-lined channel leading out of the
third box in the diagram represents this particular
possibility of "losing" P to the influence attempt.
That is, even though P may be motivated to expose himself to the induction and positively oriented to the influencing agent, the influence situation will fail to
culminate in positive influence unless the induced behavior has been transformed into a "distinguished path."

In sum, the left-hand side of the diagram tells us
that positive influence occurs if the situation is so
defined that P exposes himself to induction, if the influencing agent is so presented that P is positively
oriented to him, and if the induced behavior is so specified and facilitated that P is willing and able to
adopt it in the face of various competing alternatives.
To represent the psychological prerequisites for exposure, positive orientation, and adoption of the induced
behavior, we turn to the right-hand side of the diagram,
which depicts P's perception of the situation and his
anticipation of consequences. Taken by itself, the
right-hand side of the diagram simply says that P will
adopt the induced behavior if he sees it as meeting the
conditions for achieving a goal that he positively values. Taken together, the two sides of the diagram--
linked by a series of arrows in both directions--por-
tray the structure of a social influence situation culminating in positive influence: (1) The situation is
defined as one in which a goal that P presumably wishes
to achieve is at stake (arrow from left to right); if P
is convinced that the situation is indeed relevant to
that goal and if the goal is sufficiently important to
him, then he will expose himself to the induction (arrow from right to left). (2) The influencing agent is
presented as one who is instrumental to the conditions
for goal achievement (arrow from left to right); if P
is persuaded that O is indeed in a position to facilitate or impede his goal achievement, then he will be
positively oriented to O's induction (arrow from right
to left). (3) The induced response is specified as
the precise behavior required to meet the conditions for
goal achievement (arrow from left to right); if P perceives that response as distinctive, readily performa-
ble, and uniquely relevant to the conditions for goal
achievement, then he will indeed adopt it (arrow from
right to left).
There is no assumption that the different steps culminating in positive influence must occur in the order
that I have described and depicted in the diagram. For
analytical purposes, the steps represent a logical sequence, but in any given influence situation they may
occur in various orders and combinations. The same feature of the influence situation, the same action or com-

munication by the influencing agent, or--in the labora-
tory--the same manipulation by the experimenter may simultaneously generate two or more of the necessary inputs. The only point is that, in some order and in
some fashion, all three conditions--activation of an important goal, perception of the influencing agent as relevant to goal achievement, and transformation of the
induced behavior into a distinguished path--must be present for positive influence to occur.

This analysis also provides a systematic basis for
specifying alternative modes of reaction in the absence
of positive influence (comparable to the alternative
modes of resolving inconsistency or reducing dissonance
that the various consistency theories have proposed).
Different types of reaction are likely to come into
play, depending on the particular condition for positive influence that the situation failed to meet. Thus,
if the situation failed to activate an important goal,
the alternative reaction may take the form of minimizing the issue. If it failed to present the influencing
agent as sufficiently relevant to P's goal achievement,
then the alternative reaction may take the form of dis-
missing the agent, of derogating his message, or--in
special cases--of anticonformity. If it failed to
transform the induced response into a distinguished
path, the alternative reaction may take the form of
misperceiving or misinterpreting the message or of some
other type of avoidance mechanism.

If we reformulate the three conditions for positive
influence in terms of dimensions, we come up with what
I would propose as the three basic determinants of the
probability of influence: the relative importance of
the induction, the relative power of the influencing
agent, and the prepotency of the induced behavior.
These three variables--or, more accurately, classes of
variables--are represented in figure 5.1 by the arrows
moving from the right to the left.

(1) The importance of the induction refers to the
extent to which P views the influence situation as having motivational significance for him--i.e., the extent
to which the situation has activated goals important to
P, relative to the other goals that he is currently pur-
suing (and that he may have to sacrifice or at least
postpone by changing his behavior). The importance of

the induction depends, first of all, on the strength of
the motives that have been aroused in the situation. Second, it depends on the perceived relevance of the situation to these motives. The more important the induc-
tion--i.e., the stronger the motives activated and the
more relevant the situation to their satisfaction--the
greater P's *responsiveness* to communications offering
him new behavioral options. The probability of *acceptance* of O's particular induction depends on P's perception of O's power.

(2) The power of the influencing agent--with respect to a particular P--refers to the extent to which
P perceives him as instrumental to the achievement of
his goals. Thus, O possesses power over P insofar as
he is in a position to affect--to facilitate or impede
--P's goal achievement. The power of the influencing
agent over P depends on two factors. The first is his
capacity to control some of the conditions for P's goal
achievement, which might take the form, for example, of
controlling resources that P desires, or having the
right to apply certain sanctions, or possessing expert
knowledge that P would find useful in solving his problems. The second factor is the perceived likelihood
that O will in fact use the capacities he has in ways
that would affect P's goal achievement, which involves
an assessment of O's motives and intentions--as reflected in such characteristics as his manipulativeness,
his ruthlessness, and his trustworthiness. The greater
O's power--in terms of his perceived capacity and intention to affect P's goal achievement--relative to the
perceived power of competing influencing agents (including P himself), the greater the likelihood that P will
accept his induction. It should be noted that I am defining power independently of influence. Power, in my
scheme, is a basic determinant of influence, but it is
defined and assessed, not in terms of ability to influence, but in terms of the relationship between P and O.
Although propositions about the effects of power refer
to O's power as perceived by P, it is possible to link
O's power systematically to his objective characteristics and his position within the social system relative
to that of P.

(3) The prepotency of the induced behavior refers
to the extent to which that behavior emerges as most

clearly relevant in the context of the motivations that
have been activated in the situation. The assumption
is that, even though P may be motivated to accept the
induced behavior, he may select one of a number of alternative courses of action that are generally available to him. He may do so either because he is uncer-
tain about the exact nature of the induced behavior, or
because he considers some of the alternatives equally
effective, or because he finds the induced behavior excessively difficult or unpleasant. In short, resistances to the induced behavior may enter both at the
point of perception and at the point of action. The
likelihood that a specific induced behavior will be accepted depends on the extent to which that behavior has
become prepotent--i.e., relatively stronger than the
various available alternatives. The induced behavior
becomes prepotent to the extent to which it is strengthened within the influence situation--for example, by
making the response itself more distinctive, by linking
it clearly to the conditions for goal achievement, by
minimizing discomforts that inhibit its performance,
by structuring the situation so that the person is gradually eased into performing it, by socially facilitating
performance of the response, or by introducing situational demands and pressures that can best be met by
performing the induced response. Induced behavior also
becomes prepotent to the extent that competing responses
are weakened or eliminated in the situation--for example, by increasing the overall ambiguity of the situation, by demonstrating the ineffectiveness or counter-
productiveness of these responses for the achievement
of P's goals, by blocking performance of such responses
or making it uncomfortable, or by making it difficult
for P to engage in evasive maneuvers or to leave the
field. Typically, prepotency is achieved through some
combination of strengthening the induced behavior and
weakening alternatives--for example, by making apparent
the special advantages of that behavior relative to various other options.

I have spoken of the importance of the induction,
the power of the influencing agent, and the prepotency
of the induced behavior as classes of variables because
there are numerous forms that each of these variables
may take. By the same token, there are many ways in

which each may be operationalized in experimental studies. In one or another operational form, these three
variables typically constitute the independent variables
in experimental research on social influence (i.e., in
studies in which the dependent variable is some form of
attitude or behavior change). In many cases, the experimental manipulation clearly represents a variation of
importance, or power, or prepotency. In other cases,
however, a single operational variable may vary two or
all three of the conceptual variables simultaneously.
This is true not only for such complex operational variables as group decision versus lecture, but even for
such deceptively simple ones as size of the majority in
a group pressure situation or distance between the communicator's and subject's positions in a persuasion experiment. Sometimes, these multiple effects reinforce
each other; for example, the same operation may increase
the power of the agent as well as the prepotency of the
response, both of which are positively related to the
probability of influence. At other times, however, the
multiple effects of an operation may work against one
another in that they are related in opposite ways to the
dependent variable of social influence. For example,
one might propose that increasing the distance between
the communicator's and the subject's positions increases
the prepotency of the induced behavior but decreases the
power of the influencing agent. This kind of analysis
may help to explain the curvilinear relationships between distance and influence that have sometimes been
found, and to reconcile some of the contradictory results of different experiments on this problem. In
short, even though the three variables are not always
independent of one another, their conceptual separation
may be very useful for analytic purposes.

     In reviewing the literature eighteen years ago (Kel-
man 1956), I was able to cite various experiments showing the expected relationship between some operationalization of importance, power, or prepotency and the probability of positive influence. Many more such confirm-
ing experiments could be cited today. I attach very
little importance, however, to the confirmation of these
relationships per se at the very general level at which
I have presented them so far. Although they are stated
in the form of propositions, I really see them as more

in the nature of assumptions. Based on a logical analysis of the generic structure of an influence situation, they are designed to help us identify and organize the variables that are operative in any particular
type of influence situation. Thus, the interesting propositions from a social psychological point of view are
those concerned with the specific forms that the variables might take and their relationship to social influence under varying conditions. For example, within
my scheme, variations in the ambiguity of the stimulus
context in an influence situation can be conceptualized
as variations in the prepotency of the induced behavior.
The social psychological significance of an experiment
in this area, however, does not rest on what it tells
us about the relationship between prepotency and influence, but on what it tells us about the role of ambiguity in social influence and particularly about the specific conditions under which it is or is not a major determining factor.

   From my own point of view, the major interest of the
scheme presented in figure 5.1 is that it serves as a
starting point for qualitative distinctions between different types of influence situations. Specifically, influence situations culminating in compliance, in identification, and in internalization represent variants of
the generic situation depicted in the figure. They involve the same steps and the same classes of variables,
but differ in the specific forms that these take. Thus,
it is possible to represent a compliance situation, an
identification situation, and an internalization situation by means of separate diagrams similar in general
outline to the diagram presented in figure 5.1 but differing in some of the specific contents. In short, the
value of the generic scheme is that it serves as a framework for distinguishing the three processes and for comparing them with one another.

CONCEPTUAL STATUS OF THE
THREE PROCESSES OF INFLUENCE

I shall not describe the three processes of influence
in detail, as fuller information is available elsewhere
(Kelman 1961), and will address myself instead to the
conceptual status of the processes. However, a very

brief description of the three processes might be useful at this point:

> Compliance can be said to occur when an individual
> accepts influence from another person or from a
> group in order to attain a favorable reaction from
> the other, that is, to gain a specific reward or
> avoid a specific punishment controlled by the other,
> or to gain approval or avoid disapproval from him.
> Identification can be said to occur when an indivi-
> dual accepts influence from another person or a
> group in order to establish or maintain a satisfy-
> ing self-defining relationship to the other.   In
> contrast to compliance, identification is not pri-
> marily concerned with producing a particular effect
> in the other.   Rather, accepting influence through
> identification is a way of establishing or maintain-
> ing a desired relationship to the other, as well as
> the self-definition that is anchored in this rela-
> tionship.   By accepting influence, the person is
> able to see himself as similar to the other (as in
> classical identification) or to see himself as en-
> acting a role reciprocal to that of the other. Fi-
> nally, internalization can be said to occur when an
> individual accepts influence in order to maintain
> the congruence of his actions and beliefs with his
> value system.   Here it is the content of the induced
> behavior and its relation to the person's value sys-
> tem that are intrinsically satisfying (Kelman 1963,
> p. 400).

Each of these three processes is characterized by a
distinct set of antecedent and consequent conditions,
which are summarized in table 5.1. On the antecedent
side, I am proposing (as can be seen from the table)
that qualitative features of the influence situation
will determine which process is likely to be brought into play. Thus, to the extent that P's primary concern in
the situation is with the social effect of his behavior,
that O's power is based largely on his means-control
(i.e., his ability to supply or withhold material or
psychological resources on which P's goal achievement
depends), and that the induction techniques used are designed to limit P's choices, influence is likely to

take the form of compliance. To the extent that P's
primary concern in the situation is with the social anchorage of his behavior, that O's power is based largely on his attractiveness (i.e., his possession of qualities that make a continued relationship to him particularly desirable), and that the induction techniques
used serve to delineate the requirements of a role relationship in which P's self-definition is anchored
(e.g., the expectations of a relevant reference group),
influence is likely to take the form of identification.
To the extent that P's primary concern in the situation
is with the value congruence of his behavior, that O's
power is based largely on his credibility (i.e., his
expertness and trustworthiness), and that the induction
techniques used are designed to reorganize P's means-
ends framework (i.e., his conception of the paths toward maximizing his values), influence is likely to take
the form of internalization.

Each of the three processes generated by its respective set of antecedents corresponds to a characteristic pattern of thoughts and feelings in which P engages while adopting the induced behavior. Consequently, the nature of the changes produced by each of the
three processes tends to be different. In other words,
I am postulating a qualitative distinction between the
three processes in terms of their consequents, as well
as in terms of their antecedents (see lower half of
table 5.1). The crucial difference between the three
processes on the consequent side is in the conditions
under which the newly acquired behavior is likely to
manifest itself. Behavior accepted through compliance
tends to manifest itself only under conditions of surveillance by the influencing agent, i.e., only when P's
behavior is directly or indirectly observable by O.
Identification-based behavior, though independent of
observability, tends to manifest itself only under conditions of salience of P's relationship to O, i.e., only
in situations in which P's role is somehow associated
with O. Identification-based behavior is designed to
meet O's expectations for P's own role performance and,
therefore, remains tied to the external source and dependent on social support. Behavior adopted through
internalization, by contrast, tends to be integrated
with P's existing values, thus becoming part of a per-

TABLE 5.1. Summary of the Distinctions between the Three Processes*

	Compliance	Identification	Internalization
Antecedents:			
1. Basis for the importance of the induction	Concern with social effect of behavior	Concern with social anchorage of behavior	Concern with value congruence of behavior
2. Source of power of the influencing agent	Means-control	Attractiveness	Credibility
3. Manner of achieving prepotency of the induced response	Limitation of choice behavior	Delineation of role requirements	Reorganization of means-ends framework

Consequents:

1. Conditions of performance of induced response	Surveillance by influencing agent	Salience of relationship to agent	Relevance of values to issue
2. Conditions of change and extinction of induced response	Changed perception of conditions for social rewards	Changed perception of conditions for satisfying self-defining relationships	Changed perception of conditions for value maximization
3. Type of behavior system in which induced response is embedded	External demands of a specific setting	Expectations defining a specific role	Person's value system

*Reprinted from Kelman 1961, p. 67, by permission of the publisher.

sonal system, as distinguished from a system of social-role expectations. It depends neither on surveillance nor on salience, but tends to manifest itself whenever the values on which it is based are relevant to the issue at hand (although it does not always prevail in the face of competing demands, of course). Internalized behavior becomes independent of the original source and, because of the resulting interplay with other parts of P's value system, it tends to be more idiosyncratic, more flexible, and more complex.

Returning to the upper half of table 5.1, we can now see quite clearly the relationship between the three processes and the generic model of social influence depicted in the diagram. The probability of each process can be stated as a function of the basic determinants of influence derived from the diagram: the importance of the induction, the power of the influencing agent, and the prepotency of the induced behavior. Moreover, for each process, the magnitude of these determinants may vary over the entire range; that is, each may be generated by inductions with varying degrees of importance, by influencing agents with varying degrees of power, and by induced responses with varying degrees of prepotency. The processes differ only in terms of the *qualitative* form that these determinants take--in terms of the *basis* for the importance of the induction, the *source* of the influencing agent's power, and the *manner* of achieving prepotency of the induced response. These differences in turn make for qualitative differences in the induced behavior and in the nature of the resulting changes.

The generic model of social influence with which I started involves conceptualization at the level of social interaction. It focuses on what happens in the influence situation proper, and its basic variables try to capture the interactions between the participants in that situation. Yet, the independent variables of the model, though stated at the level of social interaction, have very definite referents to social system processes. This is particularly evident when we move from generic description of the determinants of influence to postulation of the distinct qualitative forms these determinants take when applied to the three processes.

Thus, the different bases for the importance of the induction postulated by the model can be analyzed in terms of P's relationship to the social system. Concern with the social effect, the social anchorage, and the value congruence of one's behavior represent different ways of worrying about one's integration in the social system. In the first case, P is concerned with how adequately he conforms to the rules of the system; in the second, with how securely he is embedded in one of his roles within the system; and in the third, with how fully he lives up to system values that he shares. Similarly, the different sources of power of the influencing agent postulated by the model can be analyzed in terms of the relationship between P and O in the larger social system, going beyond the immediate influence situation. Thus, means-control may refer to those agents whom P perceives to be in a position to allocate the system's resources and to apply its sanctions; attractiveness, to those in a position to define the requirements of being a good system member; and credibility, to those in a position to assess the system's needs in terms of its underlying ideology and long-term goals. The different ways of achieving prepotency of the induced behavior are most clearly at the level of social interaction, since they refer to the specific induction technique used in the influence situation. Yet, even here, the use of different induction techniques may be related to different functions of the social system. Thus, limitation of choice behavior may occur most readily in the context of the allocation of resources and the application of sanctions; delineation of role requirements, in the context of mobilizing support for the system; and reorganization of means-ends conceptions, in the context of setting and evaluating system goals.

Considerations such as these have increasingly led me to the conviction that social influence processes can be conceptualized most fruitfully in terms of the social systems within which they are generated and to which a person's acceptance of influence is directed. Thus, the three processes of influence, when viewed within the context of a particular social system, represent three ways in which P may be linked to the sys-

tem--three ways in which he meets the demands of the
system and maintains his personal integration in it.
Each process refers to a distinct component of the social system that generates standards for the behavior
of individual members and provides a vehicle for their
integration in the system. Acceptance of influence is
equivalent to meeting the standards set by a particular
component of the system and protecting one's integration
in the system by this particular route.

Specifically, compliance relates to integration
through the rules or norms of the system, i.e., the behavioral requirements that it sets for its members. In
accepting influence by this process, P is meeting the
system's normative demands--adhering to its rules--and
thus assuring himself of continued access to rewards or
approval (or avoidance of punishment or disapproval)
that depend on adherence to these rules. Identification
relates to integration through system roles in which P's
self-definition is anchored. Integration at this level
implies not just adhering to the set of behavioral requirements associated with the role, but seeing oneself
fully in possession of the role. In accepting influence
by this process, P is meeting the expectations of the
role and thus assuring maintenance of the desired relationship to the system and the self-definition anchored
in it. Internalization relates to integration through
values of the system that the individual personally
shares. In accepting influence by this process, P is
living up to the implications of these shared social
values and thus maintaining the integrity of his personal value system. In short, viewed in terms of the
linkages of the individual to the social system, compliance refers to integration via adherence to rules,
identification to integration via involvement in roles,
and internalization to integration via sharing of values.

This formulation of the three processes is not a
drastic departure from the original model. It was actually implicit in the model from the beginning, but no
explicit attempts were made to link processes of interpersonal influence to properties of the social system.
Even with the present emphasis, the model continues to
conceptualize influence from the standpoint of P; it
continues to focus on P's motivational and coping processes and to subject these to a functional analysis;

it still requires observation of behavior at the micro-
level and detailed analysis of the social actions and
interactions that mediate personal change. The only
difference is that the motivational patterns that the
model distinguishes are now clearly defined in terms of
the different linkages to the social system that they
represent. Similarly, the actions and the interactions
in the influence situation are viewed in terms of their
larger system context; that is, certain system demands
help to define the dimensions of the influence situation, and the behavior of the individuals in that situation in turn has a bearing on the functioning of the
larger system.

A special advantage of conceptualizing social influence in terms of properties of the social system is
that it helps to bridge analyses of social influence
with analyses of social control. Both are concerned
with linkages between the social system and the individual, except that social control analyzes these from
the system point of view, while social influence analyzes them from the point of view of the individual.
More generally, social influence approached in this way
may help to bridge a microanalysis of social behavior
with a macroanalysis. This kind of model may be helpful in conceptualizing individual functioning as it affects system functioning--i.e., in clarifying the ways
in which the integration of individuals into the system affects the integration and effective functioning
of the system itself, and the ways in which individual
change affects social change. Conversely, such a model
may be helpful in conceptualizing the ways in which the
structure and institutional patterns of the system (or
changes in these) affect the integration and functioning
of its individual members.

DISCREPANT ACTION AS
DEVIATION FROM SOCIETAL STANDARDS

To illustrate some of the ramifications of the three
processes of social influence, conceptualized in terms
of linkages between the individual and the social system, let me turn to a problem that has been of central
concern to experimental social psychologists: reactions to discrepant (or counterattitudinal) behavior.

For several years, my colleagues and I have been apply-
ing a functional analysis to some of the phenomena to
which dissonance theory and other consistency models
have addressed themselves. Basic to our approach has
been the attempt to distinguish qualitatively different
dilemmas that discrepant action might bring into play.
We assume that contemplation of a discrepant act
arouses different concerns in individuals, depending
on the nature of the standards from which this action
has deviated and the nature of the action itself. The
particular concern that is aroused, in turn, sets different psychological processes into motion and leads to
different ways of handling the dilemma. That is,
"modes of resolution" of inconsistency dilemmas are not
interchangeable, in our view, but are systematically
related to the particular dilemma with which the person is confronted (Kelman and Baron 1968). Some of our
studies (Kelman, Baron, Sheposh, and Lubalin, forthcoming) have distinguished, for example, between moral and
hedonic dilemmas, and predicted that the nature of the
emotional reactions aroused and of the modes of resolution utilized will be different for these different
dilemmas, and that various situational variables (e.g.,
incentives for the discrepant action) will be differentially related to the strength of arousal and resolution in these two types of situations.

We have regarded the moral-hedonic distinction, and
others suggested by our research, merely as initial
probes toward a more systematic typology of concerns
created by discrepant action. It now seems to me that
the three-process model of social influence, particularly when it is coordinated with properties of the social system, may be a useful starting point for such a
typology. Table 5.2 presents the form of the typology
as I currently envision it. The table classifies types
of discrepant action in terms of the societal standards
from which they depart. The rows of the table represent the sources of the standards from which the person's action has departed; the columns represent the
behavioral dimensions on which the deviation from standards has occurred; and the cell entries suggest the dominant emotional reactions aroused in the person by each
of the six types of deviation.[1]

TABLE 5.2. A Classification of Types of Discrepant Action in Terms of the Societal Standards from Which They Depart*

Source of Standards from Which P's Action Has Departed	Behavioral Dimension on Which P's Departure from Societal Standards Has Occurred	
	Responsibility	Propriety
External rules or norms (compliance-based)	Social fear	Embarrassment
Role expectations (identification-based)	Guilt	Shame
Social values (internalized)	Regret	Self-Disappointment

*Cell entries refer to the dominant emotional reactions that each type of discrepant action is hypothesized to arouse.

151

   The three sources of the standards, distinguished by
the rows of the table, are old acquaintances. At the
level of the individual, they refer to the social influence process by which P originally adopted the standards (acquired the attitudes) that his discrepant action has now violated. In other words, the first row
refers to actions that deviate from compliance-based
expectations, the second row to actions deviating from
identification-based expectations, and the third row to
actions deviating from internalized expectations. At
the level of the social system, the three sources of
standards refer to three components of the system in
which standards might be embedded. These are, of
course, the system components to which I have tried to
coordinate the three processes of influence: rules or
norms, role expectations, and social values. The original distinctions between compliance, identification,
and internalization readily suggest hypotheses about
P's reactions to his deviation in each of the three
rows. Thus, in the first row, we would expect P to be
primarily concerned with the way others may react to
his deviation; in the second row, he will be primarily
concerned with the implications of the deviation for
his relationship to groups in which his self-definition
is anchored; in the third row, he will be primarily concerned with the intrinsic implications of his action,
matched against his personal value system.
   The behavioral dimensions within which P may deviate
from societal standards--as distinguished in the columns of the table--are socially defined and monitored.
Each of these dimensions refers to a domain of individual behavior in which society has a definite stake and
in which it takes considerable interest, although different societies may give different degrees of emphasis
to one or another dimension. The societal standards associated with each domain may be represented at different levels (compliance, identification, or internalization) in a given individual's cognitive structure,
depending in part on the nature of his socialization
experiences. For each dimension, qualitatively different patterns of socialization and means of social control tend to be utilized. Table 5.2 presents two such
dimensions--corresponding to guiltlike and shamelike
reactions, respectively--but it may well be possible to
distinguish additional dimensions.

The first column refers to discrepant actions that
depart from societal standards of responsibility (or
morality). Most typically, these involve actions that
cause harm to others, or to society in general (e.g.,
by wasting valuable resources or failing to do productive work). Actions causing harm to the self (e.g.,
by excessive use of drugs or alcohol, or by dissipating
one's energies) also tend to be treated as departures
from standards of responsibility, perhaps because they
are seen as wasting human resources on which society
might otherwise have been able to draw. The domain of
responsibility is one in which "society" insists on the
right to make each member answerable (i.e., responsible)
to it for his actions. The social controls that are
typically exercised in this domain of behavior involve
punishment or the threat of punishment, exclusion from
"responsible" roles in the society, and disapproval in
the form of anger.

The second column refers to actions that deviate
from societal standards of propriety. Typically, these
are actions by P that are deemed inappropriate (i.e.,
not "his own") for a person in his position--or, in
many cases, for any adult in the society. P has thus
failed to live up to a particular personal image,
whether it be a strictly public image, or a self-image,
or a self-image dependent on public confirmation. He
is not accountable for his actions in the same formal
sense as he would be for behavior in the domain of responsibility, but behavior in the domain of propriety
is also subject to social controls. "Society" has an
interest in assuring that its members live up to their
images, since smooth and predictable interactions depend upon their doing so. The social controls that are
typically exercised in this domain involve ridicule,
ostracism, and disapproval in the form of contempt.

Each of the six types of discrepant action distinguished in table 5.2 should produce a distinct pattern
of reactions, predictable from the particular intersec-
tion of row and column that it represents. First of
all, a violation of societal standards will arouse qualitatively different concerns and emotional responses in
P, depending on the socially defined domain whose standards he violated and the level at which he had originally adopted those standards. Second, depending on the
type of discrepant action involved, P will go about

handling the concerns and resolving the tensions aroused
in different ways. Thus, for each cell it should be
possible to specify what P is likely to do when he finds
himself deviating from societal standards--both to avoid
or minimize the consequences of his deviation, and to
rectify the situation and come to grips with it psychologically. Let us look at some of the reactions that
characterize each of the cells, starting with those in
the domain of responsibility.

(1) *Social fear.* In this cell, P's primary concern
is with the way in which others will react to his devi-
ation--with the social consequences of his discrepant
action. He seeks to avoid or minimize the punishment
and disapproval that his action may bring about. Thus,
insofar as possible, he tries to hide or cover up what
he has done in order to evade discovery. If he has
been discovered, he tries to deny responsibility for
the action. His efforts to hide or deny the action may
take the form of somehow demonstrating that he is not
the type of person who would do such things. If he
fails in his efforts to evade discovery or deny responsibility, he engages in maneuvers designed to minimize
the severity of the consequences. He introduces exten-
uating circumstances that would reduce the level of his
responsibility--e.g., by showing that his action was
inadvertent, or that it was taken under orders, or that
it caused only minor harm. He may apologize to the person he has harmed as a way of ingratiating himself with
the other and thus mitigating the punishment that the
other might administer or demand. He may also confess
his misdeeds, again as a way of manipulating the reactions of others; confession tends to soften the social
response to deviation, since the person has demonstrated
a sense of responsibility and acknowledged the validity
of the standards that he has violated.

(2) *Guilt.* My use of this term is somewhat restricted, though quite consistent with its usage in the
psychoanalytic literature and elsewhere. I am exclud-
ing what is sometimes called "real" guilt or "existen-
tial" guilt (in contrast to "neurotic" guilt)--in other
words, a concern with the object that has been harmed
and the value that has been violated. I leave this
kind of reaction to the third cell in this column. In
the second cell, the person is concerned with his relationship to the social system and his self-definition

within it. His deviation has thrown this relationship
into question and undermined his self-concept as a well-
integrated, securely positioned member of his society.
The core meaning of this reaction is very well conveyed
by the German word *Schuld*, which means both guilt and
debt. Through his deviant action, P has incurred a
debt to the one he harmed and, most importantly, to society. To deal with the consequences of the deviation,
he must find ways of reinstating himself in the social
order, of reestablishing his desired relationship to it.
One accepted way of accomplishing this is through compensation of his victim; the form of such compensation
is socially defined and often publicly administered.
Other types of expiation and reparation are equally
effective in allowing P to "pay his debt to society."
In short, guilt is often resolved through the use of an
accounting system which allows the person to make up
for his deviation and regain his place in society. Confession represents another way of dealing with guilt,
although in the present case (in contrast to the case
of social fear) it is designed not merely to manipulate
the reactions of others, but to restore one's own position in society. Confession is a form of expiation, in
that the person humbles himself; it is a renewed commitment to the standards that were violated; and it is
a way of separating the transgressing self from the
normal self. It is important to keep in mind that in
the case of guilt P is not just concerned with being
restored to the good graces of others, but with reestablishing his own self-definition as a worthy member of
society. Though the standards he has violated are external, they function in a way similar to that suggested by Freud's (e.g., 1933) concept of the superego,
which represents an introjection of parental authority.
In keeping with the notion that the superego may be
quite rigid and severe, guilt may create a considerable
amount of inner turmoil. The person may see his deviation as so unacceptable that he despairs of the possibility of reestablishing the desired relationship to
the society. In such cases, the reaction to the deviation may take the form of varying degrees of self-punishment.

   (3) *Regret*. The societal standards of responsibility violated by P in this cell are integral parts of
his personal system of values. In keeping with these

values, he is primarily concerned with the object that
he has harmed by his discrepant action. In terms of
longer-run considerations, he is also likely to be concerned about the implications of his action for his
ability to live up to his values. One reaction characteristic of this cell is to seek ways of correcting the
wrong that has been done--not simply in the sense of
compensating the injured party in terms of a socially
established formula, but in the sense of exploring all
necessary steps for counteracting and minimizing the
harmful consequences of the action. Another type of
reaction in this cell is repentance, which involves not
only remorse for the wrong that has been done, but also
a resolution to avoid similar actions in the future. In
making such a resolution, P may engage in a process of
self-examination in order to understand why he failed
to live up to his own values and to determine how he
might want to change himself.

The three cells in the first column can be seen as
representing stages in moral development quite compatible with the three levels and six stages of moral development identified by Kohlberg (1969). I do not suggest that each individual can be placed in one of the
three boxes with respect to his moral behavior. I assume that each individual may operate at different levels depending on the particular behavior involved; for
example, he may be only complying to the norms about
cheating, but he may have internalized standards of
loyalty to one's friends. Even with respect to the
same specific behavior, a person may operate at different levels on different occasions. Nevertheless, I
would view the three cells as constituting a developmental sequence in the course of childhood socialization, with definite implications for future performance.
Thus, the child first adopts behavior in keeping with
standards of responsibility through compliance; what
he learns at this stage is to discriminate social cues
for reward and punishment. He moves to identification
initially for instrumental reasons: by taking the parent's role in his absence, he can predict more accurately what behavior is likely to be punished. Taking the
parent's role may turn out to be satisfying in its own
right, by giving him a vicarious sense of power and efficacy, and thus identification may enter into his re-

pertoire. He may then find that items of moral behavior that he has adopted through identification are in-
trinsically desirable in terms of his evolving personal
style, and these may then be internalized. Not all individuals, of course, go through the entire sequence;
for some, moral behavior--or at least certain aspects
of moral behavior--may remain fixated at earlier levels
of development. Furthermore, though a person may have
internalized a particular standard of moral behavior,
he may still react at the level of identification or
compliance in specific situations.

Let me turn now to the second column of table 5.2,
which deals with deviations from standards of propriety,
and examine each of its three cells.

(1) *Embarrassment*. In this cell, P has somehow
failed to live up to his self-presentation. He has
behaved publicly in a way that falls short of the expectations that go with a specific role to which he
lays claim or with the general role of an adult in the
society. For example, he has shown himself to be incompetent, inadequate, clumsy, or socially maladroit.
His primary concern is with the public image that he
has created--with the possibility that others will react negatively to his behavior and disapprove of him.
What is at issue for him is not his own sense of competence, adequacy, and so on, but what he has communicated about himself to others. He may be particularly
concerned that others will draw conclusions about his
general characteristics on the basis of his failure in
this specific situation. In this connection, feelings
of embarrassment may be stronger in the presence of
strangers than in the presence of friends, since friends
are unlikely to draw general conclusions on the basis
of P's behavior in this one situation, while for strangers this is the only available sample of P's behavior.
One of the ways of dealing with embarrassment is to cover up the discrepant action--to pretend that it did not
happen or that it did not mean what it seemed to convey.
For example, if P fails in a task in which he claimed
competence, he may pretend that he was not seriously
trying to succeed or that his earlier claim had really
been meant as a joke. If the fact of his failure cannot be denied, he may try to deny its implications by
finding ways of demonstrating that he possesses the com-

petence that has just been thrown into question--e.g.,
by performing a little jig as he comes out of a stumble.
Another way of dealing with embarrassment is self-ridi-
cule, which has the effect of disarming others and soft-
ening the impact of their ridicule, of showing your own
control of the situation, and of communicating that you
find it so funny because it is so uncharacteristic of
you.

    (2) *Shame*. Unlike embarrassment, shame does not
involve a mere concern with one's public image, but a
concern with one's personal image as reflected in the
public image. P's failure to live up to his self-presentation exposes what he regards as a possible underlying weakness. He is not really concerned with the
way others, in the immediate interaction situation,
will react to his deviation, but with its implications
for a role in which his own self-definition is anchored.
The deviation raises serious questions about his embed-
dedness in the role, his ability to live up to its expectations, and thus his long-term place in the social
system. As in the case of guilt, he tries to deal with
the situation by seeking ways of reestablishing his relationship to society, which has been threatened. A
characteristic reaction would involve some attempt to
compensate for his failing, for example, by achieving
success in other aspects of role performance. If his
demands on himself are excessive and he finds it impossible to reestablish his relationship to society,
his reaction may take the form of self-contempt. Self-
contempt to the point of considering oneself inadequate
to enact any of his roles in society may lead to suicide. Suicide, incidentally, is also a possible reaction to extreme guilt, where it represents the ultimate
form of self-punishment.

    (3) *Self-disappointment*. In this cell, finally, P
has failed to live up to standards of propriety that
are part of his personal value system--for example, his
own standards of quality and his own definition of what
is required in the performance of a task or the enactment of a role. In keeping with his values, he is primarily concerned with the task performance or the role
enactment in which he has fallen short. He is not wor-
ried about his social standing or the solidity of his
relationship to society, but he is disappointed in him-

self and his own achievements. One characteristic reaction to his self-disappointment is to examine his behavior in order to understand where he has failed and
to determine how he might improve in the future. Another possible reaction is to examine his standards, in
order to see whether these have been unrealistic--wheth-
er he has been expecting more of himself than he could
deliver. Such an examination may lead to a revision of
his standards accompanied by a greater degree of self-
acceptance.

The three cells in the second column do not seem to
correspond as clearly to developmental stages as do the
three cells in the first column. In fact, Nancy Thalhofer has suggested that the developmental sequence
might even be reversed. Embarrassment actually represents a high degree of social development. Along with
regret, it calls for a considerable amount of empathy.
It also presupposes an awareness that the way in which
a person presents himself is a matter of great moment
to others in his environment. By contrast, self-dis-
appointment--in a rudimentary form--may be viewed as a
more primitive reaction. In other words, disappoint-
ment with reference to a set of personal expectations
may manifest itself at an earlier developmental stage
than shame and embarrassment. On the other hand, it
should be noted that self-disappointment, as presented
in the present scheme, implies a rather high level of
development, since it involves considerable self-con-
sciousness and a well-articulated value system.

One final point can be made about table 5.2. From
"society's point of view"--that is, from the point of
view of social control--guilt and shame are often the
most desirable reactions, even though from the individual's point of view they may turn out to be the most
destructive. Societies, it seems to me, encourage
guilt and shame because social control is usually most
effective at the level of identification. Individuals
operating at the level of compliance are insufficiently
socialized; their adherence to social norms depends on
surveillance, which makes them less reliable and more
difficult to control. Individuals operating at the
level of internalization are, in a sense, excessively
socialized from the point of view of agencies charged
with social control. Since societal standards are in-

tegrated with their personal value systems, they tend
to make their own judgments about the validity of authoritative demands. Their conformity to such demands
is, thus, more conditional. Individuals operating at
the level of identification are. likely to conform to
authoritative demands with less surveillance than those
at the level of compliance, and with less questioning
than those at the level of internalization. Identification, with its associated emotions of guilt and shame,
can thus be seen as the influence process most conducive to social control.

INFLUENCE UNDER CONDITIONS OF LEGITIMATE AUTHORITY

Implicit in my discussion of deviations from societal
standards is the assumption that individuals generally
live up to societal demands at some level. The question of how individuals are induced to live up to these
demands leads us directly to a special case of social
influence: influence under conditions of legitimate
authority. Legitimate authority is a domain of influence that by its nature must be conceptualized in terms
of linkages between the individual and the social system. On the one hand, legitimacy is a property of the
social system, determined by the character and environment of the system. On the other hand, it cannot be defined entirely in terms of objective characteristics of
the system itself, since it has no meaning apart from
the individuals who perceive it and the groups that
share the norms defining it.

For a long time, I had great conceptual difficulty
in relating legitimate power to my three-process model
of social influence. Thus, for example, of the five
bases of power distinguished by French and Raven (1959),
legitimacy was the only one that could not be clearly
coordinated with the three processes of influence. However, as the model evolved to deal with linkages between
the individual and the social system, it became increasingly receptive to the linkage concept of legitimacy.
The formulation at which I finally arrived differs from
that of French and Raven. They view legitimacy as a
separate base of power, commensurate with the other four
bases. By contrast, I view it as cutting across my
three processes of influence, so that it may be asso-

ciated with any one of the three sources of power differentiated by my model--means-control, attractiveness,
and credibility. I shall return to this point later,
after examining the character of legitimate influence
more generally.

According to my present formulation, all forms of
social influence (whether or not it emanates from legitimate authorities) are seen as responsive to demands
of the social system or of one of its components, and
as mediating the integration of the individual into
the social system. What is unique about situations of
legitimate influence, however, is that the influencing
agent is perceived as having the *right* to exert influ-
ence--to make demands--within the particular domain in
question, by virtue of his position in the social system. Thus, for example, when the duly constituted administration of a legitimate political system makes certain demands, citizens feel under an obligation to accept them, regardless of their personal preferences.
Once a demand is categorized as legitimate, the individual essentially finds himself in a situation in which
his preferences have become more or less irrelevant for
determining his actions. This situation differs from
the usual influence situation represented, for example,
in most influence experiments, where the individual
chooses his behavior in terms of his personal preferences. The influencing agent in those situations has
to communicate to the influencee, in some fashion, that
accepting the induced behavior would be preferable from
the point of view of achieving his goals. O may do this
through persuasion, or negotiation, or setting an example, or offering rewards, or even through coercion. In
all of these cases, P has to become convinced that
adopting the induced behavior is preferable for him. In
situations of legitimate influence, by contrast, O does
not have to convince P that adopting the induced behavior is preferable for him, given the available alternatives, but merely that it is required of him. P's reactions are governed not so much by motivational processes as by perceptual ones. A legitimate demand has
the quality of requiredness that one often associates
with external reality. Legitimate power implies that O
has the authority to define the dimensions of the situation to which P must relate himself. This authority,

incidentally, extends to both of the domains differentiated in table 5.2: O has the right to define both
P's responsibilities as a system member and the limits
of propriety for P's role performance.

I have made a sharp distinction between influence
situations involving legitimate authority and those involving preferential choice in order to clarify what I
see as the essential nature of legitimacy. In actual
fact, most influence situations cannot be that sharply
differentiated. They involve elements of both motivated preference and perceived requiredness, which enter into conflict with one another. Situations differ,
however, in terms of the balance between the two. To
the extent that elements of requiredness predominate,
removing the situation from preferential choice, some
of the dramatic outcomes that are associated with influence under conditions of legitimate authority become possible. On the one hand, we have situations in
which individuals take actions in response to legitimate demands that are clearly against their personal
preferences and short-term interests, often calling for
considerable sacrifices. The ability of authorities to
elicit such sacrifices from system members--which in
turn depends on the extent to which the system itself
is perceived as legitimate--allows the system to function on a basis of consent, with relatively little need
to resort to coercion or to confront constant challenges. On the other hand, we have situations in which
individuals take actions that they would normally consider antisocial and immoral--as in the My Lai massacre
or the Milgram (1963) experiment--because these actions
have become legitimized. In accepting the legitimacy
of the authorities, the individuals tend to relinquish
control and responsibility to them and to obey their
demands without question (cf. Kelman and Lawrence,
1972).

Even though an influencing agent is perceived as
legitimate, his demands are not always obeyed without
question. I said earlier that P finds himself in a
situation in which his preferences have become irrelevant *once a demand is categorized as legitimate*. The
picture changes, however, if a particular demand or
series of demands is seen as illegitimate or nonlegiti-
mate--not because it goes counter to P's preferences,

but because it fails to meet certain external criteria.
To challenge the legitimacy of a demand is very difficult, particularly when O is surrounded by the trap-
pings of authority. There are great differences among
individuals in their ability to make such challenges;
the ability to do so depends, for example, on such factors as position in society, availability of appropriate models, and level of moral development. But there
are definitely conditions under which the legitimacy of
authoritative demands *is* challenged and, indeed, there
are criteria for mounting such challenges.

Criteria for challenging the legitimacy of a demand
are built into the very conception of legitimate power.
Legitimacy implies that power is exercised within certain limits and according to certain rules, rather than
in an arbitrary fashion. The perceived legitimacy of a
demand depends, therefore, on the degree to which it
conforms to the established procedures and constraints.
There is always an external reference point--a constitution, a code of laws, a set of institutionalized practices or traditional customs--to which both the system's
members and its leadership are subject. There are thus
specifiable ways of determining whether or not a given
demand is legitimate. Moreover, if the system is to be
perceived as legitimate, it provides mechanisms of re-
course (such as court tests or the ombudsman) that permit members to challenge official actions they deem illegitimate on procedural grounds--on the grounds that
they are outside the domain of O's power, or that the
way they have been executed is in violation of the
rules. The perceived legitimacy of authoritative demands depends not only on procedural considerations,
but also on the extent to which the policies in which
they are embedded conform to the basic values on which
the legitimacy of the system itself ultimately rests.
In short, then, demands from legitimate authorities can
be challenged on the grounds that they violate the established procedures or the underlying values of the
system. Thus, even in seemingly pure situations of
legitimate authority, P may resist influence; but he
would do so, not simply because he finds the induced
behavior personally undesirable, but because he feels
that acceptance is not required of him--i.e., that the
demand is not legitimate or is, indeed, illegitimate.

Given this formulation, one of the most important and most interesting questions for empirical exploration concerns the conditions under which individuals will feel free (or even obligated) to challenge authoritative demands. I would hypothesize that a key factor is the manner in which the individual is integrated into the social system, which is equivalent to the process by which he accepts the system's legitimacy. Before elaborating on this hypothesis, let me present in summary fashion a classification of patterns of personal involvement in social systems from which the hypothesis is derived. The model is specifically concerned with the national system, but it should be equally applicable to the involvement of individuals in other kinds of social systems.   .

Personal involvement in the system translates directly into perceived legitimacy of the system. That is, to the extent that a system member is in some fashion personally involved in the system--to the extent that he feels attached to it and is integrated into its operations--he will perceive the system as legitimate. Table 5.3 presents six patterns of personal involvement in (and hence perceived legitimacy of) the national system.

The six patterns result from the interaction of two qualitative dimensions. The rows represent two sources of attachment or loyalty to the system--sentimental and instrumental attachment. The columns represent three ways in which the individual is integrated into the system--ideological, role-participant, and normative integration. In other words, the rows distinguish, essentially, two types of motives of the individual that lead him to cathect the system. The columns, on the other hand, represent the three components of the system via which members may be bound into it--its values, its roles, and its rules or norms. To put it more simply, the rows define why individuals are loyal to the system, the columns define what it is they are loyal to.

For our present purposes, we are primarily concerned with the columns, which refer to the three components of social systems corresponding to the three processes of social influence. The three processes of influence contribute to the present model in two senses: they help define the way in which a particular type of inte-

TABLE 5.3. Patterns of Personal Involvement in the National System*

Manner of Integration into the System

	Ideological (Consolidation) (Internalization of system values)	Role-Participant (Mobilization) (Identification with system roles)	Normative (Conformity) (Compliance with system demands seen as legitimate)
Source of Attachment (Loyalty) to the System — Sentimental	Commitment to cultural values reflective of national identity	Commitment to the role of national linked to group symbols	Acceptance of demands based on commitment to the sacredness of the state
Source of Attachment (Loyalty) to the System — Instrumental	Commitment to institutions promotive of the needs and interests of the population	Commitment to social roles mediated by the system	Acceptance of demands based on commitment to law and order (principle of equity)

(System requirements conducive to this type of integration)

(Influence process characteristic of this type of integration)

*Reprinted from Kelman 1969, p. 280, by permission of the publisher and the editor.

165

gration is initially established, and the way in which
an individual integrated via each of these components
is likely to react to a specific system demand. Let me
briefly review each of the three columns in these terms:

(1) *Ideological integration.* An individual who
is ideologically integrated is bound to the system
by virtue of the fact that he subscribes to some of
the basic values on which the system is established.
These may be the cultural values defining the national identity, or the social values reflected in
the institutions by which the society is organized,
or both. The ideologically integrated member has
internalized these values and incorporated them into a personal value framework. When he is faced
with demands for behavior in support of the national
system he is likely to respond positively, because
support of the system is generally congruent with
his own values. The extent to which he meets specific demands, however, depends on the extent to which
he sees these demands as consistent with the underlying values of the system to which he is committed.

(2) *Role-participant integration.* An individual
who is integrated via role-participation is bound to
the system by virtue of the fact that he is personally engaged in roles within the system--roles that
enter significantly into his self-definition. He
may be emotionally caught up in the role of national
as such, with its associated symbols, and derive a
sense of self-transcendence and compensatory identity from it; or he may be functionally caught up in
various social roles that are central to his identity and whose effective performance depends on the
national system. His integration into the system is
based on identification, in the sense that he has a
stake in maintaining the system-related roles and
the self-definition anchored in them. When he is
faced with demands to support the system he is likely to respond positively, because such support is
generally required by the system role to which he is
committed. The extent to which he meets specific
demands depends, however, on the extent to which the
relevant role has been brought into salience by situational factors.

(3) *Normative integration*. An individual who is normatively integrated is bound to the system by virtue of the fact that he accepts the system's right to set the behavior of its members within a prescribed domain. Here we are dealing, one might say, with legitimacy in its pure form, in which the question of personal values and roles has become ir- relevant. Acceptance of the system's right to un- questioning obedience may be based on a commitment to the state as a sacred object in its own right, or on a commitment to the necessity of law and order as a guarantor of equitable procedures. The normative- ly integrated member regards compliance with the sys- tem as a highly proper and valued orientation. When he is faced with demands to support the system he is likely to comply without question, since he regards it as his obligation to do so. The extent to which he meets specific demands, however, depends on the extent to which these are authoritatively presented as the wishes of the leadership or the requirements of law. One important indicator of the authorita- tiveness of a particular demand is the existence of positive or negative sanctions to control proper performance (Kelman 1969, pp. 286-87).

We can now return to the question I raised earlier about the conditions under which individuals will feel free--and obligated--to challenge authoritative demands. I would propose that those who accept the legitimacy of the system by virtue of the fact that they share its basic values are most likely to challenge the legiti- macy of certain specific demands. They usually provide the most important long-run support for the system, but they are not always "dependable" in the short run, in that their support is contingent on the system's living up to its (and their) values. It is not surprising that civil disobedience is most likely to arise among this group of ideologically integrated members. By contrast, those whose integration is primarily at the normative level are most likely to accept authoritative demands without question. Though they tend to give re- liable, unquestioning obedience, they are likely to be passive and lacking in creativity. From the point of view of the system, those who are integrated at the

level of role participation are the ideal members,
since they are more dependable in their support than
the value-integrated members, but at the same time more
enthusiastic than the normatively integrated ones. This
observation is directly related to my earlier point
that identification, with its associated emotions of
guilt and shame, can be seen as the influence process
most conducive to social control.

   As I pointed out at the beginning of my remarks
about legitimate influence and demonstrated in table
5.3 and elsewhere, I propose that influence under conditions of legitimate authority may take different
forms, corresponding to the processes of compliance,
identification, and internalization, which were originally designed to handle influence under conditions of
preferential choice. While I see important parallels
between the two types of influence situations, then, I
would also hypothesize certain differences between them.
These differences can be traced to the differences in
the psychological situations in which people find themselves under conditions of legitimacy (where they acknowledge the right of the influencing agent to set behavior for them) as compared to the conditions of preferential choice.

   Perhaps the most notable differences occur in the
case of compliance. Compliance poses special difficulties because the original model postulates coercive
power as one of its possible determinants; legitimate
influence, on the other hand, is by definition noncoercive. Nevertheless, I feel that the parallelism is
sufficiently close to treat both as variants of the
same influence process. Compliance in a situation of
legitimate authority is similar to compliance in the
original model in that the influencee's behavior in
both situations is controlled by the existence of positive or negative sanctions. In the original model, however, sanctions constitute a *motivation* for compliance.
That is, the person complies in order to obtain a particular reward or avoid a particular punishment. In
the context of legitimate demands, sanctions still play
an important part in control and compliance, but primarily as *indicators* that the demands are really authoritative and meant to be obeyed, rather than as motiva-
tors for the choice that would be personally most rewarding.

I would further predict that the reactions accompanying compliance would differ in the the two situations. A person complying in a preferential choice situation is likely to experience a certain amount of resentment because his opportunities for choice have been limited. This would be particularly true if compliance is achieved through coercive tactics. A person complying under conditions of legitimate authority, on the other hand, is less likely to be resentful, because he sees it as the right of the influencing agent not only to demand compliance, but also to impose sanctions for noncompliance. By testing such hypotheses as the one just described, comparing the side effects of compliance, identification, and internalization in the two types of influence situations, we can gain some insight into the nature of legitimate authority as well as the psychological mechanisms that mediate influence in general.

NOTE

1. This clasification, and many of the ideas relating to it, developed in the course of a long series of discussions with Nancy Thalhofer, when we were both at the University of Michigan. I am greatly indebted to Dr. Thalhofer for stimulating my thinking along these lines.

REFERENCES

Bailyn, L., and Kelman, H. C. 1962. The effects of a year's experience in America on the self-image of Scandinavians: a preliminary analysis of reactions to a new environment. *Journal of Social Issues* 18 (1): 30-40.

French, J. R. P., Jr., and Raven, B. 1959. The bases of social power. In D. Cartwright (Ed.), *Studies in social power*. Ann Arbor, Mich.: Institute for Social Research, pp. 150-67.

Freud, S. 1933. *New introductory lectures on psychoanalysis*. New York: Norton.

Goffman, E. 1959. *The presentation of self in everyday life*. New York: Doubleday Anchor.

Hovland, C. I., Janis, I. L., and Kelley, H. H. 1953. *Communication and persuasion*. New Haven, Conn.: Yale University Press.

Katz, D. 1960. The functional approach to attitude change. *Public Opinion Quarterly* 24: 163-204.

Kelman, H. C. 1953. Attitude change as a function of response restriction. *Human Relations* 6: 185-214.

------. 1956. *Compliance, identification, and internalization: a theoretical and experimental approach to the study of social influence*. Mimeographed.

------. 1958. Compliance, identification, and internalization: three processes of attitude change. *Journal of Conflict Resolution* 2: 51-60.

------. 1960. Effects of role-orientation and value-orientation on the nature of attitude change. Paper presented at the meeting of the Eastern Psychological Association, New York City.

------. 1961. Processes of opinion change. *Public Opinion Quarterly* 25: 57-78.

------. 1962. The induction of action and attitude change. In S. Coopersmith (Ed.), *Personality research*. Copenhagen: Munksgaard, pp. 81-110.

------. 1963. The role of the group in the induction of therapeutic change. *International Journal of Group Psychotherapy* 13: 399-432.

------. 1969. Patterns of personal involvement in the national system: a social-psychological analysis of political legitimacy. In J. N. Rosenau (Ed.), *International politics and foreign policy*. 2d ed. New York: Free Press, pp. 276-88.

Kelman, H. C., and Baron, R. M. 1968. Determinants of modes of resolving inconsistency dilemmas: a functional analysis. In R. P. Abelson, E. Aronson, W.J. McGuire, T. M. Newcomb, M. J. Rosenberg, and P. H. Tannenbaum (Eds.), *Theories of cognitive consistency: a sourcebook*. Chicago: Rand McNally, pp. 670-83.

Kelman, H. C., Baron, R. M., Sheposh, J. P., and Lubalin, J. S. Forthcoming. *Varieties of discrepant action: toward a functional theory*. New York: Academic Press.

Kelman, H. C., and Cohler, J. 1965. Personality factors in reaction to persuasion. Dittoed (to be published).

Kelman, H. C., and Eagly, A. H.   1965.   Attitude toward
    the communicator, perception of communication con-
    tent, and attitude change. *Journal of Personality
    and Social Psychology* 1: 63-78.
Kelman, H. C., and Hovland, C. I.   1953.   "Reinstate-
    ment" of the communicator in delayed measurement of
    opinion change. *Journal of Abnormal and Social
    Psychology* 48: 327-35.
Kelman, H. C., and Lawrence, L. H.   1972.   Assignment
    of responsibility in the case of Lt. Calley: pre-
    liminary report on a national survey. *Journal of
    Social Issues* 28 (1): 177-212.
Kohlberg, L.   1969.   Stage and sequence: the cognitive-
    developmental approach to socialization.   In D. A.
    Goslin (Ed.), *Handbook of socialization theory and
    research*.   Chicago: Rand McNally, pp. 347-480.
Milgram, S.   1963.   Behavioral study of obedience.
    Journal of Abnormal and Social Psychology 67:   371-
    78.
Smith, M. B., Bruner, J. S., and White, R. W.   1956.
    Opinions and personality. New York: Wiley.
Willis, R. H.   1965.   Conformity, independence, and
    anti-conformity. *Human Relations* 18:   373-88.

The Comparative Analysis 6
of Power and Power Preference

Bertram H. Raven

Question. What do the following have in common:
(a) the analysis of teacher effectiveness, (b) the
deliberations of the Nuremberg (or My Lai) war crimes
tribunals, (c) the therapeutic examination of parent-
child or husband-wife interaction, (d) the postmortem
dissection of a deadlocked labor-management dispute?
Answer. Undoubtedly many things. All deal with the
analysis of the bases of social power and interpersonal
influence. In each case, the individual or group conducting the analysis must inevitably ask such questions
as, How does one person affect the behavior, attitudes,
and beliefs of another? How dependent is that change
upon surveillance? What is the subsequent attitude of
the changed person toward the person who initiated the
change? How long does the change last? To what extent
is any residual change attributable to the person who
initiated the influence?

It was such questions that stimulated John R. P.
French and me to develop a typological analysis of social power more than ten years ago (French and Raven
1959). In this paper, I shall present some subsequent
analyses and studies which modified and extended our
original formulation, and point out some directions for
further research. Let me first briefly present the social power typology as originally presented (French and
Raven 1959) and as modified in later statements (Raven
1965; Collins and Raven 1969; Raven and Kruglanski 1970).

THE BASES OF SOCIAL POWER

In our initial and subsequent statements, *social power* has been defined in terms of influence. *Social influence* was defined as a change in a person's cognitions, attitude, or behavior which has its origin in another person or group, the influencing agent. Power was then simply defined as the potential influence which the agent could exert on the person. Power, and its resultant influence, were then considered in terms of whether it was socially dependent or independent, whether the altered state in the person was continually related to the influencing agent. If the resultant influence was socially dependent, then we also differentiated the influence in terms of whether continued surveillance by the influencing agent was the critical factor in that dependence. Our six bases of social power were then differentiated in terms of whether the relationship to the agent was *independent, dependent on surveillance* (public dependent), or *dependent without surveillance* (private dependent).

Socially Independent Influence

Informational Power. Independent influence is the result of a basic change in cognitive elements: its basis is *information* communicated by the agent. (Informational *influence* was described in the original statement by French and Raven [1959], but we did not refer to it as a type of *power*. It was so considered in later papers.) Cognitive change is the critical factor in informational influence—the influence is immediately internalized by the influencee. He understands why he is believing or behaving differently, and his reason is related to the intrinsic nature of the belief or act rather than to the influencing agent. *Examples:* The student whose teacher has convinced him that one mathematical formula is more appropriate than another. A housewife who has been convinced by the vacuum cleaner salesman that his machine is far superior to the model she is currently using.

Socially Dependent on Surveillance

Reward and Coercion. These two bases of power are
socially dependent, and furthermore observability is
critical for influence to occur where they are the
bases of power. *Reward* power stems from the ability of
the influencing agent to mediate rewards for the influencee; *coercive* power, from his ability to mediate
punishments. Originally, we considered this to mean
material rewards and punishments only (e.g., the reward and coercive power of the teacher which stemmed
from his ability to give A's or F's, the supervisor's
ability to recommend a worker for promotion or to fire
him). But later it became clear that potential approval, love, acceptance, and liking could become commodi-
ties which also represent rewards; potential disapproval, hate, rejection, and dislike could, similarly, be
forms of punishment. These *personal* rewards and coer-
cions could be every bit as powerful as the impersonal
ones considered earlier.

Socially Dependent without Surveillance

Three sources of social power--expertness, reference,
and legitimacy--result in social influence which is
dependent upon the influencing agent, but wherein observability is unimportant. As compared to influence
stemming from reward and coercion, the effects continue
whether or not the influencee believes that his behavior
will become apparent to the influencing agent.

Expert Power. This basis of power stems from the
attribution of superior knowledge or ability to the
influencing agent. If the student in the example above
uses the mathematical formula without seeing its utility,
but in the faith that the teacher, being more skilled in
mathematics, must know that such is the road to a solution, expertness is the basis for influence, and the influence is socially dependent. Furthermore, given such
faith, the influence is private--observability is unimportant.

Referent Power. This occurs when a person uses another person or group as a "frame of reference" against

which he evaluates some aspect of himself. We tend to adopt opinions, attitudes, and behaviors similar to those held by the persons from whom we dissociate ourselves. ·Thus the process of identification of person with agent or disidentification of person from agent is the critical factor in referent power. "I am like him" --or, "I would prefer to be like him"--"so I want to behave or believe as he does."

Legitimate Power. This grows out of the influencee's acceptance of a role structural relationship with the influencing agent. It may be phrased in terms such as "I do as he says because he has a right to ask me to do it, and I am supposed to do as he asks." Legitimate power is obvious in highly structured social organizations--each member of a military organization who accepts the legitimacy of that organization feels compelled to do as his superior asks without question-- "ours is not to reason why." Legitimate power also occurs in less obvious forms--legitimate power of the experimenter over the subject has been demonstrated most dramatically by Orne and Evans (1965) and Milgram (1963, 1965). Even apparent powerlessness can become the basis of legitimate power. Such is the case where society prescribes that it is the duty of those who can to accede to requests for help from those who can't. The blind person may legitimately request the sighted person to assist him in crossing the street. Schopler and Bateson (1965), examining a number of studies along these lines by Berkowitz and his co-workers (e.g., Berkowitz and Daniels 1963; Berkowitz, Klanderman, and Harris 1964; Goranson and Berkowitz 1966), refer to such helping behavior as the "power of dependence." Ordinarily the dependent person emphasizes his helplessness, and even his obsequience. However, society may sometimes legitimate the power of the powerless, so that we see such instances as the beggar in the Jewish shtetl, as described by Zborowski and Herzog (1952), who stands at the donor's door erect and domineering, demanding his rights as a beggar. Katz and Danet (1966) describe similar devices utilized, in particular by Oriental (Sephardic) Jews, in dealing with modern Israeli bureaucrats.

Some Further Considerations

Positive and Negative Influence. There are a few
final points which should be mentioned in our summary
of the bases of power. First, we have been presenting
our influence model in positive terms--changes in the
influencee which bring him more closely into line with
the beliefs, attitudes, behaviors, and desires of the
influencing agent. Yet, in our discussion of referent
power we did allude to negative influence--changes in a
direction opposite from that of the agent. Others sometimes serve as *negative* models or referents (cf. Willis
1965). Indeed, today in particular, we can see instances of persons who have apparently rejected the
current modes of society, so that *negative* referent influence seems more predominant than *positive,* and such
persons in turn become negative referent persons for
others. If we mistrust a salesman, we may assume that
he knows more about a product than we do, but is using
that knowledge in a direction which is in his best interests but opposed to ours. The result is *negative*
expert influence. Negative legitimate influence may
occur less frequently--e.g., a prisoner of war who defines his role relationship with his captors such that,
in certain domains, he feels obliged to do the opposite
of what they ask.

Secondary Effects of Influence. Further, we must
keep in mind that, though we have emphasized the primary effects of social power, secondary effects can
also occur. The student who, because of expert power
(which is private dependent), follows his math instructor's directions in solving a math problem can learn
the logic of the formula through using it. The secondary change is then independent, resembling the results of informational influence. The boy who tastes
porridge because his mother has told him that otherwise
he cannot go out to play (coercion, public dependent)
finds to his surprise that the porridge tastes much better than it looks. The changes which result from a reduction of cognitive dissonance after forced compliance
(reward or coercive power) (Festinger and Carlsmith
1959; Collins 1969; Bem 1967) can also be seen as secondary changes following public dependent change.

Secondary changes can also occur in the perception of the influencing agent. An agent who has both referent power and coercive power over an influencee and who chooses coercive power may be successful in his influence attempt, but the use of coercion may lead to personal rejection by the influencee. The agent may now have become a *negative* referent, such that a boomerang effect may occur after surveillance is withdrawn.

Comparison with Kelman's Three Processes of Social Influence

Before proceeding further, it would be well to compare the foregoing analysis of the bases of social power with a somewhat similar analysis of the processes of social influence which was developed at about the same time by Kelman (1956, 1961). The comparison of the two systems is presented in figure 6.1. We note first that Kelman separates the influence process into its antecedents and consequents. The antecedents correspond to the sources of power in the French and Raven system. The consequents--the actual influence processes--correspond to the types of change or influence as differentiated in our system. Kelman distinguishes three "sources of power of an agent," three "resources" possessed by the agent by which he may successfully exercise influence: means-control, attractiveness, and credibility. One would be tempted to simply relate these, respectively, to "reward-coercion," "reference," and "expertise," and, indeed, in an experiment generated by this system (Kelman 1958), the independent variables are operationally defined in precisely that way. The consequents also appear to have a one-to-one correspondence--compliance, with public dependent change; identification, with private dependent change; internalization, with dependent change. Let us now look at some contrasts:

(1) "Means-control" groups "reward" and "coercion" as if they were unitary sources of power with similar effects. Our system, though grouping these together as "producing public dependent change," draws a sharp differentiation between the two; and, as pointed out above, there would seem to be good experimental evidence for making this further distinction.

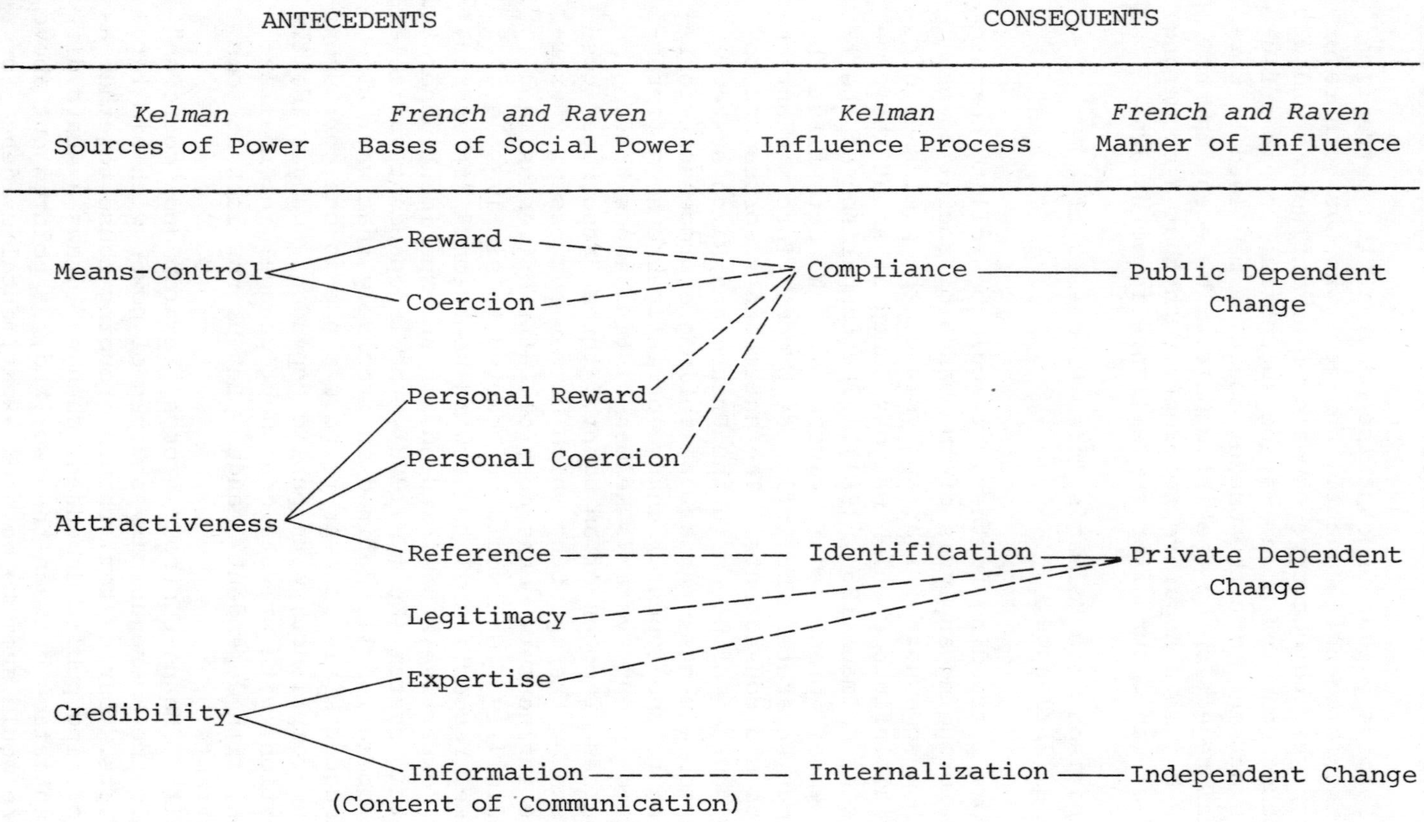

FIGURE 6.1. Kelman's and French and Raven's View of the Social Influence Processes

(2) Attractiveness might well lead to "referent power," with identification and private dependent change. However, in my revision of the original statement of the French and Raven analysis (Raven 1965), I felt compelled to consider personal coercion and personal reward, as described above. Attractiveness of an influencing agent is then a basis for wanting to be. liked by him, for fearing rejection by him. The resultant change is then more like compliance (public dependent change) than identification (private dependent change).

(3) Note further that referent power (identification can also arise from the perception of similarity, as well as from attractiveness of the agent.

(4) Legitimacy is a major omission in the Kelman analysis. Kelman has obviously considered legitimacy as a basis for influence in his presentation at this symposium. In the French and Raven system, we see this basis of power as leading to private dependent change very similar to that produced by referent power and expert power. Legitimacy is, of course, a general concept relating to propriety of behavior--it is broader than legitimate power. Indeed, in the original statement of our theory (French and Raven 1959), French and I discussed the situations wherein coercive power could be used legitimately or illegitimately--the influencee might be subjected to coercive power and conform, yet not concede that the agent has a legitimate right to utilize coercion. For example, the man on the street corner may move along if the policeman threatens to arrest him for vagrancy even though he does not concede that the policeman is acting legitimately--this, then, is illegitimate coercion. Raven and French (1958) and French, Morrison, and Levinger (1960) have examined this distinction experimentally. Though legitimacy is a broader concept than legitimate power, we would consider legitimate power to be a very important concept in its own right, by the same logic that we would apply to reward power, coercive (punishment) power, and informational power.

(5) In Kelman's definitional statements and in his experimental operations, "credibility" seems to correspond to expert power. However, Kelman suggests that credibility leads to internalization. We have indi-

cated that expertise leads to *dependent* change, at
least initially. It is true that the expert qualities
of the influencing agent might make the influencee attend more closely to the content of the communication,
but the change in that case would be informational.
Pure expert power would operate on the basis of faith--
doing what the agent asks or suggests in the faith that
he knows what is correct, even if the influencee does
not understand the intrinsic reasons for change.

Kelman's analyses have obviously been very fruitful
in furthering our understanding of the influence process and have resulted in fruitful research. It is
when two theoretical systems have most in common that
problems of translation become most difficult. The
above discussion is presented to help alleviate such
problems for readers of these symposium papers.

Interaction among Bases of Power

Initially, we described the bases of power as if they
exist independently of one another. However, the existence of one basis of power in its pure form is relatively rare. Rather, we find that the various bases exist
in differing combinations and configurations, with perhaps one basis being more dominant in one situation,
another in a different situation. Furthermore, the influencing agent may make salient one basis of power
through utilizing it. Ordinarily, the agent has some
choice as to the bases he may utilize, and, if he is
wise, he will consider what power resources he has,
which ones he will utilize, and in what combination he
will utilize them. However, even if he has the knowledge which enables him to correctly determine his resources in a given domain or situation, the task is
made more complicated by the fact that the bases of power interact with one another and, further, that the
bases of power which will be effective in changing behavior may be negatively effective in changed attitude
or belief--this is, indeed, what we were referring to
when we pointed out the positive and negative effects
of coercive power.

The interaction of bases of power is particularly
well illustrated in an experiment conducted by Raven,
Mansson, and Anthony (1962) in which expert and refer-

ent power were experimentally manipulated. The experiment was stimulated by Solomon Asch's classic study (1956) of the effects of group pressure in a line judgment task. By now, few social scientists are unaware of Asch's finding that the erroneous reports of a large majority in a group can influence a lone individual to make ridiculously erroneous reports regarding quite unambiguous line lengths. Often overlooked, however, are his even more significant extensive interviews with the "yielders" to find out why they reported erroneously. It was gratifying to note that many of the open-ended responses could be coded in terms of the bases of social power: *expert*--"a majority is usually right"; *legitimate*--"the majority rules"; *referent*--"you always like to be like everybody else"; *coercion*--"I was being pushed to give an answer that I didn't want to give." Thus it seemed particularly appropriate to vary bases of power in the group conformity situation.

Our study investigated the effects of group pressures on belief in extrasensory perception and on reported receptions of ESP images. Prior to the experiment, subjects were given semantic differential measure of the degree of belief in extrasensory perception. They were then scheduled in groups of four, with each member of the group sitting in a separate booth, in accordance with the method first reported by Deutsch and Gerard (1955). Subjects were presented with thirty trials during which they were to attempt to receive an ESP image which was presumably being transmitted by a "sender" in another room. On twenty-three trials, light signals indicated that their three coparticipants had indeed received an ESP image; on six trials, it appeared that only one coparticipant had received an image; on one trial, the light signals indicated that none of the others had received an image. In the first phase of the experiment, it seemed clear that group pressures increased the number of reported receptions and affected the belief in ESP.

The second phase of the experiment, which utilized the same basic procedures, additionally manipulated expert and referent influence. This manipulation was effected by means of verbal inductions regarding the perceptual ability of the coparticipants. It was stated that the coparticipants had been tested extensively in a "Perceptual Training Laboratory," and their perceptual ability was reported. Coparticipants in a *high attributed ability* condition were said to have unusually keen and reliable perceptual ability; those in a *moderate attributed ability* condition were said to be just slightly above average in perceptual ability; coparticipants in a *negative attributed ability* condition were described as very unreliable perceivers.

Now, we expected that these manipulations would affect both the *referent* and *expert* power of the coparticipants, since an increase in expertise would reduce reference. This was based on our assumption that referent influence stemmed from identification--if the others were seen as either very high or very low in perceptual ability, the subject (who presumably saw himself as about average or slightly above average) would not identify with them, and referent influence would be reduced. On the other hand, the greater the attributed perceptual ability, the more the others would be seen as expert. We further assumed that expertise would affect the subject's beliefs as to what was correct--thus coparticipants in the high ability condition should have the greatest effects on belief. Referent influence would most affect behavior--reported receptions of ESP images.

The differences were as predicted. *Expert* influence resulting from high attributed ability led to significantly greater belief in ESP than was true in the other two conditions. Yet, that same high attributed ability served to reduce reported reception. Influencing agents with *moderate attributed ability* had the greatest effect, whereas those with high attributed ability had no greater effect than those with negative attributed ability.

These results leave us with much to contemplate, and complicate considerably any answer to a question we are often asked, "How can I be most effective in influencing others?" For it seems that the same factor which would make us more effective in one dimension would make us less effective in other dimensions. A minister highly respected in his community tries to influence his parishioners to be more accepting of people of other religious persuasions and other ethnic groups. Does he succeed? The answer, in some circumstances, would ap-

pear to be yes *and* no: Yes, he does influence them to
believe that one *should* be more open-minded--but no, he
has no more influence on their behavior than the least
respected member of the community. It is as if his
parishioners are saying, "Yes, he is a very fine man,
and we respect him utterly and completely for defining
what is right for us. Yet he is so fine that we cannot
begin to live up to his standards of behavior--he is
just too different from us."

THE BASES OF POWER IN EVERYDAY LIFE

There have now been a number of other laboratory experiments which have examined the different bases of
social power, including studies of legitimacy and coercion (Raven and French 1958), referent influence
(Raven and Fishbein 1961), reward and coercion (Brigante
1958; Zipf 1960), referent and coercion (Zander and Curtis 1962), to mention a few examples. More recently,
increased attention has been given to the bases of power in ongoing social relationships. We find studies examining social power bases in industry (Kahn, Wolfe,
Quinn, Snock, and Rosenthal 1964), in the operations of
sales firms (Bachman, Smith, and Slesinger 1966), in
parent-adolescent relations (Smith 1970), in counseling
(Strong 1970), and in hospitals (Rosenberg and Pearlin
1962). I shall describe two further extensions--to
family power relationships and to power relationships
in school settings.

The Bases of Conjugal Power   ·

Richard Centers, Aroldo Rodrigues, and I have carried
out a field survey in which we examined the relative
power and bases of power of husbands and wives. The
data were gathered from interviews with a representative sample of 776 husbands and wives in the Los Angeles
area. One part of the study (Centers, Raven, and Rodrigues 1971) concentrated particularly on relative power, replicating and extending earlier research by Blood
and Wolfe (1960). The part of the study that I will
describe here examines the bases of power (Raven, Centers, and Rodrigues 1969).
    The respondent was told, "There are many cases where

your wife (husband) asks you to do something and you do
it, even though you may not see clearly why it should
be done. . . . I will give you some possible reasons
and would then like you to tell me how likely each of
these reasons is. . . " The five reasons, presented on
a card, represented the five bases of social power
listed in the French and Raven (1959) paper. (1) Because if you did so, then she (he) would do or say something nice for you in return [Reward]. (2) Because if
you did not do so, then she (he) might do or say something which would be unpleasant for you [Coercion].
(3) Because she (he) knew what was best in this case,
and so you did what she (he) asked you to do [Expert].
(4) Because you felt that she (he) had a right to ask
you to do this, and you felt obligated to do as she (he)
asked [Legitimate]. (5) Because you felt that you both
are part of the same family and should see eye-to-eye on
these matters [Referent].

The bases of power were rated independently on a
scale of likeliness, and then each respondent indicated
which was the most likely of the five. The findings in
general indicate that the respondents were indeed able
to make these distinctions and that their responses
were systematic. There was a clear ordering of the
bases of power, with referent and expert power being
most likely, followed by legitimate, reward, and coercion (least likely). The results showed that husbands
were more likely to say that they were influenced by
their wives because they were part of the same family
(referent power) and therefore should see eye-to-eye
on these matters. Wives were particularly likely to
attribute expert power to their husbands, with referent
power only slightly (and not significantly) lower. Thus
the major sex differences were in the expert and referent categories. There was also a relationship between
power bases and age. Expert influence was most often
attributed to the spouse by younger respondents, with
that basis decreasing with age. Referent power was relatively high even for the younger couples, but increased further with age. Both of these trends were
broken in the small group of "over 70" families. Education also affected the bases of power. Expert power increased with the amount of education, and referent power decreased, though less markedly.

As can be seen in table 6.1 the power base varies with the domain of power, the behavioral area within which influence is attempted. These data grew out of a series of questions about specific domains, e.g., "Suppose your husband (wife) asked you to go visit some friend or relative and, even though you didn't feel like it, you did as he (she) asked . . ." Note that in this case legitimate influence was predominant, as was also true for "repair or clean something around house," "change some personal habit," and "go see a doctor" even though "you didn't feel that badly." Referent power was operative in getting a spouse to go somewhere for an outing or a vacation and changing a station on the TV or radio.

Recently, the same approach has been used by Frank New ton in an interview study of the husbands (*casados*) and comon-law partners (*juntos*) in the Guatemalan peasant community of San Marcos la Laguna. Unfortunately, the domains of power sampled were not really comparable to those examined in our Los Angeles study. However, it is interesting that in San Marcos reward power was most frequently attributed in at least one comparable area--going to a fiesta. In eleven of the domains sampled, expert power of the female partner was most frequently cited; legitimate power was most frequent in four domains; referent power, in only one. It was expected that the power bases for common-law relationships would be different from those in relationships which had been legitimated and made virtually permanent in a church ceremony. This expectation does not seem to have been borne out.

In the Los Angeles study, the respondents were also asked what aspect of marriage they found most valuable. If the respondent rated "chance to have children," "love and affection," or "companionship" as the most valuable part of marriage, then referent influence predominated. If to have a partner who "understands your problems" was regarded as most valuable, then expert power was most salient. Few respondents ranked "standard of living" as most valuable; though differences in this category were not significant, it is interesting to note that reward and legitimacy were most frequent for these respondents. The relationship between marital satisfaction and attributed basis of power revealed

TABLE 6.1. Percentage Attributing Each Basis of Power to Spouse as a Function of Domain of Power

Domain of Power	N	Predominant Basis of Power Attributed to Spouse				
		Reward	Coercion	Expert	Legitimate	Referent
"Visit some friend or relative"	768	7%	8%	15%	43%	27%
"Change some personal habit"	758	6	9	35	30	20
"Repair or clean something around house"	766	5	13	28	35	19
"Change station on TV or radio"	766	14	13	8	30	35
"Go somewhere for outing or vacation"	760	10	3	10	37	40
"Go see a doctor"	768	1	2	55	22	20

Note: In comparing percentages between domains, any difference in percentage greater than 5% is significant at the .05 level of confidence.

frequent attribution of referent power among the "very satisfied" couples and a disproportionately high attribution of "coercion" among the relatively few respondents who said that they were "not at all satisfied."

To conclude, then, we have found differences in attributed bases of social power of spouses which seem meaningful and systematic. Let us now take a brief look at another empirical study of power utilization.

Power in the Classroom

For an investigation of the bases of social power in the classroom, we were fortunate in being able to include some social power items in a study of the Riverside school system. In this case, we presented junior high school students with a specific situation: "Very often students forget and leave their books, or their papers and things, lying around . . . . Suppose your *teacher* asked you to pick up the things you had left around, and you did pick them up . . ." Again, the respondents were asked to respond in terms of the likelihood and the most likely of the six power bases. The same situation was presented for a peer--"the student who sits on your right"--asking the respondent to pick up his books and papers.[1] Interesting differences were found between the power attributed to the teacher and that attributed to the fellow student. The teacher was highest in legitimate power. The fellow student was highest in referent power, with informational power as a close second. We may also note that the teacher came out much higher in expert and coercive power, the student in reward, referent, and informational power. The differences, though striking, are, of course, not particularly surprising. Rather, we look to these to again emphasize that the bases of social power typology can be presented so as to elicit meaningful and systematic responses. We are now examining our data for individual and group differences in power attributions.

Recently, David W. Jamieson conducted a comparison of the power bases ascribed to teachers by high school, undergraduate, and graduate students. In this case, the questions were phrased in general terms--"Why are you influenced by your teachers?"--rather than in terms specific to a given domain. Though the instrument was

a paired comparison questionnaire using different items,
Jamieson found significant differences between age
groups. High school students ranked legitimate power
as most likely (as did our junior high school students);
undergraduates rated coercive power as most likely (e.g.
"that person is able to harm me in some way"); graduate
students ranked expert power highest, with informational
power a close second.

Parental Power and Disturbed Adolescents

Thus far, we have presented descriptive field studies
showing regularities in the use of the bases of social
power. We now examine an application of this analysis
by a group of UCLA clinical psychologists who are concerned with the familial bases of disturbance in adolescents (Alkire 1969; Alkire, Goldstein, Rodnick, and
Judd 1971; Goldstein, Judd, Rodnick, Alkire, and Gould
1968). Particularly relevant to our present discussion
is a project described in Goldstein et al., in which
differing bases of power are specifically examined. We
will present data from that study, reanalyzed slightly,
to illustrate the utilization of our power typology.
     This study dealt with twenty families having adoles-
cent children. Their parents had sought help from the
Psychology Department Clinic at UCLA. There were six-
teen boys and four girls in the sample. On the basis
of a problem checklist and an intake interview with
both parents, the adolescents were placed in four relatively homogeneous categories. Reliability checks by
a rater unacquainted with the project supported this
classification. These four groups, presented in figure
6.2, were as follows: group 1--aggressive, antisocial;
group 2--active family conflict; group 3--passive, negative; group 4--withdrawn, socially isolated. Note that
these four groups can be further categorized along two
dimensions--active (1 and 2) versus passive (3 and 4)
and locus of difficulty outside the home (1 and 3) versus locus of difficulty inside the home (2 and 4).
     Following the intake interview and some preliminary
testing, the parents and the adolescent child were
scheduled for a session which included a standardized
interview and role playing. On the basis of separate
interviews with the three family members, a problem

Principal Locus of Disturbed Behaviors

Degree of Activity	Outside of Home	Inside of Home
Active	1. Aggressive, Anti-social Poorly controlled, impulsive acting out behavior in relation to peers, family, schools, law, etc.	2. Active Family Conflict Defiant, disrespectful attitude toward parents, belligerence and antagonism in family settings. Little aggression outside family.
Passive	3. Passive, Negative Negativism, sullenness, superficial compliance with parents. Frequent difficulties in school, underachievement.	4. Withdrawn, Socially Isolated Marked isolation, generally non-communicative, few friends, excessive dependence on one or both parents.

FIGURE 6.2. Typology of Disturbed Adolescents (from study by Goldstein, Judd, et al. [1968]).

area which was specific and critical for the parent-
child relationship was selected (e.g., use of the family car, haircut, etc.). Parents were each asked to
role-play a specific instance of the problem and, during the role-playing session, to attempt to influence
the adolescent. (Adolescents were similarly asked to
show how they attempted to influence the parent.) These
influence statements were then categorized according to
the bases of social power typology which has been described above. Four influence statements were selected
by each parent for use in a later interaction situation.
Two independent raters applied the category code to the
statements, and reliabilities for the various categories
ranged from 70 to 100 percent, with a median agreement
of 82 percent.

The data on percentage of influence attempts in each
of the power categories were tested for the extent to
which parents of adolescents with differing behavior
disorders used the bases of power differentially. Some
clear differences emerged. The private dependent power
bases--legitimate, referent, and expert--were used particularly by parents with adolescents whose problems
were principally outside rather than inside the home.
Most of the differences, on further analysis, appeared
to come from the use of legitimate power. By contrast,
parents of adolescents whose major problems were *inside*
rather than outside the home were more likely to use a
form of influence which Goldstein et al. called "re-
strictive information seeking." These included such
questions as Don't you realize this plan is bad? Do
you want to turn out like your brother? The authors
classified responses of this sort as in the "informational power" category. However, these parents were
clearly *not* seeking information. The questions were
rhetorical, and I see them as obviously expressing disapproval and reprimand for the adolescent's behavior
and would classify them as "disguised personal coercion."
It seems that this type of social influence by parents
is then associated with greater problems inside the
home--and it seems reasonable to assume that parental
disapproval would indeed have such an effect.

The remaining informational influence categories
were divided into "information seeking" and "information giving." The former included such questions as,

Where did you go yesterday? Why did you do this? Why
do you do the opposite of what we ask? The latter included the use of statements of facts and opinions to
buttress an argument for change. Information giving,
though the most frequent category of social influence,
did not differentiate much among the families. Information seeking did differentiate along the active-pas-
sive dimension; parents of adolescents whose behavior
disorders were passive were more likely to use the in-
formation-seeking means of influence. This was a mirror image of the results produced by the use of expertise indicating that the "active" groups made somewhat
more use (but not statistically significant) of expert
influence.

The authors correctly point out that there may be
problems in determining the direction of causality in
the interpretation of these results. Does parental behavior contribute to the type of behavior disorder? Or
does the behavior disorder elicit a particular type of
influence behavior from the parents? Or is there a
continuous circular process in which an influence pattern elicits behavior disorders which, in turn, maintain the influence pattern? These are problems which
would have to be examined more closely in further research. What I wish to emphasize here is the value of
social power analysis in understanding behavior disorders and pointing toward directions for their allevia-
tion.

ATTRIBUTIONS AND THE BASES OF SOCIAL POWER

Bem (1965, 1967) and Collins (1969) have pointed out
how attribution theory might account for the results
reported in cognitive dissonance experiments. In effect, they say that when reward or coercive power are
high, and made salient by the influencing agent, the
change is seen, in Michotte's (1963) terms, as a
"launching effect"--that is, the impetus for change is
seen as coming from the influencing agent, who by brute
force or an irresistible bribe seems to press the influencee in a particular direction. How well Asch's
experiment, quoted above, expressed it: "I was being
pushed to give an answer that I didn't want to give."
When the reward or coercion is small, or presented

subtly, presumably the element of choice is more obvious, as Brehm and Cohen (1959, 1962) anticipated in
their analysis of dissonance reduction some time ago.
The subject has been "released" to do what he wished to
do anyway, and the change is seen as coming from him.

What sort of attributional qualities might result,
then, from the successful utilization of other bases of
social power? We have little in the way of data at this
point. But we might speculate that informational power
would be most likely to lead to self-attribution of
change: "It so happens that he gave me some useful information to consider, but ultimately *I* decided to
change." Expert influence would presumably lead to
somewhat less self-attribution, but we might expect the
influencee to explain his behavior along these lines:
"I had to have faith in my doctor's knowledge, but ultimately I did have to decide for myself." And what
about legitimacy? Here we have something salient to
very recent events. What about the My Lai massacres
and the deliberations of the Nuremberg war crimes tribunals? What about Milgram's subjects? It seems that
once legitimacy has been clearly established, the influencee is left with a steady means for attributing
causality for behavior to the legitimate power figure.
"He told me to do it, and I was supposed to do as he
said. It wasn't my fault." An attributional copout?
Maybe, but only if we do not accept the legitimacy of
the influencing agent in the given domain.

POWER PREFERENCE

One of the areas for future research which I would like
to see followed up is the analysis of power preference.
When an influencing agent has several bases of power
available to him, how does he decide which to utilize?
When French and I first wrote our paper, the answer
seemed obvious.

On the assumption that man is rational, we would expect him to use the basis of power which is most likely
to lead to successful influence. He should prefer to
use the basis which would not require surveillance and
which would be long-lasting. Obviously, informational
power looks best, providing one has the informational
and intellectual resources to convince the influencee

logically. If not, then maybe he should prefer a private dependent basis, selecting the one which is most
likely to lead to results. Coercion should be a last
resort, since it requires expensive surveillance and
gets the influencee mad at him. Our initial, naive
assumption of a rational influencing agent would have
led us in this direction of analysis. But what about
the amount of effort and the expenditure of valuable
resources? Rosenberg and Pearlin (1962), who conducted
one of the few explicit studies of power preference,
found that nurses in a psychiatric ward who wished to
influence a patient seemed to follow a process of selection like the above. Yet, effort did play an important
part in their choices. The means considered most likely to be effective was often rejected on the ground
that it would involve too much effort.

However, Raven and Kruglanski (1970) examined other,
less subtle, bases for power preference. There seemed
to be some situations in which the use of coercive power provided personal satisfaction, as when there was
hostility toward the person being influenced. In such
instances, coercion offered a means for punishment as
well as for gaining compliance, for forcing a person to
do something under the threat of punishment was in itself a means of punishment. Furthermore, the need for
self-esteem sometimes determines the preference for a
given basis of power. If our previous analysis of coercion and attribution is correct, then we might expect
that the attribution process is utilized by the influencing agent as well as by the influencee. There are
times when it is more important for the influencee to
feel that he is the source of social influence than it
is for him to use the least effort principle or to be
successful in his use of influence. This, in essence,
is the advice that Frantz Fanon (1963) gives the
"wretched of the earth," the long-subjugated blacks and
browns who now wish to establish their independence
(p. 94). Essentially, he argues that they should use
coercive power to attain their ends in dealing with
the "colonialists" even when they can use persuasion
(informational influence) or legitimacy (the powerless
requesting their legitimate rights) to gain the same
ends. He contends that coercive power in the form of
violence "frees the native from his inferiority com-

plex . . . . It makes him fearless and restores his
self-respect." The subjugated person gains that self-
respect by seeing that *he*, not his former oppressor,
is the locus of change--persuasion and appeals to legitimacy cannot accomplish this for him. Indeed, such a
line of reasoning will sometimes lead individuals to
utilize social power to accomplish changes already in
progress--to hasten to use such power before the changes
occur without the application of power. The morning
after Martin Luther King was assassinated, I heard a
student addressing his fellow students at a meeting
held before 8:00 a.m. He was exhorting them to go to
their professors to demand that they not hold classes
that day; it seemed clear that he had coercion in mind:
"Tell them that they *cannot* hold class today, that they
will not hold class today. Tell them. Tell them." But
implied further in this was the suggestion that they
hurry up and "tell them" before they called off their
classes. The attribution of locus of control seemed
more important than the change itself.

NOTE

1. I am indebted to Dr. James A. Green for his assistance in phrasing the items and including these in
the interview schedule.

REFERENCES

Alkire, A. A. 1969. Social power and communication in
    families of disturbed and nondisturbed pre-adoles-
    cents. *Journal of Personality and Social Psychology*
    13: 335-49.
Alkire, A. A., Goldstein, M. J., Rodnick, E. H., and
    Judd, L. L. 1971. Social influence and counterin-
    fluence within families of four types of disturbed
    adolescents. *Journal of Abnormal Psychology* 77:
    32-41.
Asch, S. E. 1956. Studies of independence and conform-
    ity: 1. A minority of one against a unanimous ma-
    jority. *Psychological Monographs* 70, No. 9 (Whole
    No. 416).

Bachman, J. G., Smith, C. G., and Slesinger, J. A. 1966. Control performance and satisfaction: an analysis of structural and individual effects. *Journal of Personality and Social Psychology* 4: 127-36.

Bem, D. J. 1965. An experimental analysis of self-persuasion. *Journal of Experimental Social Psychology* 1: 199-218.

------. 1967. Self-perception: an alternative interpretation of cognitive dissonance phenomena. *Psychological Review* 74: 183-200.

Berkowitz, L., and Daniels, L. R. 1963. Responsibility and dependency. *Journal of Abnormal and Social Psychology* 66. 429-36.

Berkowitz, L., Klanderman, S. B., and Harris, R. 1964. Effects of experimenter awareness and sex of subject and experimenter on reactions to dependency relationship. *Sociometry* 27: 327-37.

Blood, R. O., Jr., and D. M. Wolfe. 1960. *Husbands and wives*. New York: The Free Press of Glencoe.

Brehm, J. W., and Cohen, A. R. 1959. Choice and chance relative deprivation as determinants of cognitive dissonance. *Journal of Abnormal and Social Psychology* 58: 383-87.

------. 1962. *Explorations in cognitive dissonance*. New York: Wiley.

Brigante, T. R. 1958. Adolescent evaluations or rewarding, neutral, and punishing power figures. *Journal of Personality* 26: 435-50.

Centers, R., Raven, B. H., and Rodrigues, A. 1971. Conjugal power structure: a reexamination. *American Sociological Review* 36: 264-78.

Collins, B. E. 1969. Attribution theory analysis of forced compliance. *Proceedings of the 77th Annual Convention*. Washington, D. C.: American Psychological Association, pp. 309-10.

Collins, B. E., and Raven, B. H. 1969. Psychological aspects of structure in the small group: interpersonal attraction, coalitions, communication, and power. In G. Lindzey and E. Aronson (Ed.), *The handbook of social psychology*. 2d ed. Vol. 4. Reading, Mass.: Addison-Wesley, pp. 102-204.

Deutsch, M., and Gerard, H. 1955. A study of normative and informational social influences upon individual judgment. *Journal of Abnormal and Social Psychology* 51: 624-36.

Fanon, F. 1963. *The wretched of the earth*. Translated by Constance Farrington. New York: Grove Press.

Festinger, L., and Carlsmith, J. 1959. Cognitive consequences of forced compliance. *Journal of Abnormal and Social Psychology* 58: 203-11.

French, J. R. P., Jr., H. W. Morrison, and G. Levinger. 1960. Coercive power and forces affecting conformity. *Journal of Abnormal and Social Psychology* 61: 93-101.

French, J. R. P., Jr., and Raven, B. H. 1959. The bases of social power. In D. Cartwright (Ed.), *Studies in social power*. Ann Arbor: University of Michigan Press, pp. 150-67.

Goldstein, M. J., Judd, L. L., Rodnick, E. H., Alkire, A. A., and Gould, E. 1968. A method for studying social influence and coping patterns within families of disturbed adolescents. *Journal of Nervous and Mental Disease* 147: 233-51.

Goranson, R. E., and Berkowitz, L. 1966. Reciprocity and responsibility reactions to prior help. *Journal of Personality and Social Psychology* 3: 227-32.

Kahn, R. L., Wolfe, D. M., Quinn, R. P., Snoek, J.D., and Rosenthal, R. A. 1964. *Organizational stress: studies in role conflict and ambiguity*. New York: Wiley.

Katz, E., and Danet, B. 1966. Petitions and persuasive appeals: a study of official-client relations. *American Sociological Review* 31: 811-22.

Kelman, H. C. 1956. Three processes of acceptance of social influence: compliance, identification, and internalization. *American Psychologist* 11: 361.

------. 1961. Processes of opinion change. *Public Opinion Quarterly* 25: 57-78.

------. 1958. Compliance, identification and internalization: three processes of attitude change. *Journal of Conflict Resolution* 2: 51-60.

Michotte, A. 1963. *The perception of causality*. London: Methuen.

Milgram, S. 1964. Group pressure and action against a person. *Journal of Abnormal and Social Psychology*. 69: 137-43.

------. 1965. Liberating effects of group pressure. *Journal of Personality and Social Psychology* 1: 127-34.

Orne, M. T., and Evans, F. J. 1965. Social control in the psychological experiment: antisocial behavior and hypnosis. *Journal of Personality and Social Psychology* 1: 189-200.

Raven, B. H. 1965. Social influence and Power. In I. D. Steiner and M. Fishbein (Eds.), *Current studies in social psychology*. New York: Holt, Rinehart & Winston, pp. 371-82.

Raven, B. H., Centers, R., and Rodrigues, A. 1969. Social influence in the dyad: the bases of conjugal power. University of California at Los Angeles (Technical Report No. 25, Nonr 233 [54]).

Raven, B. H., and Fishbein, M. 1961. Acceptance of punishment and change in belief. *Journal of Abnormal and Social Psychology* 63: 411-16.

Raven, B. H., and French, J. R. P., Jr. 1958. Legitimate power, coercive power, and observability in social influence. *Sociometry* 21: 83-97.

Raven, B. H., and Kruglanski, A. W. 1970. Conflict and power. *The structure of conflict.*New York: Academic Press.

Raven, B. H., Mansson, H. H., and Anthony, E. 1962. The effects of attributed ability upon expert and referent influence. University of California at Los Angeles (Technical Report No. 10, Nonr 233 [54]).

Rosenberg, M., and Pearlin, L. I. 1962. Power-orientation in the mental hospital. *Human Relations* 15: 335-49.

Schopler, J., and Bateson, N. 1965. The power of dependence. *Journal of Personality and Social Psychology* 2: 247-54.

Smith, T. E. 1970. Foundations of parental influence upon adolescents: an application of social power theory. *American Sociological Review* 35: 860-72.

Strong, S. R. 1970. Expertness and influence in counseling. *Journal of Counseling Psychology* 17: 197-204.

Willis, R. H. 1965. Conformity, independence and anticonformity. *Human Relations* 18: 373-88.

Zander, A., and Curtis, T. 1962. Effects of social power on aspiration setting and striving. *Journal of Abnormal and Social Psychology* 64: 63-74.

------. 1965. Social support and rejection of organizational standards. *Journal of Educational Psychology* 56: 87-95.

Zborowski, M., and Herzog, E. 1952. *Life is with people*. New York: International Universities Press.

Zipf, S. G. 1960. Resistance and conformity under reward and punishment. *Journal of Abnormal and Social Psychology* 61: 102-9.

IV

ANALYSIS OF INDIVIDUAL-SYSTEM RELATIONSHIPS

Power and Utilities in a 7
Simulated Interreligious Council:
A Situational Approach to
Interparty Decision-Making

Daniel Druckman and Richard M. Rozelle

with Roger M. Krause and Robert Mahoney

Students of interparty conflict and decision-making
have approached their subject matter with the crafts-
manlike skill of the experimentalist seeking analytical refinement as well as with the broad sweep of the
model builder seeking total integration. These disparate traditions of scholarship are represented, on
the one hand, by such monumental efforts as Boulding's
Conflict and Defense, Rapoport's work on systems approaches to conflict, represented partially in *Fights,
Games, and Debates* and elsewhere (e.g., 1964), and
Guetzkow's leadership of the Inter-Nation Simulation
school (e.g., 1968), and, on the other hand, by the
fine-tuned experimental work of Morton Deutsch, Harold
Kelley, John Thibaut, and their students. Our work,
still in its infancy, wavers between, and eventually
attempts to unite, these two tradtions. Struck by the
appeal of both these modes of thought, we have pushed

This project owes a strong debt of gratitude to Roger Krause and
Robert Mahoney of IJR, whose labors and insights contributed significantly to all stages. Mr Krause is a doctoral candidate in social
psychology at Northwestern University, and Mr. Mahoney is a graduate
student in political science at Northwestern. This data collection
was supported by General Support Grant FR-05666-02 awarded to IJR by
the NIH and by the National Institute of Dental Research Grant 5T
IDE00138-09 under the directorship of Richard I. Evans. Thanks are
extended to Dr. Evans and to John Mitchell, who served as simulation
manager. Thanks are also extended to Rev. James R. Faucette, Staff
Chaplain Supervisor from St. Lukes Episcopal Hospital, Houston, for
his consultation on certain aspects of the simulation and his assistance in recruiting ministers for several pilot runs.

201

ahead with an experimental program aimed at separating
components of variance in conflict behavior while at
the same time engaging ourselves, on a small scale, in
the construction of social simulations as tools for
model building and theory development. Both these approaches have considerable aesthetic appeal. But beyond this, from an epistemological standpoint, it is
the experimentalist's search for laws that are veridical to "nature," and the systems theorist's emphasis on
pattern-matching with its pragmatic component that make
these contrasting methodologies compelling. In this
paper, we will describe aspects of a large research program which reflects our concern for constructing models
of conflict of some generality and our concern for designing situations that permit a high degree of analytical rigor in assessing hypotheses.

While conflict resolution has been a central theme
in our diverse research efforts, we have been especially interested in the resolution of conflicts that occur
in policy-making committees whose members have different preferences for the outcome of decisions concerning
the distribution of resources. It is in this area that
the distinction between systems approaches and experimental (analytical) approaches is especially prominant.
For example, in foreign policy decision-making McClelland (1965) divides approaches into (*a*) decision-making
and foreign policy formulation and (*b*) organization and
action-patterning in the international system. The
former approach, represented by bargaining and influence models, concentrates on subsystem phenomena from
the standpoint of a particular "national actor," while
the latter emphasizes the interactions among national
actors from the standpoint of the system. More recently, Ferrar (1972) distinguished between decision-making,
situation analysis, and systems analysis as three approaches to the study of international crises. Walton
and McKersie's (1965) model of collective bargaining
reflects the distinction between contextual (e.g., laws,
public opinion, trend in price level), "personality,"
and social belief factors as influences on relationship
patterns. A distinction that is more closely tied to
theory is Gamson's (1968) separation of an "influence
approach" from a "social control approach" to the study
of political power. And, from a methodological stand-

point, investigations of committee decision-making have
been divided between experimental simulations of small
group interaction (e.g., Evan and MacDougall 1967) and
simulations of entire social systems in which these
small groups are ensconced (e.g., Guetzkow 1968). The
former studies have been characterized by considerable
analytical rigor, while the latter studies have reflected a greater concern with processes endemic to
more enduring systems than the specific laboratory situations designed to simulate decision-making conflicts.

A distinction may be made among three approaches:
situation, process, and systems. The situation approach
consists in searching for causal elements in the situation that confronts the decision-makers. Investigators
using this approach have been concerned with separating
such components of variance in decision-making outcomes
as role, structure of the outcome matrix, prenegotiation
experience, relations with constituencies, and so on
(e.g., Druckman 1971). A closely related alternative
is to look for an explanation of an observed outcome in
the *process* of decision-making and to analyze the steps
in this process leading to the events of interest (e.g.,
Landsberger 1955; McGrath and Julian 1963). A few
studies have combined these two approaches by examining
the impact of manipulated situational variables on the
decision-making process, which is in turn related to an
observed outcome (e.g., Druckman, Zechmeister, and Solomon 1972). The combination of design and measurement
rigor, as reflected in control over situational parameters, content or process analysis of the interaction
between parties, and the careful construction of criterion (outcome) measures, is necessary for convergence between these two approaches to occur (see Zechmeister and Druckman 1973). In contrast to these experimental approaches, explanations for decision-making
outcomes have been sought at the systems level of analysis. A systems approach is based on the assumption
that behavior can be understood in the context of the
structure of the system of relations, a state that exists prior to the immediate situation or persons involved in the events of interest. This approach can
be combined with a situation analysis by examining the
relationship between relatively enduring "structural"
aspects of a system (e.g., alliances in the interna-

tional system, market structure in the economic system) and decision-making outcomes in different settings varying in terms of contemporaneous-situational factors.

Our approach to the study of decision-making combines aspects of all three of these orientations. We are interested in the interaction between decision-makers and the system of which they are a part. We are interested in testing propositions about decision-making behavior, including parameters of this system as causal elements but entering them into the model in varying degrees from one experiment to another, as the behavior occurs within the context of larger systems. We are concerned with separating behavior that is systemic and general from behavior that is more closely related to contemporaneous-situational and attitudinal factors. And, finally, we are concerned with the epistemological issue of creating laboratory environments of *increasing* complexity as opposed to designing situations of *decreased* complexity for seeking reliable relationships between variables and for generalizing findings (see Raser, Campbell, and Chadwick 1970).[1]

These concerns are represented in this contribution by a methodological approach which combines systemic and situational considerations. The approach consists of a juxtaposition of model construction, simulation, and experimentation. A general model of components of interparty decision-making is explored by an experiment which is embedded within the context of a simulation of an interreligious decision-making council. This presentation reports the progress to date of a long-term research plan consisting of three stages: (a) observation of the phenomenon as it occurs under certain well-defined conditions (a situation approach); (b) determination of the extent to which the final outcome is affected by a communication process which is monitored through time and repeated interactions (a process approach); and (c) determination of the effects of contextual variables on the observed phenomenon (a systems approach). Most of this progress has been made on the first stage. The formal model is presented, following a discussion of background considerations for selecting its components, the simulation scenario, and the experimental design embedded within this scenario. The results of a series of analyses designed to estimate model

parameters and to assess the relative weighting of components are then presented. Finally, an extension of
the conceptualization in the direction of a systems
level of analysis and a preliminary analysis of the effects of context are discussed.

IDEOLOGY, UTILITIES, AND POWER

The interplay between ideologies, interests, and the
use of resources to control an outcome is a central,
and vexing, problem in the study of political decision-
making. The centrality of the problem is attested by
the large number of pages of social science literature
devoted to its conceptual clarification. These attempts
at clarification also bring out ambiguities in conceptualization and shortcomings in methodology. A major
conceptual concern is the definition and operational
delineation of these factors. A methodological concern is that of generating an analytical model which
depicts their weighting in the decision-making process.
Both of these concerns form the basis for the model and
experiment reported in this paper.

The distinction between ideology and utilities as
sources of conflict in decision-making has been made by
a number of scholars with reference to numerous contexts: e.g., international negotiations (Glenn, Johnson, Kimmel, and Wedge 1970; Rapoport 1960); cleavages
in legislative politics (Marwell 1965; Kelley 1970);
legal institutions (Aubert 1963); and the sect versus
the business enterprise (Van Doorn 1966). Two contrasting models of political decision-making have emphasized either utilities (Ikle and Leites 1962) or
cognitive factors (Hammond 1965) as the primary source
of policy conflicts. Both of these approaches derive
from more general competing theoretical frameworks,
utility theory and Brunswik's probabilistic function-
alism approach. In an attempt to unite these traditions in the study of political decision-making, an
interactionist theory has been proposed. This perspective emphasizes the *interplay* and reciprocal influences between interests and ideologies. The theory is
presented elsewhere in the form of general propositions
(Druckman and Zechmeister, 1973). Evidence supporting some of these propositions has been obtained in

several studies of political negotiations (e.g., Druckman and Zechmeister 1970; Zechmeister and Druckman 1973).
Additional support comes from Axelrod's (1970) study of
coalition formation in Italian legislative politics.
Axelrod demonstrated that when both ideological similarity and utilities are taken into account, predictions
of coalition formation and duration improve significantly over predictions based on theories that consider
only utilities. The interactionist theory gives rise
to the notion that actors attempt to *balance* ideological considerations against interest considerations in
the decision-making process. It is proposed that this
phenomenon is general, reflecting a decision-making
dilemma that exists for actors in several contexts.[2]
In this report a particular context--a simulated interreligious decision-making council--is used to investigate the process.

A third factor which enters prominently into the decision-making process is power to influence the outcome. Power is typically expressed in terms of control
over resources (viz., money or votes). Such control
obviously varies among decision-makers, making them differentially capable of maximizing their utilities. An
alternative conception considers the power of actors
with "meager" resources. An actor may be able to influence an outcome because he is *needed* by other actors
to "swing" a particular outcome. This notion is particularly relevant in situations in which the formation
of a coalition is necessary to win. A coalition can
win as easily with *many* small contributions as with a
few large contributions. These contrasting conceptualizations of power make for competing predictions of the
way in which resources will be used to influence a final
decision. In the study reported below, these alternative hypotheses are explored in a coalition formation
situation.

A definition of power in terms of control over the
resources necessary to influence an outcome conceives
of power as an instrumentality. Power may also be considered as a source of motivation. The desire for power per se may be a strong incentive for making a decisions. For example, among all possible types of outcomes (or coalitions) an actor may search for the *one*
that insures him control over other actors, control

over the division of resources obtained as a result of
the decision, or an increase in his power base over the
long run. This conception of power is especially appropriate in the system of legislative politics, where obtaining and maintaining power is a *goal* in itself. However, the problem with this definition is that power is
confused with utilities. Power *is* a utility. The research question therefore becomes: Which is the more
important source of motivation for decision-making be-
havior--power or another type of utility? This conceptualization formed the basis for Leiserson's (1970) recent experimental comparison between power and ideology
as competing incentives for entering into a coalition.
In the context of a simulated political legislature,
Leiserson compared predictions derived from a "pure"
ideology theory with predictions derived from a "pure"
power theory. His data did not confirm either "pure"
theory, leading him to propose, post hoc, a "mixed"
model in which parties weigh *both* ideological and power
considerations before deciding on a course of action.
Although there were some ambiguities in the test (e.g.,
problems of analytical separation of variables and the
post hoc method for formulating theory), this model
served as an important heuristic for the efforts reported below.

The model that we propose can be considered as an extension and clarification of Leiserson's proposed model.
The experiment that is reported is an a priori test of
this extended model. The extension is in the direction
of a more elaborate model which includes more components
than Leiserson's. The clarification consists of making
a finer distinction among types of utilities and between the conceptualizations of power considered as
utility and power considered as instrumentality. In
Leiserson's design, ideology was considered as a utility with payoffs and power was defined as both a utility and an instrumentality. His test of opposing theories was an attempt to determine whether, by their
choice of coalitions, actors were maximizing power, in
terms of decision control, or ideologies, in terms of
attitudinal similarity. Certain coalitions were considered, a priori, as either decision-control or attitudinal similarity coalitions. The instrumental definition of power resided in the fact that, in his design,

winning depended on the relative investment of resources in the coalition by different members. In our
model, explicated below, power is defined as both a
utility and an instrumentality, and the interest component is separated from ideology. These components
were defined in terms of the interreligious context
that was simulated for the experiment. For example,
ideology was defined in terms of a religious belief,
and material interests were defined as increases or
decreases in denomination membership.

Both Leiserson's model and our interactionist model
suggest that the central process in interparty decision-
making is the relative weighting (or balancing) of interests and ideology. An understanding of this weighting process is especially critical for predicting the
decision-making behavior of those actors who are conflicted between acting in the direction suggested by
their utilities and acting in the direction suggested
by their beliefs. However, to date, a methodological
strategy for characterizing this process has not been
provided. Neither Leiserson nor our previous work has
suggested a technique for measuring this process. The
weighting process is essentially a comparison of the
relative strength of the two factors. In order to make
this comparison it must be assumed that the two concepts
are equivalent in terms of scale properties. In this
report we propose, as part of a formal model, a hypothetical construct which places ideology and interests
on the same scale. In addition estimates of values for
this construct are made on the basis of data collected
from actors involved in an experimental simulation of
coalition formation in the context of an interreligious
council. Since the model is closely tied to the simulation procedures and the experimental design embedded
in the simulation, it is presented following a description of method and preceding an account of the results.

THE SIMULATION

The choice of an interreligious council as a scenario
was based on three considerations: (a) the salience of
ideology or beliefs in this institutional context (e.g.,
see van Doorn 1966); (b) a research interest in factors
affecting willingness to compromise religious beliefs

(see Rozelle and Druckman 1971), and (*c*) an interest in
comparing decision-making processes in different contexts, including the religious interdenominational council (see final section).

Participants were told at the outset that they were
going to take part in a study of the committee decision-
making process and were given some background on the use
of simulation as a method for studying this process.
The situation being simulated was a monthly conference
of the Houston Interdenominational Council of Churches,
a group made up of representatives from four denominations who meet once a month for the purpose of sponsoring joint projects in the city of Houston. Each denomination sent a representative to the "Conference."
On the agenda for this session were the following proposed projects: the construction of an interdenominational facility that could be used by members of all
sponsoring denominations for services, meetings, and
recreational activities; the administration of an advertising campaign to promote church attendance; the
construction of a community hospital to be administered
by the Council. The two-hour meeting was divided into
several phases, including a preliminary session for
role-indoctrination and procedural instructions, the
Conference, and a post-Conference session for filling
out a questionnaire and debriefing. Brief descriptions
of the instructions used for role induction and the
procedures used for conducting the conference are presented in this section.

Role-Indoctrination

Instructions given to the representatives emphasized
that they should take seriously their roles as representatives of particular denominations with differing
religious beliefs and practices. Their task would be
to initiate projects that served the purpose of the Interdenominational Council and would have a good chance
of increasing the membership of their respective denominations. Their decisions would have an effect on both
the viability of the Council and certain concerns of
their denominations. In order to increase their personal interest and involvement in the Conference, they
were told that the results of their decision-making

would be converted into real payoffs for the successful
alliance of denominations. By taking into account religious beliefs (i.e., ideology), the amount of monetary
investment, and potential membership changes in the various denominations, each representative was to decide
on whether to join with others in investing in the project or to join with others in blocking the project.
The details of Conference procedure spelled out how
this could be done.

The Decision-Making Conference

The dilemma confronting each representative was whether
to fund or block each of the three projects under consideration. Each project was considered separately,
and a decision to fund or block one project had to be
made before the next could be considered. The process
consisted of note-passing between the four parties until a decision was reached. Each representative was
assigned a cubicle from which he operated throughout
the Conference. Before an issue was "discussed," some
time was set aside to plan a strategy. The representatives were allowed thirty minutes to reach a decision.
There were three types of note cards: offer cards,
which were used to suggest an alliance in support of a
project; block cards, which were used to suggest an alliance to block a project; and answer cards, on which
a party who had been contacted with an offer or a block
could indicate an affirmative, negative, or "hold"
response.
     The process was as follows: A party who made an of-
fer to enter into a coalition with another party had to
indicate how much he was willing to contribute. If the
contacted party accepted the offer, he, in return, had
to indicate how much he was willing to contribute to
the project. This reply then was submitted to the party
who made the original offer for his approval. If the
party who originally made the offer approved, he was
required to sign a *contract* which had to be countersigned by the party who agreed to the offer. However,
if a party received and accepted an offer to join a
blocking coalition, there was no need for him to indicate how much he was going to contribute to the coalition since it was assumed that he would contribute all

of his funds in order to prevent the project from being
realized. If the party who initiated the offer to
block approved, they then signed and countersigned a
contract to form a blocking coalition. Contacted parties also had the option of replying with a rejection
or a hold response. Rejections applied only to the particular offer that was being considered and did not pre-
clude the possibility of a later coalition between the
parties with respect to other offers. When a contacted
party made a hold response, this meant that he did not
want to commit himself by either accepting or rejecting
the offer but preferred to defer his decision perhaps
in order to see what other offers he might get. In addition to making formal proposals or responses, the parties often used space provided for note-writing to explain or clarify their positions. There were ten decision-making periods, each lasting three minutes. During a single period, each party was permitted to pass
one note which was either an offer or a response to an
offer. After each period, the "simulation manager" recorded the offers and responses so that he would know
when a successful coalition, either to fund or to block,
had been formed and could have the "in" parties sign
and countersign a contract making the alliance "official." The session ended when a coalition in support
of or against the project had been formed or when ten
periods had been concluded. (In this experiment, none
of the sessions ended in deadlock.) Each successfully
funded project was endorsed by the Council as a whole
even though, almost invariably, not all parties agreed
to fund it. However, the benefits derived from the
funded project were to be shared only by the parties
who agreed to contribute to it.

Funds not allocated to a particular project were re-
turned to the general fund and could not be carried
over for use on the other projects discussed at this
Conference. These funds could, however, be carried over
to another Conference. At the conclusion of the Conference the participants received payoffs in the form of
actual money. The amount they received was based on
their success in forming alliances of benefit to their
denomination. A successful coalition could be either
a funding or a blocking coalition, depending upon the
nature and intensity of the issue-related belief and on

the projected increase in size of membership that would
be likely to occur if the project was funded or blocked.

DESIGN

The experiment was designed in order to assess the relative impact of several sources on the outcome of a
decision-making process. Two of these sources are characterized as *utilities,* while the third is regarded as
power. The two utilities were *ideology,* represented in
terms of an issue-related belief that would be affected
as a result of the decision, and *materialism,* represented by a change in membership size that would occur
as a result of the decision. The power variable was defined in terms of *initial funding potential,* with some
denominations having more funds to invest than others.
For each issue, this information was presented to each
denomination's representative in the form of positions
on three scales on an "Information Sheet." The ideology scale ranged from "completely rejects" (-5) to
"completely accepts" (+5). The scale position for a
given denomination indicated the extent to which that
denomination's representative accepted or rejected the
project-related belief (e.g., with respect to the Interdenominational Building project: "The degree to which
your denomination officially accepts or rejects the act
of praying with members of other denominations"). The
materialism scale consisted of the "projected membership change if the project is completed" and ranged
from -50% (membership loss) to +50% (membership gain).
The scale position for each denomination indicated the
membership gain or loss that would result from the
given funded project. The third scale, initial funding
potential, indicated for each denomination the "maximum
amount that can be spent on the project." The upper
end of this scale indicated the minimum amount necessary to fund the project, with different minimum amounts
necessary for each of the three projects. Figure 7.1
contains all the information on scale positions for
ideology, materialism, initial funding potential, and
minimum necessary to fund for each denomination on each
of the three projects. This information was shared by
all the representatives, who were given time to study
it prior to the Conference. The logic of the experi-

Position	Denomination	Ideology	Materialism	Initial Funding Potential
Interdenominational Building (Minimum Necessary to Fund: 650,000)				
1	C	+2	+4	505,000
2	A	+4	-2	289,000
3	B	-4	+2	217,000
4	D	-2	-4	433,000
Advertising Campaign (Minimum Necessary to Fund: 450,000)				
1	A	+4	+2	150,000
2	C	+2	-4	350,000
3	D	-2	+4	200,000
4	B	-4	-2	150,000
Community Hospital (Minimum Necessary to Fund: 850,000)				
1	A	+4	+4	283,000
2	B	+2	-2	567,000
3	D	-4	+4	472,000
4	C	-2	-2	189,000

FIGURE 7.1. Values on Three Dimensions by Position and Denomination for Three Proposed Projects

mental design determined the positions assigned to each denomination's representative on each of the proposed projects. These positions are summarized in matrix form in figure 7.1.

In general, the design combines aspects of both experimental rigor and "representativeness." Rigor is represented by some degree of orthogonality between independent variables, while representativeness is reflected in the assignment of positions that correspond closely to those of the "real" denominations and that seemed sensible to participants. However, as a result of being "pulled" in both directions, both orthogonality and correspondence to a referent universe were forfeited to some extent. The two utility variables were completely orthogonal ($r = 0$), while initial funding potential was orthogonal to both utility variables on only one issue (viz., Community Hospital). On the Interdenominational Building issue, initial funding potential correlated moderately with both ideology ($r = .30$) and materialism ($r = .10$), while on the Advertising Campaign issue it correlated moderately with ideology ($r = .29$) and strongly with materialism ($r = -.58$). In matching denominations to positions, an attempt was made to approximate the beliefs, membership situations, and monetary wealth of four real denominations (viz., Baptists, Lutherans, Methodists, and Unitarians). Figure 7.1 depicts the assignment of denominations (letters) to positions (numbers) for the three proposed projects. No single denomination was in the same position across the projects. The order of presentation of the projects was randomly determined for each session, with the stipulation that each of the six possible orders appear about the same number of times across the twenty-five replications. This procedure was used in order to assess a time order effect.

For each issue, positions 1 and 4 were "pure" cases, while positions 2 and 3 were "mixed" (see figure 7.1). Position 1 was positive on both ideology and materialism (i.e., +2, +4; +4, +2; +4, +4), while position 4 was negative on both ideology and materialism (i.e., -2, -4; -4, -2; -2, -2). The order of positive and negative scores for positions 2 and 3 were reversed, making them mirror images of each other. Positions 2 and 3 were conflicted between finding and blocking with positive

and negative payoffs existing simultaneously for each
course of action. Thus, the denominations in these
positions were "pulled" in both directions. Which way
they would go depended in part on the relative importance of ideology and materialism to them, the difference in the values on these two dimensions provided by
the paradigm, and their power to affect the final outcome. The first and second factors are conceived of as
a *utilities* problem, while the third factor is conceived of as *power*. Both of these concepts are defined
in terms of the paradigm.

THE MODEL

Utilities are defined by both subjective and objective
criteria. A representative's decision to enter a funding or blocking coalition was in part a function of the
relative gains and losses involved and in part a function of the relative importance of material and ideological concerns. The relative gains and losses for each
project were provided, but the relative importance of
material and ideological concerns was estimated on the
basis of the choices made. The model assumes that each
denominational representative attempts to maximize its
utility from the standpoint of ideology, materialism,
and other factors not represented explicitly in the paradigm. This model is represented by the following equation:

$$U_d = p_i w_i v_i + p_m w_m v_m + p_o w_o v_o + \ldots.$$

where U_d is the utility for denomination d, i is the
subscript for the ideological term, m is the subscript
for the material term, o is the subscript for some other, inexplicit resource term, and so on; and, for each
term, p is the probability of realizing the resources
in that term, w is the worth to d of a given unit of
the resource in that term, and v is the number of units
of the resource in that term. Since, according to the
paradigm, the formation of a successful coalition to
fund or block produces the changes in material and ideological resources deterministically (and is understood
by the representatives to do so), the p's are considered
to be 1.00. Also, insofar as there is no way of estimating the terms for resources not considered explicitly

in the paradigm, the sum of the third and other terms can be summarized as error. Thus the equation reduces to:

$$U_d = w_i v_i + w_m v_m + \text{error}$$

One further simplification is possible if we are only interested in the relative sizes of U_d. The worths of the two types of resources can be considered on one dimension, depicting the relative intensity of each. Thus, w_i can be set as equal to a value called θ, which ranges between one and zero, and w_m is set as $1 - \theta$. If U_d depends (for its nonerror portion) only on ideology, θ equals one and the weight for ideology is one and that for materialism is zero; if it depends only on materialism, θ equals zero and the weight for ideology is zero and that for materialism is one. More realistically, θ is likely to be between one and zero, and the weights for ideology and materialism varied accordingly. Thus the simplest formulation is:

$$U_d = \theta \cdot v_i + (1 - \theta) \cdot v_m + \text{error}$$

This formula indicates that the decision made by a representative is predictable on the basis of two parameters, θ and the number of units at stake for ideology and materialism. If a representative considers a unit of ideological resource to be equal to a unit of material resource, he would choose according to ideological concerns if there were more units of that at stake (e.g., position 2 on the Interdenominational Building issue) or he would choose according to material concerns if there were more units of that at stake (e.g., position 2 on the Advertising Campaign issue). If there were an equal number of units of each at stake (e.g., positions 2 and 3 on the Community Hospital issue), the choice would be essentially random. A representative equally motivated in both directions has a value of θ set at .5. A θ above .5 indicates that he is motivated more in the ideological direction, while a θ below .5 indicates that he is motivated more by material concerns. Thus, if there are an equal number of units of each resource at stake, the representative would choose as predicted by ideology if his θ were greater than .5, as predicted by materialism if his θ were less than .5, and randomly

if his θ were equal to .5. If one value had twice as
many units as the other, the representative would have
to be twice as motivated in the opposite direction to
be choosing at random (i.e., a θ of .33 if twice as
many ideological as material units were at stake, or a
θ of .67 if twice as many material as ideological units
were at stake).

θ is estimated by the decisions made by a denominational representative in the context of a particular
matrix or proposed project. If a representative is
motivated *equally* in both directions, his decisions
should be predictable from the values in the matrices.
These values can be summarized by an index which indicates the number of ideological units at stake as compared to the number of material units. The index, θ*,
is expressed as follows:

$$\theta* = -M/I - M$$

where *M* is the number of material units at stake and *I*
is the number of ideological units at stake. This ra-
tio-index is positive and ranges between zero and one
for positions 2 and 3. Within each matrix (or proposed
project) θ* was identical for positions 1 and 4 and for
positions 2 and 3. However, the value of θ* for positions 2 and 3 varied from matrix to matrix, including
a value of .33 for Interdenominational Building, .50 for
Community Hospital, and .67 for Advertising Campaign.
The *smaller* the value of θ*, the more units of ideology
as compared to materialism at stake, and vice versa.
Thus, for representatives who are equally motivated in
both directions, ideology is a more important determinant of behavior on the Interdenominational Building issue, while materialism is a more important determinant
of behavior on the Advertising Campaign issue. The
interaction between matrix properties, represented by
θ*, and individual motivation, represented by θ, is illustrated by the notion that the more material units at
stake, the more the ideological concern necessary for a
representative to decide in the direction predicted by
ideology alone. Hence, the greater the material attraction of the proposed project, the higher the θ*, but
the more ideologically motivated the representative is,
the higher the θ.

Stated simply, if a representative decides in an ideological direction, his θ is estimated to be greater than or equal to θ^*, while if he decides in a material direction, his θ is estimated to be less than or equal to θ^*. In terms of the paradigm, deciding in an ideological direction means: (a) having a positive ideological value and joining a funding coalition; (b) having a positive ideological value and avoiding a blocking coalition; (c) having a negative ideological value and joining a blocking coalition; (d) having a negative ideological value and avoiding a funding coalition. Analogously, material decisions can be listed for the four cases since a positive ideology implies a negative materialism.

The actual choices of representatives combined with the values of θ^* provided an estimate of θ for each denomination in each of the twenty-five replications. For each matrix (proposed project), θ was estimated to be less than, equal to, or more than θ^*. Across the three matrices a range of θ values was estimated, including the possibility of inconsistency if two of the estimates were incompatible. The range of estimated θ values was then used to construct a frequency distribution of the number of cases in each category across the twenty-five replications. This empirical distribution was compared to various alternative theoretical distributions for goodness of fit. Further details on how θ was estimated are presented in the results.[3]

But utilities are only part of the story. Denominational representatives were also constrained by the amount of resources that they could use to fund a project. Each denomination had a part of the amount needed to fund a project, necessitating an alliance between two or more representatives in order to successfully fund or block the project. Funding potential varied among denominations and, within denominations, among projects (see figure 7.1). The amount necessary to fund the projects also varied, ranging from 450,000 for Advertising Campaign to 850,000 for Community Hospital. The amount of resources that a party has can be regarded as *power*. If it is assumed that all parties are motivated to win (by either funding or blocking), then they will use their resources to control the outcome. However, there are at least two theories that make op-

posing predictions on how these resources will be used.
According to the popular *minimal winning coalition* theory, the more resources a party has at its disposal,
the more control it has over the final decision of the
coalition to block or fund. This theory predicts that
actors will behave to maximize the ratio r_i/R_j where r_i
is the resources contributed by one party and R_j is the
coalition's total resources. That is, each party will
attempt to maximize its share of the coalition's resources in order to control the coalition's members.
According to this formulation, a party behaves in such
a way as to encourage the formation of the *smallest* coalition necessary to win. A competing theory is that
of the *cheapest winning coalition*. This theory predicts
that actors will behave to maximize the inverse ratio,
R_j/r_i. That is, each party will attempt to minimize its
share of the "burden" in the hope that the *largest* possible winning coalition will form. This concept does
not, however, obviate the notion of control and power.
A party may have power because it is *needed* in order to
form a winning coalition. The party in the "pivotal"
role may be more powerful than the party with the largest share of the resources. In the context of this paradigm, positions 2 and 3 might be viewed as "pivots,"
in the sense that 1 and 4 *need* either or both of them
to win. Small contributions from three parties (e.g.,
1, 2, and 3 or 2, 3, and 4) may be as effective as
large contributions from two parties. Thus, there are
competing theories which make opposing predictions of
how a party's resources will be used in order to win in
the context of the paradigm used here.

Both of the above ratios can be added to the utilities equation presented earlier (U_d) to depict a more
general model of decision-making containing both utilities and resources. According to the minimal winning
coalition theory, r_i/R_j is added as follows:

A $$X_d = \theta(r_i/R_j \cdot v_i) + (1 - \theta)(r_i/R_j \cdot v_m) + error$$

According to the cheapest winning coalition theory,
R_j/r_i is added as follows:

B $$Y_d = \theta(R_j/r_i \cdot v_i) + (1 - \theta)(R_j/r_i \cdot v_m) + error$$

This formulation is similar to Leiserson's (1970) formulation that actors seek to maximize the expression $(r_i/R_j) \cdot W_j$, where W_j is interests or utilities. The above formulation can be transformed algebraically so that one utilities term is multiplied by one resources term (the error term is assumed). The steps, using the *X* formula as an example, are as follows:

A 1. Multiply:
$$X_d = \theta(r_i/R_j \cdot v_i) + r_i/R_j \cdot v_m - \theta \cdot r_i/R_j \cdot v_m$$

A 2. Factor r_i/R_j: $X_d = r_i/R_j (\theta \cdot v_i + v_m - \theta \cdot v_m)$

A 3. Rearrange terms:
$$X_d = r_i/R_j (\theta \cdot v_i - \theta \cdot v_m + v_m)$$

A 4. Factor θ: $X_d = r_i/R_j [\theta(v_i - v_m) + v_m]$

Thus, A4 is equivalent to A above. The notation outside the parentheses is the resources term, while the notation within the parentheses is the utilities term. It can be noted that this formulation is an expansion of the Leiserson formulation in three directions: (*a*) we have suggested an alternative resources term (viz., R_j/r_i); (*b*) we have divided the utilities into two parts (viz., v_i and v_m); and (*c*) we have added an estimate of individual subjective weights (viz.,).

The analyses were designed to determine both the extent to which representatives were responsive to the three parameters of the model (viz., ideology, materialism, power) and the nature of that responsiveness. Two types of analyses were computed. Multiple regression was used to determine the relative contribution of ideology, materialism, and initial funding potential as sources of variance in the observed outcomes. Model-fitting, described in summary fashion above, was used to determine the distribution of θ in the sample. The β weights generated from the regression analyses are somewhat analogous to the θ and θ^* constructs used in the model-fitting analyses. Like θ^*, the regression βs can be considered as estimates of the construct θ. Both analyses utilize a combination of the values of situational parameters and behavioral indices to answer three questions: (1) Is ideological or material payoff a more important incentive for decisions? (2) Are the utilities, considered jointly, a more important influence on decisions than potential power, considered in terms of initial funding potential? (3) Is the utilities formula (U_d), containing both objective and subjective parameters, a better predictor of decisions than its various components? Finally, an attempt is made to assess the relative value of the minimal winning and cheapest winning coalition theories as predictors of how the available resources will be used by the representatives.

RESULTS

All of the information for the analyses reported below was provided by the final outcomes, viz., in or out of a coalition and whether the coalition was funding or blocking. Inspection of the final coalitions for each of the three projects on each of the twenty-five runs reveals that there was no salient outcome.[4] In fact, on two of the three projects there was considerable variability with regard both to the members in the coalition and to the type of coalition. (Considerable variability was also observed in Leiserson's [1970] data.) However, in spite of this variability it will be shown that a significant amount of the variance is accounted for by *situational* parameters. In addition, a particular mixed model, similar in certain respects to that proposed post hoc by Leiserson, will be shown to depict most accurately the process used by the representatives in utilizing the information presented.

Responsiveness to Parameters:
Coalition and Individual Rationality

If the representatives were responsive to the situational parameters, it should be demonstrated that the coalitions were rational in the sense that members of a funding coalition had positive values on their ideological and material dimensions and that members of a blocking coalition had negative values on these dimensions for members in the coalition and adding these *joint sums* across the members yields a positive or negative value for the coalition as a whole.[5]

The coalition level analyses consisted of cross-tabulations between the direction of the joint sum and whether the coalition was blocking or funding. For each proposed project, the relationship between joint sum and block-fund was strongly significant (viz., $X^2_{Building} = 16.2$, $X^2_{Advertising} = 18.3$, and $X^2_{Hospital} = 20.8$; $p < .001$ in all cases), indicating that the coalitions were rational. At another level, we can examine the rationality of the individuals in these coalitions. By calculating the joint sum values (ideology plus materialism) for each of the four positional actors in a coalition, we can determine whether they should have favored a blocking or a funding coalition. An examination of their actual coalition memberships indicates the number of "hits" and "misses" in terms of their preset values. Table 7.1 presents the cross-tabulations between type of position ("mixed" versus "pure") and type of coalition (block versus fund) for each proposed project. The type of coalition variable consisted of values on a scale that ranged from being in a blocking coalition (1) to being in a funding coalition (4). The first two values were combined to form the "negative" category, while the last two values were combined to form the "positive" category. This index is described in the next section. It can be seen that the results are generally supportive of rationality. On the Advertising project all actors behaved in the predicted direction. The p values are derived from the binomial expansion. On the Building project all actors behaved predictably, with the "mixed" positions showing a tendency to go in both directions an almost equal number of times, although denomination A might have gone somewhat more in the direction of the positive category. Finally, on the Hospital project the results are supportive of rationality with the exception of those for denomination D. It was expected that, like B, D would be equally torn between positive and negative. Thus, like coalitions, the actors generally behaved rationally in terms of the created situational parameters. This finding can be interpreted as support for the effectiveness of the manipulated values for ideology and materialism.[6] In fact, additional preliminary analyses indicated that the actors responded to their utility values irrespective of how much they

had to invest. Those actors who wanted to be in a
funding coalition most (i.e., those with positive values on both materialism and ideology) invested the
most in the coalition even though on two of the three
projects they had the *least* to invest. Put another
way, those who had the strongest incentive for wanting
to get a project funded, contributed the most, both
relative to other coalition members and as a portion of
their own funding potential, to its realization.

TABLE 7.1. Rationality of Actors by Project

Denominations	Mixed or Pure	Negative	Positive	p*
Interdenominational Building				
A	Mixed	12	13	1.00
B	Mixed	17	8	.108
C	Pure	1	24	.001
D	Pure	23	2	.001
Advertising Campaign				
A	Pure	3	22	.001
B	Pure	25	0	.001
C	Mixed	20	5	.004
D	Mixed	6	19	.014
Community Hospital				
A	Pure	0	25	.001
B	Mixed	12	13	1.00
C	Pure	23	2	.001
D	Mixed	8	17	.108

*Two-tailed probabilities according to the binomial
test

Relative Weighting of Components

Leiserson (1970) proposed a "mixed model" of coalition
formation in which actors weigh both ideological and
power considerations. However, his own data analyses
did not specify the weight assigned to the various components. By using multiple regression techniques, we
were able to assess the relative impacts of the three
independent variables--ideology, materialism, and initial funding potential--on a composite outcome measure
(dependent variable) for each of the proposed projects.
The dependent variable was an index that ranged from
being *in* a *blocking* coalition (1) to being *in* a *funding*
coalition (4). Being *out* of a *funding* coalition (2)
and being *out* of a *blocking* coalition (3) were the two
intermediate values. The intermediate "out of coalition" values are based on the reasoning that failure
to join a coalition of type X is equivalent to *weakly*
supporting a type Y coalition. For each proposed project, two regression analyses were performed: one in
which ideology and materialism were regressed on the
index and one in which initial funding potential and
joint sum (ideology + materialism) were regressed on
the index. In the second analysis, the two independent
variables were correlated somewhat on two of the three
projects (viz., .28 for Interdenominational Building;
-.20 for Advertising Campaign). While multicollinearity was not a serious problem due to the low intercor-
relations (see Fox 1968, p. 257), the slight statistical dependence did have the effect of precluding the
computation of tests of the significance of the difference between regression coefficients (see Rummel 1970,
p. 31). As an alternative, the significance of the difference between the correlation coefficients were calculated according to a formula provided by McNemar
(1962, p. 140) which takes into account the correlation
among independent variables when both are correlated
with a common dependent variable.

Table 7.2 presents the correlation coefficients,
tests of significance of the difference between the coefficients, β weights, and the multiple R's between the
independent variables and the outcome index by proposed
project.[7] The data indicate that the two utilities,

ideology and materialism, both correlate significantly
with the outcome index but that on only one issue, Advertising Campaign, does materialism do significantly
better than ideology ($p < .01$). The same pattern obtains for the regression β weights. The comparisons between the joint sum variable and initial funds (a power
index) produced consistent results across the three projects. In all cases, joint sum correlates significantly
higher with the index than with initial funds. Also,
joint sum predicts (β weights) the outcome considerably
better than initial funds. The consistently high multiple correlations indicate that in each analysis the two
independent variables taken together were strong predictors of the outcome, considered in terms of the index. It is apparent from these results that the denominational representatives were responsive to the two
utilities and that this responsiveness was not mitigated by the amount of money available to fund the projects. The outcomes were not predictable from initial
funding potential, and the utilities predicted outcomes
consistently for each of the three projects, which varied in terms of the amount available for funding. This
general finding is qualified somewhat, however, by the
results of a time order analysis. It was found that
the largest difference between joint sum and initial
funding potential occurred for the first project discussed, whichever it was (since projects and time orders were assigned randomly). The difference got progressively smaller with each ensuing project, although
it was large in all cases. This result is in keeping
with a number of findings in the experimental gaming
literature, showing strong effects for manipulations on
initial trial behavior (see Druckman 1971, pp. 528-29).

These findings point to a "mixed" model consisting
of the two utilities (joint sum) as a better predictor
than either potential power (initial funds) or a mix of
power and utilities (i.e., the multiple correlation between initial funds + joint sum and the outcome index
is only slightly higher than the correlation between
joint sum and the index). This finding is similar in
some respects to Leiserson's finding that a "mixed"
model is the best fit and different from it in other
respects. If Leiserson's "power" term (r_i/R_j) is considered to be a utility that actors attempt to maximize,

TABLE 7.2. Correlations and Regression Weights between Independent Variables and the Composite Outcome Index

Variable	Simple r	Differences between Correlations[1]	β	Multiple R	Proposed Project
Ideology	.32**		.32**	.50**	Building
Materialism	.38**	.06	.38**		
Ideology	.33**		.33**	.64**	Advertising
Materialism	.55**	.22**	.55**		
Ideology	.32**		.32**	.49**	Hospital
Materialism	.36**	.04	.36**		
Initial Funds	.20*		.06	.50**	Building
Joint Sum	.49**	.29**	.48**		
Utilities Equation[2]	.67**				

226

Initial Funds	-.19*	.81**	-.07	.62**	Advertising
Joint Sum	.62**		.60**		
Utilities Equation	.66**				
Initial Funds	.18	.31**	.18*	.52**	Hospital
Joint Sum	.49**		.49**		
Utilities Equation	.57**				

1. The significance of the differences between the two correlations with the dependent variable was calculated using the formula from McNemar (1962, p. 140).

2. For this analysis, U_d was the only independent variable entered into the regression equation. In the one-variable case the simple r equals the regression coefficient. Thus, these coefficients are not reported. The fact that the utilities equation includes joint sum as a component precludes a test of the significance of the difference between the correlation coefficients for joint sum and U_d.

*p < .05
**p < .01

the findings are parallel. If, however, Leiserson's
power term is an instrumental definition of power, the
findings are in contrast. Also, this comparision between the data sets is valid only to the extent that
Leiserson's "intensity of feeling" scale (operationalization of the ideology variable) is assumed to be a
utility scale and that subjects in his experiment were
motivated to maximize this "utility." These assumptions
appear plausible since, as in the procedure used in this
experiment, Leiserson instituted real payoffs contingent on these scale values.

The joint sum variable is an additive combination of
the values on the two utility scales. This combined value is a better predictor of the outcome than either value taken separately and than initial funds. However,
the joint sum analysis does not provide information on
the relative weights assigned by the parties (viz., subjective parameters) to the two components of the variable. The analysis is based on the sum of the objective
parameters in the prediction equation. This weighting
process is summarized by the construct   , discussed
above. According to the simplified version of the utilities formula (U_d), if the parties weigh the two components equally (θ = .5; 1 - θ =.5), the outcome can be
predicted, assuming that funding potential is negligible, from the assigned values per se (i.e., v_i and v_m).
Values of θ above .5 place more weight on the ideology
component, while values below .5 weigh materialism more
strongly. We now turn to an analysis which attempts to
estimate θ and to determine the distribution of θ values for the sample participating in this experiment.

Relative Importance of Ideology and
Materialism: Estimates of θ

θ is a hypothetical construct that can be estimated
from two items of information: decisions of parties
and parameters of the matrices (see figure 7.1). It
represents the relative importance of ideology and
materialism as sources of motivation. Decisions are
operationalized in terms of a behavioral outcome index
that ranges from being *in* a funding coalition to being
in a blocking coalition. The matrix parameters are
summarized by the index θ*, which is expressed by a

ratio of the negative value of the material units divided by the difference between the number of units in
ideology and the number of material units. Estimates
of θ were made for each denomination across projects.
Estimates could, however, also be made for positions
across projects.

An estimate of the range of θ can be made only for
the mixed positions 2 and 3. For these positions it
is possible to determine whether a denomination was
motivated by one or the other type of interest. The
rotation of denominations through positions insured
that each denomination was in either of the two mixed
positions at least once (denominations B and D were in
these positions twice) (see figure 7.1). With regard
to positions 1 and 4, the best that we can say is that
the representatives in these positions were either consistent or inconsistent. The different matrices (projects) represent more or less severe tests of the importance of ideology as reflected in the value for θ*.
Thus, a denomination that stands to gain 2 units on
ideology but would lose 4 units of material resources
by funding shows a stronger ideological incentive by
agreeing to fund than one that stands to gain 2 units
of ideology when only 2 units of material resources are
at stake. It is assumed that if a denomination either
decides to fund or fails to block through a coalition
its θ is on one side of θ*, while if it decides to
block or fails to fund through a coalition its θ is on
the other side of θ*. Which side is which depends on
whether it is motivated to fund for ideological reasons and motivated to block for material reasons (position 2) or is materially motivated to fund and ideologically motivated to block (position 3). A denominational representative is assigned a θ greater than or equal
to θ* if, in position 2, he joins a funding coalition
or avoids joining a blocking coalition or if, in position 3, he joins a blocking coalition or avoids joining
a funding coalition. Similarly, a representative in
position 2 who joins a blocking coalition or avoids
joining a funding coalition is assigned a θ which is
less than or equal to θ*, while in position 3 joining
a funding coalition or not joining a blocking coalition
results in being assigned such a θ.

The range of possible estimates of θ is a function

of the assignments, prescribed by the design, of denominations to positions 2 and 3 for each project. These
assignments, contained in figure 7.1, and the θ* values
are reproduced here:

Position	Building	Project Hospital	Advertising
2	A	D	C
3	B	B	D
θ*	.33	.50	.67

A range of estimates of θ for each denomination was
determined by the θ* values corresponding to all of the
projects in which the denomination was in positions 2
or 3. These estimates are as follows:

Range of θ Estimates

A	<.33		>.33	
B	<.33	.33-.50	>.50	Inc.
D	<.50	.50-.67	>.67	Inc.
C	<.67		>.67	

Denomination

The inconsistencies for denominations B and D resulted
from contradictory behavior on the two issues (i.e., a
θ estimated at below .33 on one and at above .50 on the
other).

The proportion of cases in each of the cells depicted
above, across the replications (N = 25), was as follows:

Range of θ Estimates

A	.64		.36	
B	.04	.36	.40	.20
D	.36	.40	.08	.16
C	.24		.76	

Denomination

This empirical frequency distribution was compared to various theoretical distributions to determine goodness of fit. The seven proposed alternative theoretical distributions or patterns are defined as follows:

(1) *Null.* Resulting distribution if choices were made randomly and without regard to $\theta*$.

(2) *Ideological.* Resulting distribution if $\theta*$ was used and all parties decided all issues ideologically regardless of material stake.

(3) *Materialist.* Resulting distribution if $\theta*$ was used and all parties decided all issues materialistically regardless of the ideological stake.

(4) *Mix 1.* Resulting distribution if $\theta*$ was used and all parties had different θs for different issues.

(5) *Mix 2.* Resulting distribution if $\theta*$ was used and all parties had a θ of .50 or were equally concerned with both types of utilities.

(6) *Mix 2a.* Resulting distribution if $\theta*$ was used and θ was more or less normally distributed, with a mean of .50 but some distribution in the tails (10% have θs greater than .67 and 10% have θs less than .33).

(7) *Mix 3.* Resulting distribution if $\theta*$ was used and values of θ were distributed equally in the population (i.e., θ has a rectangular distribution).

Goodness of fit was assessed by the square root of the sum of the squared deviations between each theoretical distribution and the obtained distribution. The rank order of the models is reported in table 7.3. It can be seen that mix 2 is the best fit, doing somewhat better than mix 2 and considerably better than null. (The significance of the size of these differences remains to be determined since, to date, there does not appear to be a test of significance that can be applied to this data.)[8] Thus, it appears that the best estimate of θ for most representives is around .50. One implication of this finding is that final decisions can be predicted from the matrix values for the two utilities assigned to the denominational representatives. For each denomination an estimated value of θ was computed. These individual ranges were used in the following analyses (table 7.3).

Another method for estimating theta was through several self-report post-Conference questions. Partici-

TABLE 7.3. Goodness of Fit of
the Various Theoretical Models

Model	Fit*	Rank
Mix 2a	.2162	1
Mix 2	.2771	2
Mix 3	.3277	3
Null	.3618	4
Materialist	.5902	5
Ideological	.6232	6
Mix 1	.6951	7

*The square root of the sum
of the squared deviations between the observed frequencies
and the theoretical model corrected by the maximum possible
fit value for the pattern.

pants were asked to indicate on a seven-step scale the
relative importance of ideology and materialism with
respect to each project. Also, a question asked them
to evaluate the relative importance of the two utilities in general, assuming that both were assigned the
same scale value (e.g., +2 and +2). Comparison of the
two data sets of the construct θ. The results inci-
cated that there is substantial convergence (again,
there is a problem here with regard to computation of
a statistical test), serving to increase one's confidence in the validity of θ.[9] We now have five estimates of θ for each denomination. Each estimate can be
inserted into the utilities equation to predict the outcome index.

The Utilities Equation

The utilities equation (U_d) is a weighted sum of values
for ideology and materialism. According to the model,
the utility values, presented by experimental contingencies, are corrected (or multiplied) by an internal

balancing process, represented by the construct θ, that
consists of weighting the relative importance of ideology against the relative importance of materialism.
By inserting the various estimates of θ into the equation, its predictability can be compared with the predictability of the objective parameters alone (i.e.,
joint sum). The twenty correlations between U_d and the
outcome index for each estimate of θ for each project
and across the three projects ranged from .36 to .67.
There appears to be a similar pattern of correlations
among the various estimates of θ inserted in U_d and the
outcome index. However, the behavioral estimates of θ
are somewhat problematic due to a circularity caused by
estimates based on behavior and a predictor variable
based on similar behavioral observations, and the unit-
equivalence questionnaire item is based on incomplete
data. On the other hand, the project-specific items
are *relatively* independent of behavior and are based on
complete data. The correlations and regression coefficients between U_d and the outcome index, using this
questionnaire estimate of θ, are reported in table 7.2.
It can be seen that in all cases the utilities equation
correlated more highly with the index than joint sum
alone. The increase is especially notable for the
Building project (a difference of .18). These results
suggest that added complexity (i.e., U_d versus joint
sum) does *not* reduce predictability and even increases
it in some cases.

Minimal Winning Versus Cheapest Winning Coalitions

The analyses to this point have concentrated on the attraction of the *direction* of the coalition (i.e., to
block or to fund). Another concern of the model is the
composition of the coalition. It will be recalled that
there are two opposing theories concerning how a party's
resources might be used in order to win. One formulation asserts that a party will behave in such a way as
to maximize the ratio r_i/R_j (minimal winning coalition
theory), while an opposing formulation asserts that a
party behaves to maximize the inverse ratio, R_j/r_i
(cheapest winning coalition theory). These theories
focus on investment behavior rather than on the effects
of initial funding potential. A preliminary test of

the theories was made. This consisted of an attempt
to determine which of the two ratios members of *funding* coalitions (N = 129) were attempting to maximize.
In order to correct for unequal unit size, the ratios
were corrected by their standard deviations   (e.g.,
$r_i/R_j/SD_{mWC}$). The mean of the corrected minimal winning coalition ratio ($\overline{X}$ = 1.18) was significantly higher than the mean of the corrected cheapest winning coalition ratio (e.g., $R_j/r_i/SD_{CWC}$) ($\overline{X}$ = .67, t = 4.10,
p < .01). This result supports the minimal winning coalition theory. A second test of the theories utilized
the general formulas which contained both resource and
utility components (i.e., X_d and Y_d). These formulas
were also corrected by their respective standard deviations. Five comparisons were made, including the five
different estimates of θ. Three estimates were behavioral (i.e., low point, mid point and high point of the
estimated θ range for a denomination), while two were
based on the estimates provided by the post-Conference
questionnaire. The other terms in each formula were
parameters of the experiment. The corrected means and
the *t*-ratios for each comparison are presented in table
7.4. If it is assumed that the higher ratio reflects
more clearly what the parties are maximizing, then
these results strongly and consistently support the
minimal winning coalition theory. Members in funding
coalitions were acting to maximize their control of
the coalition's resources by making large contributions.

A series of regression analyses were also performed,
using the proportion of a member's funds contributed to
the coalition as a dependent variable and the X and Y
formulas as independent variables. The results generally support the analyses reported above. The formula
based on the minimal winning coalition theory predicted
better than that based on the cheapest winning coalition theory. In fact, further analyses in which the
three components (viz., *CWC* ratio, *MWC* ratio, and utilities) were entered in the regression equation as
three separate, independent variables, showed that, in
terms of priorities, the actors first avoided cheapest
winning coalitions (as evidenced by high negative θ coefficients), then sought minimal winning coalitions and
considered their two utilities, materialism and ideology
(moderate positive θ coefficients which were of about

TABLE 7.4. Comparison of Minimal Winning and Cheapest Winning Theories in Terms of the Corrected X and Y Formulations

Estimate of	$\overline{X}_d/SD_x$	$\overline{Y}_d/SD_y$	t
Low point	.56	.27	2.33*
Midpoint	.47	.15	2.57*
High point	.33	.03	2.41*
Project-specific questions	.56	.30	2.09*
Unit-equivalence question	.33	.06	2.17*

*p < .05, two-tailed

the same size for both the MWC ratio and for U_d, irrespective of which estimate of subjective utilities was used in the formulation).

Adding the minimal winning ratio to the utilities formulation produces a multiplicative combination of attraction of direction and preference for composition of the coalition. This formula was called X (and its cheapest winning counterpart, Y). A next step in the sequence of analyses would be to attempt to predict the outcome index from the entire formulation. However, at present this analysis cannot be performed since the ratios that enter into the X and Y formulas can only be computed for a portion of the sample, viz., those who get into funding coalitions, precluding scores on three out of the four index categories. In order to solve this problem an attempt is being made to develop a more general ratio that will include those who enter blocking coalitions. The experimental procedure would be modified somewhat by allowing actors to contribute a portion of their funds to a blocking as well as a funding coalition. The index variable will then be the proportion of funds contributed to the coalition total for *both* funding and blocking coalitions.

CONCLUSIONS AND EXTENSIONS

In concluding, we offer the following contributions derived from this effort: (a) a rationalistic model
which serves to extend previous work; (b) a methodological innovation based on the notion of a convergence
between two traditions; and (c) a few interesting findings that relate both to the model and to the more general issue of responsiveness to situational parameters
in decision-making. We contend that these three contributions are arranged in order of importance.

The model extends Leiserson's previous work by adding several components and by making explicit a decision-making process that consists of weighting these
components. The weighting process is depicted in the
form of multiple regression equations and by the hypothetical construct θ , which is estimated by examining
decision-making behavior in conjunction with values of
situational parameters. Both complementarity and convergence between these two modes of analysis were demonstrated. The regression analysis indicated that the
combined values of the two utilities (i.e., joint sum),
ideology and material payoffs, were better predictors
of the outcome than either utility taken separately or
than initial funding potential. However, this particular regression analysis did not provide estimates of
the relative subjective weighting of the two components
(represented by θ) entering into the joint sum. Such
estimates were provided for the sample of actors in the
simulation by a complex procedure which utilized both
objective parameters (i.e., $\theta*$) and behavior (i.e., the
outcome index). The most accurate model for depicting
the distribution of these values was developed by means
of a pattern-matching procedure. It was found that the
most accurate distribution of θ was a near-normal distribution of values, ranging from complete reliance on
ideology (1) to complete reliance on materialism (0),
with most actors weighting the two components equally
(i.e., .5). Convergent with these pattern-matching results was the finding generated by the regression analyses that there was not a consistent significant difference in the correlations of ideology and materialism
(taken separately) with the outcome index.

The estimates of θ for each denomination were then
inserted into the utilities equation, and this formulation was used for prediction. Insofar as a number of
estimates of θ were above or below .5, inserting these
values into the utilities equation may have had the effect of increasing or decreasing predictability based
on the objective values alone (i.e., joint sum). However comparisons of the predictability of the entire
utilities equation with joint sum indicated no appreciable difference and even, in some cases, an increase
in predictability for U_d.

A second major component of the model is a resource
term regarded as potential power. Alternative resource
terms were proposed. One term was based on the notion
that actors use their resources to control other members of a coalition. Another term was based on the notion that actors use resources sparingly, opting for
large winning coalitions with many small contributions.
A series of analyses indicated that significantly more
members were acting to maximize their control of coalition resources (i.e., minimal winning coalition). Thus,
the first term was used in the final model equation,
which is as follows:

$$X_d = r_i/R_j \; [\,\theta(v_i - v_m) + v_m] + \text{error}$$

The values for the parameters in this equation were set
in terms of variables embedded within the simulation
context as well as in terms of behavior that occurred
within this setting. We also have an interest in "contextual" behavior and have some reason to believe that
the context makes a difference (see discussion below
on effects of context). In keeping with this interest,
the distribution of θ obtained for the sample used in
this experiment can be compared to distributions of θ
obtained from other samples in different contexts. The
fact that θ is a relative measure and that it lies between zero and one makes it particularly suitable for
comparison across experimental samples and contexts.
One might posit, for example, that a rectangular distribution of θ (i.e., fewer values of .5 than a normal
distribution) is more likely to describe a sample in a
legislative setting than a normal or near-normal distribution (which presumably exists in the interreli-

gious context used here). Thus, it is conceivable that
the obtained distribution may be context-specific, just
as the best distribution for depicting Leiserson's data
is likely to be context-specific. Some of these considerations are discussed in the next section.

The weighting process depicted by the model consists
of only two components: ideology and interests. Con-
ceivably, in the decision-making process, actors take
account of other factors not made explicit in the paradigm used here (e.g., prestige, attraction). This is,
of course, more likely to be the case in the referent
system, where the limitations imposed on laboratory
models due to a concern for analytical rigor do not
exist. For this reason, it is necessary to consider an
extension of the model to the n-component case. The
algebraic extension is worked out in an addendum to
this paper.

Although some of the regression coefficients are impressive, it is evident that a large proportion of the
variance in outcomes remains unexplained by the manipulated situational variables, represented as parameters
in the model. Situational parameters were only part of
the simulation environment. There was also a complex
process of interaction among the parties, i.e., messages were being exchanged in a four-way communication
network on each of an average of three or four decision
periods. An analysis of the process of interaction can
be used to complement the situation analyses presented
in this paper. The results of such an analysis may account for a portion of the unexplained variance, presented as an *error* term in the model. We are engaged
at present in a rigorous statistical analysis of the
number and types of messages sent and received by each
party. More informally, such an analysis can be used
to explain the occasional occurrence of nonsalient or
"nonrational" outcomes (e.g., a coalition of the whole).
For example, a comparison of the outcomes of a recent
series of pilot runs in which ministers served as subjects with the outcomes obtained in the earlier college
runs showed that there were more nonpredictable outcomes in the former. An analysis of the process provided us with a tentative explanation for this difference. In contrast to the students, the ministers freely made use of religious terms (e.g., "Christ's healing"

in connection with the Community Hospital project) and appealed to such concepts as "Christian unity" in trying to persuade others to join a coalition. These appeals often seemed to transcend the more abstract cost, profit, ideology, and membership considerations defined by the model and used almost exclusively as arguments by the students. Such observations encouraged us to consider modifications in the operational definition of model parameters when actors constituted a sample more similar to the population in the referent system from which they come.

Finally, the methodological complexity achieved by a confluence between formal model construction, simulation design, and diverse methodological traditions may be a heuristic spin-off from this sort of effort. Paradoxically, complexity in methodology may be the surest route to theoretical breakthroughs represented by the clearest, simplest, and most general propositions.

Toward a Systems Level of Analysis

Lest we be "accused" of being reductionists, let us not conclude without introducing some considerations from another direction. In the reported experiment, a simulation was used as an analytical tool for separating components of variance and for providing estimates of model parameters. The formal model is a model of *individual* decision-making behavior, and two of its components, material interests and ideology, were represented in the simulation (i.e., operating model) in terms of scale values which were converted into real payoffs to the actors, contingent on the coalition outcome. Another use of simulation is as a device for reproducing aspects of the more complex (referent) system represented. The designer of a system simulation places more emphasis on *systemic* processes and less emphasis on the *analytical* separation of components. One type of systemic process which parallels the ideology and material interests components of the formal model is the interplay between conflicts of interest and ideological differences, considered as a *pattern* of conflict endemic to the system that is represented by the simulation.

The link between a pattern of conflict and the for-

mal structure of an organization or institution can be
represented in a system simulation. Some leads on how
to conceptualize such "links" are presented by van Doorn
(1966) with respect to two types of formal organizations: the sect and the business enterprise. These
settings differ in terms of the relative emphasis placed
on ideology or interests as the primary source of conflict. This difference in emphasis was shown by van
Doorn to have implications for the intensity of conflicts and for the style of conflict resolution. However, the *interplay* between the two types of conflict
is perhaps most prominent in a third setting: political decision-making. In political decision-making, conflicts of interest often derive from ideological differences. This interdependence between the two types of
conflict formed the basis for a set of interrelated propositions, reported elsewhere, depicting the effects on
the intensity of conflict of the reciprocal relationship between interests and ideology (see Druckman and
Zechmeister, 1973). Druckman and Zechmeister enumerate
the components for a simulation in which the systemic
phenomena can be observed and suggest a technique for
model construction. However, the difficulties involved
in attempting to reproduce such seemingly elusive phenomena lead to a consideration of a second strategy for
examining the effects of context. The context may be
shown to account for a portion of the variance in certain *behavioral* variables. This can be illustrated
with respect to the minimal winning versus cheapest
winning issue.

It may be recalled that we proposed two theories of
investment behavior, referred to as cheapest winning
and minimal winning coalitions. The cheapest winning
theory is based on the notion that actors attempt to
get the greatest benefit, in terms of the best projects,
for the least amount invested. They may attempt to get
greater benefits at the same cost by encouraging others
to invest more while keeping their own investment constant, or they may attempt to get the same benefit at
less cost by decreasing their own investment while the
investments of the others remain constant. (The risk
in the former strategy is that of overinvestment, while
the latter strategy incurs the danger of falling below
the minimum amount necessary to "win"). The minimal

winning theory is based on the notion that actors attempt to achieve control of a coalition through large
investments relative to the total invested by the coalition. This may be accomplished by encouraging others
to invest less while keeping their own investment constant or by increasing their own investment while the
investments of others remain constant. The former
strategy, if successful, results in achieving more control for the same investment (there is a risk here, however of falling below the amount necessary to "win"),
while the latter strategy, if successful, results in
achieving more control for a larger investment (there
is a risk here of overfunding). It is argued, although
it will not be demonstrated, that certain characteristics of the legislative setting make it more likely
that actors will be motivated by minimal winning considerations, while certain dimensions of the interreligious context make it more likely that actors will be
motivated by cheapest winning considerations.

Among the dimensions of difference between the settings that may be critical for the two theories are:
(a) responsibility for the cost of the projects; (b)
the relative advantages and ease of forming stable coalitions; and (c) the relative importance of variations
in the proposals for the projects suggested by different members of the same coalition. In the legislative
setting, the cost of projects is borne by the entire
body rather than by members of the winning coalition
only; the "payoffs" for forming stable coalitions are
high; and variations in proposals made by different coalition members are critical. Decision control (minimal winning) is necessary in order to maintain stability over time. Stability has an advantage in the legislative setting, given the large size of the body (i.e.,
re-forming for each new issue is costly) and the fact
that the total membership does not change for several
years. Decision control is also critical as a mechanism for arbitrating between alternative proposals offered by different members of the coalition. In the
contrasting interreligious setting, the cost of projects is borne by coalition members only; resources not
invested by an actor may be used for another project;
the relatively small number of parties makes it less
difficult to reorganize in order to form a new coali-

tion; the council membership is relatively fluid since
different denominations may be present at different
meetings due to different agendas; and variations in
proposals for the same project made by different coalition members (all, however, favoring the project) may
have a relatively negligible effect on potential benefits derived from its realization. For these reasons,
inter alia, maximizing the cost/benefit ratio per project is likely to be more important than control over
decisions. Thus, it is contended that the cheapest winning version is the "best candidate" for predicting investment behavior in the interreligious setting. However, it must be cautioned that since we know relatively little about the interreligious referent system (as
compared to the legislative system), these dimensions
of difference may more appropriately describe a comparison between the legislative referent system and a particular experimental model of the interreligious council system (viz., the model created for this experiment).
A clarification of referent system differences awaits
more experience by the authors with the interreligious
setting and renewed attempts to simulate this setting.
Meanwhile, we turn to a preliminary test of the effects
of context.

The Effects of Context

It was possible to reanalyze Leiserson's coalition data
in terms of the minimal winning versus cheapest winning
issue. This analysis permitted a comparison of the competing predictions in the two different contexts, political legislatures and interreligious councils. This
comparison must be regarded as tentative since, on the
one hand, all of the critical dimensions of difference
between the settings were not highlighted in the laboratory simulations and, on the other, the compounding of
several other, less theoretically compelling, dimensions
of difference makes a strict interpretation of differences in findings problematic (e.g., votes versus money
as the primary resource, the nature of beliefs, appointed versus elected representatives, representation
of members versus representation of constituents, four
denominations versus two parties, and so on). However,
the comparison seemed particularly compelling in light

of our interest in the systems level of analysis. This comparison should be viewed as more suggestive than conclusive.

Mean values for *MWC* and *CWC* were computed across all members of winning coalitions in the Leiserson Legislative simulation, using the formulas $MWC = r_i/R_j$ and $CWC = R_j/r_i$, where r_i equals the voting weight of a single member and R_j is the summation of voting weights for all members in a given winning coalition.[10] The mean values obtained were corrected by their standard deviations, and a ratio was computed to test the significance of the difference between the corrected means:

$$t = \frac{\overline{X}_{mwc,\ corrected} - \overline{Y}_{cwc,\ corrected}}{S_{mwc,\ corrected} - cwc,\ corrected}.$$

The results indicated a highly significant difference between the means (*MWC, corrected* = 3.39; *CWC, corrected* = 2.20; *t* = 10.54). Thus, as expected, Leiserson's data show strong support for the minimal winning coalition theory. The comparison between his legislative data sets and our interreligious data sets shows stronger support for the minimal winning coalition interpretation of investment behavior in the legislative setting. (The comparison between the theories in our simulation, reported above, yielded a *t* ratio of 4.10; see also table 7.4). This might be interpreted as partial support for our hypothesis, although it was expected that the cheapest winning version would "win" in the interreligious situation. Some tentative interpretations for this difference in terms of one of the critical dimensions of difference posited above can be offered.

In the interreligious situation, the actors were pulled in two directions. There were advantages in "overfunding" a project, and there were benefits in not investing all of one's resources. Overfunding (i.e., going above the minimum necessary to "win") could result in a bigger and better project and insure a win with a small coalition. The fact that actors could save unspent resources for use at later conferences was an incentive for investing sparingly. However, since for these particular actors the incentive for overfund-

ing was situation-specific (i.e., winning the "game")
while the incentive for saving was largely hypothetical
(since they might not be involved in future conferences
in their present roles), it might be argued that the
former incentive was more salient, resulting in investment behavior more in line with the minimal winning interpretation. This game characteristic perhaps mitigated against cheapest winning, which may still be the
best formulation for the referent system. In the Leiserson experiments the situation appears more straightforward. The incentives were contingent upon winning
in the immediate situations; there was no "future" for
which to save and no penalty for overfunding. Hence,
the parameters of the situation strongly favored maxi-
mal investment of resources, in line with the decision-
control hypothesis. A better test, however, would be
to compare the competing formulations under two experimental conditions, the first varying only critical dimensions of difference between the settings and the second varying only noncritical dimensions of difference
between the settings.

Yet another possibility exists and, indeed, is suggested by the informal process analysis of the pilot
minister data discussed above. Support for the cheapest winning formulation may obtain in a sample that is
more similar to the population in the referent system
than that used in our simulated interreligious council.
The minister data revealed clear tendencies on the part
of participants to be motivated by cheapest winning considerations. The wealthier denominations were reluctant to contribute large amounts to the projects and
were inundated by repeated appeals from weaker denominations for larger contributions before a contract "should
be signed." In addition, there were no apparent communications designed to minimize the size of contributions
from other denominations to fund a project. Instead,
equity was used as the principal consideration in determining the amount that each denomination should contribute to a funding coalition. Although these observations are tentative, and the number of runs on which
they are based is small, they do suggest, in keeping
with our prediction, that perhaps the cheapest winning
formulation is the best explanation for investment behavior in the *referent system*.

ADDENDUM: EXTENSION OF THE MODEL

The proposed extension to the *n*-component case pre-
serves the essential concept of the *relative* importance
of components. Instead of considering the relative importance of v_1-ness to v_2-ness, this extension considers the relative importance of v_i-ness to *all* other components. The initial utilities formulation proposed
earlier in extended form is:

$$U_d = w_1v_1 + w_2v_2 + w_3v_3 + \ldots w_nv_n$$

One salient solution, similar to that used earlier, is
to convert the weights w_i to the new weights w_i', such
that the sum of the weights is unity. Thus,

$$w_i' = w_i \bigg/ \sum_{j=1}^{n} w_j$$

In the case of $n = 2$, w_1' is the same as our former θ
and w_2' is equal to our former $1 - \theta$. The generalization of the θ formulation to the case of three or more
utilities is then:

$$\dot{U}_d = \sum_{j=1}^{n} w_i' \cdot v_i,$$

where v_i is a measure of the ith component of objective
utility and w_i' is the subjective weighting factor of
that component with a value between zero and one, such
that if $w_i' = 1$, it is the only weighting factor entering into the estimation of utility, and if $w_i' = 0$, it
has no effect on the utility at all. More typically,
it will lie between zero and one, reflecting its contribution to the estimate relative to those of all other components considered in the estimate.

To return to a more familiar formulation, w_i' can be
expressed in terms of our Greek-letter terminology.
Thus, in the three-component case, w_1' (which is equal
to $w_1/w_1 + w_2 + w_3$) is alpha, w_2' (which is equal to

$w_2/w_1 + w_2 + w_3)$ is θ, and w_3' (which is equal to $w_3/w_1 + w_2 + w_3$) is $1 - (\alpha + \theta)$. Expressed in this manner, the utilities equation for the three-component case is:

$$U_d = \alpha \cdot v_1 + \theta \cdot v_2 + 1 - (\alpha + \theta) \cdot v_3$$

If any weighting factor equals one, then U_d will equal v_1 or v_2 or v_3, as the case may be, and the other two factors will equal zero. If any factor equals zero, then U_d will be the weighted sum of the remaining two components of utility. Thus, if the third factor equals zero, U_d reduces to

$$\alpha \cdot v_1 + (1 - \alpha) \cdot v_2$$

as was the case in our two-component model ($\theta = 1 - \alpha$). If any factor equals zero and one of the two remaining factors equals .5, then the third factor will also equal .5, and U_d will be the simple sum of the remaining two objective components of utility (i.e., joint sum). Similarly, if any two of the three weights equal .33, then the remaining weight will also equal .33, and U_d will be the simple sum of the three components, and so on. Measurement and design problems for the three-or-more-component case will be a forthcoming consideration.

NOTES

1. In our research, substantive simulations are used as "tools" for studying these processes. The use of substantive scenarios (e.g., collective bargaining, political decision-making) as opposed to abstract tasks is controversial in the gaming-simulation literature (e.g., see Hermann 1967). Some investigators claim that the more abstract the task (e.g., Prisoners' Dilemma), the wider the range of generality of obtained results. It may be argued, however, that this generality is "spread thin," resulting in limited implications for *any* particular setting. Also, the use of abstract tasks precludes an assessment of the effects of context or observations of behavior that occurs within systems. This goal (viz., the assessment of context)

is central to our diverse research efforts and is discussed below.

2. For example, Lall (1966), in his classic treatment of international negotiations, devoted several
chapters to the impact of ideology on behavior. He
presented a number of examples which showed that even
the most ideological countries pay *more* attention to
their vital interests than to their ideologies when
these two factors conflict. In his words: "A country
which is imbued with a strong ideological belief does
not let these beliefs dominate its representatives in
negotiations with other countries" (p. 287). He goes
on to demonstrate that at the negotiating table and in
informal exchanges the ideological beliefs of a country
tend to have little influence on its demands and attitudes regarding matters of substance. Its assessment
of its own best advantage in terms of military power,
and the protection and promotion of its other vital interests, will predominantly determine its conduct. Taking this together with other sources, we came away with
the notion that the relative importance of these factors varies with situational and contextual variables
(e.g., international negotiations, legislative politics,
interreligious councils).

3. The details of computational procedures are not
presented here. For those interested in the step-by-
step computations, an unpublished manual may be obtained from the authors.

4. Space limitations prevent a listing of the coalition outcomes. For those interested, this data can
be obtained by writing to the senior author.

5. This analysis is based on two assumptions: (*a*)
that the units on the ideology and materialism variables are equivalent, i.e., that a +1 for ideology is
as highly valued as a +1 for materialism, and (*b*) that
a coalition can be viewed as the linear sum of its
parts. Some evidence for the first assumption is presented below in the analysis of θ, and it appears that
the second assumption is not violated.

6. Several follow-up, nonparametric analyses were
computed to assess responsiveness by the "mixed" cases
to the two components, ideology and materialism. In
support of the more sophisticated analyses reported below, it was found that the parties generally weighted

the components equally. However, rather than report these results here, we defer consideration of this issue to a later section.

7. A second dependent variable, dollars invested in the coalition, was used in the same regression analyses. This variable was highly correlated with the outcome index (.73, .61, .74 for the three projects, respectively). However, the relationships between the independent variables and dollars were not as consistent as they were with the index variable. The correlations on the Interdenominational Building project were the most impressive (.35 with ideology; .45 with materialism; .36 with initial funds, and .57 with joint sum). Also, this variable produced one "respectable" correlation with initial funds (.43 for Community Hospital).

8. On the surface this problem appears amenable to evaluation by one of the procedures suggested by Grant (1962) for testing theoretical models that make precise numerical predictions of experimental outcomes. However, a careful appraisal indicates that the problem does not conform to the parametric or structural assumptions underlying his methods. Recasting the problem by, for example, eliminating cases in order to use the recommended statistics seems at present to be too high a price to pay. Grant also argues forcefully for statistical tactics that involve estimation (with or without significance testing) rather than hypothesis testing on both theoretical and practical grounds. The strategy used above concurs with this recommendation.

9. The detailed results can be summarized as follows: for the three project-specific items, the overlap was 30% above chance; for the unit-equivalence item, the overlap was 33% above chance; and for all items, an average overlap 31% above chance was obtained.

10. Since Leiserson's w_j is not the same as our v_i, it was not included in the calculation of the *MWC* and *CWC* values. The simple formula r_i/R_j and its inverse, used on the Leiserson data, is, however, equivalent to one of the analyses computed above in connection with our data.

REFERENCES

Aubert, V. 1963. Competition and dissensus: two types of conflict and of conflict resolution. *Journal of Conflict Resolution* 7: 26-42.

Axelrod, R. 1970. *Conflict of interest: a theory of divergent goals with applications to politics.* Chicago: Markham.

Druckman, D. 1971. The influence of the situation in inter-party conflict. *Journal of Conflict Resolution* 15: 523-54.

Druckman, D., and Zechmeister, K. 1970. Conflict of interest and value dissensus. *Human Relations* 23: 431-38.

------. 1973. Conflict of interest and value dissensus: propositions in the sociology of conflict. *Human Relations,* 449-66.

Druckman, D., Zechmeister, K., and Solomon, D. 1972. Determinants of bargaining behavior in a bilateral monopoly situation: opponent's concession rate and relative defensibility. *Behavioral Science* 17: 514-31.

Evan, W. M., and MacDougall, J. A. 1967. Interorganizational conflict: a labor-management bargaining experiment. *Journal of Conflict Resolution* 11: 398-413.

Ferrar, L. L. 1972. The limits of choice: July 1914 reconsidered. *Journal of Conflict Resolution* 16: 1-24.

Fox, K. O. 1968. *Intermediate economic statistics.* New York: Wiley.

Gamson, W. A. 1968. *Power and discontent.* Homewood, Ill.: Dorsey Press.

Glenn, E. S., Johnson, R. H., Kimmel, P. R., and Wedge, B. 1970. A cognitive interaction model to analyze culture conflict in international relations. *Journal of Conflict Resolution* 14: 35-48.

Grant, D. A. 1962. Testing the null hypothesis and the strategy and tactics of investigating theoretical models. *Psychological Review* 69: 54-61.

Guetzkow, H. 1968. Some correspondences between simulations and "realities" in international relations. In M. Kaplan (Ed.), *New approaches to international relations*. New York: St. Martin's Press.

Hammond, K. R. 1965. New directions in research on conflict resolution. *Journal of Social Issues* 11: 44-66.

Hermann, C. F. 1967. Validation problems in games and simulations with special reference to models of international politics. *Behavioral Science* 12: 216-31.

Iklé, F. C., and Leites, N. 1962. Political negotiation as a process of modifying utilities. *Journal of Conflict Resolution* 6: 19-28.

Kelley, E. W. 1970. Utility theory and political coalitions: problems of operationalization. In S. Groennings, E. W. Kelley, and M. Leiserson (Eds.), *The study of coalition behavior*. New York: Holt, Rinehart & Winston.

Lall, A. 1966. *Modern international negotiation: principles and practice*. New York: Columbia University Press.

Landsberger, M. A. 1955. Interaction process analysis of the mediation of labor-management disputes. *Journal of Abnormal and Social Psychology* 51: 552-59.

Leiserson, M. 1970. Power and ideology in coalition behavior: an experimental study. In S. Groennings, E. W. Kelley, and M. Leiserson (Eds.), *The study of coalition behavior*. New York: Holt, Rinehart & Winston.

McClelland, C. A. 1965. Systems theory and human conflict. In E. B. McNeil (Ed.), *The nature of human conflict*. Englewood Cliffs, N. J.: Prentice-Hall.

McGrath, J. E., and Julian, J. W. 1963. Interaction process and task outcome in experimentally-created negotiation groups. *Journal of Psychological Studies* 14: 117-38.

McNemar, Q. 1962. *Psychological statistics*. New York: Wiley.

Marwell, G. 1966. Conflict over proposed group actions: a typology of cleavage. *Journal of Conflict Resolution* 10: 427-35.

Rapoport, A. 1960. *Fights, games, and debates*. Ann Arbor, Mich.: University of Michigan Press.

------. 1964. *Strategy and conscience*. New York: Harper & Row.

Raser, J. R., Campbell, D. T., and Chadwick, R. W. 1970. Gaming and simulation for developing theory relevant to international relations. *General Systems* 15: 183-204.

Rozelle, R. M., and Druckman, D. 1971. Role playing vs. laboratory deception: a comparison of methods in the study of compromising behavior. *Psychonomic Science* 25: 241-43.

Rummel, R. J. 1970. *Applied factor analysis*. Evanston, Ill.: Northwestern University Press.

Walton, R. E., and McKersie, R. B. 1965. *A behavioral theory of labor negotiations: an analysis of a social interaction system*. New York: McGraw-Hill.

Van Doorn, J. A. A. 1966. Conflict in formal organizations. A. de Reuck and J. Knight (Eds.), *Conflict in society*. London: Churchill.

Zechmeister, K., and Druckman, D. 1973. Determinants of resolving a conflict of interest: a simulation of political decision-making. *Journal of Conflict Resolution* 17: 63-88.

V

POLITICAL POWER

Power in Cross-Cultural 8
Perspective: Tribal Politics

Robert M. Carmack

INTRODUCTION

Before the reader discovers for himself what this paper
is, some of the things that it *is not* should be made
clear. To begin with, it is not a cross-cultural study
in the sense that this usually implies in anthropology
--i.e., a tabulated, comparative study of large numbers
of cultures, such as are described in the Yale Human
Relations Area Files. Rather, generalizations about
tribal politics are derived from a relatively small number of detailed sociocultural studies. There are two
reasons for this. In the first place, it is the author's conviction that our definitions of and concepts
about power are not sufficiently refined and general to
permit useful comparisons on a broad scale. Most studies of that kind seem to me to be hopelessly in error
with respect to comparability of the data which are manipulated statistically. As a result, the analyses seem
unenlightening (for an example of the problem alluded
to here, see Naroll 1964). One of the main goals of
the present essay is to more critically and comprehen-
sively define power concepts for purposes of cross-cultural comparison.

The author wishes to thank the members of the symposium for their
helpful comments, as well as members of his own department for their
friendly criticism. I am especially grateful to Professors William
Fenton and Walter Zenner for their useful suggestions for improving
the original essay.

255

Second, it is a major thesis of the present essay
that a rich sociocultural context is needed to properly
clarify the nature of power. That context is precisely
what is deleted in the typical cross-cultural study. I
think it significant that one often finds a heavy reliance on "case studies" for suggesting explanations of
correlations based on statistically manipulated data
(e.g., Otterbein 1968). The most meaningful questions
about power have to do with its relationships to other
aspects of culture, such as ecology, social structure,
and symbolism. These relationships are best revealed
through careful study of the context within which power
is created and used.

The present study lacks strong historical orientation, though the author feels that this would greatly
enhance its usefulness. Originally, I planned to compare the politics of tribal societies with those of
traditional states and peasant societies. When this
became impractical, it was decided that power concepts
could nevertheless be developed, using the data on
tribes alone. It remains my conviction, however, that
comparisons with more complex sociopolitical systems
are critical for further clarification of tribal politics and the general validity of the concepts developed
in this paper. Fortunately, some contrast between tribal and modern industrial politics can be drawn by comparing this essay with the other symposium papers. The
analysis of the changing political systems of tribal societies as they have come under the influence of industrial states would also be enlightening, but this is
outside the scope of the limited study presented here.

Some anthropologists will question the validity of
referring to the societies described in this paper as
"tribal." It is well known that all the peoples studied by anthropologists have had contact with complex societies and that, therefore, we lack truly aboriginal
cases. While this is true, it is not a serious problem
if the full cultural context is taken into account in
political analysis. External influence is then built
into the study, and its specific effects can be considered. Further, tribal peoples have in most cases been
in contact with more complex states for thousands of
years, so that their normal condition is one of having
to contend with powerful neighbors. Nevertheless, I

have avoided sources which deal with tribal peoples whose societies have been drastically altered through contact with modern states. This accounts for the absence in this paper of references to the literature on factionalism, a phenomenon which I believe to be closely associated with the strains on tribes under heavy external influence. Whether or not what has been called tribal society in this paper is pristine, I am confident that it represents an extremely widespread form of sociopolitical development, the characteristics of which are common and significant enough to warrant their own label (whether tribal or something else).

Finally, it may be useful to make explicit some of the theoretical assumptions of the essay. The reader will find a largely implicit evolutionary framework. The very subject matter of the essay--tribes--represent a sociopolitical stage of evolution.

Basically, however, the essay is functionalist and game theory in orientation. The functionalist approach is especially evident in the study of authority, administration, and law. It is also revealed in the many correlations sought between power and other systems-- viz., economic, kinship, ideology. Though game theory is not presented in a formal way, it is the orientation for the many statements in the paper about the ways in which aspects of culture are manipulated by powerholders. It provides the basis for studying the processes of change and development in tribal society.

BASIC CONCEPTS

Politics have to do with making decisions, deciding between alternatives when choice is involved. Inevitably, in human societies alternative choices will differentially affect persons, categories of persons, and groups according to their situations in those societies. Hence, politics necessarily involve an element of controversy, of opposition, and of contrapositioning.

On the other hand, these same persons and groups simultaneously share interests and situations, hold to choices which are so much in the common interest that differences must be submerged. This is as much a basic reality of social living as conflict and opposition. The decisions which have to be made within the context

of solidarity or united interests should not evoke opposition, but rather support and obedience.

The view that societies have two modes of decision-
making came to anthropology primarily from the study of
tribal societies. One key was provided by a peculiar
form of tribal social organization not widely found
around the world, though it occurs rather commonly in
sub-Saharan Africa. Known as the segmentary lineage
system, it was first described by Evans-Pritchard for
the Nuer of the Sudan. The politics of the Nuer seemed
like an almost anarchic process of fissioning and coalescing lineages in the conduct of feuds and wars
against other lineages and tribal peoples (such as
their neighbors, the Dinka). Anthropologists were able
to show that segments in these societies both split
apart and unite along genealogical lines, according to
the size and genealogical composition of their enemies.
Thus, if members of a minimal lineage find that their
foes in a dispute (say, over women or the injury of
some member) are organized on a major lineage level,
they seek to merge with all the lineages which together
would make up their own major lineage, exactly equivalent to that of their enemies. Within the contending
major lineages cooperation would take place, the minimal lineages of each major lineage suppressing conflicts
and antipathies which normally affect their relationships in order to effectively confront the contraposed
major lineage. In the case of the Nuer, even major lineages combine, recognizing their common descent from a
more remote ancestor, in order to attain a worthy com-
bat unit against other tribes or large Nuer groups with
whom they fail to share common ancestors.

At first, the political significance of segmentary
lineage systems was not understood, though several brilliant ethnographic descriptions of them appeared (Evans-
Pritchard 1940; Fortes 1945; Bohannan & Bohannan 1953).
It was said that societies in which such systems existed
lacked government, were instances of "ordered anarchy"
(Fortes and Evans-Pritchard 1940). Smith eliminated much
of the confusion, however, with his prizewinning essay
"On segmentary lineage systems" (1956). He demonstrated
that the whole system of segmentation and incorporation
has a political basis, and that the kinship (genealogical) organization by which the natives united and di-

vided merely provides an ideological framework for the
operation of political principles. He further argued
that while united for effective political struggle
against other lineages of the same scale the lineages
become units of internal command and obedience. Their
sublineages function to maintain rules, conduct ritual,
and generally engage in peaceful decision-making. This
makes the internal workings of these fighting lineages
administrative in character, and hence equivalent to
the bureaucracies of modern states. Smith concluded
that, far from being without government, segmentary
lineage societies epitomize and even dramatize what is
basic to the political system of all societies: a dual
structure and process in which divided, opposed units
in political conflict coesist with united, cooperative
units conducting administrative affairs in a different
context.

Once it is realized that political and administrative action may be aspects of activities and relationships ostensibly kinship, ritual, recreational, or economic in form, then it is possible to discover political process in all societies. This is true even for
those tribal societies which do not overtly recognize
the existence of rulers, laws, or politics. We may define political activity as the aspect of social action
that is oriented to the process of competitive decision-
making. The capacities which persons and groups bring
to the struggle may be termed *power*. It follows that
relations of power tend to be game oriented, in the
sense of involving the use of calculation and strategy
in order to gain victory in the contest. In maximizing the situation, men in all societies institute
change, thereby adapting their societies to a dynamic
environment.

On the question of administrative activity, that is,
internal decision-making controlled by expectations of
support and obedience, there have been strong differences of opinion. Some anthropologists have seen administrative activity as simply another form of power
--legitimated or authorized power (Tuden, Swartz, and
Turner 1968; Southall 1965; Fried 1967). This view,
however, misses the point of the segmentary lineage
clarification: viz. that administration is coeval with
and as fundamental as politics based on power, for it

functions differently. It cannot, therefore, be subsumed under the concept of power. The right by which
persons and groups make internal decisions with the expectation of support and obedience is properly termed
authority. There are many ways in which authority relations differ from those articulated by power, such as
being delegated rather than contested, being organized
hierarchically rather than segmentally, being backed by
sanctions rather than gains, tending to preserve and
conserve rather than change, etc. (Smith 1956, 1960,
1966; Mair 1965, pp. 99-125).

With the twin concepts of power and authority, we
are in possession of variables sufficiently basic to
permit broad cross-cultural comparisons. Some social
scientists have argued that the concepts are, in fact,
too broad, and that we need more refined concepts, such
as legislative and judicial authority, the power to
wage war, the power of political parties, and the like
(Eisenstadt 1959; Easton 1959). These concepts, however, bear a strong bias of our own culture, for, as
Schapera (1956) points out, the politics of tribal peoples may not include such functions, while, contrari-
wise, they often involve officials in ritual and other
activities not usually characteristic of the politics
of industrial societies. Further, each of these concepts can be shown to have both political and administrative aspects--e.g., the administration of war is
quite a different matter from its politics. A compromise would be to move in our studies from the very general to more specific comparisons, adding as needed concepts like legislation, warfare, and political ritual.
But, always, we should analyze these secondary concepts
within the context of our more abstract concepts of
power and authority.

The "field" within which relations of power and authority operate is another problem which has concerned
political anthropologists. Two well-known British anthropologists, Radcliffe-Brown (1952, pp. 32-48) and
Nadel (1969, p. 169 ff.), have argued that rights and
duties are aspects of all social relationships and that,
therefore, a condition of authority (or controlled decision-making) is inherent in all of them. With this
thought in mind, one anthropologist studying a group of
Australian aborigines was able to analyze the totality

of their social relationships in terms of the authority component. He concluded that each man's duties balanced out his rights (Sharp 1958). Even though this led him to state that the group was a "people without politics," his study is actually a clear description of authority and administration in that society.

Working from a different perspective, French anthropologists have viewed social relationships as consisting of value exchanges, whether the values be wives, goods, sex, or words (Mauss 1967; Levi-Strauss 1963a, p. 277 ff.). These anthropologists have tended to emphasize the balance and reciprocity characteristic of social relationships, and hence the obligation or expectation involved. However, this approach also leads to a recognition that in social relationships people manipulate exchanges to their own advantage, and tip the balance in their own favor. Fredrik Barth, a Norwegian anthropologist, has essayed in support of this viewpoint (1966). He claims that the manipulation of situational factors and tradtional values, rather than adherence to status rights and duties, primarily determines human behavior. He further argues for the existence of "generative" processes by which competing "entrepreneurs," seeking their own profit, mediate value exchanges between social persons for whom such transactions are either difficult or not possible. In the process, the "social brokers" aid in the construction of new values congruent with the new social bonds they help create.

If, in fact, all social relationships have power and authority aspects, are they not, therefore, universally political and administrative--i.e., don't they have to do with government? To answer yes to this question would expand the study of politics so far that it would be of little use for comparative studies. Therefore, from insights first provided by Maine (1963) and Weber (1964), political anthropologists have looked to corporations as the context for a more restricted locus of political action((Radcliffe-Brown 1952; Fortes 1953; Evans-Britchard 1940; Gluckman 1965a; Smith 1960, 1966). As long-lived, ongoing social groups, with fixed rules of membership and internal order, corporate groups appear to be what we mean by the term *society*. Corporations of single individuals--corporations sole--comprise

the offices and commissions which make up much of the
internal structure of societies (see Smith 1966, 1968;
Fichter 1957).

While recognizing that in terms of numbers per unit,
principles of organization, and degree of complexity,
corporations have varied tremendously in the social history of man, we find it significant that they seem to
be a universal feature of human society. A hunting
and gathering band differs in many ways from a nation-
state or a peasant village, but in terms of corporate
qualities it is identical to them: it has presumed per-
petuity (even should all of the band's members die, its
name and rights often continue; it has fixed rules of
membership (those living in the same territory usually
must have kinship or affinal ties with the band leader);
it possesses internal rules or order governing relationships (e.g., almost always one is obligated to seek a
spouse from outside the band); it controls an estate
of some kind (such as the hunting and gathering rights
of certain territories, and the drinking rights of water holes) (Steward 1955; Radcliff-Brown 1952, pp. 32-
48).

It is this universal tendency to establish corporate
groups that makes it possible to define and study politics cross-culturally. These groups define the "public"
spheres of social living, and it is precisely the public
arena which is of interest to the political anthropologist. The use of power to influence public decisions
defines political action, while the use of authority to
make controlled public decisions (that is, to execute
politically determined decisions) is administrative action (Smith 1956, 1960; Easton 1959).

As Swartz (1968) and others have pointed out, corporate society cannot define the entire field of political action. Influence on the public decisions of a
corporate group may come from external groups, persons,
or networks of persons--e.g., another corporate group
might go to war against the decision-making group; a
prophet from outside the group might influence the attitudes of participants in the decision-making process;
or a coterie of men might raid members of the group in
order to coerce some viewpoint. Hence, the corporate
groups of a society will define only the *locus* of political action, while the *field* of the action will in-

clude all groups and persons that bring power to bear
on the decisions in question. Administrative action,
on the other hand, will be defined by the corporate
structure, since that is the source of the authority
governing the process. Of course, outsiders might be
brought in as intermediaries and "neutrals" to aid in
the administrative process, but they have authority
only to the extent that it is allocated to them by the
authorizing body.

UNITS OF COMPARISON

Political anthropology, like all of anthropology, is
broadly comparative in its approach, and a major problem "is that of making certain that the phenomena being
compared are close enough in form, structure, or process to warrant the comparison" (Manners and Kaplan
1972, p. 7).

One of the ways the anthropologist attempts to control his comparisons is to place the samples to be compared in a developmental framework (Harris 1968, p. 633;
Cohen 1968). The procedure is to "establish a taxonomic
schema based on levels of sociocultural integration. .
. . Once this taxonomy has been established, a comparison of societies within each level of integration is
undertaken" (Cohen 1968, pp. 443-44).

There now exist in anthropology and the social sciences a substantial number of useful models of the developmental stages or levels through which human societies have passed during man's short history (White
1959; Service 1962; Steward 1955; Fried 1967; Lenski
1966; Bellah 1964; Almond and Powell 1966). Many of
these typologies are based on economic indices, which,
it is claimed, closely correlate with sociopolitical
factors. In the simplified typology of this paper, except for some comparative observations at the end, the
tribal level of development will be the subject of analysis. This level of development may be said to contrast with two other major levels of development, traditional states and modern nations (Almond and Powell
1966; cf. Eisenstadt 1967). Tribal subtypes of great
interest have been developed, but these will be touched
upon only as they aid us in our investigation of the
uses of power.

The decisive technological condition of tribal society is some combination of hunting and gathering,
fishing, simple horticulture, and pastoralism. The traditional level of society is founded on intensive forms
of agriculture, such as the use of irrigation, flood
control, terraces, fertilizers, the plow, or successful mixtures of horticulture and pastoralism (especially
of cattle). The modern stage of social evolution is
based on the complex technologies of industrialization.
Besides employing these economic factors as useful typological indicators, we will be concerned with the ways
in which they affect power and authority and with the
extent to which power and authority act as independent
forces for change in the economic sphere of society.

The tribal type is extremely general, and most anthropologists work with more specific classifications.
Fried (1967) relegates "tribes" to a position of secondary development and transitory existence. For him,
the basic types of preindustrial societies are egalitarian, ranked, and stratified. They correspond, respectively, to cases where access to roles and subsistence goods is equal or unequal, or, in the case of
stratified societies, where there is an unequal and
standardized distribution of *strategic* resources (that
is, true socioeconomic classes exist). He claims that
only with the stratified society do power and authority
become effective and stable instruments of control, as
they become encased in the structure of the state.

Smith (1965, 1968) has summarized and refined Weber's
political typology, noting that Weber's focus was on the
relationship between rulers and their administrative
staffs. For Weber, patrimonial political systems are
distinguished from acephalous political systems because
the latter lack the chiefs of the former. Acephalous
systems may be gerontocratic, where the elders rule, or
patriarchal, where the ruler is the head of a descent
group. Unlike acephalous rulers, patrimonial chiefs
act independently of their kinsmen, though they vary in
the way they control their administrative staffs. Where
the chief effectively dominates his staff, Weber refers
to him as a paramount; where his patrimony is fragmented
by appropriations to subchiefs, he is a feudal lord.
Patrimonial organizations, finally, can be distinguished
from legal-rational forms by the presence in the latter
of rule-defined, impersonal staffs called bureaucracies.

Each of these typologies conceals a variety of forms, and we may wish to recognize specific differences that exist among the societies included within any given type. As a starting point, however, the tribal type would seem most useful for broad comparisons and contrasts of salient political features among the numerous societies studied by anthropologists. Specific cases illustrating these general characteristics should provide some indication of the variety of detail we are ignoring for the moment.

BAND POLITICS

Tribal politics operate within the context of kinship relationships, and generally are not formally differentiated by the people themselves from other kinds of activity. Contrary to Fried's claim, however, there are no egalitarian societies. Even the simplest bands located in the marginal areas of the aboriginal world have inequalities based, at a minimum, on age and sex. These inequalities, plus others created by genealogical, ritual, and economic differences, provide the basis of both order (administration) and conflict (politics) in tribal society (Balandier 1970; Smith 1968).

In the most undifferentiated tribal societies—corresponding to Weber's gerontocratic and Fried's egalitarian society—virtually all power and authority reside in elders and their assemblies, the representative units of families collectively making up the corporate band. The individual elders exercise authority over their younger and female kinsmen, who are the "administrators" of public policy. Authority is tightly hedged within traditional bonds of kinship, age, and sex. It is further mitigated by the relatively secondary nature of policy (which rarely involves changes in customary rules) and by a large residual execution of policy carried out collectively by the group.

Internally, power comes into play mostly in assembly discussions, where elders try to influence and persuade one another. Their consensus decisions are misleading, for these are made only after the contest has already been won and a common front can be presented to the rest of society (Bailey 1965). Power in this context tends to be personal, based on the elders' abilities to con-

ceptualize and solve problems, speak articulately and
persuasively, and mediate with the magical world, and
on respect built up as a result of day-to-day contributions to the group. As with authority, power in these
societies is highly circumscribed, partly by an egalitarian ideology which damps conflicts and by a mythol-
ogy which emphasizes the maintenence of the status quo.

Whether or not there is political conflict between
bands, including the possibility of warfare, is uncer-
tain from the data available. We lack evidence of band
warfare in some cases (e.g., the Bushman, Shoshoni,
Congo Pygmies), while in others (e.g., the Australian
aborigines, Andamanese) bands clearly seem to have
fought each other. We may never have a final answer,
for the presence of more complex societies adjacent to
some of these band societies has altered their aboriginal situation (Service 1962, 1971; Fried, 1967, pp.
51-107).

Power relations at this simple level of tribal society may be illustrated by the Bushman bands of South
Africa. The !Kung Bushman inhabit the Kalahari desert,
living off the vegetation and small insects which the
women gather, and the antelope and other game hunted by
the men (Thomas 1965; Marshall 1960; Schapera 1956).
Though Bushman appear to consist entirely of families
wandering around in the desert, in fact they are organized into territorial and kinship groups which may be
called "bands." The bands have territorial boundaries
which "are thoroughly understood and respected" (Marshall 1960, p. 331). They also control the rights to
Veldkos (zones with nuts, berries, fruits, tubers, etc.),
and usufruct rights to game and water in the territory.
Bands are small in size, averaging only twenty-five persons. They are named, and the names persist even when
all members of a band die out or join other bands. The
band, therefore, is a corporate society, and the locus
of political and administrative action.

Unlike some of the other band societies, the Bushman
have the office of headman. There is little authority
associated with it, though the headman is followed in a
few matters, such as choosing a campsite, deciding who
will make the first fire, and mediating with persons
from other bands. He is supposed to be a descendant of
the past headman, but there are many cases of talented

men from outside the band or from the band itself serving in place of the "legitimate" heir. Most authority
in this simple society is exercised by family heads
over their children, wives, and in-laws.

Political struggle is strongly suppressed in Bushman
society. There is no ostensible conflict over the headmanship, for it is said to bring more obligation than
privilege. Elders and headman join in council to make
decisions by consensus. There was no observed conflict
between bands over territory, Veldkos, game, or water.
Still, the Marshalls mention an instance in which a
legitimate headman's family contested the fact that
another man had become the actual leader. In another
account, recorded by Thomas (1965, pp. 178-205), we are
given the biography of a man, Toma, who became the
adopted headman of his wife's band. He was attracted
to the band by his father-in-law, the past headman, in
order to increase the economic capacity of the group.
Toma exercised considerable influence (power) as headman, partly because the other members feared his physical
sical strength (as a young man he had thrown his cousin
into a crowd, with a threat that the next time he would
kill him).

No conflict between Bushman bands was recorded,
though this may be the abnormal result of their pro-
tected condition at the present time. It may be significant that men from different bands never greet each
other with weapons on their backs, for that would be a
sign of hostility. Marshall (1960, p. 347) also indicates that the band fissions which occur from time to
time are probably related to unmentioned conflicts.

Power and authority among the Bushman are limited by
an ideology which stresses kinship ties, égalité, and
sharing. The headman's authority is seen to derive
from his position as father of the traditionally chief
family of the band. Compared to the authority of the
band family heads (for example, of fathers over sons
and sons-in-law), the headman's authority is mainly
titular. Bushman males do not openly express a desire
to be headmen or leaders: "They do not want to stand
out or be above others...for this draws unfavourable
attention to them and arouses envy and jealousy" (Mar-
shal 1960, p. 351). In the distribution of game and
other "gifts," the headman is given no priority, though

he is conceptualized as the titular "owner" of the objects. All persons receive gifts according to kinship
status and are expected to return them in egalitarian
fashion.

In such a cultural atmosphere, most social control
will not be based on power or authority. In fact, the
usual mode of control is simply that of talking (public
opinion). Marshall claims that "most !Kung cannot bear
the sense of rejection which even mild disapproval
makes them feel" (1961, p. 232). The Bushman are able
by these means to depoliticize their society even
though, as we have seen, they are not a people without
politics.

A study of Bushman cosmology sheds further light on
their political system. They believe in a creator high
god, lesser gods, and spirits of the dead. The main
lesser god respects the high god, but he is not subject
to his authority (the two are in a relationship which
is informal and joking in Bushman society). The wives
and children of the high god are his workers and perform duties under his command. The spirits of the dead
operate largely independently of the gods (bringing
both good and ill to men), and are not greatly feared,
because they "are minor characters and can be driven
away" (Marshall 1962, p. 144).

Relationships between divine beings are an expression, at an ideological level, of the political relations discussed above. In the high god concept, band
authority is given recognition. As in Bushman bands,
the high god's kinsmen are his executors. The limited
nature of authority is expressed by his nonauthoritar-
ian relationship with the lesser god and by the independence of the spirit people.

Significantly, the Bushman do not believe in witchcraft and sorcery, for good and ill are dual aspects of
all divine beings. This reflects the relative infre-
quency of political conflict within and between bands.
Sometimes the gods disagree with one another, but, as
in society, they "talk things over and agree together"
(Marshall 1962, p. 245).

The Bushman term for the power by which the high god
created and now controls the world is *gaoxa*. Medicine
men can gain and use it to cure sickness. Since almost
all men practice medicine, there appears to be little

correlation between the possession of gaoxa and political power (though a closer study of the role of medicine men in band conflicts might reveal more relationship than that reported by the Marshalls). Headmen are
sometimes called gaoxa, but this usage is limited, and
the term is usually reserved for district commissioners
known to the Bushman. Some informants told the Marshalls (1962, p. 226) "that to call a man gaoxa was to
compare him to the deity, which might anger the gods."
This view would seem to be a further indication of the
limitations which the Bushman place on the use of power
by their headmen.

Usually the headmen are referred to as *kxau*, which
means "owner" (Marshall 1960, p. 348). That is to say,
the headman has titular rights to the band and its resources. By our definitions, the concept of kxau would
correspond to authority. Thus, it is authority rather
than power which dominates the Bushman's concept of
headmanship. This is mundane authority, for kxau is
widely used to define kinship relations within the band,
but is only weakly associated with deity.

The vast majority of tribal societies are far more
differentiated than that of the bushman, and, correspondingly, are far more politicized. Many of these
tribes have been the object of anthropological investigation, and in some cases their political systems have
received special attention (see the bibliographies in
Gluckman 1965b; Easton 1959; Cohen and Middleton 1967;
Smith 1968; Middleton and Tait 1958). In general, politics and administration in these societies are a mag-
nification of tendencies seen in the Bushman and other
band societies. An attempt will be made to generalize
about their political characteristics, especially as
these diverge from the patterns described above for
Bushman society.

ECOLOGY AND POLITICS

Some of the finest anthropological studies on tribal
societies have dealt with the question of the relationship between economic factors and the political system.
One consequence of this work has been the elaboration
and modification of the Marxian formula that technology
and related economic factors lead to class structure,

in support of which political organization takes its
form, which in turn is projected into and supported by
religion and ideology (Marx 1964; Harris 1968, pp. 217-
49). The complexity of the intervening variables between technology and political organization has led to
a widespread replacement of Marxian economic determinism with the concept of "ecology."

One of the earliest and most influential ecological
studies was Steward's (1955) demonstration that a band-
type sociopolitical form could be explained by a single
ecological adaptation in seemingly disparate environments: hunting nonmigratory game in marginal areas
with a simple technology (bow and arrow, sticks, spears,
traps, etc.). The simple political forms resulting
from this type of adaptation were seen as part of a
long chain of intervening ecological relationships:
family labor divided on the basis of age and sex, common ownership of strategic property, low population
density, small fragmented migratory groups periodically
coalescing into temporarily sedentary larger groups,
the prevalence of bilateral descent and band exogamy.

Just how delicate the balance between ecological
adaptation and political organization can be at this
simple tribal level has been dramatically shown by
Sharp (1968). With scrupulous care he analyzed the effects of introducing one important technological change
--replacing stone axes with metal ones--into an Australian tribal society. The changes in the political system were dramatic, though they were only part of the
changes occurring in all aspects of society. The authority of the elders was undermined because younger
males and women could now own metal axes. The stone
ax had been an important symbol of masculine and gerontocratic superiority, but metal axes ate away at this
kind of legitimacy. For the first time, political conflict was directed by the elders against the younger
generation and nonband peoples (whites who gave the
metal axes to the natives). The case demonstrates the
intricate interconnectedness of institutions resulting
from ecological adaptation. Even the myths of the tribe
were undermined because it proved difficult to incorporate the axheads into mythical accounts of the ancestors. Since all social relationships, including those
of authority, were supposed to be based on what the an-

cestors had ordained, this resulted in a serious erosion of authority.

Since the pioneering ecological studies by Steward, many well-conceived research efforts have documented the way the political system relates to the ecosystem (see, e.g., Sahlins 1958; Carneiro 1970; Stevenson 1968). Cultural ecologists have isolated critical intervening variables between technology and politics, such as total net yield of production, population density, settlement patterns, and stratification (Orans 1968; Fried 1967). Along with type of environment and technology, these ecological factors are causally connected, and in turn provide the basis for the kind of political system present. It has been shown that even subtle, seemingly slight, ecological variation can cause significant differences in tribal politics (see, e.g., Suttles' analysis of variation among Northwest Coast tribes, 1968; Hackenberg's demonstration of contrasts between the Pima and Papago tribes of Arizona, 1968).

As our understanding of the ecological basis of tribal politics has expanded, it has become clear that causation does not operate only in the direction of ecology to political system, for the latter can influence significantly the kind of ecological adaptation made by a society. This can be seen from even the most obvious cases of ecological determinism that we have, such as the transformation of the sociopolitical organization of an Australian tribe through the introduction of metal axes (see above). In an often overlooked statement, Sharp (1968, p. 91) indicated that in addition to the metal axes, ideas about authoritarian leadership also came into the aboriginal culture as a result of contact with whites. Thus, the direct introduction of new forms of authority must be placed alongside ecologically induced changes if we are to understand the erosion of the traditional political system. Further, as noted by Cohen (1968, p. 82), the very weakness of the political system of that particular tribe prevented the aborigines from either halting the intrusion of metal axes or controlling them in order to stimulate a more advanced level of technological development.

Almost without exception, students of ecology have admitted that the political system cannot be entirely

explained by ecological relationships. Politics must
sometimes be taken as independent variable and ecology
as dependent variable. An analysis which clearly defines the reciprocal relationship between these two
variables is a study by Oliver if the ecology and social
organization of the Great Plains Indians (1968). Oliver
carefully documents the basic ecological adaptation
which underlay Plains Indian society: the mounted hunting of the buffalo. Based on that adaptation, their
form of politics consisted of band-type headmen during
the winter months, when dispersed buffalo were hunted
in small groups, alternating with tribal officers and
councils during the summer months, when communal buffalo hunting prevailed. Oliver observes, however, that
there were significant differences among some of the
Plains tribes in spite of their sharing "essentially
the same ecological situation." For example, the Black-
foot tribe had an unstable leadership, mostly based on
power, while the Cheyenne had elected officers and a
well-organized council. Oliver's explanation of these
differences came from a careful study of the historical
background of the different Plains societies. He found
that the apparent nonecological political differences
among the tribes resulted from their past political organization. The kind of political system these tribes
had upon adapting to a buffalo-horse ecology *did* make a
difference, even though all the tribes were later transformed to an important extent into broadly similar kinds
of political societies.

Cultural ecologists have attempted to incorporate the
observed partial independence of the political system
into their models by insisting that the environment to
which societies must adapt has both physical and social
dimensions (Service 1962; Sahlins 1964; Cohen 1968). In
this way, tribal political organization greater than the
ecology seems to warrant is sometimes attributed to the
tribes' need to defend themselves or to provide for attack against other societies in contact with them.
Stevenson (1968) attributes the existence of acephalous
African tribal political systems with anomalously high-
density populations to symbiotic relationships with
neighboring centralized states. Using the same argument in reverse, Service (1962) claims that when tribal
societies without chiefs are in contact with societies

which have them, they may be stimulated to develop
chiefs of their own (or be destroyed or assimilated).

   Similarly, Sahlins (1961) explains the segmentary
lineage system of the Nuer as political adaptation to
a neighboring tribe, the Dinka, who by contrast are organized in fragmented, relatively isolated lineages.
By developing segmentary lineages above the village level, the Nuer can successfully raid and push outward
their Dinka neighbors. Oliver, in the above-cited study
of Plains Indian ecology, also included military pressures from competing tribes as a necessary part of the
total adaptive situation leading to the development of
Plains chieftainship. The developed, formalized nature
of authority, which contrasted these societies with
those of other North American Indian tribes (Lowie 1948),
and indeed with the same tribes at earlier periods of
their history, resulted in part from the requirement
that leaders demonstrate military skill and achievement
(Oliver 1968, p. 256 ff.).

TRIBAL ADMINISTRATION

Much administrative action in tribal society is similar
to that of the Bushman, i.e., highly limited in authority, granted on traditional principles to the aged and
experienced, and hedged against conflicts over it. Indeed, the authority of lineage headmen, village elders,
and the like seems insignificant and uninformative when
compared to that of more complex political societies.
Yet, on close inspection it reveals some interesting
general features. Wallace, for example, finds that
tribal administration shares generic features with modern forms (1971). He asserts that administrative organization is a "structural pose" that groups in all so-
cieties--whether kin-, community-, or association-based
--may at least temporarily assume. Universal features
found in administrative organization, according to Wallace, are the presence of both line and staff members
(vertical versus horizontal lines of authority), devices
to insulate the group against inefficiency (such as incest rules to prevent sexual conflict in kin-based
units), and reorganizational measures to eliminate error and rejuvenate structure (such as altering genealo-

gies to make them conform to changing relations of authority).

Focusing on tribal administration per se, we may note three characteristics which seem to occur widely (Gluckman 1965b, pp. 90-91). One of these is the tendency for tribal agents, supposedly only exercising delegated authority, to act with relative autonomy in certain spheres. In Wallace's terminology, this would mean that administration tends to be staff oriented rather than line oriented (horizontal rather than vertical). I would take this one step further and add that, within limited spheres, tribal authorities tend to exercise their authority with *considerable* autonomy. This is easily overlooked in the study of tribal authority because of the strong egalitarian ideology which pervades most societies of this type (Miller 1955).

A well-known example in the literature are the soldier societies of the Plains Indians (Llewellyn and Hoebel 1961; Oliver 1968). The Cheyenne, who, as compared to other Plains tribes, had well-defined tribal authorities, nevertheless severely limited the rights of those officials in order to zealously preserve freedom of individual action. Yet, within the context of the summer buffalo hunts and raiding expeditions, the soldier societies exercised an effective policing authority. We are told that, in the case of the Cheyenne, "the coercive authority of the military leaders bordered on the dictatorial" (Llewellyn and Hoebel 1961, p. 104). These leaders combined police, judicial, and correctional duties, and individualistic warriors as well as chiefs had to obey them within their spheres of authority.

This authoritarian kind of control was not confined to the Plains Indians. Indeed, I think it characteristic of tribal administration, though the spheres of authority are always limited and are defined by the importance of the situation. This is clear in the case of the Navaho, who were famous for their apparent lack of authority. In Shepardson's excellent account of their indigenous authority system (1967), she describes the "peace chief" as the most stable authority. His authority usually did not extend beyond the outfit, which consisted of several extended families. It was traditional dependent "upon his own personal qualities

and his ability to secure cooperation and retain respect." But there were three other kinds of Navaho
leaders: for war, the hunt, and ritual. Though these
leaders were supposed to be subordinate to the peace
chief, in fact they operated quite independently, and
each exercised complete authority in his own sphere.
"The man who organized the [war] party was in complete
command of all members. . . . The [hunting] expedition
was under [the leader's] absolute authority and was
held responsible for the outcome" (Shepardson 1967, pp.
150-51).

Navaho administration was staff dominated, and Shepardson notes the "lack of a clear hierarchy among
roles." "Commissions" of authority were temporary, new
leaders rising and falling as different situations arose
and abler men cam forward. This might be seen as exem-
plifying the informal reorganization and rejuvenation
which Wallace found to characterize all administrative
systems.

A second general characteristic of tribal administration is the close association between "mystical symbols"
and authority. Such symbols, it is claimed, stand for
"the ultimate common interests of a tribe" (Gluckman
1965b, p. 91). They legitimate authority by identifying
it with what is most valued and respected in society.
Mystical symbols make authority inseparable from nature
and the sacred by linking it with basic values like fer-
tility, health, prosperity, peace, and accomplishments.
The social (authority), natural, and sacred become so
interconnected that disturbance or action in one sphere
affects the others. Natural disaster may be blamed on
the authorities. Likewise, "failure in amity, feelings
of hostility and unspoken grievances, also spoil a sacrifice and bring mystical retribution in the form of
misfortune. Or misfortune is due to a breach of taboo,
or to a warranted curse by an elder, or even to protec-
tive mystical activity of the accredited elders of a
society" (Gluckman 1965b, p. 244).

This characteristic has profound implications for
the study of power and authority, but it is complex and
difficult for modern man to understand. In a brilliant
essay on the significance of the ritual surrounding the
initiation of tribal men into office, Fortes clarified
one aspect of the problem: beyond guaranteeing the leg-

itimacy of official authority, this kind of ceremony
also "imposes accountability for its proper exercise"
(1966, p. 86). This is done by dramatizing society's
ownership of the office and the separateness of the office from the person being initiated. More than being
a legitimizer, then, ritual and mystical symbols may
function to limit authority and to act as a check
against divisive individuals who would otherwise not
be controlled by society. In another place Fortes
(1953, p. 34) refers to this as a "polarity in religious
cult and in the political office and authority linked
with cult." The basis of his statement is the oft-
noted distribution in tribal societies of authority in
one kind of organization (e.g., patrilineages) and ritual rights in another (the matriline in a double descent system).

This is basically the same point made by Turner in
his analysis of Ndembu politics (1957), for he showed
that ritual control comes into operation precisely in
those situations which the judicial process cannot handle (such as natural crises, or conflicts based on fundamentally different value assumptions). Because ritual
is carried out after conflict has occurred, and brings
disputants into cooperation through their common acceptance of the great values of society, it can function in
ways in which authority cannot (Turner 1966).

We may apply one of Wallace's principles to the correlation between ritual and authority in tribal society
by suggesting that ritual is a kind of administrative
"insulation." Shepardson, for example, describes Navaho
war, hunting, and ritual leaders as also being ritual
specialists in their own spheres of authority (1967, pp.
150-51). This kind of association between office and
the sacred suggests that ritual activity "purifies" the
acting authorities, in the sense of requiring them to
demonstrate their commitment to the basic values of society. Personal and other distracting attitudes are
thus excluded (as we would exclude, e.g., nepotism from
bureaucratic administration) (Wallace 1971, p. 5), and
the effectiveness of group action is thereby assured.

A third administrative principle in tribal society
(Gluckman 1965b, p. 90) is highly interesting, though
it is administrative only in an indirect sense. This
is the process of achieving social control in tribal

society through the overlapping affiliation of persons in different groups. Gluckman cites the case of the Cheyenne, where the administrative function of soldier societies is achieved by drawing men from several different bands, We have many other descriptions of this process at work in tribal societies (e.g., Murphy 1957; Forde 1964), but the classic study is Colson's account of social control among the Tonga (1962).

She describes how redress for murder is achieved in that society without chiefs. The details of the case are complicated, but the principle is simple. Men of the deceased man's lineage have the right to retaliate but are dispersed in several villages. Because they are married to women from other lineages, the men from those lineages can apply pressure on the vengeance group through their wives. A "natural" death in the community may be interpreted by a ritual specialist as resulting from the disturbance, so mystical pressure is added to the social pressures. In the end, the vengeful men are tied to so many persons and groups wanting a solution that a peaceful settlement has to be worked out (in this case, the deceased was compensated with blood cattle).

Gluckman has elaborated on the significance of this process for social control (1965b, pp. 91-116). He argues that the incessant struggling and fighting which seems to go on in tribal societies without central authorities is often controlled through mechanisms such as the one described for the Tonga. Though it is true that this kind of social control appears to be the obverse of authority, it should be remembered that persons from different groups have *rights* with respect to those being controlled. While the "authority" of any one of them might be insufficient to control a conflict their combined rights may be sufficient.

While the kind of authority discussed above typifies administration in tribal society, there is a strong tendency for more centralized forms of authority to come into existence. From one perspective, this may be seen as a result of the development of more complex social structures than are found in simple bands like the Bushman, Congo Pygmies, etc. There are clans, lineages, villages, age grades, associations, and the like (Service 1962; Lowie 1961). The principles of descent,

labor, residence, cult, and alliance which such structures entail provide the bases for political competition and, eventually, increased authority.

In many tribal societies, charismatic leaders emerge
from the competition and control spheres of influence
wider than those of the traditional lineage and village
elders. Interestingly, their generosity and their conformity to the moral order is what gives them an advantage in the competition. Though these "big men," as
they are called in Melanesia, may enjoy considerable
power and prestige, it is difficult for them to convert
this into authority. They must constantly seek the support of followers, and find themselves inevitably opposed by rivals. It is especially difficult for them
to convert political position into office. Therefore,
in many cases the political norms of tribal societies
may be quite static and traditionally defined (to be
acceptable, leaders may have to be of certain lineages,
ages, locales, etc.), while the actual practice of political life may be highly dynamic.

For reasons not entirely clear, there are other societies in which wide leadership roles develop into
positions of institutionalized authority and succession.
Fortes, who refers to these positions as corporations
sole (versus lineages, villages, etc., which are corporate groups), notes that they make up the central core
of the social structure of some tribal societies in
Africa (1953, p. 37). Heirs succeed to the authority
and other rights and privileges of the offices (sometimes divided among different heirs), so that there develops a "stability of the society over time . . . pre-
served by perpetuating the status system." The existence of corporations sole is more common in tribal societies than was formerly believed. Sometimes the statuses are so totally transferred that the very names
and history of the former occupants are taken on by the
heirs, thus making it difficult to discover their true
corporate nature (Cunnison 1959; Gluckman 1965b, pp.
120-21).

Where these wider authority positions are a means for
controlling strategic ties between lesser levels of society (such as promoting needed trade between different
tribes), they may be quite stable. Often, however, that
is not the case, and the positions are limited in time.

In such instances, tribal societies will appear to os-
cillate between centralized (chieftainship) and acephalous political forms, a situation which has been described by Leach for the Kachin of Burma (1954), by
Southall for the Alur of Uganda (1956), and by Powell
for the Trobriand Islanders (1960). Even where the
chieftainship is stable, the authority vested in the
position may remain extremely limited, as with the essentially ritual status of the Tallensi chiefs and the
Shilluk "king" (Fortes 1945; Evans-Pritchard 1963;
Lowie 1948; Gluckman 1965b, pp. 116-35). Thus, while
the development of corporations sole in tribal society
represents an expansion in the scope of authority, the
changes in structure need not be great. Per se, corporations sole are not an index of a tribal society's
progress toward statehood or some other form of centralized political development.

Societies at the tribal stage of political development are usually plagued by violent conflicts between
groups similar in structure, rules, size, and culture.
When such conflicts occur within the same "tribe," they
may be termed feuds. That is, they are conceptualized
as administrative or legal problems which would be resolved peacefully if they were to occur within the most
basic corporate units. Rarely will a chief's authority
extend far enough to settle such disputes, so attempts
are made to use third parties as mediating "commissions."
The authority temporarily granted such persons is based
differently from that of big men, for the mediators are
often selected precisely because they are *not* powerful.

A particularly clear example of this kind of mediating administration is found among the Tonga (Colson
1962; Gluckman 1965b, p. 91 ff.). The Tonga lack chiefs,
and even leadership within their matrilineages and villages is weakly developed. At a higher level, the fourteen matriclans lack leaders and, in fact, never meet
as a group. Nevertheless, they have important functions
in maintaining the rules of society. The various clans
are in joking relationship with each other, and jokes
by outside clansmen are often biting castigations for
wrongdoing with respect to the rules of marriage, property, kinship, etc. As outsiders or "strangers,"
these clansmen will have no selfish interest in the
disputed matters and so can act as "arbiters of morals"

(Gluckman 1965b, p. 99)   in Tonga society.

This kind of social control is similar to the process of social overlapping discussed above. The mediating clans may lack the backing of force and the formal recognition of a quality equivalent to our concept of authority, yet they do exercise rights which are legitimate and prescribed by society. Self-help, the redress of wrongs by the same persons and groups who are offended, is simply another typical manifestation of this informal kind of administration in tribal societies. A feud usually starts when a group attempts to carry out redresses considered to be its right and privilege, but which the other party refuses to recognize as legitimate. Where, in fact, the self-executioners have the backing and support of corporate society, however diffuse that backing might be, these redresses are a form of administration. Authority in such cases is a temporary and specific delegation. The fact that it is often unsuccessful and may require the special kind of mediation described earlier does not alter its administrative nature.

Law

Since rules backed by authority are what we generally mean by law (Durkheim 1964, pp. 69, 426-27; Weber 1964, pp. 128-29), the above argument is, in effect, a claim that all tribal societies have law. This raises a hoary question in anthropology, for there are some who argue that tribal peoples lack law (Radcliffe-Brown 1940; Hoebel 1954; Diamond 1951, pp. 54-56; Redfield 1967; Fried 1967, pp. 90-91, 144 ff.). Those who deny the existence of tribal law do so by defining it in ethnocentric, Western terms--i.e., as rules backed by the use or threat of force by a state agency. What appears to be most basic to the existence of law, however is the presence of absence of corporate units with recognized rules and the authority to maintain them. As social anthropologists have repeatedly pointed out (see especially Fortes 1953), the corporate lineages, clans, association, villages, etc. of tribal society are legal units. They provide legal statuses for men in society, and they lay down rules defining relations between those statuses; they are the source of authority, whether to back officers, self-executioners, or the group as a whole, in support of the rules. Because of their legal nature these groups tend to be viewed from the outside as "single persons."

We might wish to distinguish between different *types* of law so as to contrast societies with courts from those without them, but this should not lead us to deny the fundamentally legal character of the groups found in all tribal societies. Though a number of political anthropologists have argued for this point of view (Gluckman 1965a; Malinowski 1926; Smith 1960; Pospisil 1958), Redfield's discussion (1967) is one of the clearest (despite his conclusion that our law is fundamentally different from that of "primitives"). Redfield clarifies what may be one of the principal sources of confusion for students of law, which is that tribal law is primarily civil rather than criminal (see also Elias 1962). That is to say, self-help is the primary mode of maintaining rights in tribal societies. As Redfield further clarifies, the wronged persons who retaliate are typically kinship groups rather than individuals, so that to refer to tribal civil law as "torts" is unsatisfactory.

Redfield also notes that in all tribal societies a limited amount of sanctioning exists for wrongs seen as damaging to the entire society--such wrongs as incest, recidivous homicide, desecration of the sacred. This kind of action might be termed criminal law, and its maintenance usually involves supernatural sanctions, such as witchcraft or punishment by spirits or gods. Nevertheless, there are cases of capital and other forms of punishment at the tribal level, even among band-organized tribes. The Eskimos, e.g., will execute inveterate murderers, an individual who has tacit community approval serving as executioner (Hoebel 1954, p. 89).

Anthropologists have found that, contrary to superficial appearances, most tribal societies develop well-defined procedural "codes" for maintaining law. In the remarkable case of the Yurok Indians of California, who are without courts or formal authorities, a complex code of compensation for injury exists. Under this code every kind of civil wrong has its compensation in dentalium shells, obsidian blades, and woodpecker scalps. The code takes into account the differences

in rank of the offended persons--e.g., a man of low
standing is worth only ten strings of shells, while a
highly ranked man is worth fifteen (Kroeber 1953; Goldschmidt 1951; Hoebel 1954). There are many cases of
similarly standardized legal procedures in tribal societies (Diamond 1951, p. 115; Redfield 1967; Gluckman
1965a).

It is not possible to discuss further the nature of
tribal law, but it should be noted that we now know a
great deal about its substantive as well as its procedural forms (Nadel 1969; Gluckman 1965a; Diamond 1951;
Elias 1962). The basic point of our discussion on law
has been to show that in tribal societies rules which
receive authoritative backing, and hence should be
viewed as tribal administration, are not always formally differentiated from kinship, ritual, and other
rights. Nevertheless, the lineages, clans, or mediators, taking measures supported by corporate society
for the correction of wrongs, are authorities. Their
decisions can be binding, and may carry sanctions of
great effectiveness even in the absence of the threat
of force (for a summary of sanctions in tribal society,
see Radcliffe-Brown 1952, pp. 205-11).

TRIBAL POLITICS

Anthropologists have often called our attention to what
seems to be a sharp contrast between the peaceful, consensual character of internal tribal decision-making,
and the extremely hostile side of external tribal politics. Murphy, in a famous study (1957), claims that
hostility within Mundurucu society was almost totally
suppressed, while warfare against external tribes was
mercilessly pursued. He sought to explain this in
terms of the contradiction between a matrilocal residence rule and a patrilineally organized society. He
argued that the potential internal aggression resulting
from this arrangement was controlled by having the hostility transferred to the outside (for a criticism of
his argument, see Wilson 1958).

Gluckman notes that legislation is largely absent in
tribal societies without strong chiefs and that even in
tribes with strong chiefs legislation produces few significant changes and is negligible in effect compared

to economic influences (1965b, pp. 169-72). Tribal societies without legislation give the appearance of being static from within, for decisions are made by consensus and on situational rather than basic structural
matters. Then, too, as noted above for the case of the
Ndembu, when a structurally significant dispute arises,
the whole issue may be projected into the ritual sphere.
The status quo is thus maintained through a common acceptance of valued social symbols.

To a large extent, as first pointed out by Fortes
(1953) and Smith (1956), the apparent internal tran-
quillity and consensus of tribal society is a legal fiction. Tribal societies are unspecialized compared to
modern social forms, so that the corporate units function both politically and administratively. A lineage,
village, or secret society is simultaneously struggling
for land or power against some equivalent outside political unit and distributing authority internally in an
attempt to maintain the rights and duties it already
controls. Because such units are defined by political
conflict with the outside, their power and holdings constantly change. Hence, the internal administrative order also will change in order to adapt to new conditions.

Anthropologists have fully documented this dynamic
side of internal tribal politics. As Balandier puts it
(1970, p. 69): "The discovery of antagonisms, struggles
and conflicts suggests the importance of political strategy in societies with minimal or diffused government and
encourages one to point out the diversity of its means.
The genealogical charter, kinship and marriage alliances
may be transformed into instruments in the struggle for
power, for they are never mere mechanisms that automa-
tically ensure the attribution of political status and
the devolution of office." The myth of the egalitarian
tribe is made possible by expressing conflict and opposition in ritualistic ideologies. Divination, ances-
tral worship, and witchcraft function as a "code used
in political confrontations" and provide the "arguments
that are employed in clan societies" (Balandier 1970,
p. 68).

There exists a substantial literature explaining the
political functions of tribal ideologies (see Gluckman
1965b, p. 216 ff.; Middleton and Winter 1963; Mair 1969;
Sahlins 1968; Goody 1962). Rituals based on these ideo-

logies--accusing someone of witchcraft, divining to
find a disturber, mediating with the spirits to learn
the cause of some sickness--follow the lines of conflict within tribal society. They allow tribal man to
struggle over power while maintaining the fiction that
the conflict exists outside the tribe (Evans-Pritchard
[1937] claims that this guise is necessary in societies
which cannot question their basic principles). Yet the
effects of such conflicts are socially real, for actual
power shifts and changes in status, authority, and law
do occur as a result of them. We discover that ritual
functions both to support authority and as a device for
political manipulation.

In tribal society, kinship and ritual function in a
similar way. Like ritual, kinship is both a basis for
authority and a source of power. Fortes (1953, p. 29)
sees ritual and kinship as similar but different levels
of organization and calls our attention to the "tremendous importance of the web of kinship as a counter-
weight to the tendency of unilineal descent grouping
to harden social barriers." He recognizes that lineage
structures constantly undergo "fission and accretion,"
while kinship genealogies and ties are altered as part
of the formation of new social realities (Fortes 1953,
pp. 27, 31; also Smith 1956).

Studies of tribal society in Africa have documented
the way kinship is manipulated for political purposes
and serves as an expression of political action (e.g.,
Van Velsen 1964; Mitchell 1956; Turner 1957). In sum-
marizing the results of those studies, Balandier (1970,
pp. 58-64) specifies the differences in condition between individuals and groups which provide the "energy"
for tribal politics. Typically tribal politics stem
from differences in rank between clans and lineages,
relative distances of male kinsmen from direct lines
leading to past family or lineage authorities, differences between age groups (e.g., youth versus elders),
and personal differences in wealth and leadership qualities (Balandier 1970, p. 59).

What these studies show is that to a significant degree the social organization (kinship, ritual) and even
the economic forms of a society are determined by political processes occurring within it. This is an extremely important point and calls for documentation.

Epstein's (1968) comparison of a tribal society in
Africa (Ndembu) with one in Melanesia (Tolai) is highly
informative analysis bearing on the problem.

Epstein points out that the two societies are broadly
similar in ecology and social organization. Both practice subsistence horticulture and have discrete village
organizations, and the core of both societies is a matrilineal descent group. Despite these striking simi-
larities, their politics are remarkably different. In
Ndembu society most political action pivots upon men attempting to attract matrilineal kinsmen to their villages in order to gain support in their claims to headmanship. "This situation is fraught with difficulty,
for the more successful the headman, the greater his influence and prestige in relation to other such groups.
On the other hand, the more people he succeeds in at-
tracting to his village the greater the likelihood of
the development of internal faction and fissionary tendencies. . . . In the end, of course, group unity can
no longer be maintained, and fission takes place, usually along the lines of lineage segmentation" (Epstein
1968, p. 60).

Tolai politics is of the "big man" variety found
widely in Melanesia. Most competition arises between
men seeking to exercise power over several village
units. Supporters come from outside the big man's ma-
trilineage as well as from within it, for the immediate
object of the struggle is not village office but the
acquisition of shell money. Wealth of this kind can be
used to sponsor ceremonies which create obligated clients and prestige for the competitors. Hence, struggles take place on a scale above the village level, and
villages tend to be stable. Well-established big men
may convert their power into temporary authority--com-
missions--but their kinsmen seldom succeed to these positions.

There are minor ecological differences between the
two societies which might help explain these political
differences--e.g., the Tolai geography provides a more
fertile soil and more regional variation (the latter
condition presumably underlies an indigenous trade
found in the area). Nevertheless, specific, significant structural differences in the two societies appear
to be more directly the result of their varying politi-

cal systems. Whereas Ndembu marriage is brittle and
families tend to be matricentric, neither situation
prevails in the Tolai family structure. Ndembu villages
undergo constant fission and fusion along matrilineal
lines, while Tolai communities tend to be stable. (Turner [1957] explained the instability of Ndembu villages
as the result of contradiction between virilocal residence and matrilineal descent.) Ndembu witchcraft is
local and directed against matrilineal kinsmen, while
that of the Tolai is directed against outside persons
and groups. An egalitarian exchange economy prevails
in Ndembu society, in contrast with the Tolai's "self-
interested cunning and economic calculation." The personal characteristics of leaders in the two societies
differ sharply. Ndembu headmen are older than Tolai
big men. They have "unobtrusive personalities,[are]
unaggressive, and [are] ready to share what wealth they
might acquire with their relatives"--characteristics
that are almost polar opposites of those found among
Tolai big men.

Considerable additional evidence could be adduced to
support Epstein's analysis that politics can significantly determine tribal social and cultural forms. Particularly convincing are studies by avowed ecological
determinists who in the end admit that political factors must be seen as having a degree of autonomy with
respect to ecology. As noted above, many of them simply build this into their models by including the sociopolitical field as part of the total ecological system
(Service 1962; Sahlins 1964; Cohen 1968).

Another source of evidence comes from the increasing
number of anthropologists who find that game theory can
be used to explain the "generation" of sociocultural
forms (Buchler and Nutini 1969). Many of them work
within a "formalist" economic framework (Le Clair and
Schneider 1968), but in most cases their results can be
interpreted politically as well as economically. A good
illustration of this approach is Salisbury's (1966) use
of game theory to analyze Tolai economics. Salisbury
found that, in spite of technoeconomic changes introduced from the outside into Tolai society, traditional
descent groups, land tenure, religion, and shell money
continue. These are maintained, he says, by the action
of struggling "big men."

Barth (1959, 1965), working directly with political systems in tribal society, has shown that regular structural features are the result of strategic political choices made by men. For both abstract and specific cases, this kind of political process can be analyzed with simple game theory (1959). These studies suggest that tribal man is more of a political animal than we had thought.

Most students of tribal society have commented on the chronic state of hostility and warfare which seems to prevail between tribes. Warner (1937) long ago described war, as he called it, between the clans of the Australian Murngin. He claimed that their wars were proportionately as lethal as ours--there were a hundred deaths over a twenty-year period. At issue in most of the conflicts were women, the strategic resource of this polygynous, bandlike society. Accounts of this kind led Service (1962, p. 114) to state that the "external polity of tribes is usually military only."

A more careful consideration of the evidence suggests a somewhat moderated view of the external relations between tribal peoples. It is argued by many anthropologists that the simplest hunting and gathering band societies often "lack true equivalents of warfare" (Harris 1971, p. 225; Lesser 1968; Fried 1967). Conflicts exist in such societies, but they are "generally so infrequent, brief, unorganized, and involve so few individuals that they must be considered as a distinctive form of warfare" (Newcomb 1960, p. 327). This conclusion may be controvertible, but it seems to best fit the facts as we now know them.

The militant aspect of tribal external relations has been stressed, perhaps, at the expense of many other kinds of alliances and exchanges which also characterize intertribal relations. Fried (1967, p. 178) reminds us that "most rank societies [tribes] engage with equal or greater frequency in other inter-community activities, most notably in feasts, parties, ceremonies, and other events predicated on organized hostility." The great pig-giving ceremonies of New Guinea and the Northwest Coast potlatches are familiar examples of this kind of intertribal exchange. Ecologists like Fried (see also Harris 1971; Rappaport 1968; Suttles 1968; Sahlins 1968) see these institutionalized exchanges as devices

by which villages are organized into larger economic
networks. Thus, the exchanges have ecological bases.

While not denying them these functions, it should be
noted that such "exchange alliances" are also political.
Ostensibly, the gifts exchanged--whether pigs, women,
or copper crests--are nonpolitical, but in fact they
are always partly intended to gain some measure of control over other groups (and thus enhance or protect the
internal "estate" of the acting corporate group).

It is difficult to document this claim, though we
have a few studies which do just that. For example,
Uberoi (1971) restudied Malinowski's classic description of the kula exchanges which took place between
Melanesians from different islands. He found this
strange institution to involve an intense competition
between men and lineages to control the actions of independent men and external groups. By manipulating
kula alliances, it was possible in some cases for lineages from less fertile regions to dominate groups from
more fertile regions--"the political link conditions
the economic advantage" (Balandier 1970, p. 72).

The whole question of exogamy and wife exchange, on
which there is a veritable mountain of literature in
anthropology, also has to be viewed from a political
perspective. Malinowski (1965) himself showed that powerful Trobriand chiefs increased their power and authority by seeking marriage alliances with the most prestigious and economically powerful matrilineages. Leach
(1954), in a classic study, has detailed the process by
which marriage alliances are manipulated in accordance
with political goals among the Kachin of Burma. In a
remarkably interesting recent study, Chagnon documents
the process by which the Yanomamö of Venezuela politically manipulate marriage alliances (and, incidentally,
in the process deviate from their "prescribed" cross-
cousin marriage patterns). "Over a long term the exchanges are usually balanced, but a stronger group, especially in the initial stages of exchange, will have
an advantage" (Chagnon 1968, p. 123). Weaker villages
permit this kind of exploitation, albeit with every resistance possible short of war, because of their need
for political allies to protect them against raids.

The same kind of political goals underlie Yanomamö
technological specialization and intervillage trading.

"Each group seems to create shortages of particular
items, such as bows, clay pots, arrows, . . .and relies
on one or more of its allies for these goods" (Chagnon
1968, p. 121). The Yanomamö will even produce an economic surplus specifically to attract supporting allies,
thus providing us with yet another instance of a reversal of the economic-political equation.

Not all anthropologists, of course, interpret exchange alliances politically. Levi-Strauss (1969), for
example, views the development of systems of marriage
exchange as the essential factor in the very emergence
and subsequent evolution of complex human societies.
Bohannan (1963) sees exchange alliances (including tribal "warfare") as alternatives to centralized political
systems. They allow communication and interaction between tribal units to occur, and in the process violence is kept relatively well under control. To see
exchange alliances as also political, however, is not
to deny their nonpolitical aspects. In fact, the multi-
functional nature of tribal institutions is a theme
which must run throughout any summary of tribal politics.

Warfare

Let us now turn our attention to tribal warfare, which
occurs in all but the few exceptional cases mentioned
above. Most anthropologists view warfare as a cultural
phenomenon, something learned from one's society and
not engaged in because of psychological needs (see
especially Mead 1940; Malinowski 1965; White 1949; Newcomb 1960). Its essential universality is to be accounted for, in part, by its early invention and subsequent diffusion. It is simply an available form of external tribal relations, for, as Mead put it, "If a people have an idea of going to war and the idea that war
is the way in which certain situations defined within
their society, are to be handled, they will sometimes
go to war" (1940). A growing number of anthropologists
also stress the ecological basis of warfare. It is an
adaptive institution and therefore persists in tribal
society (Fried 1967; Harris 1971; Vayda 1968). According to this argument, tribal warfare responds to population pressures by reducing total population through
military deaths and spacing out local populations (see

also Carneiro 1970; Sahlins 1961; Rappaport 1968).

The diffusional and ecological arguments have been challenged, though there is considerable evidence to support both (they are not mutually exclusive). For present purposes, the political nature of warfare is what will be stressed. Some discussion of this point seems necessary, since there are anthropologists who claim that tribal warfare is "devoid of any political relevancy" (Malinowski 1941, p. 538) or that "it may be unwise to call this sort of situation warfare. . . [for] it is merely a violent social relationship" (Bohannan 1963, p. 305).

In the classic cases, tribal warfare is a controlled form of fighting which seems more like sport than war. Military raids are short in duration, and few deaths result from them. The overt objectives seem exotic to us--taking trophy heads, scalps, bones, flesh for cannibalism, and the like. This kind of raiding, however, is not mere sport. It is a form of political activity because its unexpressed objectives include (a) the attempt by groups to demonstrate superiority over each other and, thus, to influence each other's policy; and (b) the advancement of the personal goals of individuals who use raids to enhance their power and prestige within their own groups.

The politics of raiding seem to lack the elements of conquest as we know them in modern warfare, where one power totally expropriates the resources of another. Yet, careful analysis reveals that some resource expropriation invariably takes place. It has been shown, for example, in follow-up studies of the Nuer (Sahlins 1961) and the Maori (Vayda 1967), that booty taken through raiding (women, weapons, cattle, etc.) is not economically insignificant. Further, territories are expanded in the process of driving neigboring tribes away from lands adjacent to those of the raiders--eventually, these vacated lands are occupied by the raiding tribes. Indeed, territorial expansion is the basic "function" of warfare in horticulturally based tribes, according to Vayda (1961, 1968). This may be true even where there appears to be more than enough available land, since interior crowding can exert pressure on a sparsely settled perimeter.

It has not been easy to study tribal warfare first-hand. Most tribes have long been under the domination of modern states, and their violent institutions have been suppressed. Chagnon's study shows that Yanomamö warfare perhaps comes closer than any other to being carried out under aboriginal conditions, and thus deserves our closest attention. Significantly, Chagnon finds a clearly political element in their fighting. Exchange alliances constantly break down in Yanomamö society because of political struggle, and frequently they end in war. This is true of gift-giving feasts--sometimes held only as a pretext for a planned raid--as well as arranged marriages. Another kind of "exchange alliance" with strong political overtones is the Yanomamö "contest," which may involve chest-pounding duels between hostile villages.

Lineage structure or headman authority cannot unite politically divided Yanomamö men or prevent them from fighting each other. Population pressure is a factor, for warfare is more intense in the more densely populated central part of Yanomamö territory. But there is no evidence that it creates a need to expand landholdings: "Were it not for their wars the Yanomamö could remain almost indefinitely in the same general area" (Chagnon 1968, p. 118).

Chagnon concludes that war is waged for political reasons. Men fight to gain power over other men and villages, and ultimately to control women. "The critical aspect of the cultural ecology is neighboring, hostile villages" (1968, p. 113). In a situation of chronic warfare, militant ideology and institutions to carry it out are essential "to preserve the sovereignty of independent villages" (1968, p. 112).

The evidence we have about tribal life supports Chagnon's claim that the chronic Yanomamö pattern with respect to warfare "probably obtained to a much greater extent in the past than most of us are willing to concede" (1968, p. 157). Some disagree. Harris, for example (1971, p. 229 ff.), argues that the Yanomamö are an abnormal case in which "the war system reaches maladaptive intensities." But even he admits that "excessive warfare is an ecological trap into which primitive man has fallen again and again" (1971, p. 231). Viewed

against the backdrop of our above discussion of political struggle, tribal warfare becomes simply the most
overt expression of a process which significantly influences every feature of tribal society and culture.

POLITICS AND COSMOLOGY

We now turn to the relationship between power, authority,
and cosmology in tribal society. That they are closely
interconnected has already been commented on, and some
of the ways the sacred is used to maintain authority or
as a source of power have already been outlined. The
topic is one of intense current investigation and interest in political anthropology. One scholar recently
expressed the view that our primary research objective
qua political anthropologists should be the analysis of
the "dialectical relationship" between power and symbolism (Cohen 1969). He argued that they are analyti-
cally separable variables, each with a reality of its
own.

Durkheim (1961) pioneered anthropological thinking
about the possible relationship between social structure, including the political system, and the cosmological world (which he referred to as "collective re-
presentations"). He noted that the relationship operates at two levels: a functional level, on which symbols, by being set apart (made sacred), function to control society and bring solidarity; and a semantic level,
on which the principles of organization in society are
projected into the cosmological realm. Since some of
the ways sacred symbols function in relationship to
authority and power have already been discussed above,
it is the second level of analysis, the semantic, that
will concern us in this section.

Levi-Strauss (1963b) has elaborated Durkheim's suggestion in a study of totemism. He demonstrates that
the relationship between Australian aboriginal social
organization and myth is not direct, but metaphorical.
The political struggle over game animals and women going on between moieties is metaphorically expressed in
the totem myths of the groups. One moiety is said to
be Eaglehawk and the other Crow. They both hunt for
food, but because Eaglehawk is Crow's maternal uncle he
can command Crow to bring back game. Crow cheats, eats

the game, and lies to his uncle about it. Eaglehawk
causes him to vomit up the food and prohibits him from
further hunting (he can only scavenge). As Lévi-Strauss
(1963b, p. 87) puts it, "The world of animal life is
represented in terms of social relations similar to
those in human society."

Lévi-Strauss and other structuralists have gone on to
study symbolic systems as if these were quite divorced
from the underlying sociopolitical structure (for comments on this, see Cohen 1969, pp. 225-27; Leach 1968).
However, Lévi-Strauss laid the foundation for fruitful
investigations which have important implications for
the study of tribal politics. For example, Horton
(1964) suggests that the metaphorical process by which
the social order is projected into the cosmos is similar to the way science operates for modern man. Tribal
man uses his own society as a model to explain the
events of his world, but in doing so he applies only
some of its key principles, then distorts these in order to make them applicable (the way Rutherford applied
the planetary model to explain the structure of matter).
The cosmological model necessarily becomes increasingly
abstract as the problems tribal man seeks to mediate become more diffuse and distant. It follows that political conflict and change will be projected onto lower
cosmic levels, while deep values, including authority
and the continuity of society, will be found at higher
and more abstract levels (cf. Sahlins 1968, pp. 96-113).

The relatively undifferentiated political system of
tribal society finds expression in a "magical" cosmology (Wax 1968). Nature, deity, and man are interconnected and personalized. Plants, animals, rocks, stars,
and spirits are alive and are treated with the reciprocity due kinsmen (e.g., the successful hunter must
leave an offering in exchange for the animal). Men do
not overtly dominate one another, and so the cosmological order contains few authoritative deities. In the
simple structure of the cosmos, the lower level is
filled with ancestor spirits (e.g., the dead spirits
of the Bushman mentioned earlier), totems, monsters, and
the like, who, in their struggles with each other, parallel political affairs in tribal life (Evans-Pritchard
1962; Miller 1955; Horton 1962; Lienhardt 1961). Mediated by men on earth, these beings loosely oversee the

norms of society, and in subtle ways are organized
along the lineage, village, and factional lines of society. The discrepancies between the versions by which
tribal men describe these beings are a manifestation of
their varying political bases, for different versions
correspond to politically competing groups (Firth 1961;
Leach 1954).

Some tribal societies have an uppermost cosmological
level, where they place a high god similar to the one
described for the Bushman. These otiose gods tend to
transcend the issues which divide tribal societies, and
provide symbolic expression of the deepest and broadest
tribal values (Horton 1964; Sahlins 1968; pp. 99-105).
From this level come support for the corporate groups
and corporations sole, the unity of the tribe vis-à-vis
stranger tribes (the "nonpeople"), and questions of creation, birth, and death--"the life course of the world
seen as a whole" (Horton 1962, p. 214).

A verification of the rough correlation suggested
above between the political and cosmological orders of
tribal society comes from studying the world view of
societies with a degree of centralized authority. For
example, the Shilluk of the Sudan had a chief who
helped bind together over 100,000 persons who were otherwise fragmented into typical clans, lineages, and villages. The limited authority of the chieftainship be-
longed exclusively to a royal clan. Eligible sons of
former chiefs competed for the position by killing the
reigning occupant (Evans-Pritchard 1963, pp. 66-85).

Shilluk cosmology was basically tribal in form
(Lienhardt 1963). It was magical, clan ancestor spirits
occupying a lower level and functioning to punish deviations within local units. A distant god, *juok,* helped
explain general problems like the creation, the origin
of sickness and death, and the place of neighboring
tribes in the world.

Of special significance, however, was a sacred being
not found in most tribal societies: a culture hero who
had lived on earth, had founded the royal dynasty, and
became reincarnated in each new chief (hence, the "divine kingship"). He was not like the prophets of Is-
rael, proclaiming monotheism and an ethical system, for
his myth only recounted the way the chieftainship was
formed and why men struggle over it. The biographical

features ascribed to this "demigod," combined with his substantial power and his intermediate position between lowly spirits and a high god, give Shilluk cosmology an organization different from that of tribal societies without chiefs (cf. Miller 1955, pp. 278-81).

Balandier (1970, pp. 101-6) reminds us that tribal societies generally have semantic categories to refer to what we have called authority (Balandier calls it power). As is the case for so many other social forces operating at the tribal level, the limited rights to govern which exist in these societies are referred to by terms associated with some dangerous substance (guilt and evil are also personified in tribal society) (Beattie 1964, p. 179). The danger associated with the substance derives from the belief that it emanates from sacred beings. Its possession is necessary if valued things are to be accomplished, but too much of it is dangerous. In political terms the danger expresses symbolically the jealous restrictions on authority needed to counterbalance the incessant political divisiveness of tribal life.

Political opposition to legitimate authority is usually also viewed as substance, as the power or essence of witchcraft. As already noted, this is shown by the way the power of witchcraft tends to follow the lines of political stress and conflict. The man who competes too hard for power runs the risk either of being bewitched or of being declared a witch. Hence, the powerful man in tribal society must balance his attempts to control others against the threat of social ostracism and infamy (Evans-Pritchard 1937; Beidelman 1971).

CONCLUSIONS

An attempt has been made in this essay to generalize about tribal political systems. These would seem to offer us the sharpest possible contrast with our own political forms and, hence, to provide us with a useful cross-cultural perspective on the uses of power in human society. The tribal level of society has been the traditional subject matter of anthropology, and the description of its myriad forms surely constitutes one of the lasting contributions of that field. Included within the ethnographic corpus are numerous descrip-

tions, analyses, and syntheses of tribal politics. The
results of these works have been summarized in the preceding pages. It might be useful to recapitulate briefly what has been said.

Two basic processes found in all societies and, indeed, in all social relationships are struggle between
men over choices which will bring change and cooperation
among men with respect to choices needed to maintain
past arrangements. These two processes are the basis
of political action, which involves the use of power,
and administration, which concerns authority.

The public field of politics and administration is
defined by corporate structures. However diverse their
constitution, such structures are universally present
in the societies of man. In the form of lineages, villages, associations, etc., they constitute the stable,
adaptively significant units of tribal society. They
define and create authority and provide the issues and
foci for political struggle.

As a developmental level of political organization,
tribes precede societies with state organization,
whether the latter societies are based on agrarian or
industrial technology. Within the tribal level, sub-
levels can be defined on political as well as other
grounds. One subtype, the band, is largely, though
not totally, depoliticized. This is accomplished by
decentralizing authority and socially repressing conflict through kinship and other reciprocally oriented
institutions.

Between the natural environment and society's technology, intervening variables, such as population density, settlement patterning, and stratification, can be
shown to influence the forms of tribal politics. Yet,
political action is not fully explained in this way. It
seems to be in some degree autonomous.

The underdeveloped nature of administrative structures in tribal society is partially compensated for by
the binding action of simultaneous affiliations in several different groups and by the backing of authority
and normative behavior in ritual. Within prescribed
spheres of social action in tribal society, authority
can be definitive, though even in these spheres it tends
not to be strongly hierarchical in structure. Tribal
societies have law, but it is executed primarily by the

participant members themselves.   These members usually
operate with the diffuse backing of corporate society
and under the threat of personal retaliation.

Despite a cultural screen of harmony and mystical
unity, struggle over basic structural arrangements--
i.e., public policy--is endemic to tribal society. Such
struggles for power significantly influence kinship and
other features of social organization.   Political conflict between autonomous corporate units is thinly
veiled, for all alliance bonding can be shown to have
implicit political goals.   Intertribal warfare is a
normal condition in most cases.   Though intertribal
warfare is stereotyped and any given conflict is transitory, exploitation and domination are nevertheless involved.

The political system in tribal society is a powerful
projector of images onto the cosmological screen.   The
images are distorted and transformed in the process,
but their origin in society is clearly revealed by the
similarity between semantic and social structure.   But
cosmology is dialectically related to the political system, functioning both as a conservative force backing
traditional authority and as an instrument of political
manipulation.

Having boiled tribal politics down to the paltry re-
sidue of a few sentences, one is left with a deep sense
of guilt.   The actual patterns within which the above-
summarized principles operated were rich and vibrant,
and of seemingly endless variation.   Other aspects of
tribal cultures always stood out more prominently than
politics to those who observed them.   The complicated
tribal kinship systems gave birth to anthropology as a
field, and four generations of anthropologists strove
to understand their complexities.   Tribal religious and
ritual life has defied our understanding to this day,
though first-approximation analyses revolutionized our
thinking about the religions of "civilized" society.

The consolation of the anthropologist who concentrates on the political side of tribal life may lie in
the fact that politics have been shown to be the heart
of the tribal body.   The evidence is in, and on that
point it seems clear.   Knowing this can give new perspectives to our studies of kinship and ritual.   It can
also force us to recognize that   tribes were closer to

our own human condition than we had thought.

Far from being an esoteric topic, tribal politics
have broad implications of great importance to the
modern world. They are of utmost relevance to us, just
as they were to the founders of modern social science
(men like Marx, Durkheim, Weber, Spencer, and Maine).
We can only note some of these implications in passing,
clarifying a few issues as we proceed.

We are all aware that "the world today belongs to
nation-states," tribal peoples everywhere having been
subjected to a crushing domination. The nation-state
operates in all spheres: colonialist economic exploitation of resources; imposed political systems, whether
"democratic" or "communistic"; and cultural aggression,
through the promotion of religion, science, life-styles,
etc. Incredibly, in some isolated parts of the world a
gross extermination of tribal peoples is still being
practiced.

Acculturation studies in anthropology have revealed
that political stress within tribal societies necessarily accompanies their contact with nation-states, even
where the dominant power attempts to understand the native culture. It is nevertheless also clear that an
understanding of tribal politics and culture is essential to a truly humanistic approach to the culture contact situation (for summaries of this position, see
Anderson 1972, pp. 79-86; Keesing and Keesing 1971, pp.
346-72; Goodenough 1963). In this regard, we now have
numerous studies of the political processes involved in
tribal acculturation. Apart from their theoretical significance, they have pushed the political anthropologist
into an increasingly activist role in defense of tribal
peoples. Thus, there are pragmatic and political reasons why we need to know about tribal politics.

A second implication of our study has to do with the
claim often made by anthropologists that tribes are simple systems relative to modern societies and, therefore,
fit subjects for discovering what is truly basic in all
human society. No attempt will be made to elaborate
this point, for it has been the underlying theme of the
entire essay. Using tribal society as a contest, it
has been possible to discuss some of the fundamental issues in the social sciences, and perhaps to shed some
light on them. We have discussed such basic questions

as the definition of power and authority, the relationship of power and authority to government, the economic
determinism of politics, the meaning and definition of
law, the origin and functions of warfare, the role of
politics in social development, and the relationship between religion and society. Our treatment has differed
in many ways from the definitions and emphases usually
found in studies of our own political institutions.
Clearly, these concepts provide a useful perspective
which, if applied judiciously, could lead to many insights into our own condition.

A third and final implication which I want to mention requires some discussion. It has to do with the
possibility that tribal politics and culture may represent the "natural" condition of human society and that
they continue to operate in a modern context under the
facade of complex, specialized political forms. In the
hands of popular writers, this becomes an argument for
the existence of a tribal "instinct" that propels modern man into reckless wars today as it did tribal man
in the past. One reason why this view has become current is the relatively recent recognition on the part
of anthropologists that psychobiological characteristics
which distinguish man from the other primates evolved
largely as an adaptation to culture. As Geertz has essayed (1964, 1968), man's need for group living, norms
and morals, symbolizing, and other culturally conditioned activities is so great that without them his life
"would be but buzzing, blooming confusion. . .[and] we
would quite literally not know how to feel" (1964, p.
47).

A general consensus seems to be emerging among physical anthropologists and cultural evolutionists that much
of tribal man's psychobiology was the result of an ancient adaptation to changing sociocultural forms simpler than the tribal life generally portrayed in this
paper. On the basis of the admittedly scattered ar-
chaeological remains that are now available, it appears
that the crucial phase when man's large brain evolved
corresponded to a hunting way of life probably only
roughly similar to that of the band societies known to
us. Perhaps not until 30,000 years ago did more complex tribal forms develop, and then only in a few favorable places. By that time man was fully sapientized,

and a psychology adapted to cultural living must have
been genetically established. Too little time has
elapsed since then for much significant genetic change
in man's emotional and cognitive capacities to have occurred. But during the same period cultures have
changed enormously. As soon as a tribal way of life
evolved, it rapidly pushed hunters and gatherers to
the marginal zones and reigned supreme. Tribal domin-
ance was based on plant and animal domestication, which
began around 10,000 B.C. in the Near East. By 2000 B.C.
horticultural tribes flourished from Indonesia to Ire-
land. In the New World, plants began to be cultivated
around 5000 B.C., and by the time of Christ tribal life
had spread from Peru to the American Southwest (Sahlins
1968).

The tribal way of life, then, is not the "natural"
condition of man. That honor belongs to the hunting
culture, and anthropologists are feverishly investigating hunting societies in an attempt to discover man's
underlying biological and cultural "needs" (Lee and
Devore 1968; Pfeiffer 1969; Washburn 1966; Tiger 1970).
Tribal politics, in fact, might be viewed as man's
first major attempt to control society under "unnatural"
conditions. Compared to that of the hunting way of
life, tribal technology produced larger surpluses of
food, a greater diversity of craft objects, and excess-
es of people. The conflict which resulted from these
conditions required additional control mechanisms. Generally, new wine was put in old bottles, as limited dis-
pensations of authority and alliance bonds based on marriage, ceremony, and the like were elaborated within
tribal administration and politics. The control mechanisms were good enough to give tribes an easy superiority over most hunting societies and to promote a
fairly egalitarian distribution of goods and services
among men. The price for this appears to have been
"a world continually at a low boil of quarreling, feud-
ing, and raiding" (Anderson 1972, p. 56). Further, tribal institutions took on a skewed political slant, for
they had to aid in the all-pervasive requirement of maintaining peace in the face of a continual threat of conflict. As one student put it, "By undertaking this political function, tribal institutions develop particular
forms and particular expressions, different and curious

perhaps, but each and all understandable as diplomatic arrangements for keeping a modicum of peace" (Sahlins 1968, p. 13).

All subsequent levels of political development stand in sharp contrast to the tribal, at least in the substantive features of their political systems. A break in history came with the creation of a definitive, awe-inspiring hierarchy of administrative control--that is, the state. Under the umbrella of the state, and as a direct result of its efficiency, a tremendous increase in wealth of all kinds became available. The effective internal authority of the state allowed ruling men to legally exploit other men. Man learned to domesticate man (Anderson 1972, p. 64). It was as if tribal man's fears about authority had been proven correct.

Worse still, while violent conflict between tribal and similar groups *within* states was put under authoritative control, the exploitative wealth of rulers became the object of a much broadened and less sportive kind of warfare between states. Politics at this new stage lacked even the checks and balances which alliance and ceremony provided in the tribal world. Man learned well the lesson of authority, but the even more critical lesson of power remained.

We are now in a third stage of political development beyond that of our "natural" condition. In the other two stages, we found it difficult to balance our political tendencies with the wealth produced by our developing cultures. This may be our last chance to find a more satisfying and less brutal adaptation.

REFERENCES

Almond, G. A., and Powell, G. B., Jr. 1966. *Comparative politics: a developmental approach.* Boston: Little, Brown.

Anderson, R. T. 1972. *Anthropology: a perspective on man.* Belmont, Calif.: Wadsworth.

Bailey, F. G. 1965. Decisions by consensus in councils and committees. In M. Banton (Ed.), *Political systems and the distribution of power.* New York: Praeger, pp. 1-20.

Balandier, G. 1970. *Political anthropology*. Allen
    Lane: Penguin Press.
Barth, F. 1959. Segmentary opposition and the theory
    of games: a study of pathan organization. *Journal
    of the Royal Anthropological Institute* 89: 5-21.
------. 1965. *Political leadership among Swat Pathans*.
    New York: Athlone Press.
------. 1966. Models of social organization. *Royal
    Anthropological Institute of Great Britain,* Occa-
    sional Paper No. 23.
Beattie, J. 1964. *Other cultures: aims, methods and
    achievements in social anthropology*. New York: Free
    Press.
Beidelman, T. O. 1971. Nuer priest and prophets. In
    T. O. Beidelman (Ed.), *The translation of culture:
    essays to E. E. Evans-Pritchard*. London: Tavistock,
    pp. 375-415.
Belliah, R. N. 1964. Religious evolution. *American
    Sociological Review* 29: 358-74.
Bohannan, L., and Bohannan, P. 1953. *The Tiv of cen-
    tral Nigeria*. London: International African Insti-
    tute.
Bohannan, P. 1963. *Social anthropology*. Holt, Rine-
    hart & Winston.
Buchler, I. R., and Nutini, H. G. 1969. *Game theory
    in the behavioral sciences*. Pittsburgh: University
    of Pittsburgh Press.
Carneiro, R. 1970. A theory of the origin of the
    state. *Science* 169: 733-38.
Chagnon, N. A. 1968. Yanomamö social organization and
    warfare. In M. Fried, M. Harris, and R. Murphey
    (Eds.), *War: the anthropology of armed conflict and
    aggression*. New York: Natural History Press, pp.
    109-59.
Cohen, A. 1969. Political anthropology: the analysis
    of the symbolism of power relations. *Man* 4: 215-35.
Cohen, R., and Middleton, J. 1967. *Comparative politi-
    cal systems*. New York: Natural History Press.
Cohen, Y. A. 1968. *Man in adaptation: the cultural
    present*. Chicago: Aldine.
Colson, E. 1962. *The Plateau Tonga of northern Rho-
    desia: social and religious studies*. Manchester:
    Manchester University Press.

Cunnison, I. G. 1959. *The Luapula peoples of northern Rhodesia: custom and history in tribal politics*. Manchester: Manchester University Press.

Diamond, A. S. 1951. *The evolution of law and order*. London: Watts.

Durkheim, E. 1961. *The elementary forms of the religious life*. New York: Collier Books.

------. 1964. *The division of labor in society*. London: Free Press.

Easton, D. 1959. Political anthropoloty. In B. J. Segel (Ed.), *Biennial Review of Anthropology*. Palo Alto, Calif.: Stanford University Press, pp. 210-62.

Eisenstadt, S. N. 1959. Primitive political systems: a preliminary comparative analysis. *American Anthropologist* 51: 200-220.

------. 1967. *The political system of empires*. New York: Free Press.

Elias, T. O. 1962. *The nature of African customary law*. Manchester: Manchester University Press.

Epstein, A. L. 1968. Power, politics, and leadership: some Central African and Melanesian contrasts. In M. J. Swartz (Ed.), *Local-level politics*. Chicago: Aldine, pp. 53-68.

Evans-Pritchard, E. E. 1937. *Witchcraft, oracles, and magic among the Azande of the Anglo-Egyptian Sudan*. Oxford: Clarendon Press.

------. 1940. *The Nuer*. Oxford: Clarendon Press.

------. 1962. *Nuer religion*. Oxford: Clarendon Press.

------. 1963. *The divine kingship of the Shilluk of the Nilotic Sudan: essays in social anthropology*. New York: Free Press.

Fichter, J. H. 1957. *Sociology*. Chicago: University of Chicago Press.

Firth, R. 1961. History and tradition of Tikopia. *The Polynesian Society*, Memoir 33.

Forde, D. 1964. *Yako studies*. London: Oxford University Press.

Fortes, M. 1945. *The dynamics of clanship among the Tallensi*. London: Oxford University Press.

------. 1953. The structure of unilineal descent groups. *American Anthropologist* 55: 17-41.

Fortes, M. and Evans-Pritchard, E. E. 1940. *African political systems*. London: Oxford University Press.

Fried, M. H.   1967.   *The evolution of political society:*
    an essay in political anthropology.   New York: Random
    House.

Geertz, C.   1964.   The transition to humanity.   In S.
    Tax (Ed.), *Horizons of anthropology.*   Chicago:
    Aldine.

------.   1968.   The impact of the concept of culture on
    the concept of man.   In Y. A. Cohen (Ed.), *Man in*
    adaptation: the cultural present.   Chicago: Aldine.

Gluckman, M.   1965a.   *The ideas in Barotse jurisprud-*
    ence.   New Haven, Conn.:   Yale University Press.

------.   1965b.   *Politics, law, and ritual in tribal*
    society.   Oxford: Basil Blackwell.

Goldschmidt, W.   1951.   Ethics and the structure of so-
    ciety.   *American Anthropologist*   53:   506-24.

Goodenough, W. H.   1963.   *Cooperation in change.*   New
    York: Russell Sage Foundation.

Goody, J.   1962.   *Death, property, and the ancestors.*
    Stanford, Calif.:   Stanford University Press.

Hackenberg, R. A.   1968.   Economic alternatives in arid
    lands: a case study of the Pima and Papago Indians.
    In Y. A. Cohen (Ed.), *Man in adaptation: the cul-*
    tural present.   Chicago: Aldine, pp. 145-52.

Harris, M.   1968.   *The rise of anthropological theory.*
    New York: Crowell.

------.   1971.   *Culture, man, and nature.*   New York:
    Crowell.

Hoebel, E. A.   1954.   *The law of primitive man: a*
    study in comparative legal dynamics.   Cambridge,
    Mass.:   Harvard University Press.

Horton, R.   1962.   The Kala ari world-view: an outline
    and interpretation.   *Africa*   32:   197-220.

------.   1964.   Ritual man in Africa.   *Africa* 34: 85-104.

Keesing, R. M., and Keesing, F. M.   1971.   *New perspec-*
    tives in cultural anthropology.   New York: Holt,
    Rinehart & Winston.

Kroeber, A. L.   1953.   The Yurok: law and custom.   In
    Handbood of the Indians of California.   Berkeley,
    Calif.:   California Book, pp. 20-52.

Leach, E. R. 1954.   *Political systems of Highland Burma.*
    London: London School of Economics and Political
    Science.

------.   1968.   Claude Lévi-Strauss--anthropologist and
    philosopher.   In R. A. Manners and D. Kaplan (Eds.),
    Theory in anthropology.   Chicago: Aldine, pp. 541-51.

Le Clair, E. E., Jr., and Schneider, H. 1968. *Economic anthropology: readings in theory and analysis*. New York: Holt, Rinehart & Winston.

Lee, R. B., and Devore, I. (Eds.), *Man the hunter*. Chicago: Aldine.

Lenski, G. E. 1966. *Power and privilege*. New York: McGraw-Hill.

Lesser, A. 1968. War and the state. In M. Fried, M. Harris, and R. Murphey (Eds.), *War: the anthropology of armed conflict and aggression*. New York: Natural History Press, pp. 92-96.

Lévi-Strauss, C. 1963a. *Structural anthropology*. New York: Basic Books.

------. 1963b. *Totemism*. Boston: Beacon Press.

------. 1969. *The elementary structures of kinship*. Boston: Beacon Press.

Lienhardt, G. 1961 *Divinity and experience: the religion of the Dinka*. Oxford: Clarendon Press.

------. 1963. The Shilluk of the upper Nile. In D. Forde (Ed.), *African worlds*. London: Oxford University Press, pp. 138-63.

Llewellyn, E. N., and Hoebel, E. A. 1961. *The Cheyenne way*. Norman: University of Oklahoma Press.

Lowie, R. H. 1948. Some aspects of political organization among the American aborigines. *Journal of the Royal Anthropological Institute* 78: 11-23.

------. 1961. *Primitive society*. New York: Harper Torchbooks.

Maine, H. S. 1963. *Ancient law*. Boston: Beacon Press.

Mair, L. P. 1965. *An introduction to social anthropology*. Oxford: Clarendon Press.

------. 1969. *Witchcraft*. New York: McGraw-Hill.

Malinowski, B. 1926. *Crime and custom in savage society*. London: Routledge & Kegan Paul.

------. 1965. An anthropological analysis of war. *American Journal of Sociology* 46: 521-50.

------. 1965. *Coral gardens and their magic*. Vol. I. Bloomington: Indiana University Press.

Manners, R. A., and Kaplan, D. 1972. *Culture theory*. Englewood Cliffs, N. J.: Prentice-Hall.

Marshall, L. 1960. Kung Bushman bands. *Africa* 30: 325-55.

------. 1961 Sharing, talking, and giving: relief of social tensions among Kung Bushmen. *Africa* 31: 231-49.

------. 1962. Kung Bushman religious beliefs. *Africa* 32: 221-52.

Marx, K. 1964. *Selected writings in sociology and social philosophy*. Translated and edited by T. B. Bottomore. New York: McGraw-Hill.

Mauss, M. 1967. *The gift*. New York: Norton.

Mead, M. 1940. *Warfare is only an invention--not a biological necessity*. Asia 40: 402-5.

Middleton, J., and Tait, D. (Eds.). 1958. *Tribes without rulers*. London: Routledge & Kegan Paul.

Middleton, J., and Winter, E. (Eds.). 1963. *Witchcraft and sorcery in East Africa*. London: Routledge & Kegan Paul.

Miller, W. B. 1955. Two concepts of authority. *American Anthropologist* 57: 270-89.

Mitchell, J. C. 1956. *The Yao village*. Manchester: Manchester University Press.

Murphy, R. 1957. Intergroup hostility and social cohesion. *American Anthropologist* 59: 1018-35.

Nadel, S. F. 1969. *The foundations of social anthropology*. London: Cohen & West.

Naroll, R. 1964. On ethnic unit classification. *Current Anthropology* 5: 283-312.

Newcomb, W. W., Jr. 1960. Toward an understanding of war. In G. E. Dole and R. L. Carneiro (Eds.), *Essays in the science of culture*. New York: Crowell, pp. 317-36.

Oliver, S. C. 1968. Ecology and cultural continuity as contributing factors in the social organization of the Plains Indians. In Y. A. Cohen (Ed.), *Man in adaptation: the cultural present*. Chicago: Aldine, pp. 243-62.

Orans, M. 1968. Surplus. In Y. A. Cohen (Ed.), *Man in adaptation: the cultural present*. Chicago: Aldine, pp. 204-14.

Otterbein, K. F. 1968. Internal war: cross cultural study. *American Anthropologist* 70: 277-89.

Pfeiffer, J. E. 1969. *The emergence of man*. New York: Harper & Row.

Pospisil, L. 1958. Kapauku Papuans and their law. *Yale University Publications in Anthropology*, No. 54.

Powell, H. A. 1960. Competitive leadership in Trobriand political organizations. *Journal of the Royal Anthropological Institute* 90: 118-45.

Radcliffe-Brown, A. R. 1940. Preface. In M. Fortes and E. E. Evans-Pritchard (Eds.), *African political systems*. London: Oxford University Press.

------. 1952. *Structure and function in primitive society*. Glencoe, Ill.: Free Press.

Rappaport, R. A. 1968. *Pigs for the ancestors: ritual in the ecology of a New Guinea people*. New Haven, Conn.: Yale University Press.

Redfield, R. 1967. Primitive law. In P. Bohannan (Ed.) *Law and warfare*. New York: Natural History Press, pp. 3-24.

Sahlins, M. D. 1958. *Social stratification in Polynesia*. Seattle: University of Washington Press.

------. 1961. The segmentary lineage: an organization of predatory expansion. *American Anthropologist* 63: 332-45.

------. 1964. Culture and environment. In S. Tax (Ed.), *Horizons of anthropology*. Chicago: Aldine, pp. 132-47.

------. 1968. *Tribesmen*. Englewood Cliffs, N. J.: Prentice-Hall.

Salisbury, R. F. 1966. Politics and shell-money finance in New Britain. In M. J. Swartz, V. W. Turner, and A. Tuden (Eds.), *Political anthropoloty*. Chicago: Aldine, pp. 113-28.

Schapera, I. 1956. *Government and politics in tribal societies*. London: Watts.

Service, E. 1962. *Primitive social organization*. New York: Random House.

------. 1971. *Cultural evolutionism: theory in practice*. New York: Holt, Rinehart & Winston.

Sharp, R. L. 1958. People without politics: systems of political control and bureaucracy in human societies. In V. F. Ray (Ed.), *American ethnological society*. Seattle: University of Washington Press.

------. 1968. Steel axes for Stone Age Australians. In Y. A. Cohen (Ed.), *Man in adaptation: the cultural present*. Chicago: Aldine, pp. 82-93.

Shepardson, M. 1967. The traditional authority system of the Navajos. In R. Cohen and J. Middleton (Eds.), *Comparative political systems*. New York: Natural History Press, pp. 143-54.

Smith, M. G. 1956. On segmentary lineage systems. *Journal of the Royal Anthropological Institute* 86: 39-80.

------. 1960. Government in Zazzau, 1800-1950. *International African institute*. London: Oxford University Press.

------. 1965. *Lecture notes on traditional political systems*. Los Angeles: University of California at Los Angeles.

------. 1966. A structural approach to comparative politics. In D. Easton (Ed.), *Varieties of political theory*. Englewood Cliffs, N. J.: Prentice-Hall, pp. 113-28.

------. 1968. Political organization. *International Encyclopedia of the Social Sciences* 12: 193-202.

Southall, A. 1956. *Alur society: a study in processes and types of domination*. Cambridge: Heffer.

------. 1965. A critique of the typology of states and political systems. In M. Banton (Ed.), *Political systems and the distribution of power*. A. S. A. Monographs, Vol. 2. New York: Praeger, pp. 113-37.

Stevenson, R. F. 1968. *Population density and state formation in Sub-Saharan Africa*. New York: Columbia University Press.

Steward, J. 1955. *Theory of culture change*. Urbana: University of Illinois Press.

Suttles, W. 1968. Variation in habitat and culture on the northwest coast. In Y. A. Cohen (Ed.), *Man in adaptation: the cultural present*. Chicago: Aldine, pp. 93-106.

Swartz, M. J. 1968. Introduction. In M. J. Swartz (Ed.), *Local-level politics*. Chicago: Aldine.

Thomas, E. M. 1965. *The harmless people*. New York: Vintage Books.

Tiger, L. 1970. *Men in groups*. New York: Vintage Books.

Tuden, A. Swartz, M. J., and Turner, V. W. 1966. Introduction. In M. J. Swartz, V. W. Turner, and A.Tuden (Eds.), *Political anthropology*. Chicago: Aldine, pp. 1-41.

Turner, V. W. 1957. Schism and continuity in an African: a study of Ndembu village life. *The Rhodes-Livingstone Institute of Northern Rhodesia*. Manchester: Manchester University Press.

------. 1966. Ritual aspects of conflict control in African micro-politics. In M. J. Swartz, V. W. Turner, and A. Tuden (Eds.), *Political anthropology*. Chicago: Aldine, pp. 239-40.

Uberoi, J. P. 1971. *Singh Politics of the Kula Ring*.
Manchester: Manchester University Press.

Van Velsen, J. 1964. *The politics of kinship: a
study in social manipulation among the lakeside
Tonga of Nyasaland*. Manchester: Manchester University Press.

Vayda, A. P. 1961. Expansion and warfare among Swidden
agriculturalists. *American Anthropologist* 63: 346-58.

------. 1967. Maori warfare. In P. Bohannan (Ed.),
Law and warfare. New York: Natural History Press,
pp. 359-80.

------. 1968. Hypotheses about functions of war. In
M. Fried, M. Harris, and R. Murphey (Eds.), *War:
the anthropology of armed conflict and aggression*.
New York: Natural History Press, pp. 85-91.

Wallace, A. F. 1971. *Administrative forms of social
organization*. Reading, Mass.: Addison-Wesley,
Modlue 9, pp, 1-12.

Warner, W. L. 1937. *A black civilization*. New York:
Harper & Row.

Washburn, S. L. (Ed.). 1966. *Social life of early man*.
Chicago: Aldine.

Wax, M. 1968. Religion and magic. In J. A. Clifton
(Ed.), *Introduction to cultural anthropology*. Boston:
Houghton Mifflin.

Weber, M. 1964. *The theory of social and economic
organization*. New York: Free Press.

White, L. 1949. *The science of culture*. New York:
Farrar, Straus and Cudahy.

------. 1959. *The evolution of culture*. New York:
McGraw-Hill.

Wilson, H. C. 1958. Regarding the causes of Mundurucu
warfare. *American Anthropologist* 60: 1193-96.

Legitimacy as a 9
Base of Social Influence

H. Andrew Michener and Martha R. Burt

Numerous writers have observed that the exercise of influence is based in some resource, such as competence
or wealth (Blau 1964; French and Raven 1959; Jacobson
1972; Schopler 1965, March 1966). With competence, one
person can influence another because his skills facilitate the other's goals; with wealth, he can exchange
money or materials for compliance from the second person.

Another base of influence is *legitimacy,* in which
one person complies with another's directives because
the influencer has a "right" to ask for compliance and
the target has an "obligation" to obey (Raven and Kruglanski 1970; Simon, Smithberg, and Thompson 1970). Legitimacy differs from other bases of influence because
it resides entirely in the beliefs and attitudes of
group members. If shifts occur in these attitudes, the
prerogatives enjoyed by a person will undergo change.
Many other influence bases, such as competence or wealth,
are personal resources and can be moved from one group
to another. But legitimacy is group-specific. It operates as a base of influence only within a designated
group, and it cannot normally be transferred to other
settings.

A military officer, for example, may wield considerable influence based on legitimating expectations. Within the context of his military unit, he may control important decisions and achieve compliance to his orders.
But his status as an officer would, in and of itself,

provide scant basis for influence in civilian settings.
Moreover, if he retired from the service he could no
longer issue orders and expect compliance from members
of his original unit. Legitimacy originates in specific groups and functions only in those contexts.

This paper discusses legitimacy as a determinant of
social influence. When French and Raven (1959) addressed this topic fifteen years ago, it had received
considerable attention from theoreticians but little
from empirical researchers. Although broad gaps still
prevail in the data on legitimacy and influence, more
information exists today than in years past. The present paper refines the concept of legitimacy and reviews recent social psychological research on social
influence. Emphasis is given to such outcomes as the
frequency and intensity of influence attempts, the effectiveness of influence attempts, and the emergence
of resistance against influence attempts.

ENDORSEMENT AND NORMATIVITY AS COMPONENTS OF LEGITIMACY

Since legitimacy is a collective construct, most of the
empirical research treats influence in the context of
groups *whose members share common goals*. These groups
exhibit hierarchical patterns, with certain members
exercising greater influence and control over the decisions that must be made as the group pursues collective goals. For simplicity, the present review adopts
the convention that influence flows from someone in a
superordinate or high-status (HS) position to someone
in a subordinate or low-status (LS) position. That is,
HS influences LS. While influence in natural settings
is not merely a one-way proposition--LS usually influences HS just as HS influences LS--the present treatment regards HS as the influencer in a formal hierarchical structure. Thus, HS becomes synonymous with the
source of an influence attempt and LS with the *target*
of the attempt. Although both HS and LS may draw on
legitimacy as a base of influence (see Tedeschi,
Schlenker, and Lindskold 1972), the invocation of prerogatives by HS in the context of "authority" relationships seems particularly clear.

Theoretical treatments of legitimacy differ in scope

and form, but one distinction recurs frequently in
the literature on legitimacy and influence. Various
writers (French and Raven 1959; Jackson 1964) have dis-
criminated between the *power of a person* occupying the
HS position and the *powers of the position* itself.   In
other words, legitimacy (or illegitimacy) can attach to
a person occupying a role, to the role itself, or to
both. Often these are distinct in the minds of group
members. Citizens in a monarchy may see the kingship,
for instance, as a legitimate position yet view the
king himself as a pretender to the throne.

   This is a useful distinction because the empirical
literature on legitimacy divides naturally along these
lines. Following conventional practice, the term *endorsement* will be used to denote attitudes of group
members toward the exercise of influence by a *given HS
person*. Specifically, endorsement indicates their satisfaction with HS's use of his power over collective
decisions, their generalized support for HS's policies
and leadership, and their willingness to have him continue in a position of influence within the group.
Since these attitudes can change, endorsement is a variable and might affect HS's capacity to exercise influence.

   Endorsement is distinguished from *normativity,* which
refers to influence exercised via the invocation of organizational rules. These rules designate the reciprocal prerogatives and obligations of social positions in
an organization; they stipulate procedures for making
decisions, solving problems, and settling disputes. As
with endorsement, these rules are rooted in collective
attitudes and beliefs, and thus are subject to change.
Normativity is a variable because organizational rules
differ in several important respects. Some rules pertain directly to the achievement of organizational goals,
but others do not. Some are mildly sanctioned in the
event of noncompliance, but others are severely sanctioned. Some are highly accepted by LS members, but
others fail the test of consensus. In other words, the
sentiments of LS members regarding behavior--the very
basis of normative influence--are highly differentiated.
HS's ability to gain compliance via normative invocation
will fluctuate with these factors.

Throughout this paper, normativity and endorsement will increasingly emerge as different concepts. Although. both are components of legitimacy, they differ in their impact on social influence, compliance, and political opposition. The effectiveness of HS's influence based on endorsement differs from the effectiveness of attempts based on normativity, and the form of these attempts may differ as well.

Because of these differences, endorsement and normativity receive separate treatment. Beginning with endorsement, this paper reviews several theories that treat the origins of endorsement accorded a formal leader and that hypothesize consequences of endorsement for social influence. When these theoretical expectations are compared with empirical findings, several interesting discrepancies emerge, and these in turn lead to a reformulation of endorsement's role in social influence processes.

Next, this paper considers normativity as a base of influence. It presents a conceptual framework describing the dimensions of normativity that affect compliance, and then it reviews existing empirical literature. The resulting portrait of normativity includes some unanticipated features that highlight the differences between normativity and endorsement.

Finally, this paper delineates open avenues for future research on endorsement and normativity with respect to influence, compliance, and opposition.

ENDORSEMENT

Endorsement is an attitude held by LS members in a hierarchical group which indexes their satisfaction or dissatisfaction with HS's exercise of influence and control over group decisions. At an operational level, one can measure endorsement in various ways. The following scale, which includes items that intercorrelate highly, has been used in several studies (Michener and Burt 1972a; Michener and Burt 1972b; Michener and Lawler 1972; Michener and Tausig 1971):

(1) How satisfied are you with HS's use of his power in arriving at group decisions?

(2) How satisfied are you with HS's performance in
     directing the group?
(3) To what extent do you support or oppose HS?
(4) How willing would you be to have HS head the
     group again?
(5) Consider the person occupying the HS position.
     How legitimate is it for him to occupy this
     position?

Other measures with similar content appear in related
studies (e.g., Julian, Hollander, and Regula 1969). Experience indicates that the above items respond to similar factors and can be answered readily by persons in
LS positions.

The level of endorsement accorded HS is a variable
--it can rise or fall depending on circumstances. An
HS leader may be in favor one time, out of favor the
next. To understand why these fluctuations occur, one
must consider some theories of endorsement.

Theories of Endorsement

Various writers (Blau 1964; Hollander 1960; Homans 1961)
have discussed endorsement. Although their treatments
differ in several respects, they share the basic postulate that endorsement is *earned* by HS. According to
these theorists, endorsement accrues to HS on the basis
of his performance, especially his competence and equitableness. Competence is paramount--HS earns and keeps
endorsement by demonstrating his ability to deliver valued outcomes (success) to the group. Equitable behavior by HS involves a concern for the welfare of group
members, as shown by distributing rewards in a "fair"
way within the group. Homans (1961) states this suc-
cinctly: "If [HS's] chief external job is to be successful, his chief internal one is to be just" (p. 295).

Various theories treat endorsement as a credit com-
modity that can be "spent" by HS in the exercise of influence. They maintain that a highly endorsed HS enjoys a large "credit balance" which he can disburse when
influencing the group's LS members, while a poorly endorsed HS lacks the resources to achieve compliance
from LS persons.

The view that endorsement is earnable through performance and spendable on influence has been enunciated

most clearly by Homans (1961, chap. 14). In this perspective, HS uses his skills to deliver scarce, valued
outcomes that LS members cannot readily achieve by other means. Unable to repay HS in outcomes of equal value, the LS members reciprocate by giving him endorsement (or, in Homans' terminology, "credit" and "esteem").
Homans describes the relationship between HS and LS
group members in creditor-debtor terms.

> At least for the time being they cannot make [HS] a
> return in kind, as fair exchange would require, and
> so they are his debtors. True, they do render him
> [endorsement]. . . . But from this point of view
> [endorsement] is a token of unpaid debt: it is a
> promissory note. What it promises is that at some
> later occasion they will redeem the pledge by doing
> what the creditor asks them, by submitting, that is,
> to his authority (Homans 1961, p. 298).

Through this mechanism, HS can consolidate his position
within the group. By using endorsement-based influence
to orchestrate collective efforts, HS can recurringly
provide valued outcomes. He expends endorsement when
influencing members, but he receives renewed endorsement as the group succeeds through his efforts. By
this cyclical process, Homans suggests, HS can maintain
(and even bolster) his hegemony.
    Another theorist, Hollander (1958, 1960, 1964), dis-
cusses endorsement in terms similar to those of Homans.
In Hollander's view, both competence and conformity
(especially conformity to procedural rules and equity
norms) lead to endorsement. Endorsement in turn provides a basis for influence:

> Briefly, the essential point. . .is that the leader's
> influence depends on how competent others in the
> group believe he is in helping the group achieve its
> goals, and his conformity to the group's normative
> expectations is a sign of his motivation to belong
> to the group. . . . Thus, a person gains credits,
> in terms of the positive impressions held by relevant
> others, which he may then draw on in exerting influ-
> ence, particularly regarding deviations from nor-
> mative expectancies (Hollander and Julian 1970,
> p. 36).

Thus, Hollander (who uses the term *idiosyncrasy credit* rather than endorsement) espouses a position similar to that of Homans, although he stresses conformity and deviance to a greater extent. Hollander sees endorsement as providing a basis not only for influence by HS but also for resistance to counterinfluence from LS. A highly endorsed HS could readily veto suggestions from other members and deviate from group norms of minor importance.

Another theorist, Blau (1964), also sees endorsement as earnable and concurs with Homans and Hollander that competence and equity are the bases for its acquisition. Blau writes:

> The members of the group receive social approval in exchange for conformity and [their] contribution to the group (1964, p. 259).

Endorsement based on competence and equity leads to influence:

> [LS members'] joint obligations for [HS's] contributions to their welfare and their common approval of his fairness, reinforced by their consensus concerning the respect his abilities deserve, generate group pressures that enforce compliance with his directives (1964, p. 202).

Blau construes endorsement as a function of competence and equity, but, in contrast to Homans and Hollander, he does not see it as *directly* spendable on influence (in the sense of a direct exchange of endorsement for compliance). Rather, he suggests that pressures on LS from *other LS members* enforce compliance to HS's orders because the group as a whole values the services and outcomes that HS provides.

Empirical Research on Sources of Endorsement

In general, empirical evidence substantiates the hypothesis that HSs earn endorsement via competence and equitableness. The following review of the literature covers some major findings on the sources of endorsement.

Collective Success-Failure. Research indicates that HS's endorsement rises under collective success and drops under failure, provided that LS members care about the outcome and see HS as responsible for the result.

In a study by Julian, Hollander, and Regula (1969), subjects discussed a legal case history and decided how best to defend the person described. A group spokesman was selected to defend the case before a jury panel in the adjacent room. In those instances where the HS spokesman achieved a verdict of "acquitted" (success), his endorsement from LS members was greater than in the instances where he obtained a "guilty" verdict (failure).

Studies by Michener and Lawler (1972), Michener and Burt (1972a), and Suchner (1972) corroborate this finding. Although these studies differed in format, in each case HS controlled group decisions or invested collective resources. His efforts on the group's behalf resulted in either success or failure. Findings from each study show that the successful outcome led to significantly greater endorsement of HS than did the unsuccessful outcome.

Competence. Another factor affecting endorsement is competence on tasks that pertain to group goals. The higher HS's perceived competence, the more endorsement LS accords him.

Two of the empirical studies cited above varied competence in their designs. Julian, Hollander, and Regula (1969) *manipulated* HS's competence independently of collective success-failure and found that competence contributed heavily to HS's endorsement. Michener and Lawler (1972) *measured* competence and determined that perceptions of HS's competence actually mediated the effect of success-failure on endorsement. The greater HS's competence, the more endorsement he received. Two other studies (Suchner 1972; Wahrman and Pugh 1972) also manipulated competence and obtained similar results. Higher competence produced higher endorsement.

Another study (detailed in Hollander and Julian 1970) employed hypothetical descriptions of HS leaders that included information on competence. Subjects who received information that HS was a "good performer on group activity" indicated more willingness to have him as a fellow group member and to let him serve as spokes-

man than did subjects who believed HS was a poor performer.

In sum, perceived competence affects the endorsement
accorded HS. Not only is it a strong determinant, but
it also mediates the impact of success-failure on endorsement, at least in part.

Equitableness. Another source of endorsement is
HS's fairness. Group members are concerned with HS's
fairness and group-orientation, and they prefer a leader who cares about collective interests rather than
about his own selfish or partisan interests. When HS
manifests strong motivation to serve the group, LS members anticipate that he will continue to work in their
behalf.

Empirical research indicates that endorsement responds to equitable behavior by HS, as well as to other signs of HS's motivation to serve the group. Michener
and Lawler (1972) found that when HS distributed rewards
in a manner favorable to LS members rather than to himself, his endorsement rose to high levels. But when he
retained the bulk of the payoffs for himself, endorsement fell. This effect of payoff distribution on endorsement proved to be mediated by LS's perceptions of
HS's equitableness.

In their study using hypothetical situations, Hollander and Julian (1970) manipulated HS's apparent interest in his group. They informed some subjects that
HS was interested in group members and group activities;
for other subjects, they omitted any mention of this information. Results indicated that HS received higher
endorsement when the hypothetical descriptions explicitly attributed these interests to him than when they
omitted mention of them.

Corroboration for these findings comes from research
by Michener and Lyons (1972). In this study, LS subjects received messages from another LS member indicating either support for HS and his policies or opposition to HS's regime, depending on experimental treatment. These communications affected the endorsement
that the subjects themselves accorded HS, but the important point is that subjects construed these messages
in terms of equity and assumed that the other LS's satisfaction (or dissatisfaction) arose from HS's fairness
(unfairness) in distributing rewards among group members.

Deviance and the Loss of Endorsement. Several studies on the loss (rather than the acquisition) of endorsement have shown that deviation from collective
norms leads to reduced support. If HS violates group
norms (such as procedural norms or expectations regarding equity), the endorsement he receives from LS will
diminish. Norm-violating behavior has this effect on
endorsement because it fosters the impression that HS
lacks commitment and concern for the group, that he is
self-oriented rather than group-oriented, and that he
may prove unreliable in the future. LS may therefore
hesitate to endorse HS and may feel that some other member should control the important group decisions.

Studies by Wiggins, Dill, and Schwartz (1965), Alvarez (1968), and Suchner (1972) have all shown that
HS's endorsement deteriorates when he deviates from
collective norms. In each of these studies the LS subjects had ample evidence that HS could perform well if
he wanted to, which means that they probably interpreted
his deviance as willful (rather than as due to incompetence). Interestingly, the study by Suchner (1972) also
demonstrates that the *consequences* of HS's deviance are
important to endorsement. LS members may be willing to
continue their endorsement of HS in the face of deviant
behavior, provided he facilitates attainment of the
group's goals. Should the group fail as a result of
HS's deviance, however, endorsement will plummet.

A similar result appears in the study by Michener
and Tausig (1971), in which an HS member made collective decisions binding on the LS members. In one experimental condition, LS members perceived that HS was
usurping control (giving his own preferences too much
weight) in an effort to improve the group's deteriorating fortunes; in another condition, HS stayed within
the established normative guidelines. In both cases,
the group continued to founder regardless of HS's efforts. Results show that LS members granted HS less
endorsement when he seized additional control than when
he followed procedural rules. These findings parallel
those of an earlier study (Horwitz 1963), which also
provides evidence regarding the effects of usurpation.
In this situation, a teacher (HS) arbitrarily reduced
the decision-making prerogatives of his students and
augmented his own power at their expense. This de-

viant act generated great dissatisfaction and hostility among the students (LS).

   Summary. Overall, empirical studies on the sources
of endorsement substantiate the theoretical expectations of Homans, Blau, and Hollander. Endorsement stems
from collective success, from competence attributed to
HS, from the belief that HS shares a concern for the
group's goals, and from equitable behavior by HS. Similarly, HS's endorsement drops whenever he engages in
deviant behavior that has serious negative consequences
for the group or that implies that he does not care for
the collectivity's welfare.

Empirical Research on Consequences of Endorsement

If legitimacy truly serves as a basis of influence, and
if HS's endorsement is appropriately construed as a component of legitimacy, then endorsement should affect
the processes of social influence within any given hierarchical group. Endorsement might affect such outcomes
as HS's ability to gain compliance from LS members, his
proclivity to resist influence from LS members, and his
choice of influence techniques.

   Although the empirical research on consequences of
endorsement is much thinner than that on the sources of
endorsement, some data exist on each of these issues.
The following review discusses available findings.

   Effects of Endorsement on LS's Compliance. Does endorsement serve as a basis for influence? As mentioned
earlier, several theorists (Homans 1961; Hollander 1960,
1964) have suggested that endorsement does function as
a base, in the sense that a highly endorsed HS leader
will have more success in gaining LS's compliance to
his directives than a poorly endorsed HS member. Despite these theoretical arguments, the existing empirical evidence does *not* support the hypothesis that endorsement confers influence. Several studies report
negative findings.

   Two early studies by Raven and French (1958a, 1958b)
attempted to manipulate endorsement by varying the
route through which HS achieved a position of formal
leadership. In both studies, members of laboratory
work groups elected one of their number to serve as HS.
In some groups, this elected HS continued without in-

terruption in the supervisor's role; in other groups,
the elected person was displaced by a new HS even
though the other members of the group were not consulted. This experimental manipulation affected the
LS's sentiments regarding HS, and the LS members accorded more endorsement to HS when she was elected than
when she usurped office. However, these studies yielded
mixed results with respect to compliance. Data from
Raven and French (1958b) indicate that when HS issued
orders to regulate the speed of production in the group,
she failed to receive more compliance when she was elected than when she lacked formal elective support. Raven
and French (1958a) report marginally significant differences in compliance as a function of endorsement.
In other words, one of these studies shows no effect of
endorsement on compliance, contrary to theoretical expectations, while the other demonstrates only marginal
effects.

A related study by French and Snyder (1959) also indicates no effect, although the measure of endorsement
differs somewhat from the standard pattern. Subjects
were members of aircraft maintenance squadrons led by
noncommissioned officers. Results from two experiments
indicate that the effectiveness of HS's attempts to
change LS's opinions and to regulate productivity did
not increase as a function of endorsement (where the
measure of endorsement tapped how much authority HS
exercised over the men he supervised).

A study by Michener and Burt (1972a) provides stronger evidence that endorsement does not confer influence.
This study established a hierarchical situation in which
HS sent messages to LS members, directing them to contribute tax payments to support group goals. A questionnaire obtained measures of endorsement before HS
levied these demands, and care was taken to isolate the
effects of endorsement from those of normativity (position power) and the coercive power available to HS. The
results show that endorsement does *not* confer influence.
LS subjects did not comply with HS's tax demands to a
greater extent when they accorded him a high level of
endorsement than when they gave him a low level of endorsement.

Overall, the existing data refute the hypothesis that
endorsement, a component of legitimacy, leads to influ-

ence. This lack of a causal relationship is represented
in figure 9.1 by the *absence* of an arrow from endorsement to compliance. Until more research becomes available (and certainly more would be desirable), the provisional verdict is that endorsement per se fails as a
basis for compliance, theoretical arguments notwith-
standing.

Why might theorists have expected that endorsement
would serve as a base of influence? This expectation
probably arose because endorsement often covaries with
other sentiments, such as liking and perceived competence, and these *are* bases of influence. Numerous
studies have shown that competence leads to compliance
(e.g., Bachman, Bowers, and Marcus 1968; Evan and Zelditch 1961; French and Snyder 1959). Data have also
shown that likable persons are generally more effective
in exerting influence than are less likable persons
(see, e.g., Lott and Lott 1972; Walster and Abrahams
1972). As Blau (1964) has noted, endorsement is not
the same as liking or competence, although perceived
competence is an important determinant of endorsement.
Group members might recognize that a well-liked member

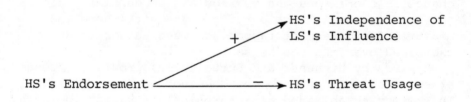

LS's Compliance to
HS's Directives

Note: (a) Solid lines indicate observed causal effects.
        (b) The absence of an arrow from HS's endorsement
            to LS's compliance reflects evidence that no
            causal effect exists.

FIGURE 9.1. Empirically Observed Effects of Endorsement
on Influence Variables

would make a poor leader, or that a highly competent
person should not be endorsed if his motivation and his
commitment to the group are in doubt. Competence and
liking may confer influence, but pure endorsement (a
component of legitimacy) apparently does not.

*Effects of Endorsement on HS's Independence from
Influence.* If endorsement does not affect LS's compliance with HS's directives, does it affect other aspects
of social influence?

Interestingly, some data suggest that highly endorsed HS members may *resist* influence more vigorously
than poorly endorsed HS members. Studies by Dittes
and Kelley (1956) and by Julian and Steiner (1961) show
that highly endorsed subjects reject the (incorrect)
judgments of their peers more than do moderately endorsed subjects. In these experiments, endorsement
feedback assumed the form of (fictitious) ratings of
perceived competence and value as a group member. Subjects who received high endorsement (or "acceptance")
from other members demonstrated greater independence
from the group's consensual judgment than did subjects
receiving average endorsement. Although none of these
groups included a formal hierarchy, the endorsement
ratings clearly heightened independence and resistance
to influence from others.

A more recent study (Hollander, Julian, and Sorrentino 1969) established a hierarchical structure in which
HS held ultimate responsibility for group decisions regarding programs to deal with urban problems. He enjoyed the legitimate right to veto suggestions from LS
members if he construed their ideas as incorrect or
tendentious. In one experimental condition, where HS
was elected to office by a vote of all members, he received endorsement feedback indicating either that he
was the "top choice" for the HS job or that he was only
the "third choice" (out of a possible twelve). Results
indicate that highly endorsed HS members were more
prone to resist influence and to veto recommendations
from LS members. Although these results are weak statistically (probably due to restricted variability in
the endorsement variable), they lend further credence
to the hypothesis that high endorsement produces greater independence as well as resistance to influence
from LS.

Obviously, further research is needed on this issue
before firm conclusions can be drawn. Figure 9.1 pro-
visionally indicates that endorsement affects HS's independence, but efforts should be made to replicate the
basic effect (i.e., that endorsement does in fact lead
to independence) and to separate the effects of endorsement from those of HS's self-attributed competence
(which may also foster resistance to influence).

Endorsement and the Use of Coercive Social Control.
Theorists have suggested that political attitudes, such
as endorsement and trust, affect the influence techniques used by HS authorities. Most explicit on this
point is Gamson (1968), who proposes that the degree of
"trust" between HS and LS will determine HS's preferences among social control techniques. Gamson (1968,
pp. 178-83) hypothesizes that HSs in a positive trust
relationship with LS members will prefer persuasion as
an influence technique, that HSs in a neutral trust relationship will opt for utilitarian rewards to influence LSs, and that HSs in a negative trust ("alienated")
relationship will interdict LSs' access to resources
and may use coercion to constrain LSs' behavior.

A study by Michener and Burt (1972b) provides data
relevant to Gamson's hypothesis on the use of coercive
power by HS. Although Gamson refers to political trust,
not endorsement, in making predictions regarding the use
of coercion, these sentiments are closely allied. Previously unreported data collected by Michener and his
associates have shown that political trust (as measured
by the trust-orientation scale detailed in Michener and
Zeller 1972) correlates substantially with endorsement.
Endorsed authorities are trusted authorities, which suggests that Gamson's predictions regarding HS's use of
coercive power may apply to endorsement as well as to
trust.

Michener and Burt (1972b) showed that HS subjects
modulated their use of threats and punishments as a
function of endorsement. HS subjects, responsible for
raising the resources to keep their group above the
"break-even point" on a collective task, levied tax demands against LS members. These tax payments cut into
LSs' individual interests, but HS could (at his discretion) threaten to reduce the LSs' personal profits if
they did not comply with his demands. Through simu-

lated feedback over a series of trials, HS received a
substantial level of compliance, but two LS members deviated from his demands, one of them seriously. HS also
received messages indicating either a high or a low level of endorsement from the LS members. Results show
that, in line with Gamson's predictions, HS used larger
threats to bolster compliance when he received a low
level of endorsement than when he received a high level.
Moreover, HS enforced these threats with greater punishments directed at noncomplying LSs under low endorsement.
Questionnaire data suggest that disendorsement heightened HS's willingness to use the prime means at his dis-
posal--threats and punishments--to increase compliance
and protect collective outcomes from erosion.

   This relationship between endorsement and the use of
threats is represented by the causal arrow in figure
9.1. Against the backdrop of Gamson's theory, the findings by Michener and Burt on HS's use of coercion are
interesting, and they should encourage further research
along related lines.

   Summary. Empirical studies on the consequences of
endorsement, while sparse, permit some provisional conclusions. In accord with Hollander's hypothesis, endorsement appears to heighten HS's propensity to resist
influence from LS members. It also affects HS's use of
coercion, along the lines suggested by Gamson's theory.
Surprisingly, however, endorsement per se apparently
does not serve as a basis for compliance-gaining, and
this refutes theoretical expections.

NORMATIVITY

The introductory section of this paper decomposed legitimacy into two elements, *endorsement* and *normativity*.
Endorsement refers to LS's attitudes regarding HS's control over collective decisions and outcomes, and it
therefore applies to a specific *person*. In contrast,
normativity refers to legitimate prerogatives residing
in a *position*. Social groups establish rules (or
"norms") that, in varying degrees, regulate the behavior of their members. These norms designate the rights
and obligations of members vis-à-vis each other. Rules
can remain relatively unchanged even though members come
and go.

A group's rules are analogous to those of a game. In
any group (as in a game), certain behaviors are prescribed and others are proscribed. Sancticns may attend
nonconformity to the stipulated rights and obligations.
When a person enters a group, he usually agrees (explicitly or implicitly) to abide by the rules. Groups differ, of course, in the extent to which their rules are
formalized and explicit; rules may range from highly
codified to very amorphous. Both in groups and in games,
participants will be expected to abide by the norms,
and failure to do so may result in sanction, such as anger or ostracism.

For present purposes, the important point about rules
is that they *provide a basis for influence.* One group
member may invoke certain rules as a means of achieving
desired behaviors from another member. This technique
of normative invocation achieves compliance, when it
does, because members value the social approval and continued group membership contingent upon compliance.
Typically, normative invocation is used not only by HS
to gain compliance from LS, but also by LS to gain compliance from HS. In fact, several studies have investigated normative invocation by LS (e.g.,Berkowitz 1969;
Schopler and Bateson 1965), and this technique may be
the *major* means of influence available to lower status
persons (who lack other resources). For consistency,
however, the present treatment will continue with the
convention that HS is the source of influence and LS
the target.

Earlier approaches (French and Raven 1959; Raven and
Kruglanski 1970; Simon, Smithberg, and Thompson 1970)
define legitimate power as *HS's right to ask LS for compliance and LS's obligation to obey.* This definition
obviously pertains to influence via normative invocation, because it treats influence as based in the expectations held by group members. These expectations
cover both the scope of the behaviors prescribed for
LS and the sanctions contingent upon their performance.

Many treatments of legitimate power imply that compliance to normative invocation is automatic: once HS
invokes a norm, LS is assumed to obey mechanically.
This approach, however, fails to note that invoked norms
are not always followed and that deviant or revolutionary activity can occur. Peabody (1964), in a field

study of welfare, educational, and police organizations,
reports that between 35 percent and 60 percent of the
respondents (depending on the organization) described
instances where supervisors had attempted an unacceptable exercise of authority. The reactions to such attempts ranged from reluctant compliance and passive
resistance to mobilization of opposition among co-
workers and efforts to go over the supervisor's head.
The point, then, is that compliance to invoked norms
must be treated as problematic. Any treatment of legitimate power must acknowledge that compliance occurs
frequently, but not always. The issue, therefore, is,
Under what conditions does HS achieve compliance to his
normatively based demands?

Properties of Norms

A brief analysis of norms will help to identify the conditions determining LS's compliance to HS's normative
demands. Norms differ in their properties and, as the
enpirical evidence cited below will document, these properties affect compliance and resistance to demands.
    A useful approach to the description of norms has
been advanced by March (1954) and, in a more elaborate
form, by Jackson (1960, 1964, 1965). One can describe
a norm in terms of two concepts: a behavioral dimension (such as that represented by the horizontal line
in figure 9.2) refers to the behavior governed by the
norm; an evaluative dimension (the vertical line in
figure 9.2) designates the positive or negative sanction expected for each level of behavior. A norm, then,
is simply a *function* indicating what sanction will attend each level of behavior. In figure 9.2, the curves
labeled norm 1 and norm 2 illustrate two possible norms.
    Suppose that norm 1 governs LS's behavior in a work
group. The behavioral dimension might refer to LS's
productive activity, as indexed by units produced per
hour. The shape of norm 1 indicates that LS should expect to receive varying amounts of approval (or disapproval) contingent upon his production. Moderate
levels of production will elicit strong approval from
the group, while extremely low or extremely high levels
will elicit disapproval.
    Empirically, how can one ascertain the shape of a

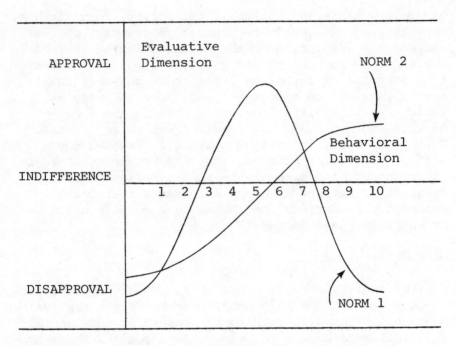

FIGURE 9.2.   Descriptive Model of Social Norms

given norm in a specific group? Since norms are based
in expectations, they can be described by *aggregating*
the responses from all group members to questions about
how much they approve or disapprove various amounts of
the behavior under consideration. Individuals may give
different responses, of course, but norms such as those
in figure 9.2 are attributes of collectivities, and
they require aggregate measures.

   This model of social norms illuminates several properties that affect one's ability to gain compliance
through normative invocation. As reflected in figure
9.2, norms differ in terms of (*a*) the range of tolerable behavior, (*b*) the intensity of positive or negative sanctions, and (*c*) the level of consensus among
group members. The *range* of tolerable behavior simply
designates those levels of behavior that meet with approval. For norm 1 (in figure 9.2), this range is
three to seven units of behavior; for norm 2, the range
is six units or more. The *intensity* of a norm refers
to the magnitude of the (positive or negative) sanctions contingent upon the behavior. Norm 1 is more in-

tense than norm 2 because it is "steeper" and involves greater amounts of approval and disapproval. The third property, *consensus*, indicates the extent to which group members agree about a norm's shape. Some norms will be highly consensual, others less so. The smaller the variance in the group members' sentiments delineating the shape of a norm, the higher the consensus.

As will become evident below, variations in these properties (range, intensity, and consensus) affect the success of HS's attempts to gain compliance from LS by normative invocation. The following section of this paper considers each of these properties in turn, and reviews empirical studies demonstrating their effects on compliance to invoked norms.

Empirical Research on Normative Invocation and Influence

Normative Boundaries and Compliance. Data from several studies show that when HS makes a demand that is not supported by the normative arrangements in the group, he is less likely to achieve compliance than when his demand is within normative bounds. That is, if HS's demand falls outside the range of tolerable behavior stipulated by the relevant group norm, LS is unlikely to comply. In this sense, group norms establish boundaries that limit HS's legitimacy-based influence over LS.

An early study by Frank (1944) demonstrated this basic phenomenon with regard to eating behavior. LS subjects were more prone to comply with an HS experimenter's demand to eat crackers when the demand appeared legitimate in terms of the experiment's structure than when the demand seemed extraneous and arbitrary.

The well-known study by Merei (1949) demonstrated essentially the same finding with respect to children's play groups. When HSs (i.e., older dominant children) were introduced into established groups, their attempts to innovate new patterns of play behavior succeeded only if their demands coincided with established normative expectations. Out-of-bounds demands met with noncompliance from the younger children.

Similar findings emerged from the study by Michener and Burt (1972a) described earlier. In this situation a formally designated HS requested LS members to con-

tribute a substantial share of their private resources
to the group's collective activity. Depending on treatment, this fixed request either fell within the range
approved by a formal written norm or exceeded the established upper limit for such contributions. Again,
LS subjects complied less to HS's directives when his
demands overstepped normative arrangements than when
they did not.

Besides incurring noncompliance, out-of-bounds demands run the risk of provoking attitudinal resistance
and hostility. In the study by Frank (1944), subjects
manifested attitudinal resistance as well as behavioral
noncompliance. An investigation of organizational behavior by Wager (1971) also indicated that negative attitudes emerge in response to out-of-bounds demands.
Using hypothetical situations, Wager found that employees resisted their company's attempts to influence
private matters, such as their voting behavior. Similarly, research by French, Morrison, and Levinger (1960)
found that LS's attitudinal resistance to HS's use of
coercion was greater when this force exceeded the normative limits than when it fell within them.

The thrust of the above studies is clear: when HS
makes demands that fall outside the behavioral range
supported by collective expectations, compliance by LS
decreases and attitudinal resistance increases. These
relations are depicted by causal arrows in figure 9.3
showing that HS's out-of-bounds demands fail to obtain
compliance and stiffen LS's resistance.

Intensity of Sanction. A second property affecting
compliance to norms is the intensity of sanction. Behavior governed by norms can be sanctioned in many ways,
ranging from verbal expressions of approval or disapproval, to monetary rewards or fines, and even to physical punishment. Moreover, sanctions may originate
either from HS or from other LS members, and in many
cases simple expressions of approval (or disapproval)
from other LS members may effectively regulate behavior
(see Gergen 1969, pp. 19-33).

Empirical studies have demonstrated the impact of
sanctions on compliance. The clearest evidence comes
from research on the magnitude of threats, which is relevant because the present model of a *norm* parallels
the definition of *threats and promises* widely used by

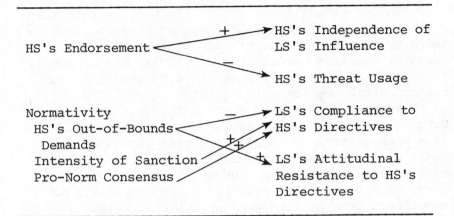

FIGURE 9.3. Empirically Observed Effects of Endorsement and Normativity on Influence Variables

investigators. Threats and promises are usually cast as contingent statements, in an "if, then" format (Kelley 1965; Tedeschi 1970; Tedeschi, Bonoma, and Brown 1971). Threats take the form "If noncompliance, then punishment" (or sometimes "If compliance, then nonpunishment"), while promises assume the form "If compliance, then reward." In both cases payoffs are contingent on compliance. In this sense threats and promises resemble norms, which generally take the form: "If you perform at (some specified) level, then you will receive (some specified) amount of approval or disapproval." Thus, norms also express contingent conditions under which rewards or punishments may be expected.

Not surprisingly, empirical studies have shown that more compliance results when sanctions are strong rather than weak. Research on threats (Horai and Tedeschi 1969; Tedeschi, Bonoma, and Brown 1971) indicates that compliance rises as punishment magnitude increases, and research on positive sanctions (Crosbie 1972) shows that increased levels of reward elicit greater compliance. In general, however, the findings with regard to promises are not as consistent as those with regard to threats, and, as Tedeschi, Bonoma, and Schlenker (1972) have noted, more research is needed to clarify the role of reward magnitude in promises.

In an investigation of the efficacy of sanctions in a *group* context, Zipf (1960) compared rewards administered by HS with punishments administered by HS. Both forms of sanction gained substantial amounts of compliance from LS, although punishment also stiffened resistant attitudes toward authority.

In another study using a group setting, Michener and Burt (1972a) varied the magnitude of punitive sanctions. HS's prerogatives included the use of punishment as a legitimate response to noncompliance by LS. The results, which corroborate studies of threat effectiveness, show that strong negative sanctions elicit more compliance from LS than weak negative sanctions.

The effects of sanctions intensity on LS's behavior are represented in figure 9.3 by a causal arrow running from sanction to compliance.

Normative Consensus. A third property affecting compliance to an invoked norm is the degree of consensus accorded the norm. Some norms achieve support from virtually all members of a given group, while others receive only mixed or partial support. The degree of consensus accorded a norm is important because norms are *collective* agreements (and in this respect they differ from threats and promises, which often involve no collective understandings). Various theorists (French and Raven 1959; Janda 1960) have proposed that the key to compliance-gaining via normative invocation rests in LS's *attitudinal acceptance* of the relevant norm. Highly consensual norms, of course, are by definition accepted by many members of a group, and there seems little doubt that if an LS member accepts a norm as binding on his behavior, his probability of compliance will be higher (for empirical demonstrations, see Campbell 1964; Bowers 1968).

But what happens when an LS member does not accept a behavioral norm invoked by HS? Certainly this situation occurs, as when LS's private goals and beliefs conflict with HS's demands, or when LS's utilitarian self-interest is at variance with normatively prescribed behavior. In this case, LS's actions will depend on the intensity of sanction for noncompliance, but they will also depend in part on the group's consensual support for HS's demands, as will be demonstrated below.

Since norms are collective agreements, they create
a network of alliances between HS and the various LSs,
as well as among the LS members themselves. As Blau
(1964, pp. 208-9) has noted, the reticulate structure
of these alliances stabilizes the normative order within the group. In essence, these alliances define potential coalitions that will emerge to suppress deviant
behavior. If an LS member dissents from a norm supported consensually by other group members, then he will
have to contend not only with HS but also with the other LS members, who become coalitional partners against
the aberrant LS. In addition to serving as agents maintaining surveillance against LS's deviance, other LSs
also support HS in his demands and may even become sanctioning agents against LS. When normative consensus
prevails, LS faces a broad coalition if he fails to comply.

Empirical research demonstrates the effects of consensus on LS's compliance to HS's directives. Several
studies have shown that consensus heightens compliance,
while dissensus encourages deviance and renitence.

A study by Bowers (1968) separated the individual's
acceptance of a norm from a collectivity's *consensus*
regarding the norm. Using survey data from over 5,000
students at 99 colleges, Bowers assessed the independent
effects of acceptance and consensus on performance of
various deviant behaviors. Indulgence in disapproved
behaviors decreased as acceptance of the norm (against
the proscribed behaviors) increased and as consensus
within the college setting increased. Interestingly,
no effect of consensus occurred until the proportion of
persons disapproving approached a *majority*; lower levels of consensual support had no impact on compliance.

Laboratory studies of fact-to-face interaction have
also demonstrated that consensus increases compliance.
But again, this seems to hold only at high levels of
consensus. Early studies by Asch (1956) on judgmental
conformity, as well as later studies in this tradition
(e.g., Allen and Levine 1968), have demonstrated that
substantial amounts of conformity (to erroneous judgments) occur when a subject confronts a unanimous majority. However, any breach in unanimity--even a single deviate-ally--will free the subject to defy the
majority and make veridical judgments.

A stronger demonstration of the consensus effect comes from Flanders and Havumaki (1960). In that study, an HS leader tried to induce LS subjects to accept a choice against their initial preferences. The experiment used a panel of lights (on which all LSs ostensibly recorded their stance on a critical issue) to manipulate perceived consensus. Depending on experimental treatment, LS subjects either perceived that other LS members were standing solidly against HS's directive or that they were gradually switching their position to form a consensus in support of HS. The results indicate higher levels of compliance by LS when the group's consensus apparently supported HS; the data also show, however, that this compliance was frequently accompanied by lack of inner conviction and high levels of attitudinal resistance.

Another study (Milgram 1965) dramatizes the impact of consensus on LS's compliance to HS's directives. This experiment employed the classic Milgram situation, in which an HS experimenter induced an LS subject to administer high levels of electric shock (ostensibly up to 450 volts) to another person strapped in an "electric chair." Depending on experimental treatment, two confederates (ostensibly occupying roles similar to the subject's) either strongly supported the HS experimenter's demands for application of the electric shock or strongly opposed those demands. This pattern of consensus or dissensus affected LS's behavior, for the use of shock was very high when the LS peers supported HS's demands, but much lower when they opposed the demands. Although Milgram's (1965) data do not show a significant difference in compliance between the consensual-support condition and a control condition where LS behaved without other LS members present, a recent replication (Larsen, Coleman, Forbes, and Johnson 1972) does show such a difference.

Further evidence for the effects of consensus on compliance comes from research by Feldman and Scheibe (1972). In this study, the members of four-man groups were directed by the HS experimenter to fill out very personal, offensive questionnaires. Three of the persons in each group were actually experimental confederates; the fourth was a real subject. In one experimental condition, all three confederates completed the questionnaire as directed. In other experimental conditions, however, either one, two, or three confederates feigned anger and stalked out of the experiment, throwing the offending questionnaire into the wastebasket. Results indicate that the percentage of subjects completing the questionnaire dropped off drastically as the number of dissenting confederates increased from zero to three.

In sum, available data indicate that LS will comply more readily with HS's directives when other LS members support the invoked norms than when they oppose those norms. This relationship is represented in figure 9.3 by an arrow between consensus and compliance.

Normative Consensus and Coalitional Alignments

Suppose that, regardless of the pressures on him, LS refuses to comply with HS's normative demands. What will happen in this case?

As Moscovici and Faucheux (1972) have noted, noncompliant behavior by LS challenges the normative structure of a group. Deviance--and especially intentional noncompliance, such as civil disobedience--compels group members to reconsider the prevailing structure of rights and obligations. LS's action, by sharpening perceived differences among members, may call existing norms into question and precipitate radical change in the group's normative structure.

If the group's LS members are not unified in support of the existing rules, then some members may align themselves with the deviant if they view change as potentially profitable. Any such movement constitutes a *revolutionary coalition* against HS and the prevailing system of rules. Thus, LS's disobedience may precipitate changes in the rules governing who makes what decisions, how conflicts are resolved, or who controls group resources.

Moscovici and Faucheux observe, however, that LS's noncompliance will not always lead to social change, because recusancy can elicit a diversity of responses from other members. If the other LSs decide to uphold the existing normative arrangements, they may simply join HS to chastise or ostracize the noncomplying LS. In this case, LS members would constitute a *conservative coalition* reaffirming the existing normative order. In everyday situations, of course, the conservative response to deviance occurs more frequently than the revolutionary response.

Nevertheless, the important point is that revolutionary responses *can* occur, and this underscores the fragility and tentativeness of normativity as a base of influence. From this standpoint the pivotal questions are: Under what conditions will a noncomplying LS face a conservative coalitional response from the other LSs, and under what conditions will he be joined by other LSs in a revolutionary coalition against the existing order? Research illustrates both the conservative and the revolutionary coalitional response to deviance. The key to the choice between revolutionary and conservative reactions seems to lie in whether the various LS members believe that valued (collective) goals are best facilitated by the existing normative arrangements or by some alternative set of rules, such as those implicit in the behavior of the noncomplying LS.

The conservative coalitional response appears in the classic study by Schachter (1951), where group members joined against a deviant. In this situation (which did not involve a hierarchical structure) an extreme deviant adamantly refused to adopt the group's consensual position. After repeated attempts to persuade him, the members finally ostracized him and refused to appoint him to any position of importance within the group. Sociometric rejection of the deviant was greater when the group was highly cohesive, and members excluded him more from important group positions when the topic of discussion was relevant to their interests. In other words, ostracism was greater when the conservative coalition was closely knit. The essential findings of the Schachter experiment have been replicated by Emerson (1954) and Berkowitz and Howard (1959).

Related studies suggest that conservative, rather than revolutionary, coalitions will emerge when LS's noncompliance obstructs the achievement of goals valued by other LS members. Early studies by Festinger and Thibaut (1951) and Gerard (1953) showed that influence pressures increase when unanimity is necessary for success on a collective task. And Videbeck and Bates (1959)

using data from long-term groups, demonstrated that the
more important and central a given behavior is to the
group's task, the more members conform to the norms
governing it. In general, these findings suggest that
conservative pressures will uphold the existing normative arrangements when deviance obstructs important
collective goals. This is not surprising, of course,
because shared goals are the very foundation of coalitional alliances.

In addition to illustrating conservative coalitional
behavior, available research treats revolutionary coalitional activity. When LS refuses to comply with normative stipulations, other LS members will sometimes ally
themselves with the deviant rather than with HS. Empirical findings demonstrate that revolutionary responses of this sort occur when HS's directives breach
shared expectations regarding equity, when they enhance
HS's private self-interest at the expense of the collectivity's welfare, and when they appear likely to produce failure on collective tasks.

A study by Stotland (1959) illustrates revolutionary
coalitional activity. LS subjects worked at a task under the supervision of an HS authority. HS frequently
nullified decisions by LS, thereby frustrating LS and
arbitrarily blocking progress toward the group goal. In
one experimental condition LS worked alone with HS, but
in another condition LS intermittently consulted with a
second LS member. This second member provided a coalitional alignment against HS's obstructionist decisions,
and subjects showed more hostility and less cooperation
toward HS in the coalitional condition than in the lone
condition.

Michener and Lawler (1971) provide a more direct demonstration of revolutionary coalitional activity under
conditions of collective failure. This study established a status hierarchy giving HS important decision-
making prerogatives, but LS members had the ability to
form coalitions overturning the prevailing order. Results indicate that HS was able to maintain his prerogatives if the group succeeded in its collective goals;
this held true even when the potential LS coalition
was very strong. Under conditions of repeated failure,
however, LS members coalesced and shifted decisional
prerogatives from HS to themselves. In other words,

LS members upheld the original status structure only
when it led to collective success.

Revolutionary coalitional behavior can also emerge
in response to inequitable decisions by HS. In a study
by Michener and Lyons (1972), HS made decisions regarding the division of rewards among group members. These
decisions were set so that HS always usurped an extra-
vagantly large portion of the rewards. Depending on
experimental conditions, the LS subjects received messages from another LS member either supporting or opposing HS's right to allocate rewards. When the other
LS member indicated opposition to HS, the LS subject
could either join the other LS member against HS or uphold HS's prerogatives under the existing arrangements.
Results indicate that when LS subjects interpreted HS's
decisions as inequitable, they joined the revolutionary
coalition against HS. A subsequent study by Lawler
(1972) manipulated HS's equity-inequity directly, and
found similar evidence for the impact of inequity on
revolutionary activity.

Overall, these studies show that coalitional alignments among LS members either reaffirm or undermine the
normative order. The form of these alignments--and the
conditions leading to their change--constitute the
foundation of rule-based influence. Shifts in coalitional alignments will cause shifts in HS's ability to
exercise influence via normative invocation.

SUMMARY: NORMATIVITY CONTRASTED
WITH ENDORSEMENT

This paper began by decomposing the concept of legitimacy into two elements, endorsement and normativity.
This conceptual distinction receives ample justification from the empirical research on legitimacy and influence. Endorsement and normativity differ sharply
from each other because, as figure 9.3 highlights, they
affect the social influence processes in diverse ways.
Endorsement apparently has its strongest impact on HS's
behavior, while normativity determines LS's behavior.

Data indicate that, contrary to theoretical expectations, endorsement is *not* a base of influence. Related
sentiments, such as liking or ascribed competence, may

elicit compliance from LS, but endorsement per se apparently does not affect the level of LS's compliance to HS's demands. In contrast, normativity does serve as a base of influence. Data show that LS is not likely to comply with directives that fall outside normative boundaries; but when HS's directives are covered by normative arrangements, LS's compliance increases under high levels of sanction and under high levels of pro-norm consensus.

Although endorsement is not a base of influence, it nevertheless serves an important function. Endorsement feedback from LS members provides HS with a means to assess his performance as leader. A high level of endorsement tells HS that his behavior is serving the group well, at least from the standpoint of morale. Under these conditions HS may feel secure in his position and take added risks through deviation from LS's expectations. A low level of endorsement, however, signals discontent with some important aspect of group functioning--probably inequity among members or failure to achieve collective goals. To maintain his position, HS must cope with this situation, either by alleviating the source of discontent or by suppressing dissident LS members.

Despite the differences in their consequences, both endorsement and normativity (especially consensus) stem from related sources. The empirical literature on endorsement and on revolutionary/conservative coalitions shows that the origins of legitimacy rest with the attainment of collective goals and the maintenance of equity among group members. Consensual support goes to individual HSs who can deliver these valued outcomes; it also goes to normative arrangements believed to foster such outcomes.

Since endorsement and normativity have different consequences (if not different origins), it is important to maintain the theoretical distinction between person-legitimacy and position-legitimacy. Normativity provides a base for compliance-gaining, which endorsement does not. And endorsement supplies HS with information about the acceptability of his policies and decisions, which normativity does not. Both contribute substantially to a smoothly operating group.

TOPICS FOR FUTURE RESEARCH

One important function of a literature review is to
identify reliable empirical generalizations and to
discard erroneous theoretical conceptions. Another
function is to delineate topics for future research.
Numerous research ideas emerge from the framework presented in this paper. Some of these are listed below.

Endorsement

(1) Future research should replicate the unanticipated
finding that endorsement does not serve as a base of
influence. This replication should treat LS's compliance to HS's directives as the prime dependent variable,
but it should also ascertain whether LS's attitudinal
acceptance of suggestions and ideas from HS varies as
a function of endorsement. In any such replication,
care must be taken that endorsement is not confounded
with competence or liking, which are distinct bases of
influence and which often covary with endorsement in
natural settings.

(2) Another important issue is whether endorsement
affects HS's propensity to *initiate* influence attempts
of various kinds. Other influence bases, such as attributed competence, will heighten HS's propensity to
initiate influence (see, e.g., Hastorf 1961; Marak 1964),
but research has not fully illuminated the effects of
endorsement on the frequency of HS's influence and leadership attempts.

(3) Although available data are weak, they suggest
that high endorsement will heighten HS's propensity to
resist pressures from LS members and to deviate from
group norms, especially when HS believes this serves
collective interests. Future research should identify
the conditions under which high levels of endorsement
actually increase HS's propensity to overstep normative
boundaries.

(4) When subjected to pressures from LS members,
HS can respond by changing relevant policies, thereby
alleviating sources of inequity or collective failure.
Alternatively, HS can try to "keep the lid on" by exerting counterpressures against LS members. These social

control efforts can assume various forms, such as persuasion or inducement or coercion. Important questions
are: Does the level of endorsement accorded HS affect
his choice among alternative social control techniques?
And, does endorsement affect the intensity with which
HS uses the various techniques? Available research indicates that endorsement affects the intensity of threat
and punishment usage. But future studies must determine endorsement's impact on the use of other techniques,
such as persuasion and inducement.

Normativity

(1) Sometimes LS members comply with HS's normative
invocations, sometimes they don't. Existing research
indicates that LS's probability of compliance increases
with the degree of in-boundedness of HS's demands, with
the intensity of sanction, and with the degree of consensus supporting the norm. Future research should
seek out other factors that heighten the probability of
compliance with normative invocations in collective settings.
     (2) Research studies indicate that LS's compliance
increases under high levels of consensus, but in many
of these studies the consensual norms are also those
most directly relevant to collective goals and thus
most intensely sanctioned. This confounding makes interpretation difficult, and future research should carefully separate the effects of consensus from those of
sanction intensity. Moreover, future studies should investigate the mechanisms that mediate the effects of
consensus. Perceived consensus might heighten LS's compliance because it strengthens LS's attitudinal acceptance of the norm, because it increases LS's subjective
probability of being sanctioned for noncompliance or deviance, or because it reduces LS's chances of creating
a revolutionary alliance (against HS) under noncompliance. Research should assess the relative importance
of these alternative mechanisms.
     (3) Little is known about the factors that deter-
mine HS's *use* of normative invocation as an influence
technique, but one might hypothesize that the level of
consensus supporting a norm will determine HS's propensity to invoke that norm. For instance, HS might

readily call upon consensual norms, but refrain from invoking weakly supported norms because this would precipitate a direct test of his legitimacy. Under such conditions, HS might resort to another influence technique, such as direct incentives. Research should explore the factors affecting HS's choice of normative invocation as a technique.

(4) Research findings show that, when HS makes demands that trangress normative boundaries, his efforts usually fail to achieve compliance. HS's ability to exert legitimacy-based influence is limited to what prevailing norms allow. Yet, HS's legitimate prerogatives can expand or contract, depending on conditions. Organizational rules often change, and these shifts may lead to greater centralization of authority (where HS enjoys added influence prerogatives) or to greater decentralization (where HS loses control). Future research should explore factors that cause such expansions and contractions in HS's legitimate influence prerogatives.

REFERENCES

Allen, V. L., and Levine, J. M. 1968. Social support, dissent, and conformity. *Sociometry* 31: 138-49.

Alvarez, R. 1968. Informal reactions to deviance in simulated work organizations: a laboratory experiment. *American Sociological Review* 33: 895-912.

Asch, S. E. 1956. Studies of independence and submission to group pressure: 1. A minority of one against a unanimous majority. *Psychological Monographs* 70.

Bachman, J. G., Bowers, D. G., and Marcus, P. M. 1968. Bases of supervisory power: a comparative study in five organizational settings. In A. S. Tannenbaum (Ed.), *Control in organizations,* New York: McGraw-Hill.

Berkowitz, L. 1969. Resistance to improper dependency relationships. *Journal of Experimental Social Psychology* 5: 283-94.

Berkowitz, L., and Howard, R. C. 1959. Reactions to opinion deviates as affected by affiliation need (*n*) and group member interdependence. *Sociometry* 22: 81-91.

Blau, P. M. 1964. *Exchange and power in social life*. New York: Wiley.

Bowers, W. J. 1968. Normative constraints on deviant behavior in the college context. *Sociometry* 31: 370-85.

Campbell, E. Q. 1964. The internalization of moral norms. *Sociometry* 27: 391-412.

Crosbie, P. V. 1972. Social exchange and power compliance: a test of Homans' proposition. *Sociometry* 35: 203-22.

Dittes, J. E., and Kelley, H. H. 1956. Effects of different conditions of acceptance upon conformity to group norms. *Journal of Abnormal and Social Psychology* 53: 100-107.

Emerson, R. M. 1954. Deviation and rejection: an experimental replication. *American Sociological Review* 19: 688-93.

Evan, W. M., and Zelditch, M., Jr. A laboratory experiment on bureaucratic authority. *American Sociological Review* 26: 883-93.

Feldman, R. S., and Scheibe, K. E. 1972. Determinants of dissent in a psychological experiment. *Journal of Personality* 40: 331-48.

Festinger, L., and Thibaut, J. 1951. Interpersonal communication in small groups. *Journal of Abnormal and Social Psychology* 46: 92-99.

Flanders, N., and Havumaki, S. 1960. Group compliance to dominative teacher influence. *Human Relations* 13: 67-82.

Frank, J. D. 1944. Experimental production of resistance. *Journal of General Psychology* 30: 23-41.

French, J. R. P., Jr., Morrison, H. W., and Levinger, G. 1960. Coercive power and forces affecting conformity. *Journal of Abnormal and Social Psychology* 61: 93-101.

French, J. R. P., Jr., and Raven, B. R. 1959. The bases of social power. In D. Cartwright (Ed.), *Studies in social power*. Ann Arbor: University of Michigan Press, pp. 150-67.

French, J. R. P., Jr., and Snyder, R. 1959. Leadership and interpersonal power. In D. Cartwright (Ed.), *Studies in social power*. Ann Arbor: University of Michigan Press.

Gamson, W. A. 1968. *Power and discontent*. Homewood, Ill.: Dorsey Press.

Gerard, H. B. 1953. The effect of different dimensions of disagreement on the communication process
in small groups. *Human Relations* 6: 249-71.

Gergen, K. 1969. *The psychology of behavior exchange*.
Reading, Mass.: Addison-Wesley.

Hastorf, A. H. 1961. The "reinforcement" of individual actions in a group situation. In L. Krasner
and L. P. Ullman (Eds.), *Research in behavior modification: new developments and implications*. New
York: Holt, Rinehart & Winston.

Hollander, E. P. 1958. Conformity, status, and idiosyncrasy credit. *Psychological Review* 65: 117-27.

------. 1960. Competence and conformity in the acceptance of influence. *Journal of Abnormal and Social
Psychology* 61: 365-69.

------. 1964. *Leaders, groups, and influence*. New
York: Oxford University Press.

Hollander, E. P., and Julian, J. W. 1970. Studies in
leader legitimacy, influence, and innovation. In
L. Berkowitz (Ed.), *Advances in experimental social
psychology*. Vol. 5. New York: Academic Press, pp.
33-69.

Hollander, E. P., Julien, J. W., and Sorrentino, R. M.
1969. The leader's sense of legitimacy as a source
of his constructive deviation. *Technical Report
No. 12*, State University of New York at Buffalo.

Homans, G. C. 1961. *Social behavior: its elementary
forms*. New York: Harcourt, Brace.

Horai, J., and Tedeschi, J. T. 1969. The effects of
threat credibility and magnitude of punishment upon
compliance. *Journal of Personality and Social Psychology* 12: 164-69.

Horwitz, M. 1963. Hostility and its management in
classroom groups. In W. W. Carters and N. L. Gage
(Eds.), *Readings in the social psychology of education*. Boston: Allyn & Bacon.

Jackson, J. M. 1960. Structural characteristics of
norms. In E. B. Henry (Ed.), *Dynamics of instruc-
tional groups*. The 59th Yearbook of the National
Society for the Study of Education. Chicago: University of Chicago Press.

------. 1964. The normative regulation of authoritative behavior. In W. J. Gore and J. W. Dyson (Eds.),
*The making of decisions: a reader in administrative
behavior*. New York: Free Press.

------. 1965. Structural characteristics of norms. In I. D. Steiner and M. Fishbein (Eds.), *Current studies in social psychology*. New York: Holt, Rinehart & Winston.

Jacobson, W. D. 1972. *Power and influence in interpersonal relations*. Belmont, Calif.: Wadsworth.

Janda, K. F. 1960. Towards the explication of the concept of leadership in terms of the concept of power. *Human Relations* 13: 345-64.

Julian, J. W., Hollander, E. P., and Regula, C. R. 1969. Endorsement of the group spokesman as a function of his source of authority, competence, and success. *Journal of Personality and Social Psychology* 11: 42-49.

Julian, J. W., and Steiner, I. D. 1961. Perceived acceptance as a determinant of conformity behavior. *Journal of Social Psychology* 55: 191-98.

Kelley, H. H. 1965. Experimental studies of threats in interpersonal negotiations. *Journal of Conflict Resolution* 9: 79-105.

Larsen, K. S., Coleman, D., Forbes, J., and Johnson, R. 1972. Is the subject's personality or the experimental situation a better predictor of a subject's willingness to administer shock to a victim? *Journal of Personality and Social Psychology* 22: 287-95.

Lawler, E. J. 1972. Factors affecting the mobilization of revolutionary coalitions. Unpublished doctoral dissertation, University of Wisconsin.

Lott, A. J., and Lott, B. E. 1972. The power of liking: consequences of interpersonal attitudes derived from a leberalized view of secondary reinforcement. In L. Berkowitz (Ed.), *Advances in experimental social psychology*. Vol. 6. New York: Academic Press.

Marak, G. E., Jr. 1964. The evolution of leadership structure. *Sociometry* 27: 174-82.

March, J. G. 1954. Group norms and the active minority. *American Sociological Review* 19: 733-41.

------. 1966. The power or power. In D. Easton (Ed.), *Varieties of political theory*. Englewood Cliffs, N. J.: Prentice-Hall.

Merei, F. 1949. Group leadership and institutionalization. *Human Relations* 2: 23-39.

Michener, H. A., and Burt, M. R. 1972a Components of "authority" as determinants of compliance. Unpublished manuscript, University of Wisconsin.

------. 1972b. The use of coercive influence under
varying conditions of legitimacy. Unpublished manuscript, University of Wisconsin.

Michener, H. A., and Lawler, E. J. 1971. Revolutionary coalition strength and collective failure as
determinants of status reallocation. *Journal of
Experimental Social Psychology* 7: 448-60.

------. 1972. The endorsement of formal leaders: an
integrative model. Unpublished manuscript, University of Wisconsin.

Michener, H. A., and Lyons, M. 1972. Perceived support and upward mobility as determinants of revolutionary coalitional behavior. *Journal of Experimental Social Psychology* 8: 180-95.

Michener, H. A., and Tausig, M. 1971. Usurpation and
perceived support as determinants of the endorsement
accorded formal leaders. *Journal of Personality and
Social Psychology* 18: 364-72.

Michener, H. A., and Zeller, R. A. 1972. A test of
Gamson's theory of political trust orientation.
Journal of Applied Social Psychology 2: 138-56.

Milgram, S. 1965. Liberating effects of group pressure. *Journal of Personality and Social Psychology*
1: 127-34.

Moscovici, S., and Faucheux, C. 1972. Social influence, conformity bias, and the study of active minor-
ities. In L. Berkowitz (Ed.), *Advances in experimental social psychology*. Vol. 6. New York: Academic Press.

Peabody, R. L. 1964. *Organizational authority*. New
York: Atherton Press.

Raven, B. H., and French, J. R. P. 1958a. Group support, legitimate power, and social influence. *Journal of Personality* 26: 400-409.

------. 1958b. Legitimate power, coercive power, and
observability in social influence. *Sociometry* 21:
83-97.

Raven, B., and Kruglanski, A. W. 1970. Conflict and
power. In P. Swingle (Ed.), *The structure of Conflict*. New York: Academic Press.

Schachter, S. 1951. Deviation, rejection, and communication. *Journal of Abnormal and Social Psychology*
46: 190-207.

Schopler, J. 1965. Social power. In L. Berkowitz (Ed.), *Advances in experimental social psychology*. Vol. 2. New York: Academic Press.

Schopler, J., and Bateson, N. 1965. The power of dependence. *Journal of Personality and Social Psychology* 2: 247-54.

Simon, H. A., Smithberg, D. W., and Thompson, V. A. 1970. Why men obey. In J. H. Kessel, A. F. Cole, and R. G. Seddig (Eds.), *Micropolitics*. New York: Holt, Rinehart & Winston, pp. 580-89.

Stotland, E. 1959. Peer groups and reactions to power figures. In D. Cartwright (Ed.), *Studies in social power*. Ann Arbor: University of Michigan Press.

Suchner, R. W. 1972. Status endorsement as a function of perceived competence and conformity of leaders in successful and unsuccessful groups. Unpublished doctoral dissertation, University of Wisconsin.

Tedeschi, J. T. 1970. Threats and promises. In P. Swingle (Ed.), *The structure of conflict*. New York: Academic Press.

Tedeschi, J. T., Bonoma, T. V., and Brown, R. 1971. A paradigm for the study of coercive power. *Journal of Conflict Resolution* 15: 197-224.

Tedeschi, J. T., Bonoma, T. V., and Schlenker, B. R. 1972. Influence, decision, and compliance. In J. T. Tedeschi (Ed.), *The social influence processes*. Chicago: Aldine-Atherton, pp. 346-418.

Tedeschi, J. T., Schlenker, B. R., and Lindskold, S. 1972. The exercise of power and influence: the source of influence. In J. T. Tedeschi (Ed.), *The social influence processes*. Chicago: Aldine-Atherton, pp. 287-345.

Videback, R., and Bates, A. P. 1959. An experimental study of conformity to role expectations. *Sociometry* 22: 1-11.

Wager, L. W. 1971. The expansion of organizational authority and conditions affecting its denial. *Sociometry* 34: 91-113.

Wahrman, R., and Pugh, M. D. 1972. Competence and conformity: another look at Hollander's study. *Sociometry* 35: 376-86.

Walster, E., and Abrahams, D. 1972. Interpersonal attraction and social influence. In J. T. Tedeschi (Ed.), *The social influence processes*. Chicago:

Aldine-Atherton, pp. 197-238.

Wiggins, J. A., Dill, F., and Schwartz, R. D.   1965.
  On "status-liability." *Sociometry* 28:   197-209.

Zipf, S. G.   1960.   Resistance and conformity under
  reward and punishment. *Journal of Abnormal and
  Social Psychology* 61:   102-9.

Campus Crisis: *10*
The Search For Power
Dean G. Pruitt and James P. Gahagan

This paper is a preliminary report on a case study of
campus conflict that occurred in 1970 on our campus,
The State University of New York at Buffalo, better
known as the University of Buffalo, or UB.

AIMS AND METHOD

Case studies are rarely performed by social psychologists. Yet they would appear to be quite useful as an
aid to theory building. Their value is in part heuristic. They bring one closer to naturally occurring phenomena than does any other sort of research. This provides the possibility of tracing causal sequences in
detail and thereby discovering new behavioral mechanisms. When several cases are compared, regularities
can often be found in long sequences of behavior, such
as are formalized in the structural change models described below. Case studies also force an integrative
stance on the theory-oriented researcher. He must read
broadly in a number of different kinds of literature in
order to comprehend the diverse features of his case;

The research reported in this paper was supported by NSF Grants
GS-2270 and GS-3227 awarded to the Center for International Conflict
Studies at the State University of New York at Buffalo.
  Four other scholars contributed to the development of the chronology
and critiqued the theoretical ideas: Steven A. Lewis, Joseph S. Maciejko,
Ira S. Rubin, and John A. Saurenman.

and as he constructs his analysis, he is almost forced
to integrate the thinking of various writers. In addition, case studies help identify gaps in existing
thinking.

Of course, case studies have their drawbacks in comparison to large-sample studies. Subjectivity is often
more of a problem, and it is hard to know how to generalize the ideas generated. Hence we favor a progressive strategy, consisting of a single case study followed by a comparison of several cases and finally by
a large-sample test of the hypotheses generated earlier.

In gathering the data for our case study, we have
employed participant observation, interviewing, and the
examination of records. In the first two approaches,
we have explicitly rejected the dictum of observer
neutrality, because of the assumption that neutral parties are not very welcome during conflict and after-
ward often have difficulty gaining full information
from participants. Hence, during the conflict Pruitt
joined a moderate faculty group that was trying to reestablish "sanity" on campus and Gahagan mingled with
the dissenting students. Subsequently, Pruitt did most
of the interviews with administrators and faculty members. Gahagan spent more than a year after the crisis
getting to know many student participants better and
was thereby able to uncover a number of intimate details that would not otherwise have come to our attention.

This division of labor has undoubtedly led each of
us to become biased in the direction of the participants with whom he has been interacting. So where does
objectivity come in? Our approach has been to discuss
the details of the case and our analyses of them with
each other and with a group of more neutral graduate
students. This forces clarification of our underlying
values and assumptions. We often disagree, sometimes
a bit heatedly. But in this way we hope to keep each
other honest and to end up with a balanced viewpoint,
or at least a split verdict that gives the reader a
choice of biases.

A brief chronology of the crisis will be presented
in the next section. Following that, three broad approaches to conflict theory will be described, along
with an integration of two of the approaches which was

suggested by efforts to apply them to our case. In attempting to understand our case, we have identified a major gap in existing theory, in the area of blame assignment. Hence we have been stimulated to develop a partial theory of this phenomenon, which will be presented in the last two sections of the paper.

While we will vouch for the correctness of most of the facts presented, we make no pretense of empirical validity for the theoretical ideas. They are speculations, stimulated, but by no means tested, by our data. We hope that the reader will find them fruitful.

CHRONOLOGY OF THE UB CRISIS

The years from 1964 to 1968 saw a progressively increasing number of instances of campus protest throughout the United States. As the school year 1969-1970 began, the expectation was for more of the same. Many university students were aroused about such campus issues as racial discrimination and complicity with the national war effort. National radical student organizations had indicated at their conventions and through their publications that universities were to be the targets of further protest activities. On the other side, state legislators, boards of trustees and university administrators were busily developing legal systems and other measures for dealing with the expected protest activity.

At UB, the year 1969-1970 began with the chief administrator on leave and an Acting President in his place. The radical students were focusing their actions on the Vietnam war, minority rights, Department of Defense research, and the ROTC program. A fragile black-white student coalition developed during the first semester under black leadership for a confrontation with the Medical School, aimed at forcing a greater responsiveness to the medical needs of black city dwellers. During this confrontation, the campus police made their first appearance in "riot control" uniforms. A series of actions were later initiated by white radicals against the ROTC, which included the destruction of equipment and records and the disruption of classes. Subsequently, a number of faculty members began pressuring the Administration to develop a viable legal structure to punish these and future transgressions.

The student judiciary, which typically handled these
cases, had broken down. The Administration, already
somewhat disorganized as a result of the President's
absence was further weakened when the President an-
nounced that he was leaving for good, and rivalry developed over his position.

Unexpectedly, at the beginning of the semester, during the bitter Buffalo winter, issues surfaced in the
Athletic Department concerning the alleged racism of a
coach, the manner of financial support of black basketball players, and alleged discriminatory grading practices for black Physical Education majors. The black
athletes and the Black Student Union (BSU) appealed for
tactical support from white students in order to force
the university into negotiations. A sit-in took place
on the basketball court on February 24, resulting in
cancellation of the varsity game and the beginning of
negotiations. The campus police were present at the
sit-in, wearing their riot-control outfits, and the
Buffalo police, alerted to the situation by administrators, were seen on campus by the demonstrators. A number of demonstrators and allied students became particularly alarmed about the presence of the Buffalo police, because they had been unilaterally summoned by
an administrator rather than at the direction of the
Faculty-Student-Administration Security Task Force,
which was believed to be the only body that could legitimately take such an action.

Negotiations with the black athletes continued
throughout the following day, February 25, with the most
immediately pressing demand being the cancellation of
the game that was scheduled to be played at 8:00 p.m.
In order to bring pressure on the Administration to
meet this demand, an early evening rally was scheduled
in the Student Union to mobilize for a sit-in if the
game was not canceled. At about 7:45 p.m., the black
athletes and the Administration reached a last-minute
agreement to cancel the game. A BSU leader informed
those present at the rally of the agreement and the
black athletes' satisfaction with the progress of the
negotiations. He thanked them for their support and
recommended that they disperse. Some more militant
blacks challenged this speaker and questioned his attitude concerning the Buffalo police presence the night

before. This challenge was supported by several white
radicals. A group of forty to fifty white students then
proceeded to the Acting President's office with the intention of demanding an explanation for the presence of
the Buffalo police on campus the night before. Thus began the escalation cycle of February 25, which precipitated a three-week crisis that involved roughly 70 percent of the full-time students in one or another kind
of anti-Administration activity.[1]

Several members of the protest group interrupted a
meeting between the negotiators and the Acting President to get the latter's explanation for the presence
of the Buffalo police and were told to leave after having gotten what they considered an unsatisfactory explanation. As they left, ice and other missiles were
thrown at the windows of the Acting President's office.
As the students were moving toward the Student Union,
the campus police arrived in their riot-control uniforms and were told by the Acting President to arrest
the window breakers. In the meantime, the students
had entered the Union and become engulfed in the usual
large evening crowd there. The campus police entered
the Union, using their nightsticks to prod and separate
the crowd, and apprehended two of the student radicals.
The two were handcuffed, and one was brutally beaten
in full view of the milling and excited onlookers, some
of whom began moving toward and striking at the officers. The officers then left the Union with their prisoners and were chased across campus by a group of students.

Back in the Union, students were milling around, discussing the events and collecting bail money. Some windows of the bookstore were broken, but calm prevailed
within ten minutes.

In the meantime, the administrators who had been negotiating with the black athletes went to the Campus
Security Office in considerable disarray. There they
formed the impression that a riotous situation existed
in the Union. Information conflicting with this impression either did not reach them or was rejected because
it did not fit their perceptions. It is not clear exactly how the decision was made, but the Buffalo Tactical Police Unit, which had been summoned earlier, proceeded to the Union and cleared it, employing seemingly

unnecessary force. A confrontation between the police
and about 500 enraged students then took place outside
the Union, resulting in the injury and arrest of several dozen people.

At an informational meeting held a few hours later
for administrators, ranking faculty, and Student Association representatives, no clear picture of the sequence of events emerged. Most of the top administrators blamed things on a small number of dedicated revolutionaries, minimizing both the level of force employed by the police and the injuries sustained by students.

On the following day, February 26, a large segment
of the student body was both angered and confused about
the events. The Student Association asked the Acting
President for an explanation of the events and guarantees that steps would be taken to prevent their recurrence, but this request was not heeded. At a large
noon rally conducted by campus radicals, militant
speeches focused on "getting the pigs off campus" and
"avenging" the student injuries. The rally culminated
in a march on the Administration Building to demand an
explanation from the Acting President, which was not
forthcoming. The students then moved on to the Campus
Security Office, where a few members of the crowd dam-
aged windows and a police car. During the remainder of
the afternoon, small groups of students, with larger
groups observing more or less approvingly, committed
various acts of property destruction on campus, aimed
mainly at the ROTC and other "political" targets. When
things seemed to be cooling down, the campus police appeared in their riot-control outfits, and the dispers-
ing students quickly massed and ran toward them, yell-
ing epithets and throwing projectiles. The campus police retreated off campus, where Buffalo police officers were waiting, and a student-police standoff occurred.

Flushed with a perceived victory of having "driven
the pigs off campus," approximately 3,000 students at
an evening rally voted to call for a strike on class attendance in an effort to keep police off campus and
force the Acting President to resign. In the course of
the discussion that led to this vote, radicals articulated a simple causal theory, which attributed blame

for the police action to the Acting President, who had
"unjustifiably" ordered the police (both campus and
city) into the students' territory. The police were
also pictured as blameworthy, but less so than the Acting President, since they had acted under orders and
were not all university controlled. The Acting President's supposed authoritarian outlook, as illustrated
by his past attempts to enforce rules and norms and
his alleged insensitivity to students, were cited as
explanations for his actions. A number of other demands, including the abolition of the ROTC and of research supported by the Defense Department, were also
discussed and informally agreed upon.

During the night, acts of vandalism occurred on campus, including a number of fire bombings. One fire
bomb narrowly missed injuring a librarian and destroyed
500-600 hard-to-replace books in the Library. These
and other acts of vandalism that occurred throughout
the crisis aroused considerable sentiment against the
students both within and outside the university community.

Friday, February 27, was a critical day in terms of
student protest leadership. The picketing of classes,
which was organized by the radicals but included many
previously moderate or inactive students, was partially
successful. Class attendance was curtailed by about
30 to 40 percent. Mass meetings were scheduled by both
the radicals and moderate Student Association leaders,
with the radicals holding theirs first.

At their rally, the radicals emphasized the necessity for adopting militant tactics in order to maintain
pressure on the Acting President and disparaged the
Student Association leaders who were attempting to moderate the situation. Efforts to discredit these leaders centered upon their close ties with the Administration and the Chancellor of the state system, which allegedly made them handmaidens or lackeys of the enemy.
Shortly after the meeting, a written set of nine demands appeared. It was signed by the Strike Committee,
a new radical struggle organization.

At the Student Association rally, challenges to those
leading the discussion began early, coming not only from
identified radical students but also from previously
moderate students. To complicate matters further, a

split developed within the Student Association, with a
number of individuals taking a position close to that
of the radicals. A proposed list of demands covering
the same issues as the radicals' demands, but more moderate in both tone and goals, was discussed. No consensus could be reached, and the demands were tabled.
Further challenges developed over the proposal that the
Student Association engage the Administration in negotiations. The meeting ended with few signs of support
for the Student Association, which was in considerable
disarray.

By Monday, March 2, the protest leadership was clearly in the hands of the loosely organized Strike Committee. On that day, the committee utilized a convocation
which had been organized by one of the experimental colleges as a Strike Support Rally. With about 2,500
strike sympathizers and only a smattering of opposition,
the demands and the strike were endorsed by voice vote.
Student Association leaders were not permitted to speak.

The public statements of the Administration during
the first five days of the crisis focused on the damage
done to physical facilities and blamed a small minority
of students, whom the Acting President called "vicious
vandals" in a television address delivered on Sunday,
March 1. Various administrators and faculty members
had attempted to persuade the Acting President to use
the television address and other means at his disposal
to apologize for the injuries sustained by students on
February 25 and to place the blame for the events on
the police, but he rejected this advice. Presentation
of the "vicious vandal" theory on TV reinforced the
outer community's negative perceptions of the dissenting students and (together with the negative reaction
of taxpayers to the property damage) contributed to the
developing pressure for strong measures to end the
crisis and punish the wrongdoers.

During the first five days, the only public actions
taken by the Administration to deal with the crisis
were to obtain a temporary restraining order from the
State Supreme Court on February 27, and to cancel
classes on Monday, March 2, to allow for a cooling-off
period. Two high administrators were working behind
the scenes with members of the Student Government in a
futile effort to "communicate" with dissenting students.

Various unpublicized, small-scale actions were taken by people at lower levels of the Administration, but there is little evidence of coordination in any of these efforts. In the words of several of our informants, the administrative "team" had broken down. The main activity of the faculty during this period was organization of a Peace Patrol, whose members spent many hours on the campus attempting to minimize violence.

For the next two days--Tuesday, March 3, and Wednesday, March 4--moving student pickets, employing mainly verbal persuasion, attempted to enforce the strike of classes with decreasing success. During this time, the Strike Committee became an effective organization, with around 400 active supporters, but general student participation in the strike fell off rapidly.

In the face of diminishing success, the Strike Committee escalated its tactics on Thursday, March 5, and began blocking the entrances to the Administration Building. Various attempts by the Administration to impress upon the blockaders the fact that they were violating the restraining order and were subject to arrest were ineffective. Efforts to identify the student blockaders were also futile. Those faculty and staff members who could have identified them were either not asked or were uncooperative. Three attempts were made to mediate the situation, two by faculty members and one by a graduate student and a high administrator. These failed, apparently for three reasons: (a) the Acting President was unwilling to bestow legitimacy on the Strike Committee; (b) the demands were represented as nonnegotiable; and (c) the identity of the legitimate representatives of the Strike Committee was not clear to the Administration.

Friday, March 6, began with resumed blocking of the entrances to the Administration Building, though the number of blockaders had diminished. The Admissions and Records Office, in another building, was occupied by strikers, some of whom wore masks to avoid identification. Later in the day, fire hoses were turned on in the Administration Building, flooding the basement and threatening the electrical system and some computing equipment. Though these incidents involved a considerable escalation of student tactics, the actual number of demonstrators was diminishing, and active support for the Strike Committee was apparently decreasing.

In an attempt to restore calm, the Administration took a number of steps on Thursday and Friday. The restraining order was continued for thirty days. A group of radical leaders was suspended pending hearings, though it turned out that few of them were actually involved in the blockade of the Administration Building. A temporary commission was set up to hear cases brought against students.

During this two-day period, a great deal of pressure for action against the demonstrators arose from segments of the faculty and staff, many segments of the local community, and the New York State Legislature. In response to this pressure, and to "protect life and property and reestablish normal university functioning," the Acting President decided that it would be necessary to call a large number of city police onto the campus.

Early on Sunday, March 8, 400 Buffalo police moved onto the campus to begin regular patrolling. Protest meetings were held, and in the late afternoon about 5,000 students and faculty peacefully marched around the campus to protest the police presence. During the course of the next week, several administrators resigned, including the Acting Executive Vice President. Many members of the faculty were clearly in opposition to the Administration, and a number of classes were canceled.

The police presence breathed new life into the Strike Committee. The activities it organized during the week were mainly symbolic protests, heavily influenced by Yippie tactics. A pig was roasted in front of the Union and a mock funeral was held for SUNY-Buffalo with the concurrent establishment of PUNY-Buffalo (*P* for People's) and the issuing of "Nth degrees." Some limit testing occurred in the form of entering buildings and chanting loudly, in clear violation of the restraining order. These actions went unpunished.

On Tuesday, March 10, the Administration rescinded the suspension of radical leaders and set up a liberal-led Academic Task Force to deal with the issues raised by the strike demands. The Strike Committee was offered and rejected membership on the Task Force. No efforts were made to negotiate with the Strike Committee. The Acting President appeared before the Faculty Senate on

Wednesday, March 11, to explain his actions, following which a motion of no confidence failed by a 3-2 majority.

At a mass rally held on the evening of March 11, in response to the failure of the faculty to vote no confidence, the Strike Committee issued an ultimatum calling for the Administration to meet the strike demands by 9:00 p.m. the next night or face the outcome of a "War Council." This ultimatum was repeated the next morning. During the day, some faculty members attempted to persuade the Acting President to meet with representatives of the Strike Committee or to communicate some flexibility on the Committee's demands in order to forestall the War Council. Their advice was not heeded because of a desire not to bestow legitimacy on the Strike Committee. The War Council was held that evening, with a bonfire and some members of the Strike Committee dressed as Indians. A painted replica of the American flag was burned, and a series of confrontations took place around the campus, with students breaking windows and insulting and throwing objects at the Buffalo police. In front of the Administration Building, the inevitable occurred--the police charged at the students with clubs swinging. A number of injuries were sustained by both students and police, and some students were arrested.

A tense calm pervaded the campus for the next two days. However, on Sunday, March 15, 45 faculty members sat in the Acting President's office, with the explicit intention of remaining until the police were removed and the restraining order was lifted. They were arrested by the campus police with assistance from the Buffalo police. On Monday, demonstrations began again, with the number of participants somewhat increased as a reaction to the arrest of the "Faculty 45." The Strike Committee was reorganized into affinity groups with designated tasks to carry out over the spring recess, so that momentum would be maintained during this period. More peaceful student demonstrations followed, but the number of participants declined as many students left early for spring vacation. The last student demonstration took place on Wednesday, March 18--exactly three weeks after the police actions in the Student Union.

Moderate faculty members began organizing after the

confrontation of March 12. They formed the University
Survival Group and attempted, with some success, to
establish lines of communication with the Chancellor
of the State University system. The intent was to use
these lines to provide a more balanced picture of the
events at UB than the Chancellor's office was apparently getting from the UB Administration. Members of the
Survival Group also went to the Acting President on a
regular basis and attempted unsuccessfully to convince
him to resign. In their last visible action on campus,
members of this group presented a motion of no confidence in the Administration to the Faculty Senate on
March 17. This body, angered by the arrest of the
Faculty 45, passed the motion by a 7-3 majority.

The police were asked to leave the campus by the
Acting President shortly before the end of spring vacation. With the exception of unsuccessful attempts to
reorganize the affinity groups into an ongoing structure, the campus was calm and quiet until the United
States invasion of Cambodia and the killings at Kent
State.

The extent and depth of the crisis apparently undermined public support for the Acting President and several other high university officials. Before the crisis,
it had been generally believed that the new president
would be chosen from the existing Administration. Instead, a faculty member with a "law and order" reputation was chosen for this position, and many of the men
who had been key decision-makers during the crisis had
left the campus by the end of the next year.

CONFLICT PROCESS MODELS

Three basic approaches have been taken in the analysis
of community conflicts of the kind that occurred at UB.
These derive from three groups of models that take contrasting positions about the conflict process (i.e.,
how conflicts grow, maintain themselves, and are resolved): the aggressor-defender models, the conflict-
spiral models, and the structural change models. In
our view, each kind of model contains part of the truth,
and the three kinds seem relatively easy to integrate.
But we distinguish between them for three reasons: (a)
most conflict theorists adopt one approach to the ex-

clusion of the other two; (*b*) the same is true of many participants in conflict, including some in our case; and (*c*) these approaches have contrasting implications for conflict management.

Aggressor-Defender Models

These models assume a basic asymmetry between the two parties to a conflict. One party (the "aggressor") is assumed to be the originator of the conflict and the major contributor to its continuation. His behavior is typically explained in terms of the motives and emotions satisfied by conflict and the failure of deterrents against aggression. In the hands of theorists and commentators on campus conflicts, the students have usually been portrayed as the aggressors and the administration as the defenders.

Some analysts who adopt this approach attempt to account for the motivation of large segments of the student body. For example, Lipset (1970) attributes campus conflict to the frustrations and tensions of student life, which, he argues, have been due to the low status of the student role in the university, the growing ideology of independence, overcrowding on campuses, youthful idealism, and the Vietnam war. Other authors adopt a more sinister view of the phenomenon, attributing it to careful planning on the part of a small conspiratorial group of students who stir up the more idealistic elements of the broader student body and "lead them around like sheep." The conspiratorial view has been most frequent among people in law enforcement and legal systems (Hoover 1968; Moore 1965) but has also been held by some educators (Hayakawa 1969; Rafferty 1969). It would appear to be a version of the "blacktop" image described by White (1970).

Aggressor-defender models also underlie much of the thinking of those who attribute campus conflict to the failure of psychological deterrents. There are at least five varieties of deterrents against student aggression that either have been or can be postulated to have weakened in recent years: anticipation of punishment for aggression (Hook 1969; Howe 1968); respect for the university authority structure and authority in general (Bettelheim 1969; Rubenstein and Levitt 1967), a sense

of hopelessness about achieving student goals through
collective pressure against the administration (Davidson 1970; Rapoport and Kirshbaum 1969); personal contact and ties with members of the faculty and administration (Kerr 1964); and loyalty to the institution.

Aggressor-defender models are also important because
they enter into the thinking of many *participants* in
campus conflict and hence must be an element of any
comprehensive theory about this phenomenon. Thus, the
Acting President and others around him appear, in the
early stages of the crisis, to have subscribed to a
conspiratorial theory of the situation. In this view,
a hundred or so "vicious vandals" were responsible for
the conflict, and the crisis could only be solved by
deterrent actions, such as obtaining an injunction, re-
building the campus judiciary, suspending alleged radical leaders, and, finally, calling in the Buffalo police for a lengthy stay.

It is interesting to note that the student demonstrators also, by and large, subscribed to an aggressor-
defender model. However, in their eyes, the Administration was the aggressor and the student body the defender.
In this view, on February 25 the Administration authorized the police to invade student territory. Furthermore, various creations of the Administration, e.g.,
the ROTC and military research, aided the military,
which was an aggressor against the youth of America. In
light of such aggression, students had to defend themselves and obtain changes in basic policies.

Such perceptions on both sides may well have contributed to the amplitude and length of the crisis.

Aggressor-defender models are very heuristic in the
sense of pointing to motivational, emotional, and deterrent preconditions of conflict. In addition, they
adequately describe some of the processes that take
place during conflict. But they also have a number of
drawbacks, which are at least partially remedied in the
two other kinds of models:

(1) They paint a relatively static picture of conflict, in the sense that they largely ignore the way
conflicts change over time.

(2) They usually lead to a one-sided analysis of
causation which looks only at the sources of the aggressor's behavior. This defect can be remedied by

viewing both sides as aggressors, an approach which is not altogether satisfying.

(3) Scholars who employ aggressor-defender models tend to adopt a moralism that places blame on one or the other party, usually the one that is viewed as the aggressor. The scholar who allocates blame must inevitably distort certain facts. Participants who employ these models are likely to place the entire blame for a conflict on their adversaries. This makes them more likely to escalate the conflict because (as will be asserted later) blame legitimates aggressive behavior.

(4) Aggressor-defender models generally treat the groups that are in conflict as units and do not attend to the structure and dynamics within these units. There are occasional exceptions to this generalization, such as the black-top image of radicals leading moderate students around like sheep, but these exceptions are not very sophisticated.

Conflict-Spiral Models

The term *conflict-spiral* apparently originated with North (North, Brody, and Holsti 1964), but the concept appears in the writings of many other theorists, including Richardson (1960) in his model of the arms race, Osgood (1966) in his theory of the reverse arms race, Heirich (1971) in his analysis of the Berkeley Free Speech Controversy, and Pruitt (1969) in his discussion of reaction functions.

The basic assumption of conflict-spiral models is that conflict develops and is perpetuated through vicious circles in which each party's conflictive action is a punitive or defensive reaction to the other party's recent behavior. The other party then reacts with more conflict behavior, continuing the circle. Where aggressor-defender models search for a party who began the conflict, conflict-spiral models assume that beginnings are hard to trace. The spiral can almost always be pushed one step backward in time and a case made for assuming that either party is the aggressor.

A significant conflict spiral, involving many actions and reactions over about twenty-four hours, appears at the very beginning of our crisis.[2] On February 24,

blacks and radical whites sat down on the floor of the
basketball court during a game, as a result of which
the city police came on campus. This event led a group
of radicals to confront the Acting President on the
evening of February 25, which led him to get angry,
which led them to break his windows, which led him to
send the campus police into the Student Union, which
led students to assault the campus police, which led
the city police to clear the Student Union, which led
students to surround the city police and assail them
verbally, which led to multiple arrests of students.
There are some changes in the identity of the antagonists at different points in this sequence; but we can
view it as a simple spiral if we put the Administration and the campus and city police together into one
loose coalition and the black students, radical white
students, and enraged moderate students together into
another.

The entire crisis at UB can also be viewed as one
long spiral, as follows: the police assault students
on February 25; students riot on February 26; the Administration obtains a restraining order on February
27; students strike on March 3-4 and block the doors
of the Administration Building on March 5-6; the police
occupy the campus on March 8; students assail the police verbally on March 9-11 and harass them physically
on March 12; the police break ranks on March 12 and hit
students; 45 faculty members conduct a sit-in in the
Administration Building on March 15 to protest the police's presence and actions; the Administration has 45
faculty members arrested; the Faculty Senate censures
the Administration on March 18. Again there are drifts
in the identity of the antagonists, but the events can
be seen as a conflict spiral if we group together the
Administration and the police on the one hand and the
aroused students and faculty members on the other.

Aside from pointing out the spirals by which conflict is often perpetrated, theorists in the conflict-
spiral tradition have mainly attempted to describe the
pattern of these spirals. Another important task to
which theorists should turn their attention is accounting for the intensity of reactions at each new choice
point where the spiral begins another turn. Conflict
presumably grows when there is an overreaction to the

adversary's recent moves and diminishes or dies out
when there is an underreaction. In the absence of
this kind of theory, we have found it necessary to im-
provise.

Overreactions in our situation can be explained by
certain *momentary* factors, such as the Acting President's extreme tiredness on the night of February 25.
(He had been engaged in efforts to solve the black
athletes' problem during most of the preceding twenty-
four hours.) But such factors are hard to deal with
systematically. Overreactions may also be due to *more
permanent* factors, such as the standard operating procedures of the Buffalo Tactical Police Unit, the importance for many students of keeping the Student Union as
a sanctuary for the youth culture, the presence on campus of a number of radical students who were ready to
lead a protest, self-protective motives on the part of
policemen, administrators' sense of responsibility for
preventing damage to campus buildings, long-term police
hostility toward students and student hostility toward
the police, mounting pressure from certain members of
the faculty to do something decisive about radical disorder, a spirit of intolerance toward student demonstrators on the part of many Buffalo citizens and their
legislators, and the fact that each side saw the other
as the aggressor who was to blame for the conflict.

Conflict-spiral models correct some of the limitations of aggressor-defender models. For one thing, they
are more dynamic, in that they portray some of the
changes that occur during conflict. They are two-sided,
in that they examine the roots of conflict behavior on
both sides. This leads to a recognition that similar
motives--of protection and retaliation--often impel both
sides in a controversy. When participants in a conflict adopt a conflict-spiral approach, they do not
place blame so completely on the opponent and hence are
less likely to escalate the conflict by overreacting to
his latest provocation.

Both the conflict-spiral and the aggressor-defender
conflict model may help interpret a controversy that
developed with the UB Administration. There were
"hawks," who advocated escalatory measures, such as
calling on the police, and "doves," who advocated de-
escalatory measures, such as apologizing to the stu-

dents for the police raids on February 25 or closing
the school for a week's cooling-off period. The hawks
seem to have subscribed to an aggressor-defender model,
in which deterrence was the major consideration, while
the doves were apparently impelled by a conflict-spiral
model, which led them to seek a way to disrupt the
spiral.

Despite the strengths of conflict-spiral models, we
find it difficult to become really ecstatic about them
because they have a number of defects:

(1) They tend to be overly symmetrical in the way
they deal with the two sides to a controversy. Actually,
there are often major differences between the sides:
e.g., one may be better organized than the other; one
may favor change while the other values the status quo;
etc. Indeed, in some instances the asymmetrical aggressor-defender model would appear to be almost totally correct, as in the British conquest of India. What we are
saying here is that each model is correct under certain
circumstances, and a mixture of the two models is often
needed.

(2) Like the aggressor-defender models, conflict-
spiral models treat the parties to conflict as units
and do not usually attend to the structure of these
units. Hence, both models ignore the question of how
the parties to a conflict change in composition and
structure during the course of the conflict. Such
changes were apparent in the series of stages listed
above--where one party changed from a coalition of black
and radical white students, to a small group of radical
white students, to a coalition of radical and moderate
white students, to a coalition of students and faculty.
But neither the aggressor-defender nor the conflict-
spiral model has anything to say about such changes.

(3) Conflict-spiral models do not recognize in any
way the role of strategic planning in conflict. In
this regard, they are more naive than aggressor-defender models.

(4) Conflict-spiral models often do not adequately
account for the perpetuation of conflict beyond its beginning stages, even in cases that begin with a conflict spiral. They attempt to do so by postulating a
continuous cycle of action and reaction, but the facts
often do not support such an interpretation. For exam-

ple, there is a gap of six days in our case, between
February 27, when the Administration sought and obtained the restraining order, and March 5, when students
began blocking the doors of the Administration Building.
During this time, the Administration was not particularly provocative. In light of this period of delay, it is
hard to believe that blocking the doors was a simple reaction to the restraining order. Something must have
happened in the intervening period to keep student activism going. This "something" is the subject of the
structural change models, which are discussed below.

(5) Given the limitation just noted, conflict-spiral
models seem overly optimistic about the possibility of
reversing conflict processes once they get started. Such
models prescribe simple remedies that can often be implemented unilaterally, such as underreaction (or, as
it is sometimes called, "measured response") to provoca-
tions from the other side; goodwill gestures, such as
those proposed by Osgood (1966) for reversing the arms
race; and cooling-off periods. But when conflicts are
perpetuated by structural changes, such remedies are
likely to be relatively ineffective even in situations
that begin with a clear-cut conflict spiral.

Structural Change Models

These models are also dynamic, describing and accounting for changes that occur during a conflict. But unlike conflict-spiral models, they hold that certain *enduring* changes take place in one or both parties that
tend to perpetuate the conflict well beyond the motives
or the escalative sequence with which it began. Such
changes may occur in the social structure of the parties; in images, attitudes, or motives; or in the salience of issues or the depth of commitment to their solution. Structural change models are often asymmetrical, postulating different kinds of changes in the two
sides to a controversy.

Several examples of structural change models are
found in the literature on international conflict. For
example, Schumpeter (1955, first published in 1919)
points out that during a war military elites often become powerful within their own society. When the war
becomes unproductive or is terminated, they may not

wish to surrender their power and the privileges that
go with it. Hence they keep fighting or begin another
war, so that their services will continue to be seen
as indispensable by their fellow countrymen. Burton
(1962) argues that wars are often begun by nations that
have developed unlimited goals as a result of having
been frustrated in the attainment of limited goals during earlier nonviolent conflict with other states.
White (1970) hypothesizes that conflict induces black-
and-white thinking about the adversary, reduces empathy
with the adversary, and produces military overconfid-
ence--and that these perceptions, in turn, perpetuate
conflict.

In Schumpeter's theory, conflict engenders changes
in the structure of society which cause conflict to
continue. In Burton's theory, conflict engenders new
goals or demands which exacerbate and perpetuate conflict. In White's theory, the initial phases of a conflict produce perceptions which keep the conflict going.

The structural change model that best fits our case
is Coleman's (1957) theory of revolt against an administration, which is presented in his monograph *Community
Conflict*. This theory was derived inductively from a
comparison of a number of case studies, most of which
involved right-wing revolts against school officials
and city managers in the early 1950s.

The basic setting for Coleman's theory is a community
in which an administration is responsible for the welfare of a large unorganized public which is acquiescent
to it. The administration might be a city government,
a school board, or a school administration. A "precipitating incident" occurs--for example, the discovery
of allegedly communist books in a school library--which
leads the administration to become the defendant in a
controversy. This incident alarms the public, and people begin to question the administration's reliability.
Now certain structural changes take place. A partisan
organization is formed to conduct a struggle against
the administration in the name of, and with the support
of, large segments of the public. This organization is
often led by people who have long opposed the administration and now see an opportunity to attack it. These
are often ideologically committed, reckless individuals
"who have not been community leaders in the past [and]

who face none of the constraints of maintaining a previous community position" (p. 12). Now issues that
were previously hidden become salient. These are often
much broader and more devastating to the administration
than those concerned with the precipitating incident.
Indeed, the precipitating incident may be all but for-
gotten as larger issues come to center stage. Images
of the administrators change so that eventually they
seem totally bad; and a new motive often emerges--to
ruin the administrators rather than just change them.
While this is going on, certain other members of the
community spring to the defense of the beleaguered administration. The community now becomes polarized,
with interpersonal associations flourishing within the
opposing camps but withering between them.

Various structural changes are postulated by Coleman's theory. Some occur in the social structure of
the community; for example, the emergence of a struggle organization and the polarization of human relations. Others involve attitudes, issue salience, and
motives. These changes cause the controversy to become independent of the precipitating incident and, in
a very real sense, *self-perpetuating*.

So much for the dynamics of Coleman's theory. Coleman also talks about certain critical elements of the
situation which predispose it to the sequence of events
just outlined. It is necessary that there be (a) a
few extreme activists in the community who oppose the
administration and draw moral support and sometimes
tactical guidance from national sources; (b) a national
climate of fear and suspicion which predisposes elements
of the public to become hostile toward the administration; and (c) a lack of close.continuous relations between members of the administration and the public. In
addition, the sequence of events is more likely to develop to the extent that members of the public fail to
identify with the community as a whole.

Many features of our case fit the Coleman model. The
unorganized public consisted of the students and some
segments of the faculty at UB. The administration was,
of course, the university Administration. The precipitating incident that caused the Administration to become a defendant was the series of police raids on the
Student Union on the night of Febraury 25. A partisan

struggle organization was formed, the Strike Committee.
Its leaders were an ideologically committed group of
individuals who had been in opposition to the Administration for a long time, the campus radicals. They
essentially replaced the existing campus leadership.
Now new issues were brought forward--in the form of
various demands that went well beyond the precipitating
incident. The leader of the Administration under attack, the Acting President, began to be seen as totally
bad, and the struggle organization developed the goal
of forcing him out of his position. The university community became highly polarized, with members and supporters of the Strike Committee engaged in heavy interaction while breaking ties with the Administration and
its supporters. This polarization was also apparent in
a physical and psychological withdrawal from the campus by most of the top administrators.[3]

As the controversy developed, the dissenting students
appear to have lost sight of the precipitating incident,
as predicted by Coleman's theory. This development is
revealed in one aspect of a student survey we performed
shortly after spring vacation (Gahagan, Lewis, and Rubin
1970). When we asked students why they got into the
demonstrations, 43 percent of them indicated that it
was because of the police actions of February 25 or the
police occupation of the campus on March 8. But when
we asked them what the most important issue was, only
20 percent mentioned the police, and a majority referred
to strike demands other than those dealing with the police.

The critical elements which Coleman feels are needed
for such a crisis to develop were all present in our
situation. We had a few extreme activists who already
opposed the Administration and gained moral support and
some tactical advice from national sources, such as
Students for a Democratic Society. We had a national
climate of suspicion and hostility toward university
administrations among many young people. We had very
weak ties between the Administration and most UB students, and little, if any, feeling for the entire university community among most students. In addition,
some of the factors mentioned in connection with the
aggressor-defender models--e.g., the normal frustrations of student life, resentment against the Vietnam

war, and confidence in the possibility of achieving
"student power" by confrontation techniques--probably
also predisposed many of the UB students to join the
demonstrations once the precipitating incident had occurred.

Structural change models correct a number of the de-
ficiencies of aggressor-defender and conflict-spiral
models:

(1) They account for some of the asymmetries that
often exist in a situation. An example of such an
asymmetry in our case is the fact that the political
structure of the student body on our campus changed
radically during the crisis while the structure of the
Administration remained roughly the same. Indeed,
structural change models can sometimes account more
profoundly than the typical aggressor-defender model
for the behavior of parties that are generally assumed
to be engaged in unprovoked aggression. The conquest
of France by Germany in 1940, for example, is generally
viewed as unprovoked aggression. Yet, in a deeper
sense, it can be traced to attitudinal and, ultimately,
political changes in Germany which resulted from its
treatment by France and its allies after the First
World War (Burton 1962).

(2) When they describe changes in the composition
and political organization of parties to a conflict,
structural change models exhibit greater sophistication
than the other two types, which treat the parties as
units like billiard balls.

(3) Perhaps the strongest point in favor of structural change models is their utility in accounting for
the perpetuation of conflict. In a nutshell, they
postulate changes in social structure, attitudinal
structure, and the like, that tend to make conflict
self-perpetuating. Conflict-spiral models portray
human beings as essentially reactive to an immediate
threat--i.e., as responding primarily to fear and anger generated by the other party's most recent moves.
While there is some truth to this picture, it greatly
oversimplifies human psychology and totally ignores
social structure.

(4) Because they view conflict as self-perpetuating,
structural change models correct the undue optimisim
which we see in conflict-spiral models. They recognize

that conflict can be very hard to reverse once structural changes have begun to take root.

Another way to make some of these points is to ask what distinctive advice to administrators would emerge from a serious consideration of the Coleman model. Coleman would probably advise administrators to be very careful about antagonizing their publics on campuses where students have little contact with the administration and little identification with the campus community, and at times when there are many radicals on campus and there exists a national climate of student suspicion against administrations. If a precipitating incident occurs, the administration must try to undo it; in our case, e.g., by apologizing for the police actions of February 25, pointing the finger of blame at certain campus policemen, and devising guarantees of a nonrepetition of similar events. At the same time, efforts must be made to strengthen existing, legitimate student or faculty leadership as opposed to the potential radical leadership, e.g., by attending to their demands so that they can appear to be adequate to the crisis in the eyes of the student body. The most distinctive advice coming out of Coleman's and other structural change models concerns the importance of *timing*. Efforts to undo the precipitating incident and block the development of new structures must be taken rapidly and decisively, before the changes take hold. Waiting in the hope that the crisis will burn itself out only strengthens the hands of the emerging antiadministration leadership.

Like the other two types of models, structural change models are useful for interpreting the thinking of some participants in conflict. At UB, for example, some of the radical students seem to have had a sense of the dynamics described by Coleman when they capitalized on the precipitating incident. There is little evidence of such sophistication on the side of the Administration.

Integrating the Conflict-Spiral with
the Structural Change Approach

Although we are very partial to Coleman's structural change model as an aid to analyzing the UB crisis, we are not willing to completely discard conflict-spiral

models, because there were several obvious spirals in
our case. Rather, we see a need for integrating the
two approaches in a theory of community conflict. Our
case suggests that this integration can come about in
four ways:

(1) The precipitating incident that brings on a
Coleman-like process may arise from a conflict spiral.
Indeed, the precipitating incident on February 25 at
UB was actually a long series of incidents--police
raids, arrests, etc.--that marked the actions of one
side in a conflict spiral.

(2) Structural changes account for the fact that
conflict spirals often go on for weeks or even years.
Thus, in order to see the causal link between provocation from the Administration on February 25 and 27 and
student efforts to block access to the Administration
Building on March 5 and 6, it is necessary to know that
a Strike Committee was organized.

(3) In crises involving relations between an administration and a public, there are often multiple,
successive precipitating incidents, each representing
an action on the part of the administration in response
to a new provocation from the aroused public. Each incident engenders or strengthens hostile images, attitudes, and goals and provides groups for creating or
reviving the partisan organization and for further community polarization. Thus, on our campus the Administration called in the police on February 25, obtained
a restraining order on February 27, called the police
again on March 8, and had the Faculty 45 arrested on
March 15. Each move was a reaction to a challenge
from the students but also served to escalate or re-
vive the crisis by precipitating changes in social organization, attitudes, motives, and the like.

(4) Structural changes often take place *within the
administration* as well as within the public as a result of actions taken by the public or its representatives during the conflict spiral. Coleman makes this
point in part when he talks about polarization of the
administration and its allies. But on the administration side of the controversy our case reveals other
elements of the sequence he has described, for example,
the emergence of new leadership in the form of conservative administrators and faculty members whose counsel was given greater weight as the controversy continued.

THE IMPACT OF BLAME ON CONFLICT AND POWER

In developing a case study, the analyst often becomes
painfully aware of gaps in the theoretical literature
--phenomena that seem important in his case but have
received little attention from scholars. One such gap,
in the area of blame, has loomed before us as we have
tried to understand our case. Blame can be thought of
as the attribution of responsibility for an unpleasant
incident or state of affairs. We view blame as central
to the development of community conflicts like the one
that occurred at UB in the spring of 1970. The present
section will deal with the importance of blame in social conflict and power relations. A brief theory of
how blame develops will be sketched in the last section
of the paper.

Blame and Aggression

It is well known that people tend to become angry at
individuals whom they blame for the frustrations they
experience. Yet, surprisingly enough, frustration-aggression theory has tended to overlook blame. For example, in the writings of Berkowitz (1962, 1965) one
gains the impression that people can always identify
the source of their frustration--that there is no ambiguity about who is to blame. If blame channels anger,
then it follows that people who are blamed will tend
either to be avoided (Thibaut and Coules 1952) or to
become the targets of aggression (Berkowitz 1962).
     Anger is presumably not the only mediating link be-
tween blame and aggression. In his useful discussion
of revenge, Heider (1958) suggests that blaming another
person leads not only to anger but also to several
future-oriented goals, including (*a*) teaching the harm-
doer not to behave in the same way again, (*b*) communicating to him that he is not as powerful vis-à-vis oneself as his actions might imply, and (*c*) thereby maintaining one's own self-esteem. Any of these goals may
motivate aggressive behavior, but there are other ways
to express them, including, for example, exaggerated
forgiveness.
     If the other person is blamed for breaking a norm,
aggression may also be an expression of what is popularly

known as "righteous indignation," a sense that he deserves to be punished for the good of society. This
feeling may have been at the root of the undue force
employed by the Buffalo police in clearing the Student
Union on February 25. In a later interview with a high
police official, we discovered that the police regard
the Student Union as a haven for immorality. Not only
did the police official complain about what was sometimes true, that drugs were used in the Union, but he
also asserted that black men had sexual relations with
Jewish women from New York on special couches set aside
for this purpose. Clearly, the inhabitants of the
Union deserved any punishment they could get. Righteous
indignation was also apparent in the hostility of many
students toward the Administration for calling in the
city police without first consulting the joint Faculty-
Student-Administration Security Task Force. Indeed,
righteous indignation may underlie much student disorder in this country.

We hypothesize that blame, in addition to its role
in the simple frustration-aggression sequence, often
serves to release pent-up anger that has been felt
toward its object but had not been expressed previously.
Often resentment and hostility toward an individual or
a group build up as a result of a series of incidents
that occur over a long period of time. None of these
incidents has been sufficiently large or clear-cut, in
view of situational constraints against aggression, to
elicit aggressive behavior. Then an incident occurs
for which this individual or group can clearly be
blamed, and the pent-up anger is released in the form
of overt aggression. Such an incident is akin to the
precipitating incident in Coleman's (1957) model of
community conflict. Nothing like this sequence of
events has been observed in the psychological laboratory,
but historians and other observers of society have often
detected it in the genesis of revolts and revolutions.
Thus Nieburg writes as follows, "One shove of a woman
picket by a plant manager or a policeman may suddenly
focus years of accumulated grievances and unrelated
suffering" (1969, p. 77).

Closely related is the probable role of blame in
channeling "displaced aggression" toward the object
blamed (Bramel 1969). (By displaced aggression is
meant aggression due to frustrations unrelated to the

object of aggression.) This role is suggested by the
results of an experiment reported by Smith (1971), in
which aggression produced by frustration from the experimenter was apparently displaced onto a fellow student as a result of his failure to comply with a request. Various other conditions, such as dislike of
the target (Berkowitz 1965), also serve to channel displaced aggression, but everyday observations suggest
that blame may well be the most important channeler of
them all. In other words, we are arguing that the pro-
verbial angry executive is not so liekly to kick the
cat spontaneously as to kick it when it gets in the
way and can reasonably be blamed for something.

Why should blame release and channel aggression?
There are two possible answers. One assumes a norm or
social contract between people, a kind of mutual non-
aggression pact, in which my willingness to avoid ag-
gressing against you is exchanged for your willingness
to reciprocate. If I begin to blame you for harming
my interests, I feel less bound by this norm and freer
to aggress against you. Another position is suggested
by Schwartz (1970). Spontaneous aggression evokes
guilt and hence tends to be inhibited. But if the target of aggression can be blamed for something, he can
"be defined as responsible for his own predicament
[and it is then possible] to ascribe responsibility
for acting away from the self" (p. 129) and thus feel
less guilty. Both positions agree that blame releases
and channels aggression by *legitimating* it.

Conflict and the Direction of Blame

The points just made suggest the importance of blame
for a theory of conflict.

For one thing, the direction of blame determines who
becomes a party to conflict. Take the case of student
reactions to the police actions of February 25. The
student demonstrators at UB might have blamed any or
all of the following: the student radicals who first
broke the windows, the director of campus police, the
campus police in general, the Buffalo police chief, the
lieutenant who commanded the Buffalo Tactical Police
Unit on campus on the night of February 25, or the TPU
officers who entered the Union. Certainly most of these

individuals or groups were disliked for their part in
the events of February 25. But blame was almost exclusively directed at a totally different target, the
higher administrators of the University and in particular the Acting President. This allocation of blame
then shaped the course of later events, which took the
form of a classical Coleman-like progression, involving
conflict between a formerly unorganized mass and the
administration serving it. Actions taken thereafter by
the higher administrators to defend the university were
also blamed on the Acting President, which further
fanned the flames. In addition, had the Acting President not become a target, he might have found people to
identify the students who blocked the Administration
Building on March 5-6 and thus avoided the unmeasured,
escalative response of calling in the Buffalo police
for a lengthy occupation.

The way in which members of an administration allocate blame presumably also shapes the course of a Coleman-like progression. More precisely, our findings
suggest that blaming the leadership of the emerging opposition makes administrators less capable of reversing
such a progression, because they are unaware of the need
to appease a large number of their constituents who are
genuinely aggrieved. In our case, it appears that several of the most influential administrators blamed the
events of February 25 and subsequent days primarily on
the radicals who first broke the windows in the Acting
President's office and then became organizers of the
Strike Committee. This is evident in the Acting President's TV address on March 1, in which he indicted a
"few hundred vicious vandals," and in an interview
statement by an influential vice-president who drew an
analogy between a flock of sheep and the rebellious
students being led around by a bunch of radicals. In
response to efforts by other members of the Administration and several faculty members to shift blame for the
February 25 incidents onto the shoulders of the campus
police, the Acting President indicated that he did not
have enough evidence to reach such a conclusion. There
is no reason to believe that he ever blamed himself or
those who participated with him in the decision-making.

The Coleman-like progression might well have been
reversed on February 26 or 27 had the Acting President

apologized for the police actions of February 25, begun
an investigation of the policemen involved, and demonstrated that safeguards were being adopted to prevent
the recurrence of such incidents. But no such statements or actions were forthcoming from his office. Besides cooling down student and faculty passions, such a
statement would probably have strengthened the hand of
the leaders of Student Government, who could quite legitimately have taken credit for eliciting it. This
might have reduced the appeal of the radical, rump leadership and thereby blocked the emergence of the Strike
Committee with its capacity for independent escalative
action. Also, if Student Government has assumed the
leadership of the struggle movement, the Acting President would undoubtedly have felt freer to negotiate
with the alarmed students, and residual issues could
have been resolved peacefully.

Conflict and the Extent to Which Blame Is Focused

In addition to determining who gets blamed, it is necessary to find out how much of the blame for an event
is allocated to each of the parties blamed. Blame may
be highly focused onto a single individual, moderately
diffused onto a group of people or an organization, or
thoroughly dispersed, as when it is directed at "the
system."

We hypothesize that a conflict will be waged more
vigorously and with more extreme tactics the more focused blame is for the incident that launches the conflict. Gurr (1970) also makes this point when he says,
"The more concrete the force identified, the more effectively is anger focussed on it. 'The establishment'
is an elusive opponent" (p. 205). It follows that the
degree to which blame is focused determines in part the
extent to which conflict will escalate and hence the
likelihood and rapidity of conflict spirals.

Many theorists (e.g., Frank 1968) have noted a tendency for the participants in conflict to blame the top
leadership of the opposing party. This leads to the
"black-top image" of the adversary which White (1970)
views as a universal element of conflict. We saw this
in our case in the tendency of student demonstrators to
blame the Acting President for everything, including

policies that were under the control of the Faculty
Senate (e.g., the academic status of credits from ROTC
courses), and in the tendency of some higher administrators to blame the entire crisis on the radical leadership.

It is inevitable that the head man of an organization will become involved in some conflicts with factions in his organization. But if the conflicts are
too severe, everybody in the organization may suffer.
There are three reasons for this:

(1) The head man is often an important key to effectiveness and morale. If he becomes discredited or
distracted with the details of conflict, the organization may lose its capacity to make meaningful decisions,
as apparently happened in our crisis.

(2) The head man is often the key mediator between
elements within his organization. There is usually
more to this mediation than simply presenting neutral
suggestions. He must use the power of his office to
bring disputing parties together and to force careful
consideration of his proposals. If he himself becomes
a defendant in a controversy, there may be nobody left
with the power to mediate effectively. This also happened in our crisis. On March 5-6, when demonstrators
were blockading the Administration Building, several
faculty members attempted mediation. In one case, the
Acting President refused to meet with representatives
of the dissenting students. In another, he refused to
talk to the would-be mediator. We are not arguing that
mediation would or should have settled the controversy
at this point, but only that the story illustrates one
problem of having the head man as a prime defendant.
The Acting President's behavior before the crisis suggests that he might well have attempted mediation had
the conflict involved any part of the organization
other than himself. At a later time, other faculty
members went over the Acting President's head and tried
to get the Chancellor of the university to send a representative to mediate the controversy. But this request was denied on the ground that it would undercut
the Acting President's authority. Again, effective
mediation was not possible.

(3) When the head man becomes a defendant within
his organization, he is likely to become cut off from

the dissenting portions of the organization and therefore to lack critical information about what is going
on.   Also, because he is angry he may misconstrue certain critical issues.   Such a state of affairs may
make him an unreliable decision-maker.   Yet, it may be
hard to reverse his decisions because he is the head
man.   This is illustrated in our case in that the Acting President and a number of his associates withdrew
from the campus, psychologically as well as physically,
and apparently did not comprehend the true nature of
their position.

Blame and Power

We come now to the basic theme of this volume--power.
It seems quite clear, in the light of what has just
been said, that being blamed can lead to the loss of
at least part of a leader's power.   This power arises
from a number of sources: the capacity to communicate
with his constituents, the extent to which constituents
identify with the leader, his legitimacy in their eyes,
and his capacity to reward and punish them.   Blame can
interfere with normal communication in several ways.
The person blamed may be avoided, or communication to
him may mainly take the form of efforts to persuade him
to change his ways.   Furthermore, the person blamed may,
for defensive reasons, isolate himself from those who
blame him.   In addition, blame can erode the attraction
and admiration which constituents feel toward a leader
and hence reduce the extent to which they identify with
him (Kelman 1958).   Hollander and Julian's (1970) work
suggests that a leader's legitimacy may likewise be a
casualty of blame, if he comes to be viewed as incompetent or as lacking concern for the interests of his
group.   Another way of making this latter point is to
say that blame tends to erode trust in a leader and
hence, according to Gamson's (1968) analysis, to produce increased demands on him in the face of eroding
willingness to cooperate with him.
    Blame is less capable of eroding reward and punitive
power than the other forms of power mentioned; hence,
the governments of alienated masses tend to rely on
these grosser forms of influence.   However, we know that
even coercive power is weakened to the extent that the

possesser of such power lacks legitimacy (French and Raven 1959). Threats from a leader who has lost legitimacy as a result of becoming a defendent in a major crisis are likely to be resented and may therefore be disregarded. Furthermore, people feel little guilt about building counterpower against the coercive capability of an illegitimate leadership.

Blame can also reduce a leader's power by giving his adversaries within an organization a cause around which to rally their forces, i.e., by setting one or more Coleman-like processes into motion.

Erosion of the Acting President's power during the 1970 UB crisis was quite apparent. Not only was he unable to control the demonstrators, but, because he became the target of blame, he lost influence over large segments of the campus community. Early in the first week of the crisis, he was forced to move to a little-known location--at a distance from the events about which he was making decisions. During the second week, a number of administrators resigned, and other administrators and faculty members tried to go over his head and establish communication with the Chancellor of the State University and members of the state legislature. Hundreds of classes were canceled, and at one time a classroom building was devoted primarily to seminars run by members of the Strike Committee and their sympathizers. The final blow was a vote of no confidence by the Faculty Senate and the elimination of the ROTC from campus, a move which the Acting President opposed. With his authority and capacity to exert informal leadership on the campus largely eroded, the Acting President was forced to rely almost exclusively on coercive power wielded by the Buffalo police. Even the police had difficulty keeping order at times, because their right to be on campus was widely disputed.

DETERMINANTS OF THE ALLOCATION OF BLAME

Determinants of the Extent to Which an Individual Is Blamed for His Actions

The rather skimpy research literature on the psychology of blame has mainly taken an attribution-theory approach, within a framework laid down by Heider (1958). Heider

was interested in the extent to which a person is
blamed for actions he has clearly taken. Heider hypothesized that, in the eyes of adults, a person will be
blamed for actions that have negative consequences only
if he apparently intended those consequences and was
seemingly not constrained to act as he did by norms or
overwhelming social pressure. In contrast, children
will allocate blame more on the basis of the effect of
an action and less on the basis of the apparent intention underlying it. Shaw and Sulzer (1964) have confirmed both of these hypotheses in a study that compared
second graders with college students. That the effects
of an action are not irrelevant to *adult* thinking is
suggested by Walster's (1966) finding that the more
harmful an action's consequences, the more responsible
an individual is held for it. However, it should be
noted that Walster's finding has not been replicated
(Shaver 1970; Shaw and Skolnik 1971). Experimental
evidence also suggests that an individual is blamed
more for actions taken in an effort to improve his circumstances than for actions designed "to prevent a de-
terioration in those circumstances" (Kelley 1971, p. 21).

Determinants of Who Will Be Blamed
for Complex Events

While the ideas and results discussed above are interesting, the framework within which they have arisen is
overly narrow for understanding conflict phenomena of
the type described earlier, in that many conflict-in-
ducing actions cannot easily be traced to the behavior
of a single individual. They are determined by a chain
of events involving many people, each of whom is a potential target for blame. An example would be the police raids of February 25. For such events, the question of who gets blamed, as well as Heider's question
of the extent to which anybody gets blamed, must be
answered. When several people can be blamed, failure
to prevent an action taken by others may be as much a
basis for blame as actually taking an action.
     As a start toward building a theory about who gets
blamed, we might look at the rules for assigning blame
under the law. Such rules often have their origin in
ordinary human interaction and hence may serve as pre-

liminary models to be tested in nonlegal settings. A
case in point would be legal responsibility for auto-
mobile accidents. At times, a concept of prior formal
responsibility is invoked; for example, the owner of a
car may be held responsible for lending it to a minor
who has an accident. At other times, blame falls on
the person with the greatest freedom of action. In
still other instances, the person who has the last
clear chance to avoid the accident may be held responsible. Intersocietal differences in legal principles
and practices for the assignment of blame may serve as
preliminary guides to the development of a theory of
cultural differences in ordinary interpersonal blame
assignment.

An interesting question concerns how blame is allocated in a conflict spiral. We hypothesize that the
party who *most overreacts* is likely to be most blamed.
This may help explain why so many relatively neutral
people at UB blamed the Acting President for calling in
the police on March 8 rather than members of the Strike
Committee, whose blockade of the Administration Building had precipitated his summoning of the police. The
"punishment" of having 400 policemen occupying the campus did not seem to fit the "crime" of blocking the
doors. The moral of this story seems clear: to avoid
blame that may erode his power an administrator should
employ a *measured response* to provocation from his adversaries.

So far, we have only discussed the impact on blame
of elements of the situation. But the significance
of situational elements is often unclear, so that a
determination of blame cannot be readily made. In such
cases, predispositions (i.e., perceptual sets) presumably come into play (Pruitt 1965). For example, when
in doubt, we tend to blame the person whose actual or
alleged past behavior has given him a bad reputation.
This principle is written into the courtroom practice
of listening to character witnesses. The stronger such
a predisposition, the less conclusive need be situational evidence of blame.

There is also undoubtedly a tendency to exonerate
people to whom we are psychologically close and to
blame people we do not know or do not like. This tendency is illustrated by Hastorf and Cantril's (1954)

famous study, in which students watching a football
game tended to blame the opposing team for rule infrac-
tions. This principle may help to explain why larger
colleges and universities have had a greater number of
and more violent student disorders in the last few
years (Long and Foster 1970). On larger campuses, students are psychologically more cut off from upper administrators and hence more prone to blame them for un-
toward incidents. As a result, Coleman-like progres-
sions are more likely to get started.[4]

The conflict model espoused by a person can predispose him to certain kinds of blame perception. A person who ordinarily thinks in terms of an aggressor-defender model is likely to find it necessary to allocate
blame to one or the other side in a controversy, most
often the side he opposes. Adherents to conflict-spiral
models more often blame both sides or neither side.

Blame allocation may also play an adaptive role. For
example, it is possible that blame tends to be allocated to individuals whose future behavior seems most
susceptible to influence (Kelley 1971) or who seem to
have the greatest capacity to prevent the recurrence of
incidents like those in question (Berkowitz 1962; Gurr
1970). We might also hypothesize that people tend to
blame vulnerable individuals who cannot easily fight
back (Gurr 1970) and individuals whom they wish to hurt
for other reasons.

Situational, dispositional, and adaptive principles
have been mentioned above as determinants of who gets
blamed for an unpleasant event. This framework constitutes a starting point for theory about this question,
but the analysis has been minimal and fragmented because of the absence of relevant literature. There is
clearly a theoretical and empirical gap here.

Sources of the Black-Top Image

We come now to the question of why blame tends to become focused during conflict and, in particular, to the
psychological origins of the black-top image of the adversary, which blames only the leaders on the other
side for the actions of their group or organization. A
literature exists on the origins of this ubiquitous
phenomenon, though unfortunately it is explanatory
rather than propositional or predictive.

One explanation, given by Toch (1965), assumes that people who are confused and frightened, as people often are during conflict, tend to seek simplifying principles that resolve both stimulus and response uncertainty. When unpleasant events are blamed on an individual or a small group of people, "everything falls easily into place, the person comes to feel enlightened, and experiences the exhilarating feeling of living in a coherent--if dangerous world" (p. 52).

Other explanations focus on difficulties inherent in perceiving oneself as in conflict with an entire group or nation. White (1970, p. 30) emphasizes the "guilt of feeling hostile to a large number of people" that is eliminated by feeling hostile only toward their leader or leaders. Frank (1968) stresses the difficulty of maintaining one's self-respect while believing that many people are hostile toward oneself, a difficulty that is resolved by believing that those people are being deceived by their leaders. He also suggests that the black-top image creates "a positive image of oneself as saving the underdog masses [on the other side] from their conniving, oppressive leaders" (White 1970, p. 30).

A developmental explanation can also be given for the black-top image. Most children see themselves as dealing with individuals or small groups rather than with organizations, and when they get angry the object is therefore usually an individual or a small group. Furthermore, the pressures of socialization ensure that this object will very often be the father or the parents. These well-learned schemata persist into adulthood, so that it is easier to feel angry toward an individual or a small group than toward an organization, particularly if the individual or group is a parental surrogate, such as the head man or top management of the opposing organization.

Tactics of Blame Allocation

While black-top images often develop spontaneously as a result of natural psychological pressures, they are also frequently induced by leaders who know that their constituents will wage conflict more vigorously if they blame the leadership of the opposition. A tactical model devised by Saul Alinsky (1946, 1971) for use by

groups working for social change will be briefly analyzed.[5] Some of the tactics employed by the radical
leadership at UB are related to Alinsky's model, though
the UB case differs in that the precipitating incidents
were not induced as recommended by Alinsky.

Alinsky starts by taking an issue (e.g., segregation
in schools) and picks his target on the basis of assumed role responsibility (e.g., the school superin-
tendent). Once the issue is chosen, anger and hostility are developed within the organized group and directed toward the target so that an overreaction is obtained. This overreaction then becomes the basis for
further blame allocation and for the escalation of the
struggle behavior. The tactics focus on the attribution of blame and the intensification of anger and
hostility in a two-step process:

(1) Pick the target and freeze it.

(2) Personalize the target and blacken both the
target and the issue.

In a complex bureaucratic society, picking the target is difficult both because of the division of responsibility and because of the tendency of bureaucrats
to try to deflect blame above or below in the authority
structure. Alinsky's position is that, whenever possible, the top man in an organization should be the target. This appears to be shrewd advice for a number of
reasons: (1) Black-top images come naturally to people in conflict situations. (2) The top man is generally the most visible and public member of the organization. (3) The top man is seen as responsible for
the policies and decisions of the organization and as
capable of influencing future policies and decisions.
(4) The top man cannot easily deflect blame onto subordinates because he is in charge of the entire organization and has no superior onto whom he can deflect
blame. (5) The top man is usually the person most
capable of altering the course of the organization.

Freezing the target refers to pinning him down by
countering his efforts to explain his behavior and by
blocking all efforts to deflect the blame onto a more
diffuse target or onto an individual lower in rank.
Freezing tactics focus on the responsibility of the top
man for the actions of his subordinates and the policies of the organization.

   Personalizing the target and blackening the target
and the issue function to intensify the anger generated
by blame and to legitimate the expression of this anger.
Personalization identifies the target as a particular
individual rather than as the role he fills. Personalization takes advantage of the anthropomorphic tendency
to ascribe the locus of causality to a person rather
than to role constraints, social dynamics, or situational factors (Heider 1958). It is necessary to see
the adversary as a person rather than a role in order
to blacken his image by attributing negative human characteristics to him (e.g., cruelty and insensitivity).
   For the anger and hostility thus generated to have a
full impact on the target, the issue must also be blackened and tied to the target. It is preferable to be
able to point to a particular decision or to a series
of decisions for which the target is responsible.
   The harm produced by these decisions is then drama-
tized so that righteous indignation will be directed at
the already personalized and blackened target, assuring
disinhibition and the release of hostility and aggression in his direction.
   Elements of the UB crisis provide a good example of
blackening the issue and the target and connecting the
two. A causal theory about the events of February 25
was articulated by Strike Committee members at rallies
following these events and was largely accepted by the
audiences at the rallies. This theory was as follows:

   (1) The Acting President made the decision to send
        the campus police and the Buffalo police into
        the Union.
   (2) Students were beaten and arrested because of
        this decision.
   (3) This decision contradicted his own rule book in
        that the decision was made unilaterally rather
        than at the direction of the Faculty-Student-
        Administration Security Task Force.
   (4) The Acting President was "bad" because he
        caused the beatings and arrests.
        (a) A derogatory variant of his real name was
             assigned to him for the remainder of the
             crisis.
        (b) A derogatory cartoon of him was also used
             to reinforce the belief in his badness.

(5) But we always knew he was bad--he just lived up
to his reputation. The Acting President's past
behavior was then cited to demonstrate his bad-
ness.

    (*a*) He set up the Advocate's Office and then
directed the Advocate to assist Buffalo
courts in bringing charges against the
ROTC 19.

    (*b*) He emphasized law and order by outfitting
police with riot-control equipment.

    (*c*) His insensitivity to students had been de-
monstrated in his continual references to
physical damage to the university while
ignoring injuries sustained by students.

This theory was quite successful in alienating many
students and some faculty members from the Acting President.

NOTES

1. The figure of 70 percent was derived from the
results of a sample survey conducted several weeks after
the end of the crisis (Gahagan, Lewis, and Rubin 1970).
Of the 125 respondents, 22 percent indicated heavy involvement in anti-Administration activities (active involvement with the Strike Committee or participation in
disruptive demonstrations); 48 percent indicated light
involvement in anti-Administration activities (attending rallies and nondisruptive demonstrations or cutting
classes as a sign of sympathy with the strike); 11 percent characterized themselves as having been involved
in antistrike activities (breaking picket lines, attending class during the strike, or arguing with demonstrators); and 19 percent said they were uninvolved in the
crisis.

2. It should be noted that we view *crises* as having
beginnings at a point where many people become aware of
an acute problem, even though *conflict spirals* may not.

3. Our case study suggests that the concept of polarization is not sufficient to describe all changes in
coalition structure within a community during conflict.
As the crisis progressed, some groups, most notably
black students and engineering students, became more
neutral rather than more polarized.

4. The relationship between size of institution
and incidence and type of student disorder may also be
due to the reduced inhibition against conflict and violence and the difficulty of getting together for effective negotiation that often accompany psychological
distance.

5. Alinsky also devised an elaborate set of tactics
for building struggle organizations, which will not be
described here.

REFERENCES

Alinsky, S. 1946. *Reveille for radicals.* Chicago:
University of Chicago Press.
------. 1971. *Rules for radicals.* New York: Random
House.
Berkowitz, L. 1962. *Aggression: a social psychologi-
cal analysis.* New York: McGraw-Hill.
------. 1965. The concept of aggressive drive: some
additional considerations. In L. Berkowitz (Ed.),
Advances in experimental social psychology. Vol. 2.
New York: Academic Press.
Bettelheim, B. 1969. Student revolt: the hard core.
Vital Speeches of the Day 35: 405-10.
Bramel, D. 1969. Interpersonal attraction, hostility,
and perception. In J. Mills (Ed.), *Experimental
social psychology.* London: Macmillan.
Burton, J. W. 1962. *Peace theory.* New York: Knopf.
Coleman, J. S. 1957. *Community conflict.* New York:
Free Press.
Davidson, C. 1970. The new radicals in the multivers-
ity. In C. Katope and P. Zolbrod (Eds.), *The rhet-
oric of revolution.* New York: Macmillan.
Frank, J. 1968. *Sanity and survival: psychological
aspects of war and peace.* New York: Vintage Books.
French, J. R. P., Jr., and Raven, B. H. 1959. The
bases of social power. In D. Cartwright (Ed.),
Studies in social power. Ann Arbor: University of
Michigan Press.
Gahagan, J. P., Lewis, S. A., and Rubin, I. 1970.
Strike issues remain. *Spectrum* (student newspaper
at the State University of New York at Buffalo),
11 December. 21 (39), 1-2.

Gamson, W. A. 1968. *Power and discontent*. Homewood, Ill.: Dorsey Press.

Gurr, T. R. 1970. *Why men rebel*. Princeton, N.J.: Princeton University Press.

Hastorf, A. H., and Cantril, H. 1954. They saw a game: a case study. *Journal of Abnormal and Social Psychology* 49: 129-34.

Hayakawa, S. I. 1969. Education in ferment. In J. McEvoy and A. Miller (Eds.), *Black power and student rebellion*. Belmont, Calif.: Wadsworth.

Heider, F. 1958. *The psychology of interpersonal relations*. New York: Wiley.

Heirich, M. 1971. *The spiral of conflict: Berkeley 1964*. New York: Columbia University Press.

Hollander, E. P., and Julian, J. W. 1970. Studies in leader legitimacy, influence, and innovation. In L. Berkowitz (Ed.), *Advances in Experimental Social Psychology*. Vol. 5. New York: Academic Press, pp. 34-70.

Hook, S. 1969. *Academic freedom and academic anarchy*. New York: Cowles.

Hoover, J. 1968. Testimony presented before the National Commission on the Causes and Prevention of Violence, 18 September.

Howe, I. 1968. The new 'confrontation politics' is a dangerous game. *New York Times Magazine* 72, 20 October, 27-29.

Kelley, H. H. 1971. *Attribution in social interaction*. New York: General Learning Press.

Kelman, H. C. 1958. Compliance, identification, and internalization: three processes of opinion change. *Journal of Conflict Resolution* 2: 51-60.

Kerr, C. 1964. The frantic race to remain contemporary. *Daedalus* 93: 1051-70.

Lipset, S. M. 1970. American student activism in comparative perspective. *American Psychologist* 25: 675-93.

Long, D., and Foster, J. 1970. Levels of protest. In D. Long and J. Foster (Eds.), *Protest! student activism in America*. New York: Morrow.

Moore, C. E. 1965. Anarchy on the campus: the law. *Police Chief* 32: 48-60.

Nieburg, H. L. 1969. *Political violence: the behavioral process*. New York: St. Martin's Press.

North, R. C., Brody, R. A. and Holsti, O. R. 1964.
Some empirical data on the conflict spiral. *Peace Research Society (International) Papers* 1: 1-14.

Osgood, C. E. 1966. *Perspective in Foreign Policy.*
2d ed. Palo Alto, Calif.: Pacific Books.

Pruitt, D. G. 1965. Definition of the situation as a
determinant of international action. In H. C. Kelman (Ed.), *International behavior: a social psychological analysis.* New York: Holt, Rinehart & Winston.

------. 1969. Stability and sudden change in interpersonal and international affairs. *Journal of Conflict Resolution* 13: 18-38.

Rafferty, M. 1969. Campus violence: a fascist conspiracy. In J. McEvoy and A. Miller (Eds.), *Black power and student rebellion.* Belmont, Calif.: Wadsworth.

Rapoport, R. and Kirshbaum, L. J. 1969. *Is the library burning?* New York: Vintage Books.

Richardson, L. F. 1967. *Arms and insecurity.* Chicago: Quadrangle Books.

Rubenstein, B. and Levitt, M. 1967. Rebellion and responsibility. *Yale Review* 57: 16-30.

Schumpeter, J. 1955. *The sociology of imperialism.* New York: Meridian Books.

Schwartz, S. H. 1970. Moral decision making and behavior. In J. R. Macaulay and L. Berkowitz (Eds.), *Altruism and helping behavior.* New York: Academic Press.

Shaver, K. G. 1970. Defensive attribution: effects of severity and relevance on the responsibility assigned for an accident. *Journal of Personality and Social Psychology* 14: 101-13.

Shaw, J. I., and Skolnik, P. 1971. Attribution of responsibility for a happy accident. *Journal of Personality and Social Psychology* 18: 380-83.

Shaw, M. E., and Sulzer, J. L. 1964. An empirical test of Heider's levels in attribution of responsibility. *Journal of Abnormal and Social Psychology* 69: 39-46.

Smith, R. B. 1971. Coercive influence as a function of frustration and fantasy aggression. *Proceedings, 79th Annual Convention, American Psychological Association,* 231-32.

Thibaut, J. W., and Coules, J. 1952. The role of communication in the reduction of interpersonal hostility. *Journal of Abnormal and Social Psychology* 47: 770-77.

Toch, H. 1965. *The social psychology of social movements*. Indianapolis, Ind.: Bobbs-Merrill.

Walster, E. 1966. Assignment of responsibility for an accident. *Journal of Personality and Social Psychology* 3: 73-79.

White, R. K. 1970. *Nobody wanted war: misperception in Vietnam and other wars*. Garden City, N.Y.: Doubleday Anchor Books.

VI

THE MEANS
OF INFLUENCE

Economic Power 11

David A. Baldwin

The study of interpersonal power cuts across many disciplinary boundaries. The purpose of this paper is to explore the nature of political and economic power, the peculiarities of economic power when exercised in a political arena, and the ways in which insights drawn from the literature on interpersonal power might enhance our understanding of economic and political power.

The need for such exploratory work was impressed upon me when I began research on the role of economic techniques of statecraft in international politics. It was difficult to adapt the standard terminology and modes of analysis of international political analysis to such an undertaking. Students of international politics had become so preoccupied with negative sanctions, threat systems, and military force that they had painted themselves into a conceptual corner which left little room for nonmilitary factors, positive sanctions, and promise systems (Baldwin 1971a, 1971d, 1971e; Sprout & Sprout 1971). It is not surprising, therefore, that the recent *International Encyclopedia of the Social Sciences* (1968) included an article on military power potential but none on economic power potential. At a time when military power is losing utility in international politics (Knorr 1966) and economic power is gaining utility, this omission was especially unfortunate. It is my hope that students of international politics

blish closer links with the literature of in-
_____sonal power and thereby lay the conceptual foun-
dations for a broader and more relevant understanding
of the role of power in the international political
system.

ECONOMICS AND POLITICS

In approaching the study of economic power, the obvious
discipline to turn to is economics. At first, the in-
quiry is likely to disappointing, since the discipline
of economics has been "characterized by a strange lack
of power considerations" (Rothschild 1971, p. 7). Explicit discussions of power are rare in economic literature, and only a few economists have contributed directly to the social power literature (e.g., Harsanyi 1962;
Lindblom 1953; Schelling 1960). The initial impression
that economics has little to say about power, however,
can be misleading. The price system is, after all, an
extremely effective means by which some people get other
people to do what they would not otherwise do. The
economists' focus on one form of human behavior should
not blind us to the fact that this behavior could be
described in terms of the exercise of power over others.
The spectacular progress of economic science in this
century is probably due to the willingness of economists
to focus sharply on a particular kind of behavior (i.e.,
buying and selling) in a particular set of circumstances
(i.e., market conditions). Just as Molière's *bourgeois
gentilhomme* found that he spoke prose, so the economists
may find that they have been discussing power.

Circumstances in which free market forces break down,
such as monopoly and oligopoly, have already forced
economists to draw closer to the intellectual perspective of the students of social power. Both the development and the application of game theory are traceable
to the economists' desire to explain price behavior in
an oligopolistic market (Von Neumann and Morgenstern
1944).

A number of social scientists seem to suspect that
economics can be useful to the student of social power.
Coleman (1963), for example, claims that monetary theory
comes closer than any other to a "theory of influence
systems." Others have suggested that the theory of
economic exchange can be generalized to other kinds of

social interaction (Blau 1964; Curry and Wade 1968;
Ilchman and Uphoff 1969). Still others are fascinated
by the prospects of finding a counterpart for money in
the political system, since the existence of money
seems to solve for the economist so many of the problems that beset the student of political power (Baldwin
1971c).

Regardless of the possibility of finding (or creating) a political counterpart for money, few social scientists would deny that politics and economics are difficult to separate. There is not much agreement, however, on just what it means to say that politics is in-
tertwined with economics. Quincy Wright has drawn what
I regard as a useful and clear distinction between the
two spheres, while specifying the way in which they
overlap:

> Economic activity includes all activity rationally
> designed to achieve human objectives when faced by
> the niggardliness of nature, that is, by the scar-
> city of material or human resources. It is there-
> fore contrasted with political activity which in-
> cludes all activity designed to achieve group ob-
> jectives when faced by the opposition of other groups.
> Scarcity is the essence of economics as opposition
> is of politics. In economics, the problem is to
> overcome obstructions to achievement arising from
> physical nature, in politics to overcome obstructions
> arising from human nature (Wright 1955, p. 237).

Wright's definition of the two spheres not only distinguishes between them, but also makes it clear that both
are concerned with overcoming resistance. Wright goes
on to spell out the interdependency between politics
and economics:

> A shortage of resources leads to competition between
> different persons or groups to obtain them and this
> may lead to rivalry, conflict, and political activ-
> ity by each to overcome the obstruction offered by
> others to attaining its objectives. Conversely, a
> group may persuade an opposing group to yield to its
> demands by offering economic rewards or withholding
> economic advantages. Economics may therefore be an
> instrument of politics. (Wright 1955, p. 239).

ALTERNATIVE CONCEPTS OF ECONOMIC POWER

The term *economic power* tends to be used rather loosely, as is indicated by a review of some common meanings.

(1) *Productive power.* Perhaps the most common meaning of economic power is ability to produce goods and services in a given time period. For a nation *gross national product* (GNP) would be the equivalent term, while for an individual the equivalent term would be *earning power.*

(2) *Productive power relative to need.* A refinement of the above concept relates productive capacity to need. Thus, one might encounter the statement that John, with two children and a $15,000 annual income, has more economic power than Tom, who has the same income but eight children. In international relations per capita GNP would be the counterpart of this example. Although India and Canada have about the same GNP, Canada has only 20 million mouths to feed, while India has 500 nillion. Therefore, many people would not regard them as equal in economic power.

(3) *Growth rate.* Another concept of economic power is the ability to generate self-sustaining economic growth. The nation with a steady GNP growth rate of 5 percent will probably be accorded more economic power than the nation with a lower or less reliable rate of growth. This concept has been especially conspicuous in post-World War II discussions of international relations.

(4) *Specialized production power.* Some analysts are not satisfied with GNP as a measure of power even when it is related to need and the rate of growth. It is misleading, they argue, to equate ability to produce luxury consumer goods with ability to produce steel, cement, heavy machinery, and petroleum (cf. Morgenthau 1967). Underlying such discussions, one often finds the implicit assumption that national power is a function of military force and that economic power should be measured by this criterion.

(5) *War potential.* A sophisticated version of the preceding concept relates procudtive capacity to war-making ability in a clear and explicit way (Knorr 1955, 1970). Every facet of the economy is measured in terms

of the contribution it could make to a nation's war effort. Although this has obvious limitations, it does provide a sharply defined measure of economic power relative to a specified goal. The other four concepts share the fault of failing to specify the scope of the power relationship. Yet many students of power regard specification of scope as essential to a meaningful discussion of power (Lasswell and Kaplan 1950; Dahl 1963, 1968).

(6) *Market position*. Another concept of economic power concerns the ability of a firm to influence the market price of its products. Thus, a monolithic firm is said to have a "powerful" market position as compared to firms in a highly competitive market, in which no single firm can affect the price to an appreciable degree. In analyzing oligopoly, economists have provided a literature with applications that go beyond the problem that concerns them. Several students of international politics have found this literature useful (Russett 1968).

By focusing sharply on ability to influence market prices, economists have been able to probe deeply into this kind of economic power. A difficulty arises, however, when one tries to generalize this kind of power to other scopes. People refer to the "vast power" of General Motors without indicating whether they mean its ability to affect price or its ability to affect a wider range of social behavior.

(7) *Self-control*. Karl Deutsch (1963) has suggested that self-control is an important element in the measurement of power. Although a rampaging elephant may unleash much "power," we are reluctant to regard such aimless behavior as an indication of "power." The relevant question is: "To what degree can the elephant define and achieve his goals with economy and precision?" Likewise, in measuring the economic power of a nation, we are interested not only in the overall productive capacity of the economy, but also in the government's ability to harness the economy in order to achieve its aims. Thus, it is often said that although the United States has a bigger GNP than the Soviet Union, the Russians have more economic power than the Americans because they have more control over their economy (cf. Wu 1952).

(8) *Wealth and purchasing power*. The concept of

wealth comes close to the commonsense definition of
economic power. There is a certain ambiguity, however,
in being wealthy. The millionaire who forgets his wal-
let may find that he has no purchasing power at all.
Behind the idea of wealth as economic power lies the
implied assumption of a market in which wealth can be
exchanged for desired goods or services. Once this
qualification is added, the relational nature of economic power becomes more apparent.

A more precise and useful concept of economic power
is that of purchasing power. This concept is very close
to the concept of power employed by students of social
power. I have argued elsewhere (Baldwin 1971b) that
purchasing power is the nearest economic counterpart of
political power. The argument may be paraphrased as
follows: Without distorting the conventional meaning
of the term *purchasing power,* such power can be considered as a subset of those social relations in which A
gets B to do something he would not otherwise do (Dahl
1968). Although rarely made explicit, the following
perspectives are often implied in common usage.

Purchasing power is a social relationship. Although
we sometimes refer to purchasing power as "command over
goods and services," this can be misleading. One can
acquire goods without purchasing them, e.g., by picking
apples from a tree. A purchase, however, requires both
a buyer and a seller. Robinson Crusoe could have neither political power nor purchasing power until Friday
appeared. Purchasing power is a relationship in which
A gets B to sell him something.

Purchasing power is not money. Although economists
are prone to say that money *is* generalized purchasing
power, this merely indicates a lack of interest in distinguishing between power and the bases of power. The
relation between money and purchasing power could be
described in conventional social power terminology as
follows: money is a power resource that will very probably allow its possessor to exercise purchasing power
that is generalized in scope and domain (cf. Lasswell
and Kaplan 1950, pp. 83-86). Such a definition makes
"moneyness" a matter of degree, since probability,
scope, and domain are all variable. The higher the probability and the wider the scope and/or domain, the more
"moneyness" a given power resource has.

Money is neither a necessary nor a sufficient condition for the exercise of purchasing power. Money does not guarantee the exercise of purchasing power. A blind deaf-mute may find it difficult to exercise purchasing power no matter how much money he possesses. Like any other power resource, money is used with varying degrees of skill. Money is only one of many resources that can be used to exercise purchasing power. In some situations an honest face or personal acquaintance with the seller can serve almost as well.

Purchasing power varies in scope, weight, and domain. Variations in the weight of purchasing power are evident to anyone who can tell a dollar from a dime, but variations in scope and domain are less obvious. Because money enables us to exercise generalized purchasing power so easily, we tend to forget about the limits on scope and domain. In our daily lives most of us, if we have the money, can buy whatever we want from whomever we want. We rarely think about the things outside the scope of the buying power of our money, such as atomic bombs, Cuban cigars, and certain kinds of friendship. Likewise, variations in domain are not very salient unless one travels outside his own country. A person who tries to insert an American quarter into a French vending machine will become keenly aware of variations in the domain of purchasing power. Like other kinds of interpersonal power, purchasing power varies in scope, weight, and domain.

(9) *Economic goals versus economic means.* The most important distinction among alternative concepts of economic power is whether they emphasize means or ends. Some analysts prefer to define economic power in terms of the scope of the influence attempt (Galtung 1965, 1967). According to this conception, any sanction designed to affect economic relations is an economic sanction (cf. Pen 1971). There is nothing particularly wrong about such an approach except that it leads to some awkward interpretations in the context of international political analysis. If economic power is defined in terms of its goals, then it includes naval blockades of shipping, bombings of civilian industries, etc. In order to be consistent, one would have to include under the heading of military power embargoes on trade with the Communist bloc, economic aid to military

allies, etc. The point is that we usually define military power in terms of the techniques used, not in
terms of the goals pursued. Most people would regard
the dropping of napalm as a military sanction regardless of the target involved.

In order to be consistent with the common understanding of the term *military power*, I prefer to define "economic power" in terms of the techniques used
rather than in terms of the goals sought. A useful
classification scheme suggested by Lasswell (1936) involves a fourfold division of policy instruments as
follows: (*a*) information (propaganda); (*b*) negotiation (diplomacy); (*c*) weapons (military force);
(*d*) goods (economic Power). This scheme is especially
useful in analyzing the external relations of a group
or a nation.[1] For the remainder of this paper, then,
the term *economic power* will be used to refer to situations in which A tries to get B to do X by manipulating
the distribution and/or production of scarce goods and
services.[2]

ECONOMIC SANCTIONS

In 1965 Galtung observed that "we know of no systematic
study comparing the impact of economic sanctions with
military sanctions--or any systematic study of economic
sanctions in the world community of nations, for that
matter" (1965, p. 247). Although this paper does not
claim to provide the systematic study that Galtung
called for, some general comparisons of economic and
military sanctions will be made, and preliminary hypotheses will be suggested.

Rosenau (1963, p. 27) has suggested a number of useful criteria by which to compare inter-nation influence
techniques. Using these criteria, we shall compare
economic and military techniques of statecraft.

Military and Economic Techniques

(1) Economic techniques have more widespread effects on B's behavior than do military techniques. Mil-
tary techniques are more limited and engage a smaller
portion of the society. Everyone participates in economic activity, while only a few participate in military
activity.

(2) Economic techniques are more future oriented than military techniques.

(3) Economic techniques have more general effects on B's behavior than do military techniques.

The above three criteria concern the scope and domain of A's influence on B. To summarize, economic techniques tend to have widespread general effects on B's future behavior, while military techniques tend to have limited, specific effects on B's present (or near-future) behavior.

(4) Economic techniques work more slowly than military techniques.

(5) Economic techniques are more likely to be continuous than are military techniques. Although the threat of using military force is continuous, its actual use is intermittent.

(6) Economic techniques are less direct than military techniques.

Hypotheses 4, 5, and 6 concern the intensity and rate of operation of the techniques. Thus, we may summarize that economic techniques tend to be slow, continuous, and circuitous, whereas military techniques tend to be fast, intermittent, and direct.

(7) Economic techniques are less likely than military techniques to have integrative effects on the target nation. Nations usually increase in social cohesion when confronted by military pressure. Their receipt of economic aid, on the other hand, is likely to generate squabbles as to how to divide it.

(8) Economic techniques are more likely to be used unconsciously than are military techniques. By relying on economic techniques, one may acquire an empire "in a fit of absentmindedness." This does not hold true for military techniques.

(9) Economic techniques are less visible than military techniques.

Hypotheses 7, 8, and 9 concern the general character of the influence techniques. In sum, economic techniques tend to be disintegrative, unconscious, and invisible, whereas military techniques tend to be integrative, conscious, and visible.

(10) Economic techniques are more reversible than military techniques. Dead soldiers cannot be brought back to life.

(11) Economic techniques are more likely to be un-

guided than are military techniques. Although military
force requires constant guidence, many economic techniques can be set in operation and left unguided. For
example, trade relations may be established in the belief that free trade will lead to economic interdependence and that this, in turn, will help prevent war.

(12) Economic techniques are more effective in pur-
suing long-run goals than are military techniques.

Hypotheses 10, 11, and 12 concern the permanence and
duration of influence techniques. In sum, economic
techniques tend to be reversible, unguided, and long-
run; while military techniques tend to be irreversible,
guided, and short-run.

Two caveats regarding these twelve hypotheses should
be stated. First, they are highly tentative, and several are probably false. The purpose is not to provide
a definitive statement but merely to focus scholarly
attention on the points made. Second, all of the hypotheses relate to general tendencies. There are, of
course, exceptions to all of them.

TABLE 11.1.   Summary of Traits of Military and Economic
              Influence Techniques*

	Economic	*Military*
Scope and Domain	Widespread Future General	Limited Present Specific
Intensity and Rate	Slow Continuous Circuitous	Fast Intermittent Direct
Character	Disintegrative Unconscious Invisible	Integrative Conscious Visible
Permanence and Duration	Reversible Unguided Long-run	Irreversible Guided Short-run

*Adapted from Rosenau 1963, p. 27.

Economic Sanctions and the International System

The twelve hypotheses suggested above concern the
general nature of economic sanctions. Further hypotheses relating to the role such techniques play in
the international system will be suggested below.

    (1) The greater the "economic surplus" over and
above subsistence needs in a system, the higher the
probability of noncoercive conflict resolution (Dahl
1963, pp. 79-82). If everyone is getting a bigger
piece of pie than he got yesterday, one is less likely
to worry about the size of his piece relative to that
of his neighbor. It has been suggested that the growing economy in the United States has permitted that nation to avoid coercive conflict resolution (Potter 1954).
If an economic surplus is available, it can be used to
compensate or "buy off" disaffected groups. The spectacular growth of the world economic system in this
century provides hope that this generalization may be
applicable to the international system. On the other
hand, environmentalists are beginning to suggest that
continued economic growth is the path to planetary disaster (Meadows et al. 1972). There is a great irony
that such a realization should come just at that moment
in history when it was beginning to make sense to talk
about an economic surplus in the world economy. If the
hypothesis is true, and if the environmentalists are
right, limits on world economic growth are likely to be
even more difficult to attain than the proponents of
such limits suspect.

    (2) Increased participation in politics by the
masses has made it harder for statesmen to use economic
sanctions (Deutsch 1968; Sprout and Sprout 1968). Many
studies have shown the modern man in the street to be
especially interested in domestic economic issues. When
foreign policy was made by and for the few, statesmen
did not have to worry much about the man in the street.
Now, however, statesmen the world over are being pressed
to use economic resources at home rather than abroad.
Although this pressure is also applied to resources allocated to other techniques of statecraft, economic
techniques seem to be especially vulnerable to such
demands.[3]

    (3) Economic techniques are more likely to involve
positive sanctions (actual or promised rewards) than are

other techniques of statecraft. Military weapons are
very useful for delivering negative sanctions, but it
is rather difficult to use them to implement positive
sanctions. An influence attempt with an economic technique, however, is likely to take the form of offering
B a reward in exchange for some desired change in his
behavior.

The higher incidence of positive sanctions gives
economic statecraft some peculiar qualities that must
be taken into account in assessing the role of such
sanctions in the international political system. Influence attempts based on positive sanctions differ
from those based on negative sanctions in a number of
important ways. I have discussed these differences
elsewhere and will not repeat the discussion here
(Baldwin 1971d). The differences concern such diverse
matters as the planning processes of A, the role of
costs, the probability of success, aftereffects and
side effects on B, the difficulty of legitimation, symbolic importance, A's view of human nature, efficacy,
effects on systemic stability, surveillance difficulties,
and vulnerability to blackmail.

(4) Economic sanctions always fail. There are two
more cautious variations of this hypothesis which say
that such sanctions *usually* fail or that they *seem* to
fail. The hypothesis or one of its variations has become a sort of self-evident truth among students of
international politics. Cautious skepticism, however,
would seem to be in order. Let us at least consider
some of the reasons why economic sanctions might fail
or seem to fail.

(a) Economic influence attempts by A to get B
to do X are likely to fail because of the low autonomous probability that B would do X in the absence of
an influence attempt by A. The use of nuclear missiles
to deter Russian attack on the United States is an attempt to get the Russians not to do something they probably would not have done anyway. On the other hand,
the use of economic sanctions to get Rhodesia to give
up its commitment to white rule is an attempt to get
Rhodesia to do something it almost certainly would not
have done anyway. The point is that if economic sanctions tend to be used in hopeless situations, the observation that they rarely succeed is likely to be both

true and misleading. I have suggested elsewhere the
reasons why one might expect positive sanctions to be
used in situations where there is a low probability of
success (Baldwin 1971a, 1971b, 1971d, 1971e). If
economic sanctions are more likely to be positive, they
are also more likely to be used in hopeless situations.

(*b*) Economic sanctions fail because they tend to
be used in situations that do not matter much to the
user. Nations use economic sanctions in situations in
which they have little stake but want to make a gesture.
Sanctions were used in this way against Italy in the
1930s and against Rhodesia in the 1960s. The user may
be more interested in demonstrating his concern to
third nations than in actually getting the target nation to comply. To the extent that A's lack of commitment is perceived by B, the efficacy of the influence
attempt is likely to be undermined.

(*c*) Economic sanctions fail because of the fungibility or substitutability of one economic resource for
another (see Hirschman 1945). If rayon can be invented,
access to silk matters less; if synthetic rubber can be
invented, access to rubber matters less. Technology
has increased the fungibility of economic resources and
has thus reduced the efficacy of economic sanctions.

(*d*) Economic sanctions fail because target nations have alternative sources of supply (cf. Hirschman
1945). The revolution in the technology of transporta-
tion has facilitated the development of a world economic system in which alternative sources of supply are
available for almost any resource.[4]

(*e*) Economic sanctions fail because they increase social cohesion in the target nations. Galtung
(1967) has pointed out that a nation which perceives
itself as the target of negative economic sanctions is
likely to react very much like a nation under military
attack. Economic deprivations which might otherwise
have been regarded as intolerable not only become tolerable but something of a unifying force in the society.
The point is that the activation of economic sanctions,
at least under some circumstances, may trigger changes
in the social organization of the target nations that
offset the intended effects of the sanctions.

The above-listed factors are possible explanations
for the tendency of economic sanctions to fail. Let

us now look at some reasons why economic sanctions
might *seem* to fail even when they succeed or partially
succeed.

(a) Since the goals of influence attempts based
on economic techniques are often either confused or
concealed, the efficacy of such techniques is often
judged by the wrong criteria. Have economic sanctions
by the United States against Cuba failed? If their
goal was to topple Castro, they have certainly failed.
If, on the other hand, their goal was to demonstrate
to other nations United States concern about communism
in the western hemisphere, their failure is not so obvious.

(b) Since the economic techniques of statecraft
tend to have low visibility, they can easily be overlooked. When the United States lands hundreds of tons
of wheat in India, it attracts much less attention than
it would attract if it were to land a few hundred soldiers. The more spectacular economic sanctions, such
as those implemented by the League of Nations or the
United Nations, do attract attention; but these are
precisely the sanctions that are most likely to fail.
The everyday sanctions of aid, trade, and investment
are more mundane and much less likely to appear on the
front page. These, however, are the sanctions most
likely to succeed.

(c) Since economic techniques work slowly, their
success tends to come by degrees and is thus difficult
to detect. The effects of the multibillion dollar aid
program in the Third World are likely to be diffuse and
to be spread over many years. This has given and will
give rise to charges that the aid program has failed.

(d) The failure of many foreign policy analysts
to consider the *strength* of A's power over B (Harsanyi
1962) also accounts for a tendency to underestimate the
efficacy of economic sanctions. Harsanyi argued that
the costs to B of noncompliance should be taken into
account in assessing A's power over B. Thus, even
though economic sanctions against Rhodesia may not succeed in getting the Rhodesians to abandon white rule,
such sanctions can make it very costly for them to hold
to their chosen course (see Baldwin, 1971d, 1971e).

There seem to be several reasons for skepticism
about the generalization that economic sanctions never

work. A simple review of the general nature of economic techniques should be enough to alert us to the dan-
gers of such a generalization. We have described such
techniques as general, slow-working, circuitous, invisible, and unguided. Is it surprising that such techniques tend to be dismissed in favor of techniques that
are specific, fast, direct, visible, and guided?

The irony is that many of the qualities that account
for the "bad press" of economic sanctions are the same
qualities that make them useful in international statecraft. There are certain situations in which one wants
to apply pressure without provoking a violent response.
This is especially important if the target nation has
already committed itself not to comply. In such situations economic sanctions may be especially useful as
ways to apply slow, unobtrusive pressure to comply without seeming to challenge the target's commitment to noncompliance. Precisely because they are so unobtrusive,
such techniques allow B to back away from its commitment
and to comply without the appearance of submission. The
following quotation from Schelling (1966, pp. 66-69)
illustrates the point:

> Landlords rarely evict tenants by strongarm
> methods. They have learned that steady cumulative
> pressures work just as well, though more slowly,
> and avoid provoking a violent response. It is far
> better to turn off the water and electricity, and
> let the tenant suffer the cumulative pressure of
> unflushed toilets and candles at night and get out
> voluntarily, than to start manhandling his family
> and his household goods. Blockade works slowly; it
> puts the decision up to the other side. To invade
> Berlin or Cuba is a sudden identifiable action, of
> an intensity that demands response; but to cut off
> supplies does little the first day and not much more
> on the second; nobody dies or gets hurt from the
> initial effects of a blockade. A blockade is com-
> paratively passive; the eventual damage results as
> much from the obstinacy of the blockaded territory
> as from the persistence of the blockading power.
> And there is no well-defined moment before which
> the blockading power may quail, for fear of causing
> the ultimate collapse.

CONCLUSION

Economic power deserves more attention than it has thus
far received from social scientists. Fruitful links
can and should be established between the literature
of social power and the study of economic power. The
looseness with which the term *economic power* has been
used contributes to the difficulty of this task. A
number of economic power concepts are worthy of consideration, but the concept of purchasing power is probably the most useful.

The development of a concept of economic power will
facilitate investigation of the role of economic sanctions in the international system. In the nuclear era
it is especially important to find alternatives to military techniques of statecraft. The preceding discussion has suggested some general characteristics that
distinguish economic from military sanctions and has
set forth some hypotheses about the role of economic
sanctions in international relations. The suggested
characteristics and hypotheses are intended to focus
scholarly attention on such issues rather than to provide a comprehensive analysis.

NOTES

1. For an opposing view that argues for a quite
different way of classifying policy techniques, see
Hermann 1972. Lasswell and Kaplan (1950) suggest combining ends and means in defining forms of influence.
For them a "form of influence is a kind of influence
relationship specified as to base value and scope"
(Lasswell and Kaplan 1950, p. 84). This allows them
to identify a number of forms of influence involving
economic power.

2. This refers only to those goods and services
for which a reasonably well-organized market exists.
Without this restriction the term *economic resource*
could be used to refer to almost any power base.

3. Foreign aid is an especially good example of
this (see Baldwin 1966; O'Leary 1967).

4. Points *c* and *d* apply to both positive and negative economic sanctions. Alternative sources of supply and fungibility reduce the effectiveness of both threatened deprivations and promised rewards.

REFERENCES

Baldwin, D. A. 1966. *Economic development and American foreign policy*. Chicago: University of Chicago Press.

------. 1971a. Thinking about threats. *Journal of Conflict Resolution* 15: 71-78.

------. 1971b. The costs of power. *Journal of Conflict Resolution* 15: 145-55.

------. 1971c. Money and power. *Journal of Politics* 33: 578-614.

------. 1971d. The power of positive sanctions. *World Politics* 24: 19-38.

------. 1971e. Inter-nation influence revisited. *Journal of Conflict Resolution* 15: 471-86.

Blau, P. M. 1964. *Exchange and power in social life*. New York: Wiley.

Coleman, J. S. 1963. Comment. *Public Opinion Quarterly* 27, Spring, 63-82.

Curry, R. L., and Wade, L. L. 1968. *A theory of political exchange*. Englewood Cliffs, N.J.: Prentice-Hall.

Dahl, R. A. 1963. *Modern political analysis*. Englewood Cliffs, N.J.: Prentice-Hall.

------. 1968. Power. In *International encyclopedia of the social sciences*, Vol. 12. New York: Free Press. Pp. 405-15.

Deutsch, K. W. 1963. *The nerves of government*. New York: Free Press.

------. 1968. *The analysis of international relations*. Englewood Cliffs, N.J.: Prentice-Hall.

Galtung, J. 1965. On the meaning of nonviolence. *Journal of Peace Research* 2: 228-57.

------. 1967. On the effects of international economic sanctions, with examples from the case of Rhodesia. *World Politics* 19: 378-416.

Harsanyi, J. C. 1962. Measurement of social power,

opportunity costs, and the theory of two-person
bargaining games. *Behavioral Science* 7: 67-80.

Hermann, C. F. 1972. Policy Classification: a key
to the comparative study of foreign policy. In
J. N. Rosenau, V. Davis, and M. A. East (Eds.),
The analysis of international politics. New York:
Free Press, 58-79.

Hirschman, A. O. 1945. *National power and the structure of foreign trade*. Berkeley: University of
California Press.

Ilchman, W. F., and Uphoff, N. T. 1969. *The political
economy of change*. Berkeley: University of California Press.

Knorr, K. 1955. *The war potential of nations*. Princeton: Princeton University Press.

------. 1966. *On the uses of military power in the
nuclear age*. Princeton: Princeton University Press.

------. 1970. *Military power and potential*. Lexington, Mass.: Heath.

Lasswell, H. D., and Kaplan, A. 1950. *Power and society*.
New Haven: Yale.

Lindblom, C. E., and Dahl R. A. 1953. *Politics,
economics, and welfare*. New York: Harper & Row.

Meadows, D. H., et al. 1972. *The limits to growth*.
New York: Universe Books.

Morgenthau, H. J. 1967. *Politics among nations*. New
York: Knopf.

Pen, J. 1971. Bilateral monopoly, bargaining, and the
concept of economic power. In K. W. Rothschild
(Ed.), *Power in economics*. Baltimore: Penguin
Books, pp. 97-115.

Potter, D. 1954. *People of plenty*. Chicago: University of Chicago Press.

O'Leary, M. K. 1967. *the politics of American foreign
aid*. New York: Atherton.

Rosenau, J. N. 1963. *Calculated control as a unifying
concept in the study of international politics and
foreign policy*. Princeton: Center of International
Studies.

Rothschild, K. W., (Ed.). 1971. *Power in economics*.
Baltimore: Penguin Books.

Russett, B. M. (Ed.). 1968. *Economic theories of international politics*. Chicago: Markham.

Schelling, T. C. 1960. *The strategy of conflict.* Cambridge, Mass.: Harvard University Press.
------. 1966. *Arms and influence.* New Haven: Yale.
Sprout, H., and Sprout, M. 1968. The dilemma of rising demands and insufficient resources. *World Politics* 20: 660-93.
------. 1971. *Toward a politics of the planet earth.* New York: Van Nostrand Reinhold.
Von Neumann, J., and Morgenstern, O. 1944. *The theory of games and economic behavior.* Princeton: Princeton University Press.
Wright, Q. 1955. *The study of international relations.* New York: Appleton-Century-Crofts.
Wu, Y. 1952. *Economic Warfare.* New York: Prentice-Hall.

Index

PERSPECTIVES ON SOCIAL POWER
edited by James T. Tedeschi

PUBLISHER   Alexander J. Morin
MANUSCRIPT EDITOR   Eugene Zucker
PRODUCTION EDITOR   Nanci Oakes Connors
PRODUCTION MANAGER   Mitzi Carole Trout

COMPOSITION BY   Janet E. Braeunig
PRINTING BY   Printing Headquarters, Inc.
                         Arlington Heights, Illinois
BINDING BY   Brock and Rankin
                         Chicago, Illinois